THE STATE AND ECONOMIC LIFE

EDITORS: Mel Watkins, University of Toronto; Leo Panitch, York University

8 BEN FORSTER

A Conjunction of Interests: Business, Politics, and Tariffs 1825–1879

The advent of the National Policy in 1879 brought dramatic changes in the structure, magnitude, and objectives of Canada's tariff policy. No longer used primarily as a source of revenue for the government, tariffs on imported goods assumed a role as protector of Canadian industry against the encroachment of foreign imports on the Canadian market.

In this detailed account of events leading up to the adoption of the National Policy, Ben Forster explores a wide range of political and economic forces and traces their influence on successive Liberal and Conservative governments. He examines the pamphlet literature of the protectionists, the private correspondence of political leaders and protectionists, the public press of the day, and legislative journals and other public documents. He weaves the threads of various interests — business, industry, agriculture, and government — into a comprehensive account of the growth of protectionist feeling in Canada.

Forster's analysis illuminates a critical chapter in Canadian political history, one with implications for current discussions on import quotas, industrial policy, and free trade.

BEN FORSTER is a member of the Department of History, University of Western Ontario.

THE STATE AND ECONOMIC LIFE

Editors: Mel Watkins, University of Toronto; Leo Panitch, Carleton University

This series, begun in 1978, includes original studies in the general area of Canadian political economy and economic history, with particular emphasis on the part played by the government in shaping the economy. Collections of shorter studies, as well as theoretical or internationally comparative works, may also be included.

1 The State and Enterprise
Canadian manufacturers and the federal government 1917–1931
TOM TRAVES

2 Unequal Beginnings
Agricultural and economic development in Quebec and Ontario until 1870
JOHN McCALLUM

3 'An Impartial Umpire'
Industrial relations and the Canadian state 1900–1911
PAUL CRAVEN

4 Scholars and Dollars
Politics, economics, and the universities of Ontario 1945–1980
PAUL AXELROD

5 'Remember Kirkland Lake'
The history and effects of the Kirkland Lake gold miners' strike 1941–42
LAUREL SEFTON MacDOWELL

6 No Fault of Their Own
Unemployment and the Canadian Welfare State 1914–1941
JAMES STRUTHERS

7 The Politics of Industrial Restructuring
Canadian textiles
RIANNE MAHON

8 A Conjunction of Interests
Business, politics, and tariffs 1825–1879
BEN FORSTER

BEN FORSTER

A Conjunction of Interests: Business, Politics, and Tariffs 1825–1879

UNIVERSITY OF TORONTO PRESS
Toronto Buffalo London

Toronto Buffalo London
Printed in Canada

ISBN 0-8020-5680-6 (cloth)
ISBN 0-8020-6612-7 (paper)

Printed on acid-free paper

Canadian Cataloguing in Publication Data

Forster, Jakob Johann Benjamin
A conjunction of interests: business, politics, and tariffs, 1825–1879
(The State and economic life)
Bibliography: p.
Includes index.
ISBN 0-8020-5680-6 (bound). – ISBN 0-8020-6612-7 (pbk.)
1. Tariff – Canada – History – 19th century.
2. Free trade and protection – History – 19th century.
3. Canada – Commercial policy – History.
4. Canada – Commerce – History.
5. Industry and state – Canada – History – 19th century. I. Title. II. Series.
HF1765.F67 1986   382.7'0971   C86-093397-0

COVER: Custom House, Montreal, 1870
(in A. Henderson, *Photographs of Montreal*; collection of the Public Archives of Canada, C-20788)

Contents

Tables

Preface

I first wrote this study as a PHD dissertation under the guidance of Michael Bliss, to whose patience and insight I am indebted. Comments and questions from my board of examiners helped stimulate me to rework and extend my subject matter. A number of friends and colleagues read chapters and remarked cogently on errors and omissions they found; the anonymous readers who assessed the manuscript for publication were especially perceptive. The book has greatly benefited from this intellectual massage. I thank Gilbert Ryle for supplying philosophical detachment and engaged intellectuality. While all of these men and women aided in making this book better, they can hardly share in its shortcomings. Those are mine.

Archivists proved their worth in expediting my research in ways uncountable and in finding, with some notable exceptions, a corner where I could happily type my notes without disturbing others. Chris Speed and Jeanette Berry displayed great good will in typing the penultimate version of the manuscript. Rik Davidson at the University of Toronto Press handled editorial matters with flair, and Lydia Burton made my writing style more lucid and consistent.

The Canada Council, and then the Social Science and Humanities Research Council, provided support during my stint as a graduate student; this book has been published with the help of a grant from the Social Science Federation of Canada, using funds provided by the Social Sciences and Humanities Research Council of Canada.

Our two-year-old son Eric has shown his father, with some success, that writing books isn't *that* important. My wife, who has more than enough work to call her own, often took on my chores so that I could research and write. For that, and for many other reasons, she has my gratitude.

I dedicate this book to my parents, Margaret and Jakob. In more ways than they know, they have taught me about the importance of the past.

A CONJUNCTION OF INTERESTS

Introduction

This book is a study in the evolution of Canadian tariffs as an expression of interest group politics, from the 1820s to the formation of the National Policy of 1879. Not the effects of tariffs, but the making of them, in terms of motivation and process, provides focus for the following pages. This is meat enough, as everyone who had something to make, grow, buy, or sell had a stake in import duties. So did governments, who gained the bulk of their revenue from, and defined national interest through, customs imposts. Indeed, so did foreign states whose economic position might be affected by Canadian policy. Setting tariffs was, to say the least, a complex matter.

Political and economic conditions established the material context of tariff making. Until 1846, the primary defining agent for the tariffs of British North America was not any colonial government but the British imperial one. Though even in 1879 the Canadian government could express great concern about British opinion on Canadian tariff manipulations, Confederation was crucial in solidifying growing colonial independence in tariff matters. The union of 1867 created a common market, forced the development of a more sophisticated tariff structure to meet a greater diversity of needs, and provided a constitutional framework for the emergence of a national interest quite separate from that of Britain.

Commercial, staple-producing, and manufacturing activities defined the character of agitation on tariff matters. Certainly until the 1850s, agricultural, lumbering, and mercantile interests were paramount, as the struggle of these interests to improve their position in the British imperial, the American, and the domestic colonial markets showed. Throughout the early period there was a certain demand for a fostering care of manufactured goods among artisans, but only after the late 1840s – with the development of fair-sized factory industries – did pressures for protection to more than a handful of 'manufactures' emerge. Thirty years later, though agriculture accounted for nearly one-half, manufacturing of all kinds made up some 28 per cent of Canada's gross commodity production.[1] So widespread was industrial manufacturing, so great was the allure of growth it carried, that by then its needs largely demarcated the debate over tariffs.

Superimposed on these structural changes were the ups and downs of economic activity: each downturn of the business cycle produced a protectionist reaction of greater or lesser degree. The crises of the mid 1830s and later 1840s, the sharp contraction of 1857–59, the slight slump in 1869, and the major depression of 1874–79 all brought about demands for higher tariffs. At the same time, such downturns sharply reduced imports, which lowered government revenue, and thus generated a need for adjustments in the customs duties.

For an interest to get what it wanted in the way of tariff changes depended on its ability to exert pressure, private and public, on the government. Although everyone prized influence with politicians, few people had or could easily exercise it. Besides, it smacked of privilege in an increasingly democratic age. An interest had to act in a cohesive manner in petitioning, in public meetings, through joint action and organization. In the 1870s, farmers had the Grange, businessmen generally had the Dominion Board of Trade, industrial workers had their tenuous unions and a Trades Congress, and manufacturers had organizations like the New Brunswick Manufacturers' and Mechanics' Association. Such groups did not easily achieve unity of purpose. Any façade of unity could rupture along regional lines, or on the basis of narrow conflict of interest. Market farmers and fruit growers were protectionist because of their concern with local, domestic, demand. Wheat farmers could be free trade oriented. What then of rural solidarity?

These disagreements were obvious among businessmen and more specifically manufacturers, the groups that receive the bulk of attention in this work. While by the later 1870s vocal free-trade manufacturers were few in number, sharp disagreements arose, as earlier, among protectionists. Family squabbles, some might say, yet the process of conciliation and compromise among businessmen before 1879 involved the *incomplete* formation of an ascending élite, which had both a sense of national mission and a consciousness of class.

Tariffs were, however, put into place by governments, not by interest groups. Party advantage, political ideology, the personalities of leading politicians, and the need to pursue national interest gave governments a considerable autonomy in tariff formation. Moreover, the politically necessary accommodation of interests took place within the structure of the fiscal needs of the state. Revenue remained the overt primary consideration in framing tariffs from the 1840s up to, though not including, 1879. Of course, wisdom would have it that governments should effectively mediate between the multitude of agricultural, mercantile, extractive, and manufacturing interests to achieve balanced policy. Such mediation was possible if all interests were alive to pressing their concerns and had effective means of doing so, if the number of interests was relatively limited, and if the members of the government, particularly the finance minister, chose to listen. Taken together, these were major qualifications in an era of rapid economic, demographic, and geographic growth. Consequently, both the interests and the governments attempted to find methods of systematizing the tariff-making process, with what success we shall see.

British North American and Canadian tariff policy was a product not only of internal but of external stimuli. In Victorian Canada, both protectionists and free traders had at command persuasive concepts the intellectual expression of which was adopted from abroad. Few will dispute that the fountain-head of free trade was Britain and that Canadians offered no theoretical enhancement to the concept; likewise protectionists in Canada contributed little to the development of their pet theory.

In a material sense, protectionism in the colonies owed a great deal to British mercantilism, though in terms of ideas the connection, while seductively evident, is rather weaker. The subdued monetarist emphasis and concern with the balance of trade in Canadian protectionism was without doubt of mercantilist inspiration. Mercantilism flowered at the same time the nation-state emerged; mid and late nineteenth-century protectionism was also an aspect of nation-building. Mercantilists made the employment argument for protection: seventeenth-century French policy-maker and bureaucrat Jean Baptiste Colbert urged the development of industrial employment as a means of keeping the social peace.[2] Nearly two centuries later a similar argument had been extended into a social theory of appealing simplicity. But the differences between mercantilist and protectionist thought were profound. In its full glory, mercantilism was associated with formal empire, and was a practice that placed a great deal of emphasis on trade, on the closed character of the economic world, and thus on the impossibility of real economic growth. Protectionists, in contrast, rejected imperial domination in their fervent nationalism, and recognized that they lived in an era of great economic fecundity. Victorian Canadians, to say the least, would have found puzzling the bland mercantilist assumption that world-wide growth was unattainable. So while protectionism owed a great deal in practical terms to the mercantilist-derived British imperial preferential system, the most obvious debts owed by Canadian high-tariff pundits from the 1840s onward were to contemporary British, German, and most especially American protectionist thinkers.

Canada participated in international commercial policy trends. For some twenty years after the mid 1840s, an international movement toward lower tariffs existed. The popularity of economic liberalism as well as more pragmatic considerations culminated in Great Britain with the repeal of the Corn Laws and the reduction of timber preferences in 1846, and British North America's preferred relationship with the mother country crumbled. In Germany, leaders committed to liberalizing trade within a common market or *Zollverein* among the numerous German states had by that point met nearly total success. The *Zollverein* not only lowered its tariffs to the outside world unilaterally, it went on to conclude tariff-lowering treaties with France, Britain, Austria and Belgium in the 1860s.[3] The regime of Napoleon III lowered French tariffs: the corn laws of France were suspended in 1853 and, later, customs duties on livestock, coal, iron and steel, cottons, machinery, and other items were greatly reduced. The Cobden Treaty of 1860 between Britain and France set off a further round of tariff reductions in Europe through an interlocking web of treaties.[4] Even the heavily protectionist United States followed the trend, bringing in lower tariff levels in 1846 and 1857.[5]

Customs duties in British North America were sharply reduced in 1842 and 1846 by the imperial government, and climbed upwards only slowly thereafter. Nova Scotia, New Brunswick, and the Canadas made efforts to mutually reduce tariffs beginning in the late 1840s, and all sought better trade relations with the British colonies in and rimming the Caribbean. Excluding Confederation, the crowning achievement of the BNA colonies' attempt to liberalize trade was the Reciprocity Treaty of 1854, which made a wide variety of natural products mutually free between the colonies and the United States.

Did mere ideological conviction motivate this apparent shift to free trade? This is doubtful, for countries engaged in careful calculation of national advantage before taking any decision to lower customs duties. Protection could actually be increased by selective tariff reductions on raw materials; this was one of the effects of the 1854 Reciprocity Treaty. The Canadian efforts to arrange mutual tariff reductions with France and Spain in 1878–79, while the Canadian protective tariff was being set in place, underline the calculated quality of tariff manipulation.

Even as the tide toward lower tariff barriers was at the flood, counter-currents were felt. In the Canadas, growing revenue needs (in part the product of practically insolvent railways), the economic slump after 1857, and a rise in protectionist feeling combined to bring about increased tariffs on finished goods in 1858 and 1859. New Brunswick imposed higher tariff levels in 1859 as well. The American Morrill tariff of 1861 was a response to the same economic downturn, and the Civil War forced yet further tariff increases.[6] The system of high protection that resulted was not abandoned in the aftermath of the struggle, and partly in a retaliatory attempt to force her way into the American market, Canada raised her customs duties in 1870.

The Franco-Prussian war brought in its trail a drift towards higher tariffs in Europe. Through a combination of resurgent nationalism, protectionist leadership, and the massive war indemnity demanded by Prussia, some French customs duties were raised. The depression after 1873, in addition to heavy grain imports from the United States, helped bring about an alliance between well-organized manufacturers' and farmers' groups. Only a strong freetrade group and the web of treaties in which France was bound kept the massive protectionist assault of 1878–82 from success. Thereafter, France moved steadily in a protectionist direction.[7]

The Franco-Prussian war also sealed a German statehood that had its mundane origins in the *Zollverein*. The depression of the 1870s was, however, the key needed to release victorious protectionism in the new state, as intense internal and external competition on a wide range of goods, including ironware and textiles, developed. The process of centralization and concentration in industry accelerated greatly. Organizations representing a broad spectrum of industrial concerns were formed to limit competitive excesses. Allied with some agricultural interests, renewed in their protectionist faith by the writings of the American Henry C. Carey, the men of these organizations met with success in the German tariff of 1879.[8]

Knowledgeable Canadians were well aware of these developments; protectionists found them inspirational in the framing of the 1879 Canadian tariff. 'The change in [the membership of] this House was suggestive of the change of feeling and opinion that had certainly taken place in the country,' the MP and businessman John McLennan pronounced in the Commons early that year. 'The change they were making in this respect was in the same direction, and in accord with that going on in all the civilized world around, and he must heartily congratulate the Minister of Finance upon his good fortune in having to deal with this whole question, from the foundation, at a time when the country and the world at large was so ready to deal with it.'[9] The National Policy was a Canadian aspect of international tendencies.

As with tariffs before it, the National Policy involved a wide variety of compromises among agricultural, extractive, mercantile, and manufacturing interests, based either on prior understandings or on the mediation and arbitration of party and government. None the less, industrial enterprise increasingly became the focal point of commercial policy discussions from the late 1850s onwards. And as the variations in interest-group behaviour and argument grew partly out of the regional differences in British North American and Canadian economic development, it makes good sense to examine the potential and actuality of industrial growth on a regional basis.

During the 1850s and 1860s, economic expansion was rapid, though sometimes interrupted. The impact of war and major gold discoveries, the emergence of new technology, and the rapid reduction of transportation costs were factors in this expansion; enormous population growth was perhaps the most important impulse within the provinces. Some 618,000 more people made the British North American colonies their home in 1861 than in 1851. Though this record was not surpassed until the turn of the century, the 1860s also saw substantial population growth. Heady optimism, an enlarged consumer demand, the importation of capital, and the large labour force necessary for building the infrastructure of the colonial economies followed. Upper Canada (Ontario) benefited the most, however; Nova Scotia received the equivalent of only one-sixth of Upper Canada's population growth. New Brunswick did not fare even that well.[10]

The Maritimes lacked the potential of what was to be central Canada. Geography inhibited agriculture in New Brunswick and especially Nova Scotia; in many cases farming was an avocation for lumbermen and fishermen. In addition, while a seaboard location offered advantages in terms of fostering trade, it gave native industry little protection in the way of transportation costs. Proximity to New England proved a disadvantage in this regard. Metropolitan control was difficult to assert from Halifax: the small ports in the province had their own ocean access, and many were in the direct metropolitan ambits of the Englands, both old and New, which made it difficult to establish manufactories serving the domestic population.[11] Nor was fishing an adequate fertilizer for the seed bed of industrialization. The traditional and dominant dried salt cod required little onshore capital equipment, and the 'truck' system often left fishermen in debt to the local merchant and unable to patronize local producers. So while a number of fishing ports such as Lunenburg enjoyed a modest prosperity, fishermen were in no position to provide a major stimulus to manufacturing.[12]

The great shipbuilding boom of this era in the Maritimes was fostered not by the fisheries, but by the trade in staples, the strategic location the region held in world shipping, and an international and especially British demand for vessels. But when wooden vessels began to give way to ships with iron hulls, shipbuilders there and at Quebec City failed to meet the challenge of the new mode of production because of a lack of capital, industrial and technological shortfall, a continuing though increasingly marginal demand for wooden vessels, and because the shipbuilders were moving their investment landward.[13] As well, a large proportion of manufactured fittings for vessels, from spikes, to copper fittings, to rope, was imported rather than purchased from local producers.[14] Devoted to an export market, and often involved in more general mercantile endeavour, shipbuilders evidently favoured free trade.

Coal and lumber might also have provided a staple basis for industrialization. Coal was not only heavily exported, but it was viewed as a vital element in a potential iron and steel industry, though the hope for such an industry only began to bloom after Confederation. The ability of the coal industry to generate high levels of income and substantial increments of capital in Nova Scotia was, however, undermined by the increasing competition the Nova Scotian product faced in the American seaboard markets from American anthracite.[15]

Cyclic gluts were characteristic of the lumber market, but the 1850s and the early 1860s were good years overall. Lumbering was New Brunswick's great staple industry, for only there in the Maritimes were the drainage basins of the rivers sufficiently large to encourage widespread exploitation. Lumbering methods were destructive, however, and while large, the New Brunswick lumbering hinterland was cropped of its finest timber by Confederation. Other than the North Shore, that hinterland was dominated by Saint John, around which the sawmills (cutting more and more small pine and spruce) that proliferated with the decline of the square timber trade were concentrated.[16] The St John River valley provided a captive market for the city; the lumber industry created demands for machinery and men; the relatively large urban and rural population required manufactured goods; railway construction needed support industries; the port facility made Saint John a major mercantile centre; and it was here that shipbuilding created its strongest demand for ironware and rigging locally manufactured. A degree of industrialization resulted. Steam power came into common use in a variety of small factories, and cessation of American supply during the Civil War brought a flurry of expansion. William Park's New Brunswick Cotton Mill was established, a sugar refinery that rapidly proved unsuccessful was set up, and boot and shoe factories came into being. By 1875, the cotton mill employed 150, as did one city boot and shoe firm. Several large foundries were active by the same date: the Phoenix Foundry had about 125 on its payroll, and the New Brunswick Foundry of James Harris & Co. provided work for between 200 and 300, making railway cars, stoves, and other kinds of ironware. Still, Saint John remained very much a shipping and lumbering entrepôt. The port facility required several thousand men at the height of the season, mostly to move wood. Lumber mills in the city and environs, some twenty-seven in number, employed 2225 hands in 1875, accounting for over 3 out of every 10 industrial employees in the city.[17] The provincial economy remained heavily dependent on export markets; the provincial market remained constricted.

The problem of market, while important in New Brunswick, was crucial in Nova Scotia. Saint John supported much more manufacturing than did Halifax. The census of 1871 shows that there were twice as many industrial workers in the former than in the latter, though Halifax had a greater population than Saint John.[18] The Nova Scotian historian Duncan Campbell complained in late 1873: 'The sister Province of New Brunswick, with a much smaller population and proportionately inferior in wealth and other resources, displays enterprize far in advance of this Province. It has a number of manufacturing companies with large capitals, and the industries of St. John present greater variety than those of Halifax, although the latter city has greater wealth.'[19] Campbell's observations were acute; the average number of employees in the industries of Saint John was a touch over thirteen; in Halifax the average was somewhat under seven.[20] The chief solution the historian envisaged was in establishing enclave industries along the lines of the successful Starr Manufacturing Company with its European market for strap-on skates. The limiting factor of a small provincial population might be overcome if export markets were found. None the less, Campbell found the ready competition of British and American manufactures in the province worrisome, especially as the American market was largely closed to Nova Scotian manufactures.[21] If these negative conditions were not sufficient, a further could be discovered in the attachment of the mercantile community to international commerce. The emphasis on international markets continued to be apparent in 1870 when the organizers of an association to encourage joint stock factories in Nova Scotia took care to reject protectionism and affirm a belief in free trade.[22]

A different situation prevailed in the Canadas prior to Confederation. Lumbering offered a greater spur to industrialization, for the physical limits to exploitation were not as sharply defined as in New Brunswick. While the decline in the square-timber trade injured shipping and shipbuilding in Quebec, there was a growing demand in the American market for sawn lumber and domestically for the products of lumber mills, furniture factories, and the like.[23] The industry encouraged the construction of railways also, and some lumbermen rapidly accumulated capital.

The wheat staple in Upper Canada proved decisive in the early phase of industrialization. High grain prices in the 1850s made farmers eager buyers of farming equipment, cast-iron stoves, bricks for new houses, and, as time passed, even luxuries such as pianos.[24] Rapid urban growth fostered a fair degree of agricultural diversification, and the diversification provided a basis for agricultural product processing that, by the 1870s, led to the upward spiral of cheese, butter, and processed meat exports.[25] The well-to-do farming community was a vitally important domestic market for central Canadian manufacturers.

Industry in Ontario was geographically dispersed because of such broad-based demand. So in Toronto, industrial employees made up only 10.8 per cent of the total of such workers in the province in 1871, while Montreal stood at 26.3 per cent for its province and Saint John at 38.8.[26] Agricultural-implement manufactories, breweries, woollen manufactories, furniture manufacturing, and tanneries were liberally sprinkled on the Ontario map. Yet rapid railway construction countered industrial diffusion, and in major urban centres such as Hamilton or Toronto and at points where there was a bountiful supply of water-power, there was a concentration of firms and a consolidation of industrial activity.[27] Toronto had a high average number of workers per industrial establishment with 18.4 – more than Montreal, Saint John or Halifax. The emphasis on efficient factory production was apparent even in the layout of the Toronto Rolling Mills, which by 1866 employed more than 300 men, and in the growing dependence on machinery in the factory production of boots and shoes in the city.[28]

If railways aided in the concentration of industry, they also directly stimulated manufacturing. Huge imports of capital for railway construction were characteristic of the 1850s, and though much went out of the country to purchase equipment and hire expertise, much remained. From 1850 to 1860, railway mileage in the provinces had grown from 66 miles to 2065, and in response, locomotive and car works were erected in Kingston and Hamilton, and an iron rail manufacturing facility appeared in Toronto by 1860. The manufacture of rail spikes became an attractive proposition, and to choose a further random example, the Belleville foundryman James Smart did well out of a contract to supply stoves for Grand Trunk stations.[29]

Given this analysis of background conditions in Upper Canada, one would not expect great industrialization to have taken place in the Montreal region prior to Confederation. But it did, despite the relative poverty of agriculture and the absence of heavy, growing demand within the province of Quebec. Large export-oriented, enclave enterprises had tremendous advantages in Montreal and region. Capital was readily available in the city, labour was cheap and plentiful, and the Lachine Canal provided a fine power source. Montreal was the nexus of a major transportation network (the Grand Trunk maintenance and manufacturing facilities were there), and the city's manufactories had access to the Upper Canadian, the Maritime, the American, and even overseas markets.[30]

In fact, the growth of manufacturing in Montreal and environs between 1850 and Confederation was remarkable. In 1851, Lower Canada had only thirty-six industrial establishments with more than 25 employees. Nine of those were shipbuilding yards involving very limited capital investment, and a further fifteen were sawmills.[31] Factories began to open up along the Lachine Canal after 1847 however, to take advantage of the water power. The City Flour Mills, established that year, employed 200 men by 1856; two foundries set up about 1850 employed 250 men by the middle of the decade; a cotton mill on the canal provided work for 70 hands by that point; and other foundries, woodworking plants, and a paint and a medicine factory were found on the canal's banks. Elsewhere in the city, the Redpath Sugar Refinery opened in 1855, soon to be followed by the St Lawrence Sugar Refining Company, and in 1866 the two gave work to more than 400 people. Such a listing could be readily extended to include the numerous boot and shoe concerns, the puddling and rolling mills, the straw works, the tanneries, and many other large plants.[32] Suffice it to say that if the number of industrial workers in Halifax in 1871 were given a value of 1, Saint John would rank at 2 and Toronto at 2.7. Montreal, without peer, would rank at 4.8.[33] While many of the establishments in Montreal were undoubtedly small, contemporaries were awed and pleased by the great factories, so evidently a sign of progress.

To return to the point of departure: the potential for manufacturing-related protectionism in British North America grew sharply, beginning around 1850, and accelerating in the following decade. In Saint John and environs, in the Montreal region, and in a diffuse pattern throughout Upper Canada, a degree of industrialization was under way after that date. The process was uneven: concentration of industry was limited, the use of machinery far from pervasive, and firms of large size and capital investment limited in number. Yet, high tariffs to foster economic expansion did not appear in British North America because of the factory system. Nationalist protectionism had more complex roots in the province. They will now be explored.

1
Protection in an era of colonial transition, 1825–1854

Industrialization in British North America did not give birth to protection. The theory was mostly adopted from abroad, the sentiment carried over from the 1840s and earlier, and the practice of demanding tariff protection in the colonies came before significant factory production. Later Canadian policy inherited some basic elements from the decaying mercantilism of the post-Napoleonic British colonial system. That system emphasized protection within the empire to commerce, to agriculture, and to manufacturing. British commercial policy, so the colonials widely believed, provided a fine place for the British North American economies within the imperial whole by giving their staple products a preferred or tariff-protected place in the British market, favouring colonial and British vessels in the colonial trade, and providing British manufactures with a tariff-protected colonial market. But Britain had constant difficulties adjusting imperial policy to meet the needs of the rapidly developing provinces. Colonial interests always wanted to improve their positions in the imperial tariff structure; they tried to manipulate the low colonial tariffs to their advantage; and they pursued greater independence from Britain for colonial commercial policies.[1]

This last effort involved the adoption from abroad not only of free-trade ideas, but also of nationalist-tinged protectionist theories. However, these ideas were not popularized in the provinces until Britain herself dismantled the imperial trade system in two decisive steps in the 1840s. The imperial tariff in force in the colonies was sharply reduced and British preferences for the staple products of its dependencies were in part lowered in 1842. The second step was taken in 1846, with the repeal of the Corn Laws, the associated removal of the British preferences on colonial grain by 1849, the drastic reduction of the preferences on timber, and the amendment of the British Possessions Act to give the colonies control over what had been the imperial tariff. Almost the last tatters of the old system were swept away in 1849 with the repeal of the Navigation Laws. The alterations were vertiginous. The existing order of political economy was called into question, and the apparent dependence of the colonials on the British imperium laid bare. The colonials generally responded by attempting to make their existing economy more efficient, but they also began to explore alternative lines of economic growth.

When William Huskisson, the head of the British customs and revenue department (the Board of Trade), undertook his 'Great Reforms' in 1825, the character of the imperial commercial system was altered from one of mercantilism towards one that emphasized imperial preferences and liberalized trade relations. Still, Huskisson had every intention of fostering trade within the empire. The colonies gained most of the revenue necessary to run their governments with a low (generally 2½ per cent) duty that was imposed on goods from *all* sources. However, imperial customs duties placed only on *non-empire* goods ranged from 7½ to 15 for goods not named in the tariff – 'unspecified' as they were called – to 30 per cent and more. The imperial duties generated only a small part of colonial revenue; they were designed mostly to protect imperial markets. For a further twenty years, most British North Americans had difficulty imagining their economic existence outside the structure of the much modified mercantilist system. Only some had any desire to do so: the existing state of affairs was widely seen as beneficial.

Staple-producing and mercantile interests found British policy very useful. The lumbering industry especially gloried in its hinterland supply role. After all, the timber preferences Britain formulated when cut off from Baltic supplies during the Napoleonic Wars practically created the industry in British North America. When preferences were lowered in 1821 and then yet again in 1842, the dismayed though unproductive protest that erupted among colonial lumbermen and their British connections highlighted their sense of dependence on the metropolitan market. 'Our great ground of complaint,' the Quebec *Gazette* revealingly asserted at the later date, 'is that British Acts of Parliament created the trade, causing capital to be invested in the trade, trusting to these acts, which by the uncertain character they now assume may ruin thousands. We never asked for protection: it was given on grounds of national policy.'[2]

Lumbermen were not alone in their imperial attachments. The great merchants of the Maritimes functioned profitably as middlemen in their imperially guaranteed trade with the West Indies, shipping American manufactures and colonial fish and lumber to the British Caribbean, and taking back raw sugars and sugar by-products for colonial consumption or for shipment elsewhere. Whenever the British promised to or actually did give the Americans access to the West Indies trade, there was wailing and gnashing of teeth in Halifax and Saint John.[3] Farmers and grain exporting merchants in the Canadas enjoyed imperial preferences on colonial grain and flour; in fact, they made persistent efforts to have the preferences improved.

Merchants were particularly attached to the imperial system. They argued that their activities were the engine of colonial progress; the British market was the necessary fuel. As one merchant-politician urged, 'we must encourage commerce by every possible means,' which naturally meant the fullest possible access to the British market.[4] In fact, the commercial élite of the St Lawrence ports actually obtained modifications in imperial economic policy to suit their particular needs. The attractions of the river were enhanced, for example, when Quebec was made into a free port in 1825, allowing vessels of any nationality to engage in trade there. Nor were Navigation Law distinctions between British and American shipping on the Great Lakes enforced. Laurentian merchants also obtained favourable alterations in the imperial customs duties on breadstuffs, which strengthened the position of the trade route they dominated.

But harmony did not reign among colonial interests. Conflicts arose involving a partial rejection of British, mercantile, and colonial entrepôt dominance over commercial policy decisions; this opposition was expressed both in demands for freer trade and for domestic colonial protection. A desire to find compromise through the constructive modification of imperial policy tempered this conflict, though when customs duties on agricultural products were discussed, compromise proved difficult.

Unlike the timber industry, colonial agriculture developed important domestic markets even before 1840, which encouraged agrarian protectionism of various shades of intensity. However, commercial and consumer interests opposed the imposition of high tariffs on farm products. Nova Scotia was a case in point. The West Indies merchants of Halifax imported American foodstuffs for home consumption as well as re-export, a great annoyance to provincial farmers. Repeatedly, the popularly elected Nova Scotian Assembly moved to bring in tariffs on agricultural products; repeatedly, the moves were blocked by the merchant-dominated appointive council, the province's upper house. When agriculturists' demand for protection were partly successful, representatives of merchants and fishermen claimed that the assembly wanted 'to make other classes hewers of wood and drawers of water to the Agriculturists.'[5] None the less, the demand for protection on farm products continued to meet with modest success in the Maritimes, even during the free-trade offensive of the 1840s.

Changing market conditions, an expanding agricultural frontier, and the centrality of the Laurentian trade route made a similar conflict of interest in Upper and Lower Canada more complex. From before the turn of the nineteenth century, the internal markets of the Canadas were of great importance. The expanding Upper Canadian farming frontier increased its productivity rapidly, and the decline of wheat production in Lower Canada enlarged these markets.[6] However, a considerable exportable surplus existed from the War of 1812 to the crisis years of the mid 1830s: the surplus was sold to the Maritimes, the United States (despite the high American customs duty of 1824), and especially to Great Britain. Because after Huskisson's reforms colonial wheat did not have preference in the British market under normal price conditions, colonial farmers and corn merchants alike wanted the preference improved. But agriculturists also wanted protection from American farm products in the sizeable domestic markets. The Laurentian wheat exporters disagreed with domestic colonial agricultural protection, as it was to their advantage to import American wheat duty free either for re-exportation as 'Canadian' flour or to replace Canadian wheat already exported. The conflict of interest came to a head in the 1830s. In 1831, British commercial policy was changed to favour the merchants, leaving farmers to face an unrestricted American competition; this was unfortunately followed by poor prices and then poor crops.[7] A crisis of sorts was in the making.

The demand for policy changes from the agrarian community became insistent and provided the context for a prismatic display of ideas about commercial policy in Upper Canada. At one extreme there was a cry for freer trade in the form of reciprocity with the United States – a blow for freedom against what in some circles was seen as Britain's debilitating economic domination. Much more widespread and powerful was the protectionist reaction, which asserted the need for a tariff wall to foster Upper Canadian artisanal and especially agricultural production. This, too, was a rejection of imperial policy. In the end, it was a third option that proved most popular: compromise between the exponents of agricultural protection and mercantile interests facilitated through a modification of the empire's policies to meet special provincial needs.

The leading exponent of the free-trade option in Upper Canada by 1835–36 was the journalist-politician William Lyon Mackenzie. In the 1820s, it is true, Mackenzie had wanted artisanal manufacturing to grow in the province; he also had read some American protectionists and obliquely referred to their ideas in his newspaper.[8] But his protectionism had been one of subsidies and bonuses rather than tariffs, and had always been heavily muted by his belief in the moral primacy of agriculture and his conception of himself as a spokesman for the farming community.[9] Though his persistent opposition to the domination of the colonies by Britain through the imperial commercial system was attuned to the nationalist elements found in American protectionism, he and those who agreed with him none the less saw protection as essentially an imperial device, the intention of which was to 'protect BRITISH CAPITAL, shipping and manufactures, and to give BRITISH MERCHANTS a monopoly of the Canadian Market, or, in other words, to prevent the Farmers of these Colonies from buying the articles ... at the best market, unless under disadvantage of heavier taxation.'[10]

So sharp was Mackenzie's consequent opposition to the principle of protection that he was willing to seize almost any weapon to do battle. He did so when in 1836, Toronto-based merchants led by the banker William Allan petitioned to have British goods shipped via the United States without payment of imperial duties. It is in retrospect comical to consider that Mackenzie misinterpreted this petition – signed by the allies of the ruling Tory clique he so endlessly attacked – as prime evidence of a desire for reciprocal free trade with the United States.[11] Imperial domination, imperial protection hurt the province and the colonial farmer, Mackenzie made clear when debating on tariff matters during the 1835 session of the Upper Canadian Assembly; he was only willing to support tariff protection on agricultural goods because of public demand for retaliation against the high American tariff and in order to reduce the difficulties faced by Upper Canadian agriculturists.[12] As the putative representative of a beleaguered class, Mackenzie's free-trade principles had to have practical limits.

Mackenzie's inconsistency was produced by the quite powerful agrarian protectionist reaction to the crisis of the mid 1830s. A swelling number of heavily signed petitions told the members of the assembly that 'the people of the Province are labouring under great distress, arising chiefly from the present depression in the price of agricultural produce ... [In] particular the markets of this Colony are thrown open to American Citizens for almost all the staple productions of their soil.'[13] A 'prohibiting duty' was needed. Nor were the demands purely for protection for wheat or for unprocessed agricultural products generally. Many of the petitions sent to the assembly combined a demand for protection to both agriculture *and* manufactures, urging the legislature to provide a 'protecting Statute' for 'articles of produce and mechanism.'[14] Such petitions bore witness to close economic and social ties among farmers and artisans in many locales.

There was no great degree of industrialization in the province, of course, so one might wonder why a demand for manufacturing protection even arose. It emerged more from the realities of imperial customs duties than from abstract reasoning. The trade reforms of 1822 and 1825, like the laws and regulations that preceded them, were partly designed to keep colonial markets for British manufactures. However, colonial enterprises with low capital investment developed when high transatlantic transportation charges offset British advantages in mass production and low labour costs, and when local sources of raw materials were available and special frontier needs could be met through small capital investment. Moreover, American goods suited for colonial needs faced imperial customs duties of 15, 20, and even 30 per cent or more after 1825, as well as low colonial tariffs. As one Upper Canadian politician noted, the 'mechanics of this province are protected ... by duties on American manufactures.'[15] So there was room for a degree of growth in 'manufacturing,' if tariff protection had any role in the matter.

Still, large quantities of American goods entered Upper Canada, especially with the completion of the Erie Canal and the rapid development of upstate New York. Cyclical downturns, like the one of the later 1830s, encouraged the inflow of American furniture, wagons, tobacco, some types of iron castings, and especially leather and leather goods to compete with those of Upper and Lower Canadian manufacture. Such goods were often smuggled in or could be grossly undervalued at the customs house to reduce the amount of duty paid, undercutting the protective function of the tariff. Even in the 1820s, tanners in both of the Canadas were asking for better customs protection. By 1831, Upper Canadian furniture producers and other manufacturers petitioned their assembly for a more rigid enforcement of the imperial customs duties. As economic pressures increased and these pleadings reached a high point in 1835, they were transformed to demands for higher *colonially imposed* tariffs.[16] Almost imperceptibly, a nationalist tendency was appearing.

The public was partly aware of the arguments in favour of such protection. A few newspapers pointed out the utility of local 'manufacturing' even in the mid 1820s; sometimes American protectionists were cited. The work of John Rae, a young Scottish immigrant to the Canadas, reflected a growing sense of nationalist protectionism, though his sophisticated political economy had no immediate or direct impact on the colonials.[17] Nevertheless, Upper Canadians knew of the arguments for tariff protection, as an 1835 report of their assembly's Committee on Trade showed. Making heavy use of American sources, the committee compiled a wide-ranging though haphazard list of reasons for higher tariffs: protection was an assertion of nationality; it would allow self-sufficiency in case of war; it was a rejection of the exploitative character of British commercial practices; domestic competition would ensure low prices in a protectionist regime; under such a regime the foreign exporter – not the domestic consumer – paid the customs duty; and it would provide good wages and jobs for workingmen.[18]

As the committee's report suggests, the public concern with 'American intercourse' had an impact on the Reform-dominated assembly of 1835. Despite furious debate, the assembly passed a bill intended to impose high levels of duties on American farm produce: cattle, meat, dairy products, grains, flours, and some fruits. Less important sections of the bill established price scales for various types of leathers, stoves, cast iron, mill machinery and axes, to prevent undervaluation of the goods and the consequent payment of low *ad valorem* (percentage of value) duties.[19] The bill trespassed on the powers of the imperial government and was intended to impose duties on American goods being shipped through the province to overseas destinations. This colonial arrogance, this attack on the Laurentian trading system, was unacceptable to the entrenched Tory élite with its strong imperial attachments. In Upper Canada's Legislative Council, the bill was rejected, never to pass into law.

The American Intercourse Bill, and the public demands on which it was based, indicated an uncertain groping towards a more independent and protectionist colonial commercial policy, but it reflected an abortive wisdom. Just like the free-trade option, it militated against the existing commercial and political framework. The opposition to it, even within the assembly, was great. The necessity for compromise should have been overpoweringly evident to the disputing parties, but the crisis that dominated the Canadas from 1837 to the union of Upper and Lower Canada in 1841 prevented any elegant solution to the existing nexus of tensions. Soon thereafter, however, the same problems reasserted themselves.

In the first years of the new Province of Canada's existence, pleas for agricultural protection, led by the 'great agricultural petition' of 1842, again increased in number.[20] The political representatives of the Canadians, possibly chastened by events, now looked for solutions that might satisfy both commercial and agricultural interests. Even in the mid 1830s, compromise proposals were being put forward by the transportation promoter and politician William Hamilton Merritt. Rather than rejecting the framework of the imperial trade system, he had asserted that the provincial role was essentially that of a staple-producing hinterland tied into a mutually beneficial commerce with imperial Britain. Surely both farmers and merchants could be satisfied within that, he thought.[21] The resolution of the conflict of interest in 1842 and 1843 followed lines similar to Merritt's recommendations. The Canada Corn Act of 1843 gave greatly improved British preferences on Canadian grain. But that was not all. Three provincial acts, based on an understanding with the British government, placed duties on American wheat and other agricultural products, but at the same time allowed American grain to be milled in bond and the flour shipped to Britain as a Canadian product; similar bonding privileges were extended to other farm goods. The Canadian market was to be protected for the provincial farmer, and the British market not only for the farmer but for the grain miller and shipper.[22] Only in French Canadian Lower Canada, which could not produce sufficient grain for its own consumption, was the solution unsatisfactory, and in the political context of 1842–43, the French Canadians lacked the clout to block the changes.

Manufacturing interests (outside of milling) played no role in these manoeuvres. In part, manufacturers already had a considerable degree of protection from American competition; however, commerce and agriculture were overwhelmingly recognized as the two crucial great interests of the Canadas. When in 1843 disgruntled manufacturers, mechanics, and artisans began to press for more protection, the politician Malcolm Cameron suggested the free importation of raw materials and machinery would satisfy these interests. That was the proper proportion of protection 'as will leave them no room to complain of the measure of protection [afforded] to the more numerous and influential body of Agriculturists.'[23] The developments of 1842–43, then, fused imperial and colonial protection into a workable whole: a creative adaptation of the imperial commercial system had been achieved. Yet at the same time, the adaptation signalled the rapid decay of the existing imperial political economy. It bore witness both to the growing independence of the colonies in mercantile policy, and the willing relaxation of British metropolitan control, and it brought on new uncertainty.

In 1842, the British sharply lowered the imperial tariff, and reduced preferences on lumber, and – briefly – wheat. This resulted in a renewed bout of agitation that hastened the resolution of the conflict between commercial and agricultural interests in the united Canadas, as discussed above. But it also encouraged both articulation of a nationalist protectionist ideology, and attempts to provide strictly colonial tariff protection to manufacturers.

Such changes were particularly well illustrated by events in New Brunswick. After the reduction of the timber preferences in 1842, the lumbering industry remained in a slump for some time, a slump fueled by falling British demand and high levels of production and further enhanced by commercial and industrial depression in the North Atlantic world. A lack of employment opportunities forced people to emigrate from the city of Saint John to the United States, while local manufacturing endeavours suffered from the dumping practised by New England competitors.[24] Some interests developed strong hostility to American competition, a hostility that readily coupled with the widespread feeling that the British were exploiting the province without conscience. The imperial commercial system had resulted in provincial forests ravaged without permanent benefit to the colony and had discouraged industrial diversification; so began the refrain. The end result was a perceived provincial vulnerability to shifts in the British timber market.[25] These proto-nationalist rumblings soon fused with protectionist argument. Early in 1844, Saint John manufacturing interests such as grain millers, iron founders, and shoemakers formed the protectionist Provincial Association, an organization that also received widespread though short-lived support from farmers and fishermen. Even though many merchants opposed tariff increases as harmful to their concerns, some supported the association because of their investments in manufacturing enterprises, because they felt their hinterland markets would expand through protection, or simply because of nationalist impulses.

The association's solution to the woes of the province was attractive; it was identical with that used by the journalist Horace Greeley in the United States in 1842.[26] An independent local economy was to be created through tariff protection, in which local manufacturers would provide a source of jobs and so stimulate the market for other domestic producers. A great array of petitions – one sample is given here – urged protection on the Assembly of New Brunswick in early 1844: 'A constant and steady interchange of commodities would thus take place, the wants of the population would, in a great degree, be supplied from among themselves, and a neighbourly intercourse and feeling would spring up, which would make the interests of any one class, equally the interests of all, and result in rendering the people prosperous and contented.'[27] Mercantile resistance to these demands made them unfruitful in 1844, but in 1845 the colonial New Brunswick tariff was modestly increased. When the British government made it possible, the protectionist impulse in New Brunswick would receive much more vigorous legislative enactment.

A similar movement took place in the now united Province of Canada, though it was organizationally more diffuse and ideologically less decided. Manufacturing as an alternative to the dominant commercial and agricultural economic sectors was under public consideration. The sudden reduction in the imperial tariff level in 1842 was difficult to bear. In the light of the 17½, 20, and even higher percentage (*ad valorem*) duties the artisans and small manufacturers of the Canadas had previously enjoyed against American competition through the combined action of imperial and colonial tariffs, the new rates were very low: the rate on unspecified goods fell from 15 to 4 per cent; and though specific rates on a few agricultural items increased, the highest *ad valorem* level was 15 per cent. Now exposed to American protectionist arguments, such men let loose a barrage of petitions to the legislature of the Province of Canada between 1842 and 1846: higher duties on such goods as leather, boots and shoes, timber from the United States, beer, soap and candles, manufactured tobacco, biscuits, iron castings and axes, and scythes were requested, some of which already had a marginal protection under the colonial tariff.[28]

The outburst of petitioning reached a climax in 1845, and the provincial government made an effort to respond. The tariff of that year continued the important agricultural duties, but manufacturers were appeased by the reduction of duties on their raw materials, and an increase of rates on British goods. As well, the Laurentian trading system was coming under renewed attack through the first of the American Drawback Acts, which allowed British goods to be imported through the United States to the Canadas without the payment of American duties. The Canadian response was to impose some discriminating duties on these goods, repugnant as this was to the merchants of western Upper

Canada. These duties also had the effect of increasing protection on some Canadian manufactures. But when the British government indicated a benign disapproval of such duties, the province hastened to eliminate the most offensive items in 1846.[29] Colonial attempts to favour manufactures through the tariff remained constrained by the recognized centrality of agriculture and commerce, and by the imperial watchdog.

If the shifts of 1842 encouraged British North America in hesitant steps towards more independent commercial policies, the colonial dependencies were unprepared for the severe shock that met them in 1846. Originating in the repeal of the British Corn Laws and the removal of preferences on colonial grain and flour over the following three years, that shock was progressively worsened by a sharp reduction in the timber preferences, by an amendment to the British Possessions Act (which gave the colonies control over what had been the imperial tariff), by the abolition of the Navigation Laws, and by the commercial depression that took hold in this crucial period. To some, the great changes in British policy were only further steps in the inevitable and glorious progress of the colonies to greater independence and did not involve any reordering of economic structures. But to many others, the imperial nationality seemed shattered and the economy severely weakened.[30]

Frantic efforts were made to stabilize the suddenly chaotic universe. Many colonials demanded a return to the preferential system. Isaac Buchanan, a leading Upper Canadian merchant, rushed off to England to lobby for the grain preferences. In New Brunswick, the provincial legislature made the nostalgic gesture of providing substantial preferences to British products in the tariff of 1848, a move that the British rejected in free-trade righteousness. A public meeting in Saint John petitioned to have the Navigation Laws retained.[31] Too many powerful interests were bound up with the old commercial system for it to pass peacefully away.

Yet in other circles, free trade was accepted with quiet resignation and sometimes alacrity. Rather than establishing preferences for Britain, the Liberal government of Nova Scotia imposed a low revenue tariff in 1847 that treated trading partners equally. New Brunswickers enamoured of the free trade ethic formed the Reform Club in Saint John, which persistently advocated freer trade with the United States.[32] In the Canadas, the Free Trade Association of 1846 in Montreal manfully claimed that free trade produced the best of all worlds, urged the repeal of the Navigation Laws and colonial duties on American grains and provisions, and announced eternal vigilance in defence of revenue tariffs. Large meetings were held by the organization, and it fired off petitions and generated an audience for the free-trade publication, the *Canadian Economist*. The men involved had a firm grip on their pocketbooks of course, for the association's spokesmen and core membership were mostly Montreal grain exporters who wanted to ship American grain to Britain without impediment.[33]

The provincial government also approved of the move to free trade. Empowered by the British Possessions Act of 1846, they wiped away the imperial tariff structure and equalized the tariffs on imported goods, whatever their place of origin. The 1847 tariff stripped away much of the old imperial shield against American competition with a general rate of 7½ per cent. It was not free trade, for leather products and a few other goods obtained relatively high rates, but it was a shift in that direction.[34]

The colonials also searched in a modest way for markets other than the British. Already in 1847 there was talk of expanding trade between the colonies. After a number of unsuccessful attempts, an accord was reached between the Canadas, New Brunswick, and Nova Scotia in 1850, which Prince Edward Island joined in 1851, but this brought about no remarkable surge in trade. Adequate interprovincial transportation facilities were lacking, and the agreement only included natural products in which the colonies were each largely self-sufficient. Only in grain and flour, of the items listed, was there a notable Maritimes demand for Canadian products.[35]

Provincial eyes also naturally turned to the United States. Reciprocity with America offered economic advantages without political liabilities; that is, it could result in demand for British North American staples without offending the colonials' imperial attachments, and it could generate a greater supply of goods to be shipped via the St Lawrence. The eagerness for reciprocity is none the less puzzling, for it was a reciprocity in natural products that was most wanted in the Canadas, which contrasted strangely with the history of agricultural protectionism there. Of course, the demand for high duties on farm products had a strong retaliatory tinge to it, for the Americans guarded their market for foodstuffs jealously. Upper Canada's position rapidly altered in the 1840s however. Land devoted to the growing of wheat expanded greatly; this and several years of excellent crops yielded heavy exportable surpluses of grain. Farmers in the eastern United States had shifted away from wheat culture, as the agricultural frontier moved west. In a purely economic and geographic sense, Upper Canada was part of that frontier, and with deficient American wheat crops in the late 1840s, Canadian farmers could make money exporting to the United States despite the high American duties on breadstuffs.[36] Tariff protection of the provincial market was for this transitory period virtually useless, except perhaps as a bargaining tool to gain reciprocity. Likewise, the depressed condition of the lumber industry obliged that interest to look to urban America for continuing growth. And merchants in Upper Canada who had strong trade ties with the United States – ties reinforced by the expansion of commerce on the Great Lakes and by the American Drawback Acts of 1845 and 1846 – found a trade agreement very appealing. Reciprocity might undermine the St Lawrence route even more than the Drawback Acts did, but the considered opinion of the Free Trade Association of Montreal was that free access to American grain supplies would greatly strengthen the Laurentian trading system. Such access was half of the system the grain merchants of the city had always wanted; the other half, British preferences, were now out of the question. But the merchants had done good business before without any substantial preference, and if transportation costs in the interior could be kept low and reciprocity gained, Montreal could readily compete with New York.[37] The Quebec Board of Trade agreed: closer commercial ties with the United States were beneficial, as long as the St Lawrence was kept open to American shipping and a free trade in ships was included in the agreement.[38] Indeed, this commitment to the Laurentian system and continued trade with Britain dominated the economic policy perspectives of the Reform government that took power in 1848.[39]

Opposition to reciprocity was strongest in the Maritimes. The major sticking point for the ocean provinces was the American demand for access to the inshore fisheries, something Nova Scotia in particular was reluctant to give. The intercolonial convention on reciprocity that met in Halifax in 1849 failed because of this issue.[40] Powerful pro-reciprocity forces did, however, exist. New Brunswick lumbermen were enticed by the American market and the Saint John Reform Club was constantly issuing panegyrics on the subject. In Nova Scotia, commercial men and even farmers were attracted by the possibilities of selling ships and fish to the Americans, or engaging in American coastal shipping, or importing American products cheaply. As the depression worsened towards late 1849, the Maritimes found reciprocity an increasingly good solution to their economic woes.[41] Still, the Americans only proposed reciprocity bills in Congress; they did not pass them. So there was room for colonial protectionists to operate.

Developments in New Brunswick carried a familiar ring. R.D. Wilmot, a member of the provincial legislature for Saint John, joined with others to generate a vigorous protectionist campaign by early 1849. Wilmot had been an important figure in the 1844 high tariff thrust; now, in conjunction with political and business allies, he redoubled his efforts, citing American examples, quoting American protectionist texts, presenting the broad range of his cause. His cousin L.A. Wilmot had once said that England had abandoned her true 'National Policy' and her colonies through the adoption of free trade;[42] R.D. Wilmot outlined his scheme for breaking out of the economic trap in which he believed the province was placed. Colonial dependence on staples exports and manufactured imports meant a low level of prosperity, he argued, so industrial diversification was the only means of achieving a higher level of wealth. The consumption of local production within the province would increase its population and prosperity. But, 'a sufficient amount of patriotism and intelligence does not exist, to bring about such a result' through the spontaneous actions of individuals; protective tariffs were the only alternative.[43] A protective tariff was not class legislation – in this Wilmot's voice was joined by a chorus of local manufacturers: '*we do* contend that the public *will be* benefitted, for, as the ocean is formed of congregated drops, so, in this instance, our population (we mean our population of working men, not drones) will in a certain degree be increased, and every sensible man knows that labour begets labour, that is, the workmen and their families employed in manufacturing hats, requires clothes, boots, food, etc; should we lack mechanics or farmers to supply them with those articles, we must procure others, and they in their turn require other necessaries of life.'[44] The protectionists carried weight: the rate on goods not otherwise specified was set at 7½ per cent in 1849, but leather manufactures, vehicles, furniture and wooden ware, corn brooms, snuff and cigars, and hats were placed at the comparatively high level of 20 per cent.[45]

Nova Scotian high tariff men were not nearly as successful. In 1848 and again in 1853, heavy protectionist petitioning resulted in positive legislative reports. As the depression reached a crisis in 1849, Halifax artisans met to demand either a return to the mercantilist system or the imposition of tariff protection. They saw the continuity between the two. But though some provincial Conservatives took up protection as a pet cause, the Liberal government remained devoted to low tariffs. In 1849, the level on unenumerated goods stood at 6½ per cent, and until Confederation this general rate rose only slightly.[46]

A high tariff campaign was undertaken in the Canadas in 1847–49 as well, as the protectionist ideology that had emerged as early as 1844 in New Brunswick now became fully articulated in the westerly provinces. Hugh Scobie, born and raised in Scotland, and since 1838 the editor of the Toronto *Colonist*, waxed eloquent about the dangers of free trade, that latest enthusiasm of the British and colonial commercial world. Free trade mercantile interests were essentially parasitic, he stated in several 1847 editorials; they fed off the truly productive and destroyed the organic and harmonious society that had existed in an earlier agricultural and manufacturing Britain, erecting in its place a society divided along class lines and full of conflict. The same process now threatened the colonies. Only tariff protection would allow harmony to regain a paramount position.[47] The lawyer and politician Robert Baldwin Sullivan articulated a whole mass of protectionist arguments in a late 1847 address to the Mechanics' Institute of Hamilton. Limited though his final proposals were – he thought that Canadians generally had sufficient protection, and only needed to show more entrepreneurship – his flood of polemic about the evils of a staple-producing economy, the unacceptability of exploitation by Great Britain, the need for diversity of employment, and the fruitfulness of an economy in which a large population of urban mechanics provided a market for diversified agricultural production, marked him as a protectionist ideologue.[48]

These issues were discussed in the provincial election of 1847–48 with Reform leaders such as L.H. Lafontaine and Francis Hincks stating a strong preference for free trade, and some of their opponents advocating various degrees of protection. However, the protectionists' campaign swung into high gear only when they were able to take advantage of the government's growing need for revenue. Customs duties brought in roughly 80 per cent of government funds, and imports were declining as expenditures rose by 1848 and 1849. The tariff would have to be altered.[49]

The short-lived Brockville Association for the Encouragement of Home Manufactures met in November 1848 to demand protection, reasoning that since the Canadas had been thrown into world competition by Britain's free-trade actions, the best alternative was fostering domestic industrial production for a home trade. American progress, and the large scale emigration from the Canadas to the United States, made higher tariffs appealing to these Brockville folk. Similar meetings took place in Toronto, where an unsuccessful effort was made to persuade farmers of the benefits of industrial protection, in the District of Colbourne where protection was urged as the alternative to reciprocity, in Boucherville, and especially in Montreal.[50]

There, where the rapid growth of industry along the Lachine Canal seemed convincing proof of the value of manufacturing, a crusade of sorts gathered force in 1849. In mid January, a major protectionist meeting was held, inspirational speeches were given, and the large crowd passed protectionist resolutions, asserting sympathy with the labouring classes in their distress and urging incidental protection and low duties on necessaries. William Workman, the merchant and industrial investor who spearheaded the movement, spoke at length about the splendours of protection, heavily illustrating his thesis with examples from the United States. The protectionists circulated a petition that was signed by over 4000 by the time a meeting was held to form the 'Association for the Encouragement of Home Industry.'[51] In the meantime, the key protectionist paper, the *Gazette*, put together appropriate editorials, and in its pages were to be found enthusiastic letters from major employers clearing up the fine points of protectionist theory, and emphasizing paternalistic solidarity between employers and employed. A prohibitive level of protection was not demanded. Rather, 'incidental protection' was the principle employed. 'The expenses of the Government, and the interest of the public debt, form a burden which must be proportionately borne by all,' it was carefully explained, 'and the great principle for which we contend is, that *the burden must be so leveled* that it will give the largest possible protection to the employment of the industrial classes.' This meant low duties on 'necessaries' such as tea, sugar, and coffee, and a 'moderate amount of protection' on the industrial products of the country, 'giving both revenue and protection.'[52]

Among French Canadians, the message was spread by *La Minerve*, which carried lengthy diatribes attacking the writings of the French free-trade publicist Frederic Bastiat. Free traders were accused of being concerned with meaningless abstractions rather than practicalities, of creating a false conflict between producers and consumers, and of fostering anarchy rather than harmony and social order. Protection provided for the opposite, of course, treating all social groups with an even hand and bringing about progress within the national framework. The paper added pointedly that the harmony produced by protection made it obvious that agriculture was not French Canada's exclusive vocation. Some French-Canadian politicians agreed. Worried about the high level of emigration to the United States, they advocated not only the time-worn nostrum of agricultural expansion, but more industry via protection to keep the wandering French Canadian at home.[53]

All this battering at the walls did not have the desired result. Low-tariff men raised considerable and sometimes successful opposition in public protectionist meetings; they had numerous newspapers on their side, like Montreal's *Pilot* and *Herald*; they were backed by the weight of British opinion. Then also, solidarity on the question of protection between the French- and English-speaking peoples was undermined by the Rebellion Losses Bill, which encouraged racial antipathy.[54] After mid January 1849, Rebellion Losses became the keynote of *La Minerve*, with occasional glosses on reciprocity. Most important of all, the free traders were well entrenched in the Reform party and government – a government unwilling at that time to prejudice the chances for reciprocity with unwarranted tariff changes. Inspector General Francis Hincks, in introducing the tariff alterations that year, took a strong free-trade position despite vociferous opposition, and emphasized the importance of revenue. The duties on some raw materials used in Canadian manufacturing were increased, those on selected manufactured items decreased, and on necessaries they were maintained at high levels. The rate on unenumerated goods (those not specifically listed in the tariff) was lifted to 12½ per cent. Though the tariff inevitably contained an element of protection, the truth of the matter was reflected in the morbidly acidic comment of one protectionist paper: the 'great trunk principle' of the administration was to 'Get Money.'[55]

Hincks also attempted, though not with complete success, to make the tariff entirely *ad valorem* rather than mixed specific and *ad valorem*. Dollar-value or

TABLE 1
Number and tonnage of vessels entered inward at Montreal, 1844–49

Year	Number	Tonnage
1844	207	49,635
1845	210	51,848
1846	219	55,566
1847	234	63,381
1848	162	41,811
1849	144	37,425

SOURCE: Province of Canada, Legislative Assembly *Journals* 1850, appendix A

specific duties could not be used effectively to protect transportation routes, while percentage duties could. For the merchants of the St Lawrence, Hincks's proposal was a chance to return to a kind of commercial protection they had enjoyed under the imperial system, which had fostered British trade via their river. Their cause was urgent. The United States Drawback Acts (the first had allowed duty-free imports through the United States to the Canadas; the second duty-free exports), and the removal of British preferences and imperial duties seemed to worsen the commercial depression of the late 1840s. Montreal's port traffic declined sharply; the Laurentian trade network was seemingly threatened (table 1). Concurrently, Toronto's international trade grew. The value of goods imported at Montreal fell, but at Toronto they rose from £197,225 in 1847 to £326,863 the following year. Customs duties collected at Toronto increased from $30,000 in 1846 to nearly $400,000 in 1850.[56]

Hincks's proposal would structure the *ad valorem* system to favour direct importation via the St Lawrence. The percentage duties were to be calculated on the cash value of goods in the country from which they were last exported directly to the Canadas. Thus, goods imported from Britain directly to Quebec, Montreal, or other provincial ports of entry paid duty on their estimated value in Britain, while those same goods imported via the United States paid duty on their estimated value in the United States, which included the cost of ocean freight and insurance. The difference could be substantial: contemporaries placed transoceanic freight rates on pig iron at about 21 per cent of the Canadian value, and for fragile items such as crockery, the freight costs doubled the value of the goods. Upper Canadian merchants protested strongly, but without effect, for in 1853 Hincks closed the loopholes in the system.[57]

The crisis of the established political economy in New Brunswick had, by early 1849, been met by an upward movement in the customs tariff, and in other provinces by moves towards freer trade. Yet neither was sufficient to avert annexationists from blaming the commercial depression of the late 1840s on the shift in British commercial policy.[58] Annexationism – political fusion with the United States – had a particular popularity in Montreal, where several of the newspapers gave it partial or hearty support, and where major public meetings could be called in its favour. Large numbers of both free traders and protectionists in the city's élite signed the annexation manifesto that circulated in the autumn of 1849.[59] To annexationists, all other solutions to the economic quandary were insufficient because impermanent or because they could not generate a large enough market. A return to the preferential system was impossible, a union of the colonies would be one of competitive not complementary economies, independence would leave the province too weak, protection would bring stagnation because of the small internal market, and reciprocity with the United States was only a stopgap.[60]

However, though sometimes popular outside Montreal in the British North American colonies,[61] the annexationist passion was a passing one.[62] Annexationists did try to capture the British American League, the short-lived Tory party revival, but they were beaten back at the league's convention by a combination of protectionists who passed resolutions demanding a tariff wall for both agriculture and manufactures, and proposals for a union of the colonies.[63] Defeated in its efforts to co-opt an organizational base, faced with the hostility of colonial and British governments, lacking widespread fervent support, the annexationist movement quickly faded in 1850 as better economic times returned. It provided no genuine option in the policy choices the colonies faced.[64]

The entire business did have the effect of making the pursuit of reciprocity a compelling task for colonial and British officials.[65] Unfortunately, the Americans were not seduced into a trade agreement by the conciliatory stance taken by Britain and her North American dependencies. To politicians from the American south, reciprocity was a preliminary to annexation and the growth of free-state political power, which was unacceptable in the ever more tense American sectional struggle. The active work of the various protectionist lobbies in this context could readily stall not only pro-reciprocity agitation from eastern American entrepôts and western grain states, but also the persistent efforts at negotiation by the British.

Retaliation was therefore one of the few methods the Canadians had to pressure the United States. By January 1851, Hincks was hinting to the Americans that in the absence of a reciprocity agreement, the government of the Canadas might choose to close canals to American shipping and greatly increase the tariff, ideas that had some popularity.[66] As inspector general and premier, Hincks in 1850 introduced a change in the law that made it possible for the governor general in council (the cabinet, in effect) to remove duties on raw materials going into Canadian manufactures, a subtly protectionist move. Pressures for higher tariffs mounted. The boards of trade convention at Quebec City in September 1852 resulted in a compromise between commercial and industrial protectionists. Montreal manufacturers wrote an open letter to the convention, asking that it recommend an increase in customs duties. The delegates took heed, and urged not only protection to the St Lawrence commercial route, and retaliatory duties against the United States, but that home manufacturers be given incidental protection.[67] The Montreal Board of Trade made similar points in a petition of early 1853, 'praying for the establishment of a system of Commercial Policy, which, while it would tend directly to foster the trade of the Province, by way of the River St. Lawrence, would at the same time be incidentally protective to the manufacturing interests of the country.'[68] The proposed policies reflected the experiences of the old imperial system.

Hincks used such public demands in planning to get reciprocity. He intended to impose greater tariff protection and discriminate against American use of Canadian canals as a means of pressuring the Americans towards a trade agreement. Opposition overwhelmed his plans however, for they were revealed in early 1852 by a resigning member of Hincks' ministry, effectively crippling them before they had a chance to mature. Despite the strong protectionist advocacy of John Gamble, who both congratulated Hincks on his conversion from free trade to protection and denounced the proposals as insufficient, Hincks could only bemoan the lack of common purpose in the assembly in seeking reciprocity.[69] The retaliatory policy was put aside for nearly twenty years, until Hincks returned as finance minister of the new Canadian nation.

As it turned out, winning reciprocity in 1854 depended heavily on hardening colonial attitudes on the fisheries. Plans for protecting the inshore fisheries more effectively were laid in 1851, and in 1852, the British government agreed to supply the naval muscle necessary for enforcement.[70] Access to the inshore waters was important both for the mackerel fisheries and for the catching of bait fish for cod, but now the many American fishermen who illegally harvested the inshore waters or who operated in jurisdictions over which there was dispute, faced a more vigorous assertion of colonial rights. American interest in reciprocity grew markedly, and in 1854, a final grand round of lobbying took place in Washington to move a proposed treaty through the Senate.[71]

The final product of what was a complex diplomatic and political process need not be described in detail here. The British North American inshore fisheries were opened to the Americans; the United States opened a portion of their fisheries in partial return. Canal transportation concessions were made on both sides. Though some processed goods were included in the free list of the agreement, they were of a strictly limited character: flour, smoked and salted meats, dried fruits, butter and cheese, sawn, hewn but unfinished lumber or timber, and a further handful of like items. This left untouched the wide variety of more complex manufactured goods required by the colonial societies. There was, therefore, no threat to merchants importing manufactures along trade routes from Britain; nor was there any immediate danger to colonial manufacturing. For provincial staple producers, the treaty seemed a godsend because it gave free access to the American market for their timber, fish, coal, wheat, and other products. And the merchants who exported wheat or other goods to Britain via the St Lawrence faced no barriers in gaining access to the American hinterland. The tensions between the major colonial interests had seemingly been resolved. The national, international, and economic conditions for which the resolution was adequate were, however, in flux.

The meaning of the treaty was not clear-cut in ideological terms. Reciprocity was justified in the colonies on grounds of free trade; in fact, the goods listed in the treaty were, by 1856, allowed free into most of the colonies from the world at large.[72] Though undertaken partly at the insistence of Great Britain, this unilateral lowering of colonial tariff barriers confirmed and enhanced the mid-Victorian liberalism so common in the transforming colonial world.[73] None the less, despite the hints and promises Canadian politicians gave the Americans about the possibilities of a wider reciprocity in the future, the treaty left room for greater tariff protection of colonial manufactures. The treaty made clear the continuing primacy of the trade in staple products and the primacy of the Laurentian transportation system in the central British North American colonies, for the intent behind the agreement was obviously to capture the exports of the American interior of the continent. After a decade of tumult in the British North American political economy, a broad course had been decided upon. Markets for colonial raw or partly processed products seemingly had been retained or gained, and the protection that existed for colonial manufactures had not been lost.

For a long time, provincial products, including manufactures, had received some protection from American competition by means of imperial and colonial tariffs. After the alterations of 1846, New Brunswick moved most sharply in a protectionist direction, Nova Scotia the least. In the Canadas, the tariff of 1849 was unsatisfactory to protectionists, but did not strip them of all policy encouragement. The Reciprocity Treaty did little harm to established manufacturing industries, and in fact guaranteed free entry to a variety of useful raw materials. While commercial policies had been altered, the alterations had gone far to maintain the existing political economy.

As it happened, the growth of the 1850s ensured that the protectionist voice gained in volume and resonance. But it repeated the same things. The protectionist position had been fully stated by the end of the 1840s throughout British North America. The dangers of staple production, the importance of economic diversity in fostering harmony and growth, the defence against free trade attacks about the impact of protective tariffs on prices and about class favouritism, and the appeals to proto-nationalist sentiment as expressed in hostility to Britain or the United States found expression between 1842 and 1849. The regular citing of American and sometimes British or other examples about the positive effects of protection, and the occasional quotation from protectionist pamphlets and texts of foreign provenance gave strong indication of the derivative nature of the articulate British North American protectionist's views.

Ironically enough, it was in the later 1850s that protectionism truly found a secure niche in the minds of the provincials. Not John Rae, the schoolteacher who formulated his sophisticated and protectionist political economy in Upper Canada in the 1830s (but who was a prophet without honour in his own land), not R.D. Wilmot, or Hugh Scobie, or Robert Baldwin Sullivan, or John Gamble, or William Workman was much quoted in later years. Nor were they considered fathers of the National Policy. Isaac Buchanan, the Hamilton-based merchant who yearned for the imperial commercial system and whose advocacy of proto-nationalist protectionism only became strong in the later 1850s, was the public man to whom primacy of place was given. In recalling great moments in history, protectionists of later times ignored the function and impact of colonial and imperial tariffs prior to 1846, and almost uniformly failed to mention the high tariff agitation of the late 1840s in favour of citing the protectionist campaign of 1857–59 and the tariff of the latter year. They fashioned history out of their memories, and with the favouritism of memory, chose to ignore a painful and troubled time.

2
Continuity and change: making tariffs in the late 1850s

The Canadas witnessed a ferment for high tariffs between 1856 and 1859. The economic crisis beginning in 1857 encouraged protectionist organization and partly fostered the fiscal emergency in government that made tariff changes necessary. Pressures for protection to manufactures, demands for commercial protection, and the need for revenue coincided. Determined to 'Get Money,' the financial officers of the provincial government sought arrangements that might improve the well-being of the province while satisfying a variety of interests.

Revenue needs formed a point around which the competing demands of interests in other provinces balanced also. Conflict between commercial low-tariff interests and protectionists took place in New Brunswick in the 1840s, with the latter gaining considerable, though incomplete victories. Stable commercial policy required that this struggle be abated, and a sharp increase in government expenditure provided the means. Compromise between interests on tariff matters after that decade became such a normal feature of political life that the provincial secretary of New Brunswick, Samuel Leonard Tilley, claimed that the tariff revisions of 1859 were free of the usual clamour of petitioning and counter-petitioning.[1] Tilley was evidently seen as a trustworthy broker, a reputation that would stand him in good stead twenty years later when he was finance minister of Canada. The compromises between the interests that Tilley helped foster resulted in the steady reduction of the extremely high protectionist duties imposed in 1849 and 1851, though by 1862 these still stood at 18 per cent. At the same time, rates on unspecified goods rose steadily from 7½ per cent in 1849 to 15½ per cent in 1862.[2] The customs duties had a positive effect, so some contemporaries thought. Manufactories were 'gradually springing up' as a government report phrased it in the latter year: 'The heavy Provincial debt incurred on account of the Railroad, requiring much larger revenue to be raised now than was necessary in former years, has no doubt operated as a guarantee to those persons who were willing and desirous to invest their capital in local manufactories, as it is now apparent that our tariff cannot in future be much reduced.'[3] Revenue needs provided the basis for an incidental protection.

Government expenditures mounted in the Province of Canada also. Total ordinary government expenditures rose from £450,913 in 1849 to £923,039 in 1854,[4] and to this had to be added the constant infusions of funds into railways. It was almost exclusively because of the railway problem that the tariff had to be raised in 1856, though the form of the increase was influenced by Montreal-based protectionist agitation.

Manufacturing had grown explosively during the preceding decade in the city. Along the Lachine Canal, flour mills, foundries, rolling mills, and other industries had been established; in 1854 the Redpaths undertook their sugar refinery, which provided employment for several hundred men; boot and shoe, rubber goods, and other manufactories added to the industrial base.[5] The mounting imports of the mid 1850s, encouraged by the railway boom, by excellent grain and lumber prices, and by the expansion of credit, had by 1856 produced sharp competitive conditions that encouraged protectionism among manufacturers. They were instrumental in calling a large public meeting in late February 1856, complete with inspirational speeches and robust protectionist resolutions. Raw materials and necessaries should have low duties placed on them, the gathering agreed, and duties on luxuries and manufactures 'competing or likely to come into competition with Canadian Productions' should be increased. In fact, the Canadian tariff should be raised to the same height as the American. The Tariff Reform Association, formed to give coherence to the excitement, put these demands in a petition signed by between 4000 and 5000 manufacturers, mechanics, merchants, and farmers.[6]

A few days after this impressive memorial was presented to the provincial assembly, Inspector General William Cayley announced that the Grand Trunk Railway would not be able to pay interest on its bonds. From Hincks' time, the provincial government had been closely involved with the Grand Trunk scheme and had guaranteed the GT bonds, so the possible insolvency of that railway threatened to destroy the province's credit in the London money market. It was impossible to allow such destruction. Cayley proposed to rescue the Grand Trunk: the customs revenue, which supplied roughly four-fifths of total government income, would have to be increased by 25 per cent.[7] The coincidence of protectionist demand and government revenue needs was almost too perfect.

Though the resulting tariff may have relieved the minds of the Grand Trunk officials, it did not satisfy the protectionists. Iron, leather, and India-rubber manufacturing interests had been favoured, and unenumerated goods had been raised from 12½ to 15 per cent, but Cayley was accused of being partial to low-tariff interests. Men who favoured high tariffs were greatly annoyed by the higher duties on many necessaries, which undercut understandings between manufacturers and grocery importers and made protection less attractive to the consuming public. The Tariff Reform Association passed resolutions condemning Cayley's effort. At the heart of protectionist dissatisfaction lay the dominant revenue function of the tariff and Cayley's failure to mollify more than a small number of industrial and mercantile interests.[8]

The organized agitation did not come to an end, but was sustained by the financial crisis of 1857 and the economic downturn that followed at its heels. For a time in 1857, commercial failures were common, but when this rash of insolvencies came to an end, faltering railway construction, poor demand for lumber, and low unit prices for poor wheat harvests made chances of recovery slim in 1858 and 1859. As the main motors of the economy faltered, imports fell sharply, especially in Upper Canada. Demand for domestically produced manufactures slumped, and urban centres suffered.[9]

The situation fostered organized protectionism. During the provincial election campaign of January 1858, for example, only those candidates in Montreal who made believable high-tariff pledges were elected. And early in the year, the executive committee of the city's Tariff Reform Association framed the customs duties changes they wanted to see, and sent them off to the government.[10] Protectionist outcries came from elsewhere as well. The Quebec Board of Trade petitioned for the now familiar commercial protection to the St Lawrence route, combining this with a request to 'give such Tariff protection to our own manufactures as may tend to promote and encourage them.'[11] The upsurge of protectionist sentiment in Upper Canada was impressive, orchestrated as it was by the Association for the Promotion of Canadian Industry. Nominally open to all who cared to join, the organization was dominated by manufacturers, and its political thrust was guided by the businessman, politician, and ideologue Isaac Buchanan. Late in March 1858 the movement went into high gear: manufacturers and 'others favourable to the movement were to be encouraged to press their views on members of the Legislature.' A controlling committee was set up to distribute a printed memorial blaming 'the difficulties now experienced by all classes of the community' on unfair foreign competition.[12] The concerted effort produced a wave of favourable reaction; many were desperate for curative measures. A meeting of those favouring protection was held in Hamilton; a Kingston branch of the association was formed at the beginning of May, and similar branches were established in Belleville, Galt, London, and Dundas. Protectionist newspapers in Toronto and Montreal began to editorialize endlessly, and even a number of Reform journals advocated higher customs duties.[13] If protection had formerly 'suffered from a fancied identity with Montreal,' such an identification could no longer be made.[14] The cause caught a wave of genuine popularity.

Not least among the sources of that popularity was the seductive charm of protectionist ideology. When the Upper Canadian high-tariff men published a widely distributed pamphlet outlining their proceedings and resolutions in convention, they included an essay by Horace Greeley that they believed 'expresses, as well as can be expressed, the principles advocated by the Association for the Promotion of Canadian Industry.'[15] The essay, which expressed opinions Greeley had held since the early 1840s, undoubtedly had the full approval of the chief Upper Canadian high-tariff propagandist, Isaac Buchanan.

Buchanan's protectionist outlook was rooted in his personal history. During the 1840s, he had been firmly wedded to the vision and practicalities of the empire of the St Lawrence, with Hamilton as the entrepôt of a western hinterland. As a grain exporter, he belonged to the larger imperial economy framed by the preferential system, and he knew himself as a citizen of the British empire. Born in Scotland, he had come to the Canadas in 1830 at 19 years of age, and he returned to Great Britain at regular intervals to arrange business matters. Nor did he see himself as a merchant only. His father had first been a manufacturer of textiles and then a commercial man at Glasgow, and had owned an estate of over two square miles in Scotland. Isaac, naturally enough, fancied himself as something of a landed gentleman.[16]

Buchanan's sharp and despairing reaction to the repeal of the Corn Laws in 1846 was, therefore, more than that of a Canadian merchant having the rules changed on him. It was also the reaction of a man who identified with the British country gentry. Quite appropriately, he rushed to England at the time of the repeal and generated evidence for the use of Lord George Bentinck, who was leading the parliamentary struggle of the landed gentry against the removal of agricultural protection.[17]

The removal of the Corn Laws would utterly disrupt England's harmonious organic community and set class against class, Buchanan felt. The only solution was to consciously preserve the community by forming an alliance between a paternalistic aristocracy and the working classes in order to defeat the rising liberal bourgeoisie – who were dominated by the 'German Jews' of Buchanan's darker conceptions.[18] John Barnard Byles, the British protectionist Buchanan constantly quoted in the late 1850s, and who articulated concerns like Buchanan's with a lucidity the Hamilton-based businessman could never match, asserted that the individual without social restraint was destructive, and that the organic character of English society was being torn apart by free-trade liberalism.[19] To Byles and Buchanan there was no invisible hand. Class conflict was to be countered by a nostalgic bourgeois vision of an ideal society.

Buchanan's protectionism went beyond this, to take the form of long-term self-interest. With the loss of the imperial preferential system, alternative economic policies had to be developed within the Canadas. As a grain exporter, Buchanan's interests had been tied to that system; as an importer/wholesaler, his fortunes had been dependent on the rapid growth of the Upper Canadian farming frontier prior to the contraction of 1857. Such growth was coming to an end by then, and intensive growth on the pattern of Hamilton's industrial expansion of the early and mid 1850s seemed the only possible means of expanding domestic markets. His long-range personal interests could here mesh with protectionism and the half-formed nationalism that had been forced on him by the Corn Laws disaster. Thus the idea of a hierarchical, quasi-corporate society – which persisted with Buchanan despite the sad lack of landed gentry in Upper Canada – was transferred to the colony in the form of a paternalistic interest in the labouring man. To this curious mixture he added the developed protectionism available from Britain, Germany, and especially the United States. Buchanan freely acknowledged the debts he owed to Byles, to Greeley, to the British monetary theorist Johnathan Duncan, to the German protectionist Friedrich List, to 'American System' Henry Clay, and especially to Henry C. Carey, 'an American Economist, whose writings have raised for him a monument, *Aere perennius* [more lasting than brass].'[20] Extensive and fearless quotation from these authorities made up a large portion of Buchanan's bulky and rambling protectionist outpourings.

As the merchant understood matters, manufacturers were vital for the progress of an underdeveloped nation. Not only would manufacturing employ those unsuited to other types of work, not only would it encourage immigration and discourage emigration, it would also provide concentrated urban markets to allow farmers to escape the soil-degenerating process of persistent wheat production through the growth of a variety of products and through crop rotation. Without manufacturing, the colonial economy would be caught in a downward spiral, losing productive capacity, exporting staple products at a discount, and generally suffering under the sting of an adverse balance of trade.[21]

This was vintage Carey. The American, who perhaps cynically has been identified as an apologist for Pennsylvanian iron founders, provided intellectual underpinnings for Buchanan's sense of colonial grievance. Carey's concerns reflected the profound changes in marketing that had occurred in the late 1700s and early 1800s when a structure of wholesale merchants, discount houses, and agents developed to distribute goods internationally.[22] Carey glorified the advantages of domestic commerce as opposed to international trade. He went so far as to assert that the mercantile and banking interests of England were sucking dry both the industrial population of that country and the agricultural population of the United States through financial manipulation and debilitating transportation charges. By bringing farmer and manufacturer to live side by side, such costs would become not a levy paid to a parasitic commercial class, but part of the profits accruing to real producers of wealth.[23]

Some of Buchanan's analysis also paralleled the historical developmentalism of Friedrich List. The German, who matured his protectionist ideas during a lengthy stay in the United States in the 1830s, codified the historical approach prevalent there in his *The National System of Political Economy* (1841). When translated into English in 1856, this book, in combination with his tracts from his American period, assured List a place in the pantheon of high-tariff heroes. Nation-states, he argued, moved through a cycle of development, from simple staple production, to industrialization and economic diversification through the use of protection, to a mature economy in which free trade was the norm. Abundant historical example, much of it from Britain, illustrated List's thesis.[24] Similarly, Buchanan felt that the only way to break the cycle of stagnation or degeneration characteristic of simple economies was through protection to manufactures. After all, foreign manufacturers had an excessive lead time, skilled and cheap labour, and a malevolent attitude toward new competition; without protection, the youthful economy and infant manufactures of the Canadas could never become independent. Deserted by Great Britain (the loss of the preferential system still rankled Buchanan after more than a decade!), the Province of Canada had to look after its own interests, to the exclusion of others.[25]

In Buchanan's writing, as in those of List, Byles, Greeley, and especially Carey, the social vision of protection was of a society without debilitating conflicts. What had once been a mere economic theory about the mutual stimulation of various economic sectors[26] had by the 1840s evolved into an increasingly formal doctrine positing, as Henry C. Carey put it, the *Harmony of Interests* (1851). A properly diversified economy negated class conflict, List had asserted.[27] Carey took the matter further: interests naturally operated in harmony; conflicts between groups or classes were the consequence of an artificially induced imbalance among interests or the absence of a vital sector from the national economy.[28] In fact, the influential Carey scorned to call his three-volume masterwork of 1858 an essay in economics; rather he brought forth *The Principles of Social Science*. Buchanan's conceptions about harmony can only be seen as derivative in this context. 'THE LABOURING MASSES ARE NO LONGER OPEN TO BE HUMBUGGED BY THE SILLY DOCTRINE THAT LABOUR IS A SEPARATE INTEREST,' he trumpeted. 'THE WORKING MEN NOW SEE THAT THE ONLY POSSIBLE CAUSE OF INCREASED WAGES, IS INCREASED EMPLOYMENT, WHICH CAN ONLY ARISE FROM IMPROVING THE CONDITION OF THE EMPLOYERS OF LABOUR!' And those working men would provide a market for diversified agricultural production; 'raising up factories alongside our farms, is to benefit the Canadian farmer.'[29] It was little wonder that the working population of major urban centres attended protectionist meetings, or that petitions for protection to manufactures even came from the farming population.

Perhaps the national and society-wide vision of the ideologues of the Association for the Promotion of Canadian Industry was belied by its actions. Manufacturers dominated the major meeting of the organization in Toronto in April 1858, where tariff-change proposals were discussed. They created, and sent off to the government, a model tariff that reflected their special interests. All raw material (including some partially processed) should be allowed in duty free or nearly so, the association stated. A second level of 15 per cent should be imposed on goods that might be made in the province beginning in the near future. Components requiring assembly and many manufactures in the rough were included. The manufacturers then wanted a third level to be at 25 per cent to include all articles coming into competition with Canadian manufactures. On necessaries such as tea, sugar, and molasses, duties should be low or non-existent, to propitiate the ordinary consumer and to neutralize possible opposition from powerful grocery importers.[30]

The provincial government by no means simply accepted these demands. The Conservative government was so weak in 1858 that it could hardly afford to offend low-tariff interests with impunity. As Inspector General William Cayley told one early protectionist delegation, they could only expect minor concessions.[31] Revenue needs would dictate tariff changes.

Cayley actually made the financial position of the government look quite good when he made his preliminary estimates for the upcoming fiscal year in the middle of June. The major worry was in providing financial support for the railways, and Cayley announced he would deal with those burdens, amounting to £260,000, almost entirely by methods other than the increasing of customs duties on manufactures.[32] The bright picture Cayley painted was politically necessary, for the opposition persistently attacked the government as spendthrift. The attack reached a peak of intensity in the Committee on Public Accounts, where Cayley was sacrificed to the inquisitorial instincts of the leading figure of the opposition, the journalist/politician George Brown. The government was charged with gross financial mismanagement. Cayley himself was accused of illegal financial manipulations, the improper tendering of contracts, and rank peculation. While these accusations were never proven, Cayley's lax administrative habits gave them a degree of believability, and he failed to convincingly disprove them. The 'gentlemanly,' 'timid' Cayley[33] was goaded to such helpless fury by Brown's loaded questions at one June meeting of the committee that he was barely restrained from hurling an inkpot at his tormentor. Thus the presentation of a reasonably good financial picture was a triumph, not only for the government, but for Cayley personally.[34]

It was a pity that the ground was torn out from beneath him before the month was out. Not many days before the budget was to come down, Cayley received a letter from Auditor General John Langton telling him that the estimates for the coming year were almost blindly optimistic. 'Since I wrote you a few days ago upon the state of our finances,' Langton wrote on 27 June, 'I have been frequently turning the matter over in my mind, and the more I think of it, the more I am convinced, that I very much underestimated our difficulties.' Langton estimated a deficit of slightly more than one million pounds for the past fiscal year. Even if the support to the railways was subtracted from this, the total remained frightening: £587,500, equivalent to nearly 50 per cent of the average revenue. 'This has all the appearance of a permanent deficiency upon our present basis,' Langton went on inexorably, 'which no one can hope to meet by borrowing or by temporary expedients.' He saw no easy or obvious means of balancing the budget: cutting expenditures could only make up a small proportion of this huge deficit and would be highly unpopular politically; customs and excise duties could only be increased to a limited degree (he undoubtedly feared increased smuggling and an overall decline in revenue if the tariff was made too high); and he uneasily concluded that 'before we reach the end of the £600,000 we must come to direct taxation.'[35]

With what energy of despair or in what fashion Cayley changed his contemplated tariff in the next few days we do not know. All we can be sure of is that the tariff resolutions brought down in early July surprised observers. 'Mr. Cayley made it appear,' the *Globe* tartly editorialized, 'when moving to go into supply [some weeks earlier], that there was to be no great increase in the duties, that he was to reduce some things and to raise others, but the general average was to remain the same.'[36] Though the proposed tariff kept many of the major revenue-producing items at specific rates, and left the existing rate for unenumerated goods at 15 per cent, a large 20 per cent list was proposed, containing a mix of luxury goods and manufactures made in the province. Revenue and incidental protection were the obvious motives for the alterations.

The protectionists did not sing Cayley's praises. Buchanan, in fact, threatened to withdraw his support from the administration. He sent a circular to the other MPPs urging them to fight for more protection, and outside the assembly, the Association for the Promotion of Canadian Industry met again, with some 20 MPPs attending as observers. The organization demanded a tariff increase on woollens and clothing. Cayley gave way on these items, as he did to pressures for increasing the duty on a variety of iron products. By the time the lobbying process came to an end, Cayley had placed about one-third of the items on which the protectionists had wanted 25 per cent on the 20 per cent list. Fearful of alienating government supporters, the inspector general did not increase the tariff on obvious revenue-producing items such as necessaries or industrial-input goods. Politically isolated, his government endangered by his actions, his reputation ravaged, Cayley spent more of his time defending his integrity than his tariff in the budget debates.[37]

The protectionism of the tariff did not arouse much opposition in the assembly in and of itself. Government finance was the instrument on which the opposition played, and from it they wrung mournful tunes about the need for retrenchment, counterpointed with the horrors particular duties would visit on those affected.[38] Opposition spokesmen found it unwise to annoy protectionists in their ranks as the defeat of the government was a tangible possibility. Before the proposed legislation moved through all the necessary parliamentary procedures, but after the substantive debate was over, the much-weakened Conservatives fell on the seat-of-government question. The brief Reform administration that followed, and the events leading to the infamous 'Double Shuffle,' have been described elsewhere;[39] what should be noted here is that when the Conservatives returned to power, Cayley was no longer in the cabinet. Alexander Tilloch Galt, financier and politician, had replaced him. Fresh blood was needed to meet the immense difficulties ahead, for a new fiscal structure had to be erected. The tariff had to be reformulated, clarified, given direction.

When Galt rose in the Assembly of the Province of Canada to give his first budget speech on 11 March 1859, he stressed four aims. He intended, he told his audience, to cut back (to 'retrench' as it was then known) government expenditures, to increase revenue, to create a system of tariffs to favour the use of the St Lawrence shipping route, and to provide incidental protection to the budding manufactures of the Canadas.[40] These had been his aims, though the balance between them had not been clear, when he first joined the government in August 1858. They pivoted around one crucial factor: the financial position of the government.

It was bleak. A large deficit had been run in 1857. A very sizeable one was accumulating in 1858, despite the hasty final passage of Cayley's tariff under Galt's guidance after the Conservative return to power. Privately, Galt complained that Cayley had failed to take the revenue bull by the horns.[41] Burned into the memory of the finance minister (the title was changed from inspector general as part of Galt's general departmental reforms) was the fateful letter in which Auditor General Langton had warned Cayley of prospective annual deficits of £600,000. The immediate future offered no hope of unforced improvement, for the depression that followed the crash of 1857 had not yet lifted, and poor crops and low prices made demand for imports very soft.[42] The most attractive way of overcoming the deficit was thus not by increasing taxes, but by cutting expenditures.

Galt outlined a number of arenas in which government spending could be reduced in his budget speech, but he did have to admit that the projected savings would be modest.[43] The government establishment could not be decimated, he knew. Moreover, much of the government's political influence grew out of an elaborate system of log-rolling and pork-barrelling. So when John Rose, a confidant of Galt's and political head of the Board of Works, told an English correspondent that 'We shall put an end to all this local bloodsucking if we live,'[44] he promised a course of action that would have severely damaged the governing party. Rose's heroic scenario was not played out.

Other approaches were, however, available. Public works had absorbed huge amounts of capital, and operating expenses required yet further funds. 'Our debt is about 10 millions – direct and indirect,' Rose had gone on to tell his correspondent. 'Three fourths of this has been incurred for public works – you have the Welland Canal – the St. Lawrence Canals – the Grand Trunk R.R. – light Houses in the Gulf, etc.' Galt knew that such expenditures had to be cut back. In late 1857, he had told the British banking house of Glyn Mills, who were the representatives of the English stockholders on the Grand Trunk Board of Directors as well as financial agents of Canada in England, that he thought the Canadian government could not provide further funds for the railway.[45] Galt, after he became finance minister, tried to limit the government's further involvement with the Grand Trunk, though strategic withdrawal of government support was impossible. The Great Western Railway failed to pay a promised large instalment on its debt to the province in 1859, which only made Galt unhappier.

As with railways, so with canals. The waterways system was already extensive, but Galt was convinced that it required further expansion. 'Our past experience leads me to doubt the propriety of the Province engaging directly in these new works,' the finance minister boldly wrote the British capitalist Thomas Brassey, 'as I am satisfied they can be cheaper constructed and more cheaply worked by private enterprize than by public Department.' He then proposed a method by which future canal construction would be privately financed and the entire canal system be taken over by private capital. The scheme would have involved the government, but it would have reduced the potential for a growing government debt in canal matters.[46] The plan, however, did not stir Brassey's acquisitive instincts, for it failed to move beyond the realm of private correspondence.

A third aspect of retrenchment involved the re-financing of the Canadian debt.

Galt intended to issue consolidated debentures to save on interest payments. Similar savings were to be obtained in arrangements concerning the Imperial Loan and its Sinking Fund. But legislative and other difficulties arose, and though his borrowing schemes met with some success in the 1860s, in 1859 Galt failed to realize these plans.[47]

'The Policy I propose is to make all possible reductions in the Provincial Expenditure, meeting the then ascertained deficiency by taxation *if necessary*,' Galt had emphatically declared to the British banking house and provincial financial agents, the Baring Brothers, when he had first become finance minister.[48] His 1858 budget estimate of savings amounted to about $1,000,000 – far short of what was needed. Actual savings, as it turned out, came to less than half those projected. Further increased taxation, as Galt had likely recognized even when he wrote to the Barings in August 1858, would be necessary: the tariff would have to be revised.

Galt's approach to remaking the tariff reflected careful political calculation. He decided to go armed beforehand, and sent out a circular in January of 1859 to the boards of trade of London, Hamilton, Toronto, Kingston, Ottawa, Montreal, and Quebec City. Such systematic consultation was unusual. So also was Galt's effort to involve the boards directly or indirectly in the policy decision-making process. They were asked to consider the customs duties: how high they should be? Should they be specific or *ad valorem*? At what level should the related excise duties be set? He urged the boards to weigh their responses in the light of the fiscal needs of the government, and to take into consideration the impact such duties had on trade, patterns of consumption, and on the industrial development of the province. There was to be a collective involvement in the process of policy formation.[49]

The boards reached no consensus, however: their answers reflected only patterns of regional economic specialization, metropolitan dominance, and hinterland rebellion. The London Board of Trade went so far as to reject the idea of low duties on necessaries (tea, coffee, sugar, and molasses) that the other boards requested. High duties on necessaries would generate government revenue under free trade, the London board pointed out. The western opposition to commercial protection was also strong. The St Lawrence ports of Quebec, Montreal, and even Kingston favoured the last point of purchase *ad valorem* tariff as it would increase their control over trade; Toronto and London were opposed, as it would increase the costs of trade with or through the United States. The London board rejected industrial protection outright; the Toronto board was so divided on that issue that it refused to comment on it. Commercial protection provided a basis for compromise between merchants and manufacturers: the Kingston board was strongly protectionist and its Montreal counterpart moderately so. Quebec City, with fewer manufactories than Montreal, and with its larger shipbuilding industry oriented to external markets, was more grudging in its advocacy of tariff protection to manufactures.[50]

This disparate advice suited Galt, for he had his own views – defined by his conception of national interest, the needs of practical politics, and the potential of economic growth given the existing depression. His economic policy ideas were consequently flexible. Galt had been attracted to annexationism in 1849; yet despite the annexationists' vehement rejection of reciprocity, he was highly satisfied with the 1854 trade agreement. Some free trade in that direction was welcome, and if the siren charm of American trade became too strong, it could be balanced by closer ties to the other British North American provinces. If his idea of a federal union of British North America was somewhat visionary, Galt showed his practicality in attempting to broaden reciprocity between the provinces in 1859. He told the British government at that time that the colonies should enter an economic union; at the least, Galt wanted free trade among them in a wide variety of goods, including manufactures. When the British denounced this as an heretical conception of free trade, Galt admitted that the ideal 'was the unrestricted interchange of the labor skill and capital of mankind,' but asserted that 'the circumstances of the world and jealousies of nations will probably forever prevent its adoption.' His proposed economic union was 'an approximation' of the ideal.[51] The same practicality and national interest informed Galt's assessment of protection. Progress, he reasoned in a memorandum to himself, was dependent on comparative economic advantage, so in a period of depression, legislative interference in the economy was justified if advantage resulted. In pioneer countries, such interference was doubly justified because it attracted population and encouraged the economy to move away from simple staple production. Historically, new countries indulged in protective devices such as free land grants and heavily subsidized roads, canals, and railways. Galt could call on precedent to support protection.

The key consideration, however, was whether protection raised the average value of labour in the country. Though in his free flow of ideas he did not effectively distinguish between per capita and gross national income, the finance minister felt that careful application of tariff protection to industries using raw materials available in the country, involving limited capital investment, and utilizing unskilled labour could provide impetus for growth. As long as income accruing to manufacturing did not reduce income in farming, no negative effects would be experienced. As long as there was free entry into protected industries for prospective manufacturers, high tariffs would not be class- or special-interest legislation.[52] Yet Galt was not a protectionist. Tariff protection, as he saw it, was a temporary and selective device, to be used when 'the tide ebbs instead of flowing,' when the economy slowed from lack of other inducements to growth, such as an expanding agricultural frontier. He sought that new impetus for economic growth through the formation of a transcontinental Canadian nation and the opening of an agricultural northwest,[53] and when that prospect seemed secure in the mid 1860s, he lowered the tariff and attempted to broaden reciprocity with the United States to include manufactures. Tariff protection was not integral to Galt's economic ideas. He simply sought comparative national advantage, temporary though it might be. As he stated years later, 'Free trade and Protection as abstract principles are both inapplicable to Canada from its situation and circumstances. My own views on this subject have refined, but have in no respect changed since in 1859 ... The policy adopted then, and which to a large extent remains still, was properly known as Incidental Protection, though it might more appropriately have been termed Modified Free Trade.'[54]

The concrete expression of the government's need for revenue, Galt's ideas, and the pressures exerted on the politicians of the province was the highest tariff British North America would see until 1879. Where Cayley's tariff had created a long list of items at 20 per cent, and left unenumerated goods at 15 per cent, Galt eliminated the 15 per cent level, shifting the items in it up to 20 per cent. A wide range of semi-manufactured iron, brass, copper, and other metal items needed as component elements in Canadian manufactures were elevated by Galt to 10 per cent from Cayley's 5. Leather manufactures and ready-made clothing remained at 25 per cent; these interests could not be offended. Galt conscientiously favoured the St Lawrence trade route by putting virtually the entire tariff in *ad valorem* form. And to raise yet more revenue, duties on tea, coffee, and other necessaries were substantially increased, though for political reasons and because of the dangers of smuggling, such increases could not be taken too far.[55]

From a protectionist perspective, the structure of the tariff reflected broadly accepted principles. It was commonly understood that the spread between the customs duty rates on finished items and on the inputs going into their manufacture defined the degree of protection given to the finished products. Low tariffs on raw materials, intermediate levels of duty on partially processed inputs, and high duties on finished products: this was the logical tariff structure that followed from the premise. Such a tiered structure had been in evidence in the tariffs of the late 1840s in two levels, and in 1856 it appeared in a more complex fashion in the Canadas. The Association for the Promotion of Canadian Industry had advocated a three-tiered tariff in 1858; the Montreal manufacturers did so in 1859. Galt was willing to explain the approach in detail to a British free-trade audience in 1862: 'The principle adopted in Canada had been that of admitting all raw materials free. The next class of articles were those which had received a certain amount of manufacture, but which could not be used till they had received a certain amount of re-manufacture, and upon them a 10 per cent duty was imposed; and upon articles manufactured the duty was 20 per cent.'[56]

Another principle was crucial: incidental protection, which was the imposition of revenue-generating customs duties on imported goods that were also domestically produced. Getting money for the province was the primary purpose of these duties, but incidentally, that is in a subordinate and accessory manner, protection would be provided. The protectionists of the late 1840s and early 1850s requested such incidental protection. Galt knew this meaning. So did those who pestered him on tariff matters.[57]

The limits of protection were, therefore, defined by revenue needs. The principle at stake was evident in the way Galt responded to the steady flow of unsatisfied protectionists who came to see him after the tariff proposals were made public. 'Mr. Galt is obdurate,' wrote the Toronto correspondent of the Hamilton *Spectator* for the 12 March issue: 'Deputation after deputation waits on him, but their reports are all similar – "courteous reception, can't promise any change, difference of opinion, he says revenue must be had, *duty increased where article could bear it, duty reduced where it could not to increase importation and thus revenue*" '[58] (my emphasis). When defending his tariff to the British government, Galt made the same case: 'The point to be desired is evidently to fix such a rate of duty as will not by a diminution of consumption, defeat the object of obtaining revenue and the undersigned contends that this point has not been exceeded in the 20% duties.'[59] Galt intended to maximize incidental protection. He was mistaken, as it turned out. The revenue did not surge upward dramatically as a result of the tariff. That does not place his motivation into question, for in 1862 he attempted to lower the tariff in order to increase revenue.

Though the Conservative government in 1859 did not have a secure hold on power, the tariff was not pushed through into law by a massed army of protectionist lobbyists. Because of the rapid growth in the variety and size of business interests in the 1850s, a general consensus was always difficult to obtain. The interests were more disunited than ever in 1859, and Galt played a game of divide and conquer, manoeuvring his tariff past the opposition of commercial and manufacturing groups.

Protectionists in later years put forward the view that the 1859 tariff was their creation, and that it had been a highly satisfactory one.[60] In 1859, however, there were important groups of manufacturers disappointed with, in fact horrified by, the tariff. Manufacturers of metals were particularly upset. William Rodden, a Montreal ironware manufacturer and a spokesman for the strongly protectionist secondary iron industry, complained to his MPP, John Rose, in no uncertain terms:

> I hasten to inform you of the great dissatisfaction displayed by Manufacturers here at the proposed changes in the Tariff ... I have not got time now to write to Mr. Galt or to go into details, yet I would remark that many of us are now being placed in a worse position than we were for years past. We have 20% of protection ... Iron, sheets, plates, Brass etc. ... were only 2½% up to last year & now it is made worse by putting them at 10% ... If there really is no other way to get a revenue & 10% must be charged to Balance it, there should be a large increase in the 25% list, to it should be added the leading articles in the wood, Brass & Iron trades.[61]

The excitement in Montreal grew. A meeting of manufacturers styled the Tariff Reform Association (they claimed to employ almost 4000 hands), put together a petition of protest against the high duties on materials going into the goods they manufactured. An alternative tariff of three levels was provided. The limits of Canadian manufacturing were sharply profiled on the 25 per cent list offered: simple items such as brooms, furniture and other household goods, cut nails and other hardware, and finished clothing predominated. The most complex items were sewing machines, steam engines, and some unspecified machinery.[62]

As first proposed, the 1859 tariff provided obvious increased protection to a number of industries such as sugar refining, shipbuilding, book publishing, and rope manufacturing. Galt took some steps to satisfy a few of those discontented with his first proposals: he placed some iron products used in shipbuilding at a higher rate of duty, raised the rate on ready-made clothing, and likewise increased suggested levels on soap, starch, cigars, and cement. Galt's manoeuvring to cause divisions in the ranks of the interests went further. Any potential agreement between supporters of commercial protection and their manufacturing counterparts was undercut. Sporadic attempts at separate organization by Montreal manufacturers beginning in 1856 may have encouraged tensions between the groups. Be that as it may, Galt's wholesale adoption of the *ad valorem* system ensured that the tariff would receive full support from the river port's merchants. Within days of the Montreal manufacturers' protest against the proposed 10 per cent list, the council of the Montreal Board of Trade held a special meeting at which a memorial approving the tariff was framed and letters to Montreal MPPs were sent out, 'urging on them the necessity of supporting the Bill.'[63] Montreal businessmen had no effective unity.

Nor did the commercial community of the province. The American Drawback Acts, combined with the removal of the preferential system and the Navigation Laws, further eroded already weak western mercantile support for the Laurentian commercial system: the growth of Upper Canadian trade through American channels made any sort of common front impossible. The *ad valorem* system, which insured the support of commercial men along the St Lawrence for the tariff, only provoked outrage in the western portions of the province. Galt's refusal to reconsider the matter spurred western interests to great heights of activity. A Toronto petition opposing *ad valorem* duties was widely signed. The Toronto Board of Trade called upon its fellow organizations in Upper Canada to work up similar petitions, and to organize deputations to oppose the *ad valorem* system in meetings with MPPs. Objections of the desired type came from Windsor, Stratford, Brantford, and Oakville; the fear of Montreal commercial domination was widespread.[64]

However, the major locus for a united mercantile opposition to Galt's tariff proposals lay in the high duties he imposed on necessaries: tea, coffee, and sugar. This upset grocery importers; it ran contrary to the protectionist promise of low duties on necessaries that attracted the support of ordinary consumers and permitted neutrality on the part of grocery men in protectionist campaigns. Not only did boards of trade from western Upper Canada oppose these duties, but also those from Kingston and Montreal. Galt's clever attempt to defuse this opposition to one of his key revenue proposals through an innovative sliding scale on tea, coffee, sugar, and molasses (which would have steadily reduced the duties on these items in four yearly instalments), did not prove attractive. Business instability would result from the sliding scale, merchants claimed.[65]

Aptly enough, Isaac Buchanan became the leading opponent of Galt's proposals in the Province of Canada's assembly. As a major importer and wholesaler, he was both lord over an army of retailers and dependent on them. A leading member of the commercial class, he still was welcome among protectionist manufacturers. He was not personally opposed to the last point of purchase *ad valorem* system, as the size of his direct import operations made him immune to its possible negative consequences, but he was willing to oppose it, just as his sympathies with the condition of the workingman led him to oppose the duties on necessaries. He was joined in his opposition to the reduced protection given to clothing and other items by Malcolm Cameron, who found that Galt's tariff did not display the high principles of Cayley's.[66] The interests of Montreal manufacturers were represented by John Rose and D'Arcy McGee, the latter boldly declaring that the Cayley tariff had been 'in great measure' the work of 'he, and some two or three of his friends.'[67] Buchanan tried to gather together the elements of opposition through a motion in the assembly, which rejected the sliding scale, the duties on necessaries, and the *ad valorem* system. In private, he told Galt that the protection given to a number of manufactures was insufficient.[68]

A back-room agreement between Galt and Buchanan, arranged through the good offices of John A. Macdonald, let the motion slide to defeat, but Galt did make concessions. The duties on necessaries would be held off for a few months, and the level of the sliding scale lowered. The duties on soap, starch and ready-made clothing also would be increased from the levels originally proposed.[69] Galt, however, did manage to keep separate Buchanan and the Montreal metals manufacturers who together would have formed a most potent protectionist alliance. The continued isolation of the metals trades was necessary for revenue purposes. Iron was one of the nine items that yielded some 77 per cent of the total customs revenue. Galt stated in the tariff debate that 'the principle items to which I look for the increase not raised by my predecessor are cottons and iron.'[70] Iron, with tea and sugar, he classed as necessaries in his budget speech, for this and other metals in various partially manufactured forms would be heavily imported by the loudly protesting Montreal manufacturers for years to come, providing the province with revenue.[71] An analysis of the revenue income from customs duties in 1860 shows that Galt's assertion was truthful. The sharpest revenue increase from 1858 to 1860 came from textiles that produced about 48 per cent of the total customs revenue in 1860, up from 35 per cent in 1858 (cottons had produced 15 per cent of the customs revenue in 1858; they produced 24 per cent in 1860). Iron and steel must have been a disappointment to Galt, for its contribution to the customs revenue only rose from slightly under 10 per cent to nearly 12 per cent from 1858 to 1860. The government's need for money underlay the inclusion of many items on the 10 per cent list on which metals were so prominent. It is unlikely that Galt had any intention of creating any massive amount of intermediate manufacturing. In fact, the 10 per cent list was eliminated in Galt's 1866 tariff.

The method of divide and conquer utilized by Galt was made possible by the altering realities of the Canadian business world. Manufacturers had to some degree outgrown the compromises based on commercial protection and the limited encouragement provided by the reduction or removal of duties on input items. They were flexing muscle in their own right: this is the lesson of the protectionist organizations that appeared in 1856 and after. Cayley, in a weak position, and desperate for more revenue, gave way to the combinations. Yet by 1859, the Association for the Promotion of Canadian Industry was not active, nor were its leading members influential in formulating the tariff proposals. Isaac Buchanan complained stiffly that Galt had not consulted *him* before the tariff was announced that year.[72] In fact, the association had fallen apart, largely because of financial problems.[73] Other than in Montreal, manufacturers responded as individuals to the 1859 tariff proposals.

Moreover, agreement among commercial interests proved impossible. Galt extended the system of commercial protection to the St Lawrence through the *ad valorem* system, though he failed to close the loophole that permitted direct importation to the Canadas through New York from other countries. Merchants from Toronto westward had their own geo-economic interests, and forced the concession. The expansion of the Canadian economy made organization and agreement more desirable for businessmen, but also more difficult to achieve.

The fashion in which Galt formulated the tariff reflected his understanding of the colonial political economy. Staple production and export (with the consequent import of finished goods) formed its crux, as the commercial policy of the colony was to continue to be geared towards capturing the western trade, both from Upper Canada and the American midwest. Galt's deliberate and full consultation with the various boards of trade reflected his great concern over these matters. A system of commercial protection would, he evidently hoped, make the Canadian canal and railway routes successful, defeating the attractions of American trade, and perhaps then the financial burdens these public works imposed on the government would be removed.

Manufacturing was, in contrast, a relatively new, though rapidly growing, interest. Galt wished to encourage it within the limits of government revenue needs, especially in the absence of an expanding agricultural frontier to animate the economy. Key protectionist interests were sorely disappointed by the 1859 tariff; ironically, later protectionists pointed to the 1859 legislation as a shining example of what they wanted. While the tariff's structure did provide a significant degree of protection, later observers may have confused the impetus to industrial growth provided by the American Civil War with the effects of Galt's provisions. Certainly they had forgotten a great deal, especially Galt's threatened tariff reductions of 1862 and his actual ones of 1866.

The finance minister's vision of the federal union of the provinces combined with transcontinental growth and his connections with the Grand Trunk Railway did not prevent his actions on railway matters from being defensive and reactive. His tariff was not made 'to raise money to build railways,'[74] for after 1860 to Confederation, little railway building took place. The money on railways had already been spent, and rather more of it than first planned. Hincks had to come to the aid of the railways, Cayley did also, and Galt was inevitably forced onto the same path. Any other approach would have been suicidal. As it was, Galt was not especially partial to the Grand Trunk while in office. The British banker G.C. Glyn, to whom the railway's business was an endless burden, welcomed Galt's removal from government in 1862 with relief. The former finance minister might produce better results for the railway now than 'when crippled by the duties & responsibilities of office.'[75]

While Cayley had responded to the political and fiscal exigencies of the late

1850s by seeking more revenue and granting some industrial protection, Galt wanted not only more revenue with industrial protection granted to the limits of revenue needs, but also sought to strengthen the position of the traditional economy. His was a realistic view: the Canadas remained dependent on trade. So the continuation and extension of trade agreements loomed large.

3
Larger markets, 1860–1866: reciprocity and Confederation

The 1860s witnessed British North American efforts to strengthen and perpetuate the commercial policies put into place during the previous decade, though with limited success. Political leaders in some provinces viewed those policies – American and interprovincial reciprocity, and in the Canadas and New Brunswick, incidental protection – as highly popular. Despite the generally satisfactory situation, uncertainties and dynamic imbalances abounded. Population and industry grew. Railways and the evolution of agriculture changed the structure of some economic sectors and stimulated market expansion. Moreover, the fiscal position of several colonies was serious, which inevitably meant changes in commercial policy. If that were not enough, the American Civil War altered the economic landscape and provided incentive to the Americans to become more and more dissatisfied about their country's relations with Britain and her colonies, leading to the Reciprocity Treaty's abrogation. While these circumstances were by no means sufficient to bring about union of the provinces in Confederation, they were necessary. And the Confederation of 1867 was the single greatest change in the colonial political economies since the coming of British free trade; its consequences in terms of the scope and character of governmental policy decisions was profound.

Population growth, the railway boom, and the American Civil War all had a greater impact on the structure of the colonial economies than did American reciprocity.[1] But the great importance contemporaries attached to the treaty was not merely the end product of a social psychology of dependence, of an abject colonialism, or of a gross error in mistaking fancied for real needs. Reciprocity expedited trade and it enlarged the possibilities for individual profit.[2] The potential to buy goods for a lower price than formerly, to sell goods for more or sell more of them – these were the considerations that made reciprocity attractive to colonials. Whether structural economic change was involved was of little concern to them.

A window of opportunity existed during the years of reciprocity. The massive railway integration in the northern United States that tied the eastern seaboard to Pennsylvania and Ohio coal supplies and brought eastern and overseas markets and western wheat production into easy conjunction was only beginning when the cry for reciprocity was first satisfied, and it was not effectively completed until some time after the American Civil War. In the interim, high transportation costs forced economies into a more regional mould, in which Upper Canadian wheat producers, for example, exported to upstate New York, where prices better than those offered by the British and the domestic colonial markets could often be obtained.[3] Though the subject of trade under reciprocity awaits a price historian, it is difficult to conceive of reasons other than steadier markets and greater profitability underlying the shift of opinion about the treaty in the Maritimes from 1854, when it was widely held that too much had been conceded the Americans, to 1859 when Canadian Auditor General John Langton reported that Maritimers were particularly pleased with American demand for their fish, lumber, and farm products.[4] Trade between the region and the United States increased overall and the rapid, though brief, growth in the coal exports from Nova Scotia to the neighbouring coastal states was just beginning. Clearly enough, the agricultural interests of Upper Canada favoured reciprocity because of good American prices for barley, hops and wheat, and during the Civil War, for oats, cattle, horses, sheep, wool, and flax.[5] Lumbermen appreciated the larger market, though there was displeasure that only partly manufactured timber was included under the treaty. That the upsurge in trade during the life of the agreement took place in a once-and-for-all fashion in the year following its implementation did not at all worry British North Americans with their more prosaic and immediate concerns with price.

The treaty excluded practically all manufactures, and for those who had protectionist inclinations, that was to the best. Many raw materials were included under the agreement, which lowered input costs for manufacturers. It seemed possible to some of these men that they could compete in the United States, especially with the high price for some materials induced by the American Civil War, and from this point of view, the treaty was a positive step.[6]

Isaac Buchanan expanded this aggressive industrial perspective into an argument for a North American common market or *Zollverein* (the German model was implicit in the word). As he saw it, the economies of North America shared common problems in competing with European industries, which were based on huge amounts of capital and skilled, cheap labour. Competition within North

America was more equitable. The removal of tariffs between the Canadas and the United States, and the erection of common external tariff walls would, it followed, be an excellent solution to some of the problems facing the provincial economy. An immense American market would be laid open, and British capital and manufacturers would be attracted to the provinces in order to gain access to the United States. The St Lawrence transportation route would gain from such an arrangement as well.[7]

Such untempered enthusiasm for closer trade ties with the United States was unusual. A.T. Galt repudiated the *Zollverein* idea, and some contemporary observers felt that few manufacturers could adapt to Buchanan's scheme. 'The idea of an "American Zollverein," ' William Weir cautioned Buchanan, 'might fairly be viewed as the ultimate object to be attained, *but in the infancy of our manufactures, and while we are large importers of foreign manufactures, it is very questionable whether immediate free trade with the U.S. would be advantageous ... it would render of little value the smaller establishments set on foot under the present circumstances and which we are bound to protect to the utmost extent.*' 'Consistent,' he added almost as an afterthought, 'with the general good.'[8]

Moreover, the Reciprocity Treaty was threatened by the United States. The Canadian tariffs of 1858 and 1859 ran counter to what the Americans understood as the spirit of the treaty, and the Civil War further endangered the agreement. The coalition of interests that had brought reciprocity into existence in the United States was broken by the war; Anglo-American relations deteriorated with English and British North American sympathy for the south; and under tension-heightening incidents such as the *Trent* affair and the *Alabama* raids.

Consciousness of the delicacy of the situation permeated the thinking of the Canadian provincial government, even though it was stoutly asserted that the Reciprocity Treaty was in no real danger. A.T. Galt recognized the necessity of British military protection and the need to appease both British and American opinion, and combined these perceptions with the unique opportunities provided by the Civil War to frame his proposed but unimplemented 1862 tariff.[9]

The province's declining revenue and growing defence expenditures brought on by the Civil War made a tariff revision apparently inevitable. The United States' higher levels of internal taxation, the finance minister suggested in his budget speech, could allow the province to impose heavier customs duties on necessaries without encouraging smuggling. According to his plan, a surplus would result, and the higher duties on manufactures imposed in 1859, which had reduced consumption and government revenue, could be lowered. As the connection with Britain had to be maintained for reasons of defence if not for sentiment, and good trade relations with the United States were too important to jeopardize (Galt touched on the potential American military threat very lightly), 'it should be an object with us to endeavour to satisfy parties with whom we have large commercial transactions' by lowering customs duties.[10] He urged that the dependence of the province on trade with these two major partners be lessened by opening commerce with other nations. But what struck Galt's political peers the most was his express intention to reduce the duties on manufactured goods, to lessen protection. The already weak government was battered by attacks on Galt's proposed policy: the majority of MPPs from Upper Canada, including Tories, opposed the changes; Isaac Buchanan, as the most vocal of the protectionists, spoke out strongly against the reductions, and sent out telegrams to manufacturers throughout the Canadas to whip up public opposition.[11] The tottering administration could not force the passage of the tariff, and resigned after being defeated on another bill. And though the protectionist interests were by no means very powerful, a weak government – as in 1858 – proved vulnerable to highly committed interests.

The subsequent Sandfield Macdonald governments vocally asserted their good intentions to protectionist interests, but at the same time busied themselves on reciprocity matters.[12] There were great political advantages to be gained through a long-term renewal of the Reciprocity Treaty, as it would 'give our party a hold on the farmers that ... [would] be difficult to overestimate,' as George Brown pointed out. While Brown begged off when he was requested to go to Washington to test the waters, a few months later in early 1864, the government persuaded Montreal merchant and politician John Young to visit the American capital to estimate the chances of renewal in the face of worsening Anglo-American relations and growing hostility towards the treaty.[13]

Young's report was quite gloomy. His gloom spread to the provincial administration, which immediately begged the British government to start negotiations, and hinted at the growth of annexationist feeling if the treaty were abrogated.[14] But the Sandfield Macdonald regime had little chance to do more. The highly dramatic political events in the Canadas, beginning with the late March 1864 resignation of that government, and culminating in the Great Coalition and the move toward Confederation, seemed to leave reciprocity in the shade. But it was not forgotten in the continuing deterioration of British relations with the United States.

There was an attempted Confederate raid from Canadian soil on a prisoner of war camp in the U.S. north; and there was the adventurist southern raid on St Albans, Vermont, which was executed from Canada. These had their impact on commercial relations with the American north, which were already uncertain. Both the American ban on the export of cattle, and a ban on the export of anthracite coal to British North America caused much worry and excitement. Meat packers complained of the sporadically enforced American ban on cattle exports. The prohibition of the export of anthracite coal from the United States (the Washington government suspected that the smokeless coal was being sold to southern steamers for blockade-running purposes), which was suddenly and strictly enforced in early 1864, struck directly at industrial Upper Canada. A burst of diplomatic activity resulted in the lifting of the ban, though in the interim an interest in Nova Scotian coal had been stimulated.[15] Overall, an aura of uncertainty now surrounded the commercial relations of the colonies and the United States.

Not all these events had taken place when the J.A. Macdonald–E. Taché government took office, but the drift toward the cancellation of the Reciprocity Treaty by the United States was apparent. The new government pressed the British to open negotiations between the colonies and the United States immediately, and informed the imperial government that the desired means of reaching a decision was through an international commission. However, the British refused to act until the treaty was under actual notice of abrogation.[16] Caution was justified in the face of worsening Anglo-American relations, but the decision hampered Canadian efforts to meet the problem in ways the provincial government found most congenial. Secret support of pro-reciprocity endeavours by Americans was the only interim recourse.[17]

With the passage of the notice of abrogation in Congress in March 1865, the union of the Canadas government and important groups of businessmen finally swung into action. The delegation of government members sent to Great Britain in spring 1865 to discuss the 'existing critical state of affairs' was instructed not only on the topics of Confederation, defence, and the settlement of North West Territory and Hudson Bay claims, it was also ordered to press forward on the matter of reciprocity negotiations.[18] Canadian politicians and businessmen made active use of their American contacts. Israel D. Andrews, who had been closely connected with the original passage of the Reciprocity Treaty, now turned to save the product of his toil, though with faded capacity and vigour.[19] A number of businessmen, such as Isaac Buchanan and C.J. Brydges, the managing director of the Grand Trunk Railway, had contacts with James Wilkes Taylor, the ubiquitous midwestern lobbyist with a presumed influence in the American government. A.T. Galt, once again finance minister, was in touch with Senator Fessenden of Maine, chairman of the American Senate's Committee on Foreign Affairs. Perhaps the most important of these informal contacts was the amiable connection Galt developed with David Wells in the summer of 1865. Wells, a ranking American economist who was known to favour free trade, was at the time newly appointed as chairman of the U.S. Revenue Commission, and his political powers were thought to be great.[20]

Both the pursuit of reciprocity and the striving for Confederation were exercises in expansion, but in the background remained the threat of annexation. The fear was widespread that the end of the treaty might foster the desire for union with the United States, as the Sandfield Macdonald administration's communications with the British government made clear. While Galt was in London, England, in spring 1865, the Montreal capitalist Peter Redpath wrote him in pessimistic tones, fearing the emergence of a movement in the Canadas to join the United States. 'Many look upon it as inevitable,' Redpath noted with alarm; 'Do preserve us from annexation if you can.'[21] Yet annexationism was to be found not only in the Canadas, but also in the United States.[22] Certainly it was widely believed in the provinces that the Americans desired to control British North America and that a constant struggle had to be waged against the spread of this view among Americans.

At the Detroit Boards of Trade Convention in July 1865, the tension between annexation and reciprocity came to a head. The Detroit Board of Trade had chosen to invite a number of British North American boards to participate in the convention – a curious act in itself – and the latter had seized the opportunity to struggle for the renewal of reciprocity. Many boards of trade in the Canadas actually attended a preliminary meeting to formulate a common position, and to arrange for the collection of factual material on the benefits and possible extensions of the treaty. The 50-odd delegates from the provinces, among the roughly 600 who attended the convention, acted very much in concert there, refusing to give themselves votes for fear they would prejudice the case for reciprocity; they devoted their efforts to lobbying their American counterparts on the issue.[23]

The convention 'was called to discuss questions of Finance, Currency, Revenue, Transit, and Reciprocity,' but reciprocity – and annexation – came to dominate the four-day meeting. As the Saint John, New Brunswick, delegates reported, the passage of a pro-reciprocity resolution appeared unlikely because many Americans 'were opposed to Reciprocity under our present relations, hoping, by refusing this, to force the Provinces from their allegiance to Britain, and for trade benefits, to join them.'[24] This idea was openly discussed, and all the more so after the Montreal-based American Consul General B. Potter took to speechifying on the glories of annexation at the meeting, using as an example of Canadian sentiment an injudicious letter written by a leading Montreal businessman. The colonials had no choice but to argue the case for reciprocity with the greatest force possible. Only an electrifying speech by the great Nova Scotian journalist and politician Joseph Howe in the plenary session of the convention made a resolution favouring reciprocity secure. Besides outlining the advantages of the trade under the treaty in glowing terms, Howe boldly took up annexation and declared it an impossibility due to the loyalty of British North Americans to the mother country. Howe's oratory overwhelmed the Americans: 'At one point the whole of the Americans rose and cheered as if they were mad, and it was some minutes before they were calm enough to allow him to continue,' railwayman C.J. Brydges enthused. 'I never heard any speech which had such a wonderful effect upon hard-headed businessmen.'[25] Immediately afterwards, the convention unanimously passed a pro-reciprocity resolution requesting the American president to enter into negotiations on reciprocity and the free navigation of the St Lawrence and other rivers.

At this point, the colonial drive for a renewed reciprocity was caught up in a harsh battle within the Great Coalition government of the Canadas. Finance Minister Galt was not the only member of the provincial cabinet to claim expertise on the trade agreement; George Brown, businessman, newspaper publisher, and leader of the Reformers in the coalition, rivalled Galt in influence in the United States and in knowledge about the treaty. Brown felt Galt's diplomatic bargaining techniques were suspect; the finance minister had a reputation for rash action. Galt wished to rush to Washington in the wake of the Detroit convention victory and reach a quick agreement with the Americans; but Brown, through the cabinet, forced Galt to make the visit one of a much more cautious and preliminary character.[26] This caution was possibly an error, though the political conditions at Washington were hardly good, despite the Detroit resolution. Whatever the case, the consultations at Washington in summer 1865 produced no concrete results. The positive effects of the lobbying of British North American businessmen and the spell of Howe's oratory faded all too quickly.

The desire for reciprocity and the infighting over it in the Canadian government, however, remained. George Brown looked for assistance in his effort to trammel Galt: he found it in the Maritimes, where strong suspicions existed that Canada placed its own interests far above those of the ocean provinces in reciprocity matters. Acting on complaints from the Maritimes, the British forced the convention of a Confederate Council on Commercial Treaties, in which all the provinces involved in the Reciprocity Treaty had representation.[27] Galt's desire to handle the trade agreement on his own was implicitly repudiated even by the calling of such a convention. Not surprisingly, he was generally absent from the meetings of the Confederate Council at Quebec in 1865. The resolutions George Brown and the Maritime delegates pushed through the convention would have, if enforced, greatly limited Galt's freedom of action, and would have effectively placed reciprocity negotiations in the control of the council. Five of the resolutions dealt with British North American strategy to gain a trade agreement with the United States, one arranged for a trade commission to the Caribbean and South America, and only one dealt in the most general terms with the planning of commercial policy in the event of the abrogation of the treaty.[28] The trade commission was not a forlorn alternative to an arrangement with the Americans, but part of a broad-ranging effort of which reciprocity with the United States was a key element, an effort to gain greater and more diversified markets. The reciprocal trade arrangements earlier reached among the British North American provinces, the attempt to reach a trade accommodation with France in 1860,[29] and Confederation itself reflected the same drive. Galt had voiced an intention to broaden trade contacts in his 1862 budget speech: the conflict between Brown and himself was one of tactics and personalities, not one of fundamental aims.[30]

The conflict still had its effect on the push for reciprocity. Galt's impetuosity, his dislike of Brown, and his cavalier attitude towards the place of the Maritimes in renewing the treaty led him to ignore the restrictions imposed by the Confederate Council resolutions and by earlier understandings in the Canadian cabinet. In November 1865, he left for New York for private discussions as to how the treaty might be continued until after Confederation. Once there, he decided or was persuaded to go on to Washington, where he became convinced that the Americans would only agree to reciprocal *legislation*. Galt, without much evident thought about the political implications of his actions, then outlined what the Canadas would barter for such an agreement.[31] As C.J. Brydges understood Galt, the latter

> proposes that by mutual legislation the area of the interchange of commodities should be largely increased, extending to manufactures as well as to natural productions – that the list should include agricultural implements – all kinds of tools, boots & shoes, iron & hardware, cotton & woollen goods, and a large variety of articles – duty upon these, if any, to be equal to their internal taxes. Whatever is to be admitted from them into Canada free or at a low rate of duty, to be admitted from England or elsewhere at the same rate of duty. This plan if adopted would very largely increase our free list, and very largely reduce our scale of duties upon importations from the manufacturing districts of England.[32]

This would not have been just a continuation of the treaty as Galt later misleadingly asserted;[33] this would have been an enormous step in the direction of free trade.

Galt's activities created a potentially explosive situation within the Canadian government, for Brown was outraged. The finance minister had not only gone beyond the restrictive mandate enforced on him after the Detroit convention, he had also usurped the functions of the Confederate Council on Commercial Treaties. Brown's efforts to direct or strongly influence reciprocity matters had been rudely thrust aside. He was unable to share the political sensibilities of the other Reform cabinet members who sought to build on what had been done whatever

the correctness of Galt's opportunistic negotiations. Brown alone resigned office. The others remained to carry through Confederation, a scheme that Brown continued to support strongly.

The government of the Province of Canada then hurried to generate pressures to ensure the passage of reciprocal legislation in the United States. David Wells was willing to write a supportive report. Another positive report from a supposedly independent source in Boston would be underwritten. The Canadian cabinet approved the hiring of the peripatetic journalist, George Sheppard, to act as lobbyist or author of positive articles in Washington. Various American boards of trade were encouraged to apply pressure on the American government.[34] However, this hectic activity proved inconsequential. For when a British North American delegation led by Galt went to Washington in early 1866 to save reciprocity, it met with a cold response in talks with the American House of Representatives' Committee of Ways and Means. The galling list of items the American committee finally chose to offer was used as justification for the Canadian refusal to initiate reciprocity negotiations in the years that followed: rags, firewood, unground gypsum or plaster, and unfinished grindstones or millstones.[35]

Despite the humiliation of the January 1866 negotiations, hope for a trade arrangement with the United States was not immediately laid aside. For several months thereafter, as something of a backlash to abrogation took place in the United States, a potential for a return to the bargaining table was seen by Galt and others, including Americans.[36] Because hope had not yet died, the tariff of 1866 in the Canadas was in part constructed to improve chances of obtaining reciprocity. But it had numerous other purposes.

The last tariff of the Province of Canada embodied a variety of major changes. Protection to commercial routes was reduced by removing *ad valorem* rates on a number of goods, such as coffee, sugar, and tobacco, and by imposing specific (dollar-amount) duties on them. An important element of agricultural protection was introduced. Customs duties on manufactures were slashed as goods not otherwise specified were placed at 15 per cent (formerly they had been at 20), and items on the former 10 per cent list were now duty free, as was mill machinery. Galt, as finance minister, was certain that these alterations would produce an increase in government revenue, but to make doubly sure, he raised excise duties.

Reciprocity had a place in this. The finance minister had introduced the tariff as a move away from the American system of protection towards the European system of free trade through interrelated trade treaties.[37] Higher excise duties made reciprocity with the United States more possible because of the high

American excise duties; lower duties on manufactures, as Galt had suggested in 1862, would blunt the American distress over the tariff of 1859; and higher agricultural customs duties posed the threat of retaliation against the U.S. and applied pressure on the midwestern American grain interests, which had failed to push the American government sufficiently for reciprocity in 1865 and 1866.

More obviously, the tariff was supposed to expedite Confederation, for it was to be the first tariff of the new Dominion as well as the last of the old union of the Canadas. Some balance between the regions of the prospective nation had to be reached,[38] especially as there was a wide disparity between the rates of customs duties imposed by the different provinces: in Nova Scotia and Prince Edward Island the common rate was 10 per cent, and in New Brunswick it stood at 15½ per cent, while the Canadas stood at 20 per cent for goods not otherwise specified. Maritimers, who imported more on a per capita basis than the Canadians, would have suffered very heavy increases in taxation if the old Canadian tariff would have been imposed on them. The 1866 reduction from 20 to 15 per cent on unspecified goods would surely ease growing resentment in the eastern provinces, and make union more palatable, leading Canadian businessmen and politicians thought.[39]

Galt's creation represented rather more complex considerations than those of reciprocity and Confederation alone. The Maritimes themselves posed considerable difficulties for any tariff-maker. No longer could their economies be readily summarized as Atlantic and international, based simply on staple production and commerce. That would have been a cruel caricature of their hopes and immediate prospects, even their realities. The late nineteenth century saw those economies undergoing a shift from the Atlantic towards the continent. The discerning eye could see prospects for rapid industrial development. Confederation, the hopeful ones argued, would provide an enlarged market for tariff-protected industry, and railways would provide the necessary transportation network. The availability of coal would fuel the consequent massive growth of manufactures.[40] 'In view of the abrogation of the Reciprocity Treaty,' one heavily signed Nova Scotian union manifesto pronounced, 'we are of opinion that every reasonable encouragement should be afforded for creating and sustaining a manufacturing interest in Nova Scotia, in order that the farmer may find a home market as far as possible, for [his] productions, and the manufacturer, in turn, a nation for the proceeds of his skill and labor. Otherwise we believe that a heavy drain [on] the precious metals in return for foreign manufactures, will speedily set in upon our people and tend greatly to the impoverishment of the country, and the embarrassment of all classes.'[41] In such statements, the protectionist creed was fully apparent.

It is fascinating to discover that Isaac Buchanan's writings were known by a considerable number of political figures in the Maritimes. Even in the planning of Confederation at the Quebec Conference, background rumblings were to be heard as Buchanan made sure that a thick compendium of his prolix pennings were distributed to delegates and onlookers. Leonard Tilley, the New Brunswick Father of Confederation, possibly trained in the protectionist traditions alive in his province, felt regret at Buchanan's absence from Quebec; he expressed hope for industrial expansion in his home province as a consequence of provincial union. He was supported by New Brunswick North Shore interests led by the politician and capitalist Peter Mitchell, who wanted the intercolonial railway as a means of gaining access to the central Canadian market.[42]

A continental orientation did not necessarily mean a pro-Confederation or protectionist stance, however. Reciprocity and the American market offered an alternative to the union. Nova Scotian coal interests persisted in wanting duty-free access to the American seaboard cities through reciprocity long after Confederation. In southern New Brunswick, ambitions to gain a continental hinterland focused on railways to the United States and implicitly, on reciprocity. Saint John manufacturers also had divided opinions as to the value of Confederation. Some favoured union, but others feared that it would only mean that Canadian manufacturers would destroy their hold on the local market. Some New Brunswick manufacturers strongly expressed a localistic rejection of union and the wider field, even from a protectionist perspective, for they were already well shielded from competition by substantial customs duties.[43]

Because of the great pressure from interests in the Canadas, it was difficult to meet the Maritimes' wide variety of concerns. The tariff was of course designed to silence critical free traders, a vital consideration given the coalition nature of the Canadian government and George Brown's prominent position in the opposition.[44] Lower tariffs would make the new nation a haven for immigrants, as Toronto financier David Macpherson told John A. Macdonald. 'The effect should be to make this country more attractive than the great republic. To do this we must make it cheap to live in ... Free land to actual settlers and cheap living would be our motto.'[45] Lowering the tariff, moreover, was quite feasible. American competition was for the time being limited because of high rates of internal taxation made necessary by the American effort to reduce national debt and convert from a paper currency to gold.[46] Moreover, Galt stated that the high customs duties of 1859 had actually reduced total government revenue, and he thought a reduction in duties on non-necessities would lead to a rise in government income.[47] The increase in the excise and on import duties on necessities made the government revenue doubly safe. High protective rates could, as a result, be lowered or eliminated. Indeed, the tariff revenue generated in the Province of Canada by iron and steel and their products in 1860 had made up nearly 12 per cent of total customs revenue, but in 1868–69 the same goods only produced some 5.5 per cent the total customs income of the new Canadian nation; customs income from woollens and cottons also fell from 48 to 26 per cent and duties on alcoholic and and non-alcoholic beverages produced a significant 23 per cent of the new nation's tariff income as opposed to 10 per cent for the Canadas in 1860. Sugar and related goods produced nearly 18 per cent of customs revenue in 1868–69, somewhat higher than at the earlier date. While these changing proportions reflected an altering Canadian industrial structure, they also reflected the impact of tariff revisions. On two counts then, the move toward Confederation was a move to freer trade: Confederation itself created a larger common market, and the new country's tariff would be an incentive to greater international commerce.

Still, the move to free trade was equivocal. Agricultural protection was an important element in the tariff. The rural demand for retaliation against the United States for the abrogation of reciprocity had to be satisfied,[48] but the hefty duties on foodstuffs were designed to do more. George Brown suspected that the government was attempting to erect a political alliance between manufacturers and farmers,[49] an interpretation that perhaps overestimated Galt's cleverness; nevertheless, the new duties were certainly designed to wean farmers away from a Reform allegiance. Control of the markets of the Maritimes, where large quantities of foodstuffs were imported, was being offered to central Canadian grain growers, dairymen, millers, and shipping interests. The ocean provinces did not react kindly to these duties, which they saw as an exercise in central Canadian hegemony, and after Confederation, when the pacification of the Maritimes was of crucial importance, the duties were removed.[50]

Protection to manufacturers also remained a significant aspect of the new tariff. The elimination of the 10 per cent level, while offending some producers, also made important raw and semi-processed materials available duty free to producers of finished goods, effectively increasing their protection. Few manufacturers immediately realized they were being benefited. An outcry came from manufacturers on the proposed tariff, largely on an individual basis. The Association for the Promotion of Canadian Industry had faded after 1858, and the proposed tariff of 1862 found the provincial Canadian manufacturers quite unprepared for action, with Isaac Buchanan making hectic efforts to gather the interests together. Protectionists generally did not organize their political activity in good times, as could be seen in their demands and appeals on tariff matters. Confectionery manufacturers, for example, individually complained that the duty on their finished product in the 1859 tariff was lower than the duty on the sugar out of which it was made; in 1860 this lamentable oversight was rectified through an increase on the duty on confectioneries. There were sharp protests from individual publishers when the rate levied on books was reduced in 1860; the threat of a lower tariff in 1862 brought out yet other protests from producers.[51]

Most individual demands were, however, directed toward gaining increased protection, though some could work with insidious effect. The great capital expenditure required for factory machinery (which could be made locally only at great expense) prompted manufacturers to ask for special dispensation on the duty payable on imported machinery. This was particularly true of those setting up woollen textile mills during the American Civil War: they requested that the machinery be allowed in duty free or that they be allowed to bond the machinery or declare their mills bonded warehouses. Machinery then could be set up and worked without the payment of duty. The usual argument was that the prospective manufacturer did not have the funds to pay the duties at time of importation. The government was assured, of course, that as soon as profit was being made, the duty would be paid. In practice, the bonds were repeatedly renewed and the payment of duty left in abeyance. The badgering that accompanied requests for renewal of bonds simply eroded the will to collect the duty. Moreover, port collectors of customs more than once interceded on behalf of such petitioning, and in other cases there is some suggestion that collectors turned a blind eye to the importation of machinery that was to be locally used.[52]

Manufacturers came to expect special treatment of this sort. George Stephen, the Montreal capitalist much involved in the woollen industry in the 1860s, wrote to A.T. Galt in a rather chummy style on these matters. 'I regret to trouble you so often but it seems unavoidable. I am interested in a small woollen mill at Waterloo, C.W.,' he informed Galt.

> I am helping the owners to increase their machinery. They have now at Galt or on the way thither machinery to the amt. of $5000 or $6000.
>
> Will you give orders to the collector at *Hamilton* to take Paton & Bucker's bonds for the amt. of the duty (Paton is the same man who is to manage the Sherbrooke mill now in the course of erection). Will you do the same for B.W. Rosamond Co. of Almonte. *Brockville* is their *port* of entry. I have recently taken an interest and become a partner with the Rosamonds ... I hope by the time the bulk of the machinery for the new mills comes to hand that such things will be included on the *free list*.[53]

Galt in 1866 merely rationalized the tariff along the lines that Stephen had somewhat imperiously suggested. Such sporadic and generally individual actions on the part of manufacturers had some effect on the formation of tariff policy, but it left the finance minister relatively free to act in the way he saw most fit.

And that, in the form of the tariff of 1866, had the manufacturers scrambling once more.

The proclaimed free-trade direction of the tariff was strongly protested by Montreal manufacturers as early as 30 June 1866. The entire structure of Canadian manufacturing was about to be dismantled, they cried.[54] Commercial interests protested the needless disruption of commercial and industrial development. Dry goods and hardware merchants indicated a cautious approval, on the basis of a reduction of duties on goods they imported, but those connected with the importation of groceries felt that the move away from *ad valorem* duties and the increase in the levels of the duties on their goods would be damaging.[55] A.W. Ogilvie, a major Montreal miller, said that the tariff 'would do the manufacturers as much, if not more, injury than the merchants. He pointed to the rolling mills, to the manufactories making woollen mill machinery, on which the change would have a most damaging effect, and said the duty on Indian corn would probably result in closing up the Edwardsburg starch mill, just beginning to enter upon a prosperous business.'[56] A Hamilton Board of Trade meeting found the tariff change inopportune. The Toronto Board of Trade passed a similar motion, with discussion at the meeting centring on the many interests the tariff would damage, especially manufacturing. The London Board of Trade petitioned that no change be made until after Confederation.[57] Delegations began to converge on Ottawa, all intent on persuading the government to limit the changes proposed or to make them more acceptable.

Yet protests were not extravagantly vehement. Good economic times were partially responsible, but more was involved. The removal of duty on factory machinery pleased many capitalists, particularly in the rapidly expanding textile industry; it pleased George Stephen who, always a political ally of Galt's, spoke out in favour of the tariff.[58] Isaac Buchanan's opposition was muted. Though the new policy perhaps had annexationist overtones, 'he did not so much object to the actual changes at present proposed as to the announcement that we were about deliberately to adopt as our permanent policy, a European trade system.'[59] Indeed, the *Globe*'s Ottawa correspondent noted a degree of softness about the delegations from Montreal who were protesting the planned changes. Of course they threatened their Montreal MPPs, but the 'outside impression here is that the Montreal delegations are not taking the bull by the horns as resolutely as they might do.'[60]

The pro-administration Montreal *Gazette* was not slow to point out the tariff's advantages to the business community. The finance minister had no intention of introducing absolute free trade; he only expressed a personal wish for such a desirable future state, and that day was hardly likely to come.[61] Politicians were practical men, and Canada required a policy that promoted both trading and manufacturing – incidental protection. Theorists might argue that protection and generating revenue were contradictory, that they could not be reconciled. 'But look at the facts: We have a revenue tariff, and with it a fostering of manufactures that has built up a great industry.'[62] The alterations were not inconsistent with the principles of incidental protection, and the planned tariff would place numerous manufacturers in a better position to meet their American competition. The shift of most items on the 10 per cent list to the free list accomplished this.

If one strand in Galt's thinking had been to sow confusion in the ranks of the opposition and to recruit support from sectors that traditionally supported the reformers, the opposition was not slow to try and gain recruits from among manufacturers and others who opposed the tariff. Luther Holton exemplified this trend. Holton's Montreal supporters were involved in the organization of a 'monster' meeting on 11 July, attended by between 2000 and 6000 people, which orchestrated Montreal's disappointment with the tariff proposals.[63] Holton effectively used the meeting as a weapon against the government; he was a free trader, he proclaimed in the legislative assembly, but he never would have brought in such immense changes so suddenly. A similar line was adopted by other Reform leaders, including George Brown.[64]

Galt did make a number of changes in his proposals to bring offended interests to his side. Starch, soap, tobacco, and agricultural machinery manufacturers were appeased to one degree or another. So were sugar refiners and tanners.[65] These manoeuvres nearly isolated manufacturers of machinery and a few who made the semi-finished goods that had formerly prospered under a 10 per cent tariff. John Rose, connected to the latter group, which was strongly represented in Montreal, moved that rolled iron be placed at 10 per cent as formerly, but his motion was soundly defeated: the manufacturers of finished iron goods had too much to lose.[66]

So the tariff was completed. Its proposal had occasioned hasty organizational efforts on the parts of various interests; the continuing threat of the 'European system' and the possibility that the tariff might be reconsidered soon after Confederation encouraged further combination. Toronto witnessed the formation of a Manufacturers' Association for Upper Canada in September 1866, and a month later Montreal followed suit with its Tariff Reform and Industrial Association.[67] The existence of both was brief. John Rose, who replaced Galt as finance minister, removed the agricultural duties and then, true to Montreal interests, placed low duties on some intermediary iron products. Other than that, the tariff was not greatly revised for four years, and protectionist groups had difficulty cohering without the stimulus of prospective tariff changes. Formal organization was not urgent in Montreal where capitalists and manufacturers daily rubbed shoulders. The same did not hold for Upper Canada. There, fear and jealousy of Toronto control and a desire to maintain local independence, as well as disagreements about the nature of membership made the 1866 association unstable.[68] No record has been found of either group as instituted in 1866 meeting more than once.

A degree of success in meeting the needs of various regions and interests in the incipient Dominion of Canada was reached in the tariff. It was not complete because free access to the United States for Canadian staple products had not been gained, and no alternative had been offered to the Nova Scotian coal industry and to the lumber industry. Nor was the West Indies market enlarged through a trade agreement. Even more strikingly, the place of the great western region that was to be included in the new nation in due course had no obvious niche in the tariff scheme, other than of making Canada a place of potentially cheap land. Galt provided no vision of the west tied to central Canada's economy through the guiding power of the tariff.

Galt followed pragmatic instincts, even though the hallmark of his political style was executive and individual action. The high tariff of 1859 was good policy to meet revenue needs and the adverse effects of depression, but it was not useful in a time of growth, difficult international tensions, and declining trade barriers. The European system of lower tariff walls and trade agreements was superior during a time of prosperity to the American system of protection. In economic terms, it was frequently stressed that Confederation was the creation of a larger free-trade area, even if it was in part a reaction to the loss of reciprocity with the United States. Broader trade horizons were sought in the Caribbean and elsewhere, and even if the Reciprocity Treaty had been abrogated, the pursuit of better trade ties with the United States did not end. Instead, it began anew.

4
From a conciliatory to a national policy, 1867–1872

In hindsight, the abrogation of the Reciprocity Treaty appears virtually inevitable; the efforts at renewal in 1865–66 and later seem embarrassingly futile. But this inevitability was not comprehended at the time. Failure to obtain a continuation of reciprocity in 1866 was due, in the eyes of politically minded Canadians, to causes that were removable. George Brown, for example, thought Galt's precipitate actions in agreeing to legislative reciprocity naturally resulted in the rapacious Americans offering next to nothing.[1] Nor did the finance minister ever make good use of the Maritimes' desire for reciprocity. In Galt's 1865 effort to achieve reciprocity, he left the lower provinces to one side entirely, and during the discussions with the Committee of Ways and Means of the American House of Representatives in January 1866, the Maritimes delegates played a minor part. Joseph Howe, in Washington at the time, eagerly offered his services but was ignored. And Galt's forceful executive approach to action, his belief that the Americans would listen to reason and be impressed by facts, led to poorly planned lobbying, executed through deficient agents.[2] American ideas about potential annexation of Canada ('Political Consideration,' as W.P. Howland so solemnly and euphemistically put it) were not fully countered, and references to the matter by members of the Ways and Means Committee rang with false jocularity.[3]

But for some months following the rebuff of January 1866, there was hope of an American reconsideration of reciprocity. There was hope beyond hope as well. The passage of time and the continuing independent existence of Canada would, Canadians thought, free Americans of their annexationism and their hostility to Great Britain, and permit them to find a more rational commercial policy. Antagonizing the United States was, therefore, unwise: this idea dominated Canadian policy decisions on tariff and other matters from before Confederation at least until 1870.

There seemed little point in Canada actively trying to get reciprocity with the

Americans, however. Given the paltry list of goods the committee offered to Galt and his colleagues, the Canadian government took a stand on dignity and presented a feigned official indifference about reciprocity after Confederation.[4] The Americans would have to take the first steps towards any future agreement. Yet public pressure to acquire some trade concessions from the United States remained considerable. Rumours that the Conservative government was involved in trade negotiations in 1869 resulted in parliamentary debates replete with anxious curiosity about the matter. Quebec Liberal Lucius Huntington's parliamentary resolutions on Canadian independence in 1870 were largely motivated by a perceived need for Canada to have an independent treaty-making power.[5] And from a purely partisan perspective, any agreement with the United States by Macdonald's government would have been a devastating blow to the Reformers in Ontario, where farmers wanted access to the American market.[6]

Similar pressures existed in the Maritimes. Nova Scotia's and New Brunswick's dissatisfaction with Confederation could be diluted by the attractions a new reciprocity held for fishing, lumber, shipping, and coal interests. Much support for Confederation had come from the coal industry; so efforts had to be made to re-establish the American market for the Nova Scotian mineral. 'You can quite understand how intensely they feel the present depression in their trade,' one Maritimer told Sir John A. Macdonald. The associated anti-government feeling would disappear if a trade arrangement was reached, the prime minister was assured.[7]

The policy of conciliation that grew out of these considerations found expression in the two best levers Canada had for obtaining reciprocity: the fisheries and the tariff. With the end of the treaty, the Americans no longer had legal free access to the Canadian inshore fisheries, but they were allowed to use them until 1868 on the payment of a modest tonnage fee. The enforcement of the fee regulation was not rigid, for many American fishermen evaded payment. Only a nominal sovereignty was asserted over inshore waters. Similarly, the government advised restraint when tariffs of a retaliatory or protective character were demanded by some interests. None the less, Macdonald recognized that high-minded moderation and calculated inactivity might not bring the Americans to the correct point of view. The development of events in Washington had to be carefully observed, and even nudged in the right direction. A secret agent in Washington was necessary.

George W. Brega was one of an army of lobbyists and political agents that clustered at the American capital. He had been associated in a minor capacity with the gaining of the Reciprocity Treaty of 1854, and saw himself as having a vested interest in the reciprocity issue. He personally approached Sir John A. Macdonald and by the autumn of 1867 had been accepted as a confidential agent.

From early 1868 to early 1870, practically all organized American pro-reciprocity developments bore Brega's mark. He absorbed more than $20,000 (American, and in gold) in funds from Canada in less than two years pursuing what he conceived to be his duty: orchestrating pro-reciprocity forces to apply pressure on the American administration and Congress, ensuring that appropriate newspaper articles appeared, wining and dining politicians, and judiciously bribing key members of the House of Representatives.[8]

Brega's work reached a fruition of sorts in March 1869. The House of Representatives passed a resolution calling upon the American executive to open negotiations with Great Britain on the subject of commercial intercourse with Canada, and to press the negotiations to a conclusion. The initiative for renewed bargaining had come from the Americans – with a little help from Canadian government funds.

It was not the most auspicious time for negotiations. A number of the southern, free-trade states had not yet been readmitted to congressional representation. Protectionist views were strongly expressed in industrial New England, in Ohio, in Pennsylvania, and in other politically crucial states. The Republicans, who were in the ascendancy, had protectionist tendencies. Yet not all was lost. The wheat-exporting American west, and key commercial cities, such as Chicago, Boston, and New York, strongly supported reciprocity. And now the Americans had extended an invitation to the bargaining table, while Brega was assuring Macdonald and his colleagues of the pliability of the American executive and Congress. If that was insufficient, Finance Minister John Rose did his best to pave the way for his negotiations with American Secretary of State Hamilton Fish in the summer of 1869 by making pompous statements in his budget speech about instituting a 'national policy' if reciprocity was not obtained.[9] The meetings with Fish, a cautious man given to the long view, brought no immediate resolution, but Fish did promise to give Rose's proposals (essentially a renewal of the arrangements of 1854) full consideration. The Canadian government clearly believed that something would come of this: in the fall of 1869, Macdonald wrote to one political supporter that he and the new finance minister Sir Francis Hincks might at any time leave for Washington 'as to Reciprocity matters.'[10]

Such great expectations were undercut by the end of the year. First came the irritating rumour that Montreal businessman and politician John Young, an advocate of Canadian independence, had told Americans that a denial of reciprocity would lead to annexation. The Riel uprising in Manitoba compounded the problem by heightening tension between the two countries and bringing about an outburst of annexationist sentiment in the southern neighbour.[11] Then the reference to reciprocity in the American president's December message to Congress seemed to indicate that all was lost. President Grant announced that a renewed reciprocity treaty 'has not been favorably considered by the Administration. The advantages of such a treaty would be wholly in favor of the British producer.'[12] Congress' vote of approval on the message seemed like reciprocity's death rattle. 'Do you not think,' Macdonald asked Brega sharply, 'that the vote of the House of Representatives on the paragraphs in the President's message effectively disposes of the question and renders useless any efforts in the cause of Reciprocity and common sense?'[13] Brega put the best face possible on the vote, saying that it was only a matter of form, and Macdonald in turn reassured his correspondents, so necessary did a trade agreement seem.

At long last, in February 1870, Hamilton Fish replied to the proposals John Rose had made some eight months earlier, offering the reduction or removal of duties on fish, salt, coal, and lumber. The British minister at Washington reported that the offer was accompanied by Fish's assertion that 'he was receiving constant written and verbal communication from people of all classes in Canada representing to him that nine tenths of the inhabitants were in favour of separation from the Mother Country.'[14] To Fish and to many Canadians, that was virtually annexationism. Brega began to lose the trust of Macdonald with increasing rapidity, and worked on sufferance until his employment as Canadian agent effectively ended in April 1870. A reconsideration of Canadian policy was under way.

The Canadian government now recognized that the policy of moderation was endlessly one of hope, not of realization. A new strategy, more active and aggressive, was necessary to gain reciprocity and to satisfy diverse demands within Canada. The Atlantic fisheries were central to the altered plan.

The inshore fisheries was an issue of great importance in its own right. Inshore waters were the source of bait fish, lobster, and of mackerel. The Reciprocity Treaty had accustomed American fishermen to open access to the fisheries; after the treaty's abrogation, the Americans' fishing habits had to be changed through a strong colonial assertion of sovereignty over inshore waters. With the union of the provinces, there were multiplying demands that the Americans be excluded entirely, rather than being allowed to fish inshore on the payment of a licensing free. These demands made some sense, given the poor 1867 fishing season and the great privation in some of the Nova Scotian outports the following winter. American competition was too keen, and the fisher-folk wanted retaliation against the American duties on foreign-caught fish.[15] A greater exclusion of the Americans from the inshore waters would not only alleviate anti-government feeling, but would neatly point out the need for a reciprocity agreement to the Americans. Licensing fees were raised to two dollars per ton in 1868, and enforcement became more rigid. The move to a less accommodating policy was held in check only by the caution of the British, who had to enforce fisheries policy, and by the prospect of trade negotiations with the United States.

The developments of late 1869 partly removed the latter consideration. Peter Mitchell, the New Brunswicker who was minister of marine and fisheries, took the opportunity to reiterate the Maritimes' unhappiness with the policy of conciliation. He urged vigorous protection of the fisheries: reciprocity was hopelessly lost and Canada should pursue her own interests in an act of 'National Policy.' The cabinet took Mitchell's advice. Despite Great Britain's well-known opposition to any policy carrying the flavour of anti-Americanism, a January 1870 order in council barred the inshore to the Americans.[16]

A shift away from conciliation was also to be seen in tariff policy. It was more than a response to American inaction on reciprocity, of course. From 1866 to 1869, good economic conditions and minor alterations to the tariff had kept a variety of interests quiet. Rose had imposed small duties on some secondary iron products in 1868 to calm the tempers of the industry in Montreal and had appeased the Maritimes by removing the duty on breadstuffs. He had also imposed export duties on unmanufactured lumber – pleasant news to sawyers and lumbermen with integrated operations.[17] In 1869, however, a minor economic slump took hold, and the government deficit was large. The moment for raising the protectionist banner had come.

A brief look at the economic conditions of the country provides further clues about the attractions of protection. Some 70 per cent of the consumer durables available for purchase in the country in 1870 were imported. The contrast with the United States was striking: that country could have supplied over 93 per cent of such goods available there in that year. While the contrast was less notable in other commodity groups, even these showed that Canada had a stronger tendency to import finished goods than the United States.[18] Yet in a number of industries, Canadian production came close to meeting domestic Canadian demand, mostly because of substantial factory expansion during the 1860s. In such industries there were often a number of large mechanized plants in production by 1871.

The boot and shoe trade makes a useful example of such industrial conditions. In the United States, sewing machinery for shoes had been introduced in the 1850s, and had rapidly taken hold with the use of the McKay stitcher after 1862, accompanied by devices such as sole cutters and, later, heeling machines. By 1870, the conversion to the factory system of shoe-manufacturing was widespread there; by 1880 virtually all aspects in shoe manufacturing involved the use of machinery.[19] Major shoe manufacturers in Canada were only slightly behind; they made a practice of importing the latest of American technology. Four factories in Montreal were using the McKay stitcher by 1864; a decade later the Bigelow heeling machine was introduced. That time period framed a major bout of growth for the industry. In 1861 there were in Montreal 5 boot and shoe factories; not long after the American Civil War ended there were 8 very large ones and 6 smaller ones; in 1871 the 117 boot and shoe firms of all sizes in Montreal employed 5175 workers.[20] The same phenomenon could be observed in other urban centres in the country. Robinson and Ralston, a Saint John, New Brunswick, firm with 150 employees, boasted in the early 1870s that its machine work was 'performed by the best American inventions' and that its 'whole building vibrates with the tremor of the works' driven by a steam-engine of 25 horsepower.[21] Yet impressive as the emergence of boot and shoe factories was, shoemaking in the country as a whole was not fully a machine or factory industry. Many of the seventy establishments in Saint John in 1871 continued to practise hand-stitching, despite the example of Robinson and Ralston.[22] The average number of employees in a boot and shoe firm in Canada as a whole in 1870 was 4.5; in rural areas, the number dipped much lower than that – Brant North, for example, averaged 1.7 and Durham East 2.[23] In 1870 this broad and unstable spectrum of productive facilities was capable of meeting virtually all domestic demand.[24] The slump of 1869, combined with modestly rising imports, therefore created a degree of competitive congestion.

There existed a variety of industries in which a similar broad spectrum of productive facilities seemed capable of meeting most of the domestic demand in 1870. This was the case in agricultural-equipment manufacturing, for example. The industry produced at least the equivalent of 95 per cent of such equipment available in Canada that year. The industry could boast of some large factories, with the four in York West in Ontario sharing 226 employees, yet the average number of employees for such firms for Canada as a whole was somewhat less than 10, and there were many listed that only had 1 or 2. Carriage manufacturing was in a similar position: the firm of Price and Shaw in Saint John employed 50 hands in the early 1870s; their plant was steam driven, had 'all the most improved modern machinery' and was on this basis comparable to American carriage factories.[25] Yet the average number of employees in such plants nationally was only 3. A high level of domestic capacity was to be found in other industries. One might note a few: cabinetware and furniture, edge tools, refined oil, ropes and twine, starch, tanned leather, and soap and candles.

If these conditions implied a potential for defensive protectionism, there were also conditions that allowed for a more expansionist perspective. In all industries, more efficient factories allowed for market expansion at the cost of less efficient producers. Moreover, the propensity to import finished products showed that there was tremendous room for expansion by many industries in the country.

Cotton manufacturing, a heavily mechanized industry with 93 employees per plant in 1871, produced less than 10 per cent of domestically available cottons in 1870, a situation that made it possible for the industry to expand even during depression conditions. In earthenware – a major mass consumption item, like cottons – domestic production only came to about 38 per cent of domestic availability. The domestic production of paints was perhaps slightly lower than that in comparison to total availability in Canada in 1870. There were many industries in this situation. The statistics, though by no means accurate, none the less indicate that growth was possible. And Confederation implied national markets.

Consequently, possibilities for a broad-ranging national protectionist coalition existed. A basic element of such a coalition emerged with the gathering of manufacturers at Toronto in March 1870, which resurrected the Ontario Association for the Promotion of Canadian Industry. The association agreed that a general increase in the *ad valorem* rate to 20 or 25 per cent was only proper. The millers present decided that flour should be protected, and in a move intended to ally farmers with manufacturers, demanded the same for all agricultural products.[26]

The move was clever, though obvious. Among the mass of protectionist petitions that reached Parliament in 1870 were a large number from Ontario farmers. Fruit growers wanted defence against American competition. Market gardeners, especially in areas bordering the United States, desired duties on vegetables. Others wanted higher tariff rates on hops and cattle. Many petitions bore witness to incipient local alliances between the farmers and manufacturers in a number of locales, though retaliation against the United States for its high tariffs remained a major rural protectionist motive. One petition from Oxford County summarized the case: 'That while your petitioners are favorable to the principles of free trade, they do feel that under the present trade relations between the Dominion of Canada and the United States, it is desirable and necessary, in order to promote the growth of the agricultural, commercial, manufacturing and all the industrial interests of the Dominion, to impose an import duty on wheat, flour, corn, salt, [and] coal.'[27]

The inclusion of coal was noteworthy. Sir John A. Macdonald had been anxious to reassure the Nova Scotian industry that the Americans would lower or remove their duty on coal,[28] but the chances for this actually happening were fading. A protective duty on coal was the only other choice. Such protection would at one and the same time push the United States towards reciprocity and open the market of Quebec and Ontario to the product. The publicist Robert Grant Haliburton (who had a material interest in Nova Scotian collieries) offered a related perspective: the exchange of coal for Ontario breadstuffs through the fostering agency of protective tariffs was the only way to block the nefarious American plan to starve Nova Scotia into annexation; it was, at the same time, a basic method of creating a common British North American nationality. The Coal Owners' Association of Nova Scotia, which Haliburton did much to organize, urged the institution of an 'independent policy' for coal, for it was the central government's responsibility 'as far as possible to secure to us an outlet for our products in the Dominion, as a substitute for the market which has been, for political purposes [annexation], denied to us by the American Government.'[29]

A culmination of sorts took place in Ottawa, where Charles Tupper gathered together a sizeable deputation of MPs in March 1870 and paid a visit to Sir Francis Hincks and Samuel Leonard Tilley. The 'tentative and conciliatory policy pursued by the Government and Parliament of the country,' Tupper told the ministers of finance and customs, 'had obviously failed to induce any reciprocal concessions on the part of our neighbors ... The time has come to adopt a purely national policy of our own ... irrespective of those of foreign countries. It was believed by many that the imposition of a moderate duty upon the imports of various articles, coming into competition with our own industries, and now admitted free or at a nominal duty, would tend to promote our internal commerce, and cement the union among the several parts of the Dominion.'[30] Tupper's deputation was followed, some two weeks later, by one from the newly organized Ontario Association for the Promotion of Canadian Industry, urging protection on manufactured goods, coal, and agricultural products.

Yet the tariff of 1870 was not really defined by pressures from manufacturers. Sir Francis could with reason feel that protectionists did not find the tariff of much use to them.[31] A 5 per cent surcharge on all duties slightly increased the general tariff rate. Users of iron wire, book publishers, and some machinery manufacturers received minor advantages. Grain milling and shipbuilding received significant concessions, but these were not exemplars of the new industrialization. The tariff alterations were a reflex to the denial of reciprocity, and secondarily a means of gaining more revenue, not a response to protectionist demands from manufacturers. The coal interest had to be pacified, so 50 cents per ton duty was imposed on coal and coke. Canadian farmers were separated from American consumers by the United States tariff wall, so Canadians would be encouraged to consume the home products. Duties were placed on fruits, vegetables, butter, cheese, animals, and meat. More dramatically, a wide variety of grains and flours were given protection – the quid pro quo for the coal duty. Also faced with a high American tariff, the staple product salt found favour. The government's attachment to the traditional political economy was made all the clearer by the imposition of a more sophisticated *ad valorem* system to foster the St Lawrence transportation route.[32] The whole system related to the established staple-producing and exporting sectors of the economy that had been ostensibly damaged by the loss of reciprocity, not to the manufacturing sector.

The decision to shift from external to internal markets was an emphatic restatement of the fundamental economic function of Confederation, a function that marked a decisive change in the colonial conception of markets. But at the same time, the tariff was a retaliatory one intended to convince the Americans of the desirability of an older economic pattern. Hincks had used the same ploy prior to 1854, with the same end in mind. 'The duty on coal, wheat & flour is of course very much objected to,' Hincks confided to John Rose,'but it is part & parcel of our whole scheme of Protection & I believe will have a good effect. Suppose it does what they say divert trade ... It will be a pity no doubt but *if trade* be diverted Chicago will also feel it & depend on it until we can get the western men & those interested in our fisheries to work the Congress we won't get reciprocity.'[33]

Despite the pressures for higher tariffs, bringing the 1870 tariff into law was not easy. Protectionism was far from dominant in the new nation, and the half-formed protectionist alliance was a tenuous affair. Low-tariff feeling was widespread in the Maritimes. The coal interest was as eager to get reciprocity as protection. A major rise in customs duties, in a region where per capita imports were greater than in central Canada, meant an unfair shift in the burden of taxation and an increase in the cost of living. The 1866 duty on breadstuffs had produced such a storm of protest that they were removed in 1868. With the passage of the 1870 tariff in Ottawa, the Nova Scotian Assembly reacted by unanimously passing a resolution condemning this 'national policy'.[34]

From all appearances, central Canadians also appreciated low customs duties. Though the Guelph Board of Trade approved of protection – especially of breadstuffs – the boards of trade of Toronto, Kingston, Montreal, and Quebec City repudiated the idea, because they were interested in tapping the American grain-producing hinterland or exporting to the United States. In political terms, the Ontario Reformers were committed to low tariffs, at least at the leadership level: one of the resolutions at their 1867 convention promised to lower customs duties as quickly as possible if they were returned to power.[35]

Conservative ranks were riddled with free traders. At a Toronto meeting late in March 1870, the public was treated to the edifying spectacle of watching powerful monied men sling verbal dirt at each other. J.G. Worts, Conservative distiller and banker who otherwise did not seek the political limelight, dominated the first part of the meeting with a defence of free trade and a sharp assault on some well-known protectionists for their greed. At least one of the individuals so honoured was in the audience, and Worts found his own position analysed as one of self-interest: it was easy to be a free trader if one imported 8000 tons of coal and large quantities of corn from the United States each year to run a distilling operation. Yet Worts was not alone among the Conservatives.[36]

The vigour of the opposition to protection was reflected in the House of Commons, where defeat threatened the government as the tariff proposals were debated. Hincks at one point thought it best to give way to opposition demands and promised to remove the proposed duties on coal and wheat. Heavy pressure from Tupper and others forced the government to return to the original proposals. The opposition heaped scorn on the demoralized government for this peculiar double reversal of field. Sir John A. Macdonald, absent from the Commons because of the worrisome Manitoba troubles, had to be dragged in to bring fractious Conservatives into line.[37]

The tariff barely escaped in the Senate. David Macpherson, the Conservative senator and Toronto financier, who was strongly committed to free trade and reciprocity, found the tariff to be replete with '*odious* characteristics.'[38] He was a central figure in the rebellion of Conservative senators against the tariff, which passed by a bare majority of four in the upper House.

A whip to cow the Americans into reciprocity was one of the functions of the tariff. The fisheries, however, were to provide the occasion for renewed trade negotiations.

Alexander Campbell, the postmaster general, was sent to England in the spring of 1870 to discuss with the British not only the outstanding issues of imperial troop withdrawals, fortifications, and the Fenians, but also the fisheries and the headlands question. If the inshore fisheries were to be protected, the boundary of inshore waters had to be defined. Were those waters limited by an imaginary straight line drawn between points three miles off headlands, or did the three-mile line follow the convolutions of the coast, opening up bays and inlets to foreign fishermen? The matter touched Canadian, British, and American interests.

On 1 July 1870, the Canadian Privy Council proposed a mixed or joint commission with one imperial, one American, and one Canadian commissioner to decide the matter.[39] The proposal was rather unrealistic in terms of representation, but commissions to decide points of conflict between Britain and the United States had a long history. Only a few years earlier, a government of the Canadas had advocated a commission to formulate a new reciprocity agreement. The one suggested in 1870, though it would have dealt with the important fisheries dispute, was beyond a doubt a means of having reciprocity reconsidered.

Any attempt to improve the poor Anglo-American relations of the time was bound to be a delicate affair, and months passed before any action was undertaken on the proposal. President Grant's December 1870 message to Congress precipitated action: he termed Canada's efforts to control her inshore fisheries the 'unfriendly' exercise of powers by a 'semi-independent but irresponsible agent' that might require the United States to protect her citizens. The president then asked Congress to give him the power to suspend trade with Canada.[40]

A negotiated settlement was now crucial; Canadian policy had, on the face of it, proven effective. But both the British and the Americans seized on the idea of a commission as an opportunity to thrash out major issues that had no direct bearing on Canada. The matter of the Fenian disturbances, which would have given the Canadians an excellent means of broadening their claims, was by error or design left off the agenda. The commission membership grew to five, leaving a lone Canadian (appointed as a Britisher) in the midst of the predominantly British and American Joint High Commission of 1871. But the die was cast. Canadian participation was necessary. Sir John A. Macdonald became that lone Canadian.[41]

From the Canadian perspective, reciprocity was the key issue at stake in the following deliberations. This is evident not only from the Canadian desire to establish such a commission, but from the way the entire cabinet was involved in framing the negotiating strategy.[42] Sir Francis Hincks' closely reasoned memorandum to Sir John A. Macdonald on the eve of the prime minister's departure to Washington shows that Macdonald was no loner.

Nothing, Hincks felt, could be lost by Canadian involvement in the negotiations, and if the Alabama question (the Alabama was a Confederate raider built in Great Britain; the United States wanted reparations for the damage it had caused) went well, so surely would matters of concern to Canadians. On these grounds, Macdonald should undertake to negotiate a trade agreement with the Americans. The U.S. members of the commission would naturally insist on the free navigation of the St Lawrence because American access to that water route could be threatened by Canada and, above all, they would demand the free use of the Canadian fisheries. Macdonald's duty would be to get 'Reciprocity on the old terms, or nearly so (ie a 10 per cent revenue duty)' using these and other, lesser negotiating points. Quite probably, Hincks judged, the Americans would not grant a renewal of the old reciprocity; in particular a free trade in breadstuffs and livestock was most unlikely. Still, 'we cannot yield the fisheries without *at least* free importation of our fish, and free or low duty on coal, lumber and salt, particularly the first,' the finance minister insisted.[43] To mollify Ontario farmers who would be disappointed by such a limited reciprocity and, on the side, to make Hincks' job in finance easier, Macdonald was supposed to make a strong case for an imperial loan guarantee for purposes of railway construction. The chief desire expressed was for a return to the old reciprocity. The Conservative government was not pursuing free trade as such, but the removal of tariff barriers on staple products. The re-creation of the system of combined reciprocity and incidental protection with its support for the Laurentian trade route was the government's aim.

The prescription Hincks outlined was followed by Macdonald during the Washington negotiations and was nearly successful. The Americans did offer various tariff concessions for the fisheries; their best offer came to free coal, fish, salt, and lumber (the last to be free after 1 July 1875). Macdonald, unlike the British, was not eager to accept this, for he argued that monetary compensation would be necessary to make the offer a fair one. Macdonald had in mind manoeuvring the British into making a loan guarantee if the Americans did not provide the compensation, and he was pleased when the British accepted the necessity of a money payment in principle.[44] The confidence the Canadian government felt at this juncture was soon crushed. The U.S. commissioners, for reasons they chose not to disclose, decided to interpret the demand for a money compensation, in addition to their offer of trade concessions, as a rejection of their offer.

The Americans had not been two-faced in their offer of a limited reciprocity, Macdonald was certain. His letters, overall neither excessively hopeful or wildly despairing (one gets the impression that he knew the whole negotiation was a chancy business) were at first disappointed and puzzled, and then quite harsh on the withdrawal of the American proposal. From his viewpoint, the American action had its roots in the removal of Canadian duties on coal and salt during the 1871 parliamentary session. Greedy American monopolists, he wrote in an acid outburst, had without a thought for the future snapped up the chance to gain the Canadian market while keeping the American protected, if only for a season. The 'weak as water' American government had succumbed to pressure from business interests.[45]

What had happened in Canada to disrupt – as Macdonald felt was the case – the carefully choreographed diplomatic dance he had tried to perform in Washington? The opposition to the imposition of the tariff in 1870 had been great and nearly successful. The positions of many MPs were volatile, the agreements of 1870 were fragile: Macdonald's personal authority had to be exercised to push the tariff through. By 1871, opposition had consolidated, and Macdonald was absent in Washington. The attack on the duties on coal and breadstuffs mounted to levels Sir Francis Hincks could not manage. '*Any good excuse* to repeal the duties at once is what we want,' the finance minister wrote Macdonald with frantic urgency in March, seeking assurance that some trade concessions from the Americans were at hand.[46]

Sir John did his best, but could not comply. Hincks pinned the defence of the 1870 tariff not on its intrinsic worth, but on its presumed importance in aiding the delicate negotiations taking place in Washington. This only whetted the appetite of the Commons opposition. Outside of Parliament, protectionists did not rally to the cause – disappointed as many were with the tariff, and too busy taking advantage of the ongoing boom. In the end, the government found it impossible to control the House. From the opposition, Luther Holton's motion to make wheat, coal, and coke duty free, after being amended to include all grains and flours, passed handsomely. Sixteen MPs who had supported the government on the tariff in 1870 voted the other way in 1871, and others were absent when the vote was taken. The 'National Policy' of Charles Tupper (who later incorrectly claimed to have coined the phrase) had been shed quickly.[47] The time had not been ripe, the interests imperfectly reconciled, the ulterior motives in government too dominant.

The Treaty of Washington that resulted from the commission negotiations was a dividing line for the Conservative government. True, the Maritimes could be consoled with the free entry of fish into the United States under the treaty; true, the British guarantee for a Canadian loan was an offering to soothe central Canadian irritation; and in the future there was the potential for a large American compensation in return for entry into the fisheries, but these were limited gains. The aggressive policy, as well as the policy of conciliation, had not proved fruitful. The political possibilities of protection became ever more attractive, especially as the people who would find industrial protection appealing were growing in number.

The early 1870s were a period of remarkable expansion; businessmen recognized the economy's potential for explosive growth even in the depression that followed. In the inflating dollars of the years 1868 to 1873–74, exports rose in value from $57,000,000 to $89,000,000. Some twenty-eight new bank charters were granted and banking capital increased over 80 per cent between Confederation and the middle of 1873. Railway construction, negligible from 1860 to 1866, underwent a sharp spurt with the building of the Intercolonial. Some $15,500,000 was spent on the line between Confederation and 1874; more than 1500 miles of track were built in Canada in those years. Not surprisingly, after the slight economic slump of 1869, price inflation took strong hold until 1873, and the potential of great profits brought businessmen to extend themselves to the limit.[48] Markets were expanding; it was a time of great business optimism. The period thus was a juncture of some importance in the political economy of the country, for growth in many industries – explosive during the boom of the early 1870s – coincided with the virtual elimination of some basic choices in economic policy. Protectionism had much greater opportunity to flower as a consequence.

The nationalism fostered by the potential of the young country was readily fused with protection. Witness the enthusiasms of the Canada Firsters, so well seasoned by ideas inherited from Isaac Buchanan. Henry Morgan, Buchanan's biographer and anthologist of the merchant/visionary's written outpourings, shared patriotism and protectionism with others in the civil service; R.G. Haliburton spread Buchanan's conceptions of intercolonial trade fostered by protective tariffs to fellow Nova Scotians and Ottawa sachems by speech and pamphlet. Heir to the milling, shipping, and banking investments, as well as the fading political influence of his father, W.H. Howland became a convinced protectionist by 1870, and also a member of Canada First. He had shipped Nova Scotian coal to Toronto in 1869–70 as visible evidence of his beliefs, and was one of the leading protectionist lights of the new decade.[49]

A protectionist mood flourished in the Province of Quebec as well. Debates over protection and free trade took place in a number of newspapers in the province in 1871–72. Discussions of the issue took place regularly in the Quebec Assembly, in blithe disregard of the constitutional division of powers, and French-Canadian members of the Montreal Board of Trade pressed protectionist resolutions on their organization. French Canadians felt more strongly than ever that industrial protection was vital to prevent French Canadians from emigrating to industrial New England.[50]

A new nationalist and protectionist party appeared in the province. 'The new party says that Canada is dying out,' wrote the Montreal journalist and politician Sidney Bellingham to Sir John A. Macdonald, '& that unless we enjoy commercial freedom & the right to impose differential duties this province must sink into obscurity. Therefore you will hear the protectionist cry throughout the land as the elections approach.' The protectionist journalist John Maclean had already advised Sir George Cartier to take the lead in the new movement favouring home manufactures, a procedure that Bellingham also thought wise.[51] The Conservatives did not move quickly enough to bottle this effervescence, however. The new party, the Parti national, soon became an adjunct of the federal Liberals. Policies on commercial independence from Britain and electoral and Senate reform espoused by the Parti national brought it closer to the liberalism of Ontario lawyer and politician Edward Blake than to the Conservatives.

There were other pressures and portents. Representatives of the Toronto Board of Trade and the Saint John Chamber of Commerce were united in their advocacy of protection at the annual meeting of the Dominion Board of Trade in January 1872, though the Dominion Board avoided a split in its ranks by postponing discussion to the next year. Then, during the parliamentary session of 1872, Charles Magill, the Hamilton MP, moved for a committee to enquire into the condition of the manufacturing interests. A committee on agriculture was also formed, headed by the protectionist agricultural implements manufacturer D.G. Jones. The questionnaire the Jones committee planned to send to farmers, millers, and others had an obvious protectionist slant. Magill's committee went further than Jones', collecting answers as well as framing questions. On this basis, they concluded that raising the tariff to 20 per cent was advisable, even though manufacturers were doing well.[52]

Facing an election, the Conservative government was sensitive to these developments. Two tariff changes in 1871 made the sensitivity concrete. Both removed from the public eye subsequent alterations in the tariff that would favour manufacturers. The governor general in council (the cabinet), could authorize the free admission of machinery to be used in factories on the presentation of evidence that similar machinery was not being made in Canada. That took most of the sting out of the duty on machinery imposed in 1870. Even more important, the cabinet could move to the free list any natural or manufactured products 'used as materials in Canadian manufactures.'[53] Protection could thus be increased by reducing input costs. A sustained series of applications in 1871 and 1872 came before the Treasury Board under this latter provision. On the whole, the requests were treated generously; perhaps this is not surprising, given the imminence of a federal election.[54]

The Conservatives also decided to make protection a motif in their election campaign in 1872. Sir John A. Macdonald mentioned to one important Hamilton businessman, as early as December of 1871, that he thought 'a cry for readjustment for Revenue purposes, but affording incidental protection to our own manufactures & products, would go down well.'[55] The idea hardened into certainty in the next few months. The prime minister told Montreal financier George Stephen that he was amazed at the excitement among farmers at the removal of the duties on breadstuffs in 1871. There was strong feeling in favour of fostering home manufactures, he added. Stephen well knew that his opinion was being sought and agreed that protection was popular among the farmers in the eastern townships also. As for himself, Stephen went on with calculated lightheartedness, he was personally convinced that free trade was the best policy, but '*I* as a manufacturer could not be expected violently to oppose a policy which would tend to secure the more complete control of our own market for my products.'[56] To committed free traders such as Senator David Macpherson, who might break with the party on the issue, the prime minister put the case for the National Policy as a mere election ploy, necessary if the Tories were to be returned to office.[57]

The cities were most open to protectionism, which was why the Conservatives had redistributed seats to manufacturing centres in 1871. As Charles Tupper wrote to one Halifax newspaper during the election campaign, that city had not obtained another federal seat though its population might have warranted it, while Saint John, Ottawa, and Hamilton had, for the latter 'have great manufacturing interests to represent, while the interests of Halifax are identical with those of at least half the other counties in the Province.'[58] Though the idea of a 'National Policy' was talked about in Halifax, it naturally followed that protection was emphasized in the more industrialized cities. 'Hamilton is more interested in a policy which will encourage manufactures than any other part of Canada,' Macdonald informed Donald McInnes, the Hamilton financier, merchant, and manufacturer: 'Now our taking the duties off tea and coffee [two major revenue producers], ought to be a sufficient proof to the manufacturers that the present Government will adopt a principle of incidental protection. With our increased engagements for the enlargement of the Canals, and the construction of the Pacific Railway, the deficiency in the revenue caused by taking the duties off tea & coffee must be made up in some way, & this can only be done by a duty on manufactured goods.'[59]

Protection was also an issue in Toronto. Robert Wilkes, a merchant with very strong free-trade proclivities, ran for the Liberals in Toronto Centre. Here was the evidence, the Conservatives claimed, that the Liberals had every intention of reducing tariffs and introducing direct taxation if they came into power. Wilkes had to come forth with an admission that as revenue came from customs, he would necessarily accept incidental protection, which was the same stance that the *Globe* took at the time.[60] Montrealers had protection as an election issue as well: George A. Drummond, the directing manager of the Redpath sugar refinery and a Conservative candidate, advocated tariff protection. The approach undercut some of the appeal of the Parti national. Promises of incidental protection were made during the election campaign by Macdonald and Hincks at Hamilton, Peterborough, and Brant County, where Hincks was running.[61] But to the west of Brantford, in the heart of Liberal Ontario, the two campaigners generally avoided direct reference to protection. There, much was made of the Treaty of Washington, and how the emasculation of the tariff in 1871 had ruined the chance at reciprocity.

All this is not to argue that protection was the key issue in the election of 1872, or even that it did the Tories a great deal of good. In seventy-two Ontario seats – which excludes problematical ridings – the correlation between the ratio of Conservative votes to Liberal and industrial value added per capita as calculated from the 1871 census was .216 (see chapter 9 for further analysis along these lines). The Treaty of Washington had some positive impact in the Maritimes, as fish had free entry into the United States under its provisions. In central Canada, the treaty aided the Liberals: Macdonald admitted, in the aftermath of the election, that the Tories had lost ground in rural Ontario because of the treaty's inadequacies.[62] Moreover, many Ontarians still smouldered over the death of Thomas Scott, an Orangeman, during the Manitoba troubles. Also, political battles had a powerful orientation to immediate constituency concerns, not to issues of national import. A national policy was itself viewed from a strongly localistic perspective, for railway and coal-producing constituencies in Nova Scotia saw it as providing local benefit and voted Conservative.[63] Though protectionism proved its worth in Hamilton, it was less effective in other urban ridings. Robert Wilkes won in Toronto Centre, and in Montreal, George Drummond lost to the free trader John Young. The voters' verdict on higher tariffs was equivocal.

Between Confederation and 1871 the Conservative government (which included or had the support of such one-time reformers as William McDougall, W.P. Howland, and Sir Francis Hincks, and was at least nominally a coalition for some time after Confederation) sought to return to the commercial policy that functioned so splendidly before 1866: a mixed system of reciprocity, a revenue tariff, and incidental protection. The American cancellation of reciprocity was folly from the Canadian perspective, and the government of the new nation awaited with a degree of patience a return to common sense south of the border, a return to be hastened with surreptitious Canadian aid. Patience, in this case, did not receive its reward. By late 1869, more forceful methods were undertaken to gain reciprocity. The fisheries provided one mechanism, the retaliatory tariff of 1870 another. The tariff also offered a sop to staple producers by protecting the enlarged internal market created by Confederation, but even before the failure of the Joint High Commission to bring forth a new trade agreement, the tariff had proven to be a politically ineffective alternative to the older mixed commercial policy.

No stable accommodation of interests underlay the 1870 customs duties; their passage in Parliament had been enforced by a desperate appeal to personal and party loyalties. The defeat of the tariff's central provisions in 1871 flowed from this. Manufacturers had largely been ignored in the 1870 tariff, even though they were among the most vigorous protectionists and had shown signs of restiveness under the regime of incidental protection by late 1869. Ironically, Canadians did not generally recognize the shifts in the American economy that rendered a reciprocity in natural products worth rather less than in the 1850s.

A demand for low tariffs and reciprocity dominated commercial policy decisions from Confederation until after 1871, but some consolidation and strengthening of the protectionist perspective had taken place by that time. The faltering of the economy in 1869 brought an upsurge in high-tariff sentiment; the lull that followed after 1870 was temporary in the face of the pressures of nationalism, economic growth, and the expansion of competition. The Conservatives responded by playing protection as an issue on a regional basis in the election of 1872. It was a caution to them that their stance gained them so little; none the less, they had small opportunity to follow through on the tendencies they had displayed. Scandal brought down Sir John A. Macdonald's Conservative government, and a period of renewed uncertainty in commercial policy followed. Concurrently, the regional and national economies of the country were undergoing cyclical and structural changes that had an important impact on the social and political history of business, and in turn on political life.

5

'The obscurity of private enterprise': business and the economy, 1870–1879

The National Policy of 1879 was precipitated by the business experience of the 1870s, which consisted of a severe swing of the business cycle superimposed on the long-term processes of economic diversification, technical advance, and market integration. Between 1873 and 1896, Canada's lot consisted of economic expansion and monetary deflation, the oddly matched products of a wide array of interrelated social and economic forces, the chief of which included a constricted money supply, an altering work-force, technological and organizational innovation, and the integration of markets. Yet the census data that show long-term growth mask the shorter-term occurrences of recession, boom, or depression. In fact, the country endured a major downturn from 1874 to 1879, as E.J. Chambers has shown. All sectors of the Canadian economy (with the partial exception of agriculture) suffered, and did so more severely than their American counterparts whose performance they generally followed.[1] Contemporaries called it a depression.

This slump did not come suddenly in Canada; there was no railway panic or banking crisis in September 1873 as occurred in the United States. But the economy became congested, and in 1874 prices began to drop, with business activity slowing in the third and fourth quarters. Merchants were left with huge inventories. Importing commercial houses were immediately affected, and the impact in Montreal, where the failure of a few major wholesale firms dragged down their connections, were sometimes shattering. The early 1874 insolvency of Montreal woollens importer Messrs H. Davis & Co. for example, led to the collapse not only of his English partner, but also of two other Montreal firms, a Quebec auction house, and a Hamilton wholesaler.[2] Sloppy business practices had a role to play in such developments as righteous contemporaries complained, but they blamed equally the widespread, bloated credit system, which could make one failure the first of many. It took time for the effect of the business

TABLE 2
Business failures, 1873–80

Year	Number	Liabilities
1873	944	$12,334,191
1874	966	7,696,765
1875	1968	28,843,967
1876	1728	25,517,991
1877	1890	25,510,157
1878	1615	23,152,262
1879	1902	29,347,937
1880	907	7,947,063

SOURCE: *Monetary Times*, 7 January 1881

slowdown to have its impact on the domestic manufacturing sector, but soon the chief financial paper in the country, the *Monetary Times*, began detailing the punishment manufacturers had to endure.

The financial journal announced a typical case in its assertive prose: 'The firm of Messrs. Johnson Bros., who in 1870 succeeded their father in the tanning business in Fergus, has been in difficulties for some months. The partners were pushing and energetic, but heavy losses by bad debts and the lock-up of capital in machinery and stock which has greatly depreciated of late, have combined to bring about their present insolvent condition.'[3] Failure. In this the Messrs Johnson had the comfort of company (see table 2). The figures in table 2 include both industrial and mercantile failures of course, but the data gathered by the 1876 parliamentary Committee on the Causes of the Present Depression show that at least one-third of the failures (both in number and liabilities) during the fourteen months to February 1876 were manufacturers. And in the year ending 30 September 1878, of the 1588 who were insolvent according to government statistics, slightly more than half were defined as 'industrial.'[4] Though the depression struck unevenly and businessmen's optimism continued well beyond the beginning of the slump because of tariff increases, municipal bonusing, and a tenacious belief in industrialism, the downswing of the business cycle took hold.

The iron and steel industry provides an excellent illustration of the slide from boom to slump, and how that slide was accelerated by technological change. In the boom of the early 1870s, enthusiasm for the industry increased partly because of massive railway construction and because of a precipitous international increase in the price of ferrous metals (pig-iron doubled to roughly $50 per ton from 1871 to late 1872 in unadjusted Canadian dollars). Prices did not decline to 1871 levels until mid 1875 and optimism among manufacturers seemed further warranted by the profits of some firms.[5] Men and money rushed in. In primary production, the Moisie Iron Company, largely financed by W.M. Molson, was formed in 1869 with a nominal capital of $600,000 and expanded works rapidly. The Haycock Iron Mines opened in the winter of 1873, and the associated Ottawa Iron and Steel Manufacturing Company began construction of works in 1875. The Titanic Iron Company opened at the same time. Canadian and British capitalists provided massive investment for the Steel Company of Canada in Nova Scotia in 1873. Ambitious and hopeful men laid preliminary plans for setting up blast furnaces in Toronto. At the secondary level, the Montreal rolling mills expanded, as did numerous foundries. Many new firms were put into place, such as the Nova Scotia Forge Company in 1872, the large Coldbrook Rolling Mills of New Brunswick, or that of H.H. Date who opened a steel-making works in 1873 using a gas process of his invention.[6] While the domestic market grew rapidly, so did the international one, though total exports were admittedly not large. But international production had also been greatly stimulated by the Franco-Prussian war, and by the railway boom in North America. When the depression came, the iron industry in Canada wilted. Greatly expanded capacity clashed with declining domestic demand and falling world prices. The wholesale cost of pig-iron dropped to one-third of its 1872 high by 1879. The Haycock company suspended operation, the Moisie firm went insolvent, the Titanic Iron Company went bankrupt, and the Date firm went out of business.

Failures in the primary iron industry in Canada were not due merely to the business cycle, however. As Kris Inwood has shown, the narrow market that Canada provided, especially in depression conditions, prevented existing companies using charcoal iron furnaces (like Moisie) from undertaking the technical innovations necessary to remain competitive. When coke pig-iron and mild steel (produced by the new open-hearth technique) cut off two major portions of the charcoal iron market in Canada, what remained was too limited to permit a rapid shift to new charcoal technology. The charcoal iron industry was plagued with failures during the 1870s; production plunged, while some of its remaining market was taken over by more efficient, large-scale and technically innovative American firms.[7]

But even in the coke-fired iron and steel industry, which dominated Canada's domestic production by the 1880s, the depression severely weakened Canadian firms. Here, too, the rapid advance of technology and a limited internal market had an impact.[8] The Haycock iron and steel firm barely scraped its way past the conceptual stage. Heavily capitalized, but facing formidable technical problems, the Canada Steel Company steadily lost money during the depression, though it endured until 1883. The secondary level of the industry saw many failures; among the more specialized of the insolvent firms were the Nova Scotia Iron Works, the Canada Car Company, the Canada Bolt Company, and the Dundas,

Ontario, screw manufacturing firm. Near or actual insolvency was frequent in the ranks of foundrymen. One might note Messrs Whitehead & Sewall of Toronto, W.S. Symonds & Co. of Halifax and Dartmouth, and E.E. Gilbert, H.R. Ives and W. Clendinneng, all of Montreal. Though some of these firms compromised and rebounded, and yet others, such as the rolling mills in Montreal, continued to make a profit, the juncture of structural change and cyclical crisis made the situation grim.[9]

Nor were matters pleasant in the associated sewing-machine industry, though it imported many of its steel and iron parts. Having gained a foothold in the late 1850s, the Canadian industry expanded with great rapidity in the 1860s and early 1870s, supplying not only domestic but foreign demand. Other than a sharp slump in 1874–75, exports remained fairly steady, but only half the sewing-machine manufacturers known to mercantile agent W.W. Johnson made it through the trying period. Large domestic capacity was as crucial a competitive factor as imports, and though Johnson admitted that internal Canadian competition had much to do with the firms collapsing, his calling led him to emphasize poor management, lack of enterprise, watered capital, and a 'lack of brain fertility.'[10]

A similar cycle of expansion followed by sharp rivalry and widespread failure took place in the textile industry. Productive capacity in the woollen manufacturing industry had burgeoned from the 1860s to 1873; substantial new mills were established, most often through a system of interlocking partnerships. Even before the depression, older small mills with local markets faced serious difficulties from greater domestic competition and from heavy imports from Britain. But falling prices, shrinking domestic demand in the depression, and the dumping of coarse woollens (including shoddy) by foreign competitors made the pinch severe – all the more so because the rapid expansion of the industry in the 1860s had made it capable of supplying a major portion of domestic demand, while many firms in the industry remained small and unproductive.[11] By the beginning of 1875, the industry as a whole was being tortured. Some mills, such as Waugh & Company, were closed for much of the duration. Others shut for lengthy periods when competitive pressures grew too great in order 'to allow an overstocked market to get relieved.'[12] And others failed: the Southampton woollen mills in Nova Scotia, George Lister and Company of Saint John, the Strathroy Woollen Mills, the Redford and Sugden mills, the Elora Carpet Manufacturing Company, and many others.[13]

Cotton manufacturing, too, underwent massive expansion in the first part of the 1870s, though the industry had been established in British North America in 1844.[14] The number of cotton factories was nine in 1871 with 745 employees; there were nineteen with 3529 employees a decade later. The Cornwall Cotton mills of Donald McInnes, the Hamilton financier and dry-goods wholesaler, opened in 1872, and with 20,000 spindles was for a time the largest factory of its kind in Canada. In February 1874, the large Victor Hudon mills at Hochelaga near Montreal began operation, having been in the planning stage since 1872. This operation was only slightly smaller than the Cornwall plant. The great factory at Valleyfield in Quebec's Eastern Townships was finally opened in 1876, and had greater productive capacity than the Cornwall mills. While there were few major technological advances, machinery was refined and operated at greater speeds. In this highly mechanized industry, which enjoyed considerable efficiencies of scale, domestic manufacturers nevertheless complained of their comparatively high costs due to an inability to specialize as extensively as their American competitors. Thus, despite the great expansion of the industry, and despite a sharp drop of the existing modest exports of cottons after 1874, imports of cottons remained high.[15]

Though the domestic industry held less than 10 per cent of the domestic market in 1870, international competition had harsh effects. The Merritton mill, one of the oldest in the country, closed for a lengthy period in 1877. Donald McInnes claimed in 1878 that only one mill in Canada had paid a dividend over the previous five years. His letter of late 1877 to Sir John A. Macdonald expressed the agitation of a man in despair: 'We are *starving* here & cant make both ends meet. [He spoke metaphorically about the Cornwall mills.] *Market market* is the great cry. We must be able to sell our *things* after making them, that is a *first* necessity & any little imported displaces just so much of our stuff. When the market is *oversupplied* even a sacrifice price will not enable *order* to be made.'[16] And, indeed, similar conditions existed in the United States.[17]

Of all industries, perhaps the hardest hit was lumbering. The depression greatly accelerated changes in an industry in which the basic products, organization, and business practices had not greatly altered in the fifty years before Confederation. Of course, from the 1850s onwards, square timber had been increasingly supplemented by sawn lumber, and the dominant British market by the American. But the process of change picked up speed from the later 1860s through the depression. After the removal of British preferences in 1866, the exports of square timber to Britain declined quickly, mostly because of ever spiralling production costs and sharper competition from European and American suppliers. The depression speeded up the shift to sawn lumber mostly for the American market and deals (very large planks) for the British. At the same time, the structure of the trade changed: more and more sawn lumber and deals were, in the 1870s, moved out of the Ottawa region by barge; and after 1876 an ever larger portion of the wood products intended for Britain was shipped by steamer out of Montreal, rather than by lumber drogue from Quebec City. Matters were complicated by a temporary competition in deals for the British market from

TABLE 3
Wood products, imports and exports, 1869–78
(current dollars)

Year	Imports	Exports
1868-69	139,008	65,037
1869-70	170,558	86,532
1870-71	225,464	124,179
1871-72	280,543	152,463
1872-73	383,213	98,617
1873-74	470,756	70,567
1874-75	483,858	107,563
1875-76	376,270	314,377
1876-77	478,077	297,454
1877-78	370,205	309,193

SOURCE: *Sessional Papers* 1869–79, Trade and Navigation Returns

Michigan in the mid 1870s, and the challenge to deals by sawn lumber. A transformation of the industry was under way.[18]

Exports and prices had risen substantially from Confederation to 1873. In that year, exports reached a value of $20 million, while demand fueled by housing and railway construction within Canada was solid. Exports of wood to the United States were high from 1865 to 1874 (from 1870 to 1874, exports of planks and boards to the U.S. reached a level unsurpassed until after 1908).[19] After that date, there was a sharp decline in exports, with those to the United States shrinking more rapidly than those to Great Britain. Price levels broke; exports were limited to $13 million by 1878. Failures took place even among the most substantial lumber enterprises. Late in 1875, E.B. Eddy faced closure of his large operations, and by the end of the following year, this major lumber manufacturer compromised some $640,000 of debt at 20 cents to the dollar. Senator Robert Skead of Ottawa also failed in early 1876, and by March 1878, so had the important Ottawa lumberman Edward McGillivray. In the fourteen months after January 1875, sixty-five lumber merchants had assigned their businesses, with total liabilities of over $2 million.[20]

Wood-products manufacturers also found the depression traumatic (see table 3). E.B. Eddy, involved in the industry, admitted his inability to compete with rising American imports and asked for protection as early as 1874. Rapid expansion in the early 1870s created debt loads difficult for such firms to carry. For example, during 1875, 'the firm of Tees Brothers, extensive manufacturers of desks and cabinet ware in Montreal, were obliged to get an extension having so large a portion of their means invested in buildings, machinery and plant. Had the year been an ordinary one, it is probable that they could have paid in full, but owing to the untoward condition of commercial affairs they were unable to meet even the extension and consequently were served with a writ of attachment.'[21] They compromised with creditors, but their case was but one of many.[22]

A shift from the use of cloth-fibre to wood accompanied the technological changes during the expansion of the paper-manufacturing industry in the 1860s and in the boom of the early 1870s. These alterations were combined with an enlargement of productive facilities by companies such as Alexander Buntin & Co., the Barber mill at Georgetown, the New Brunswick Paper Manufacturing Company, and the Merritton Paper Mills owned by Charles Riordan. New mills were opened in Ontario and Quebec. Higher levels of capitalization and technology created efficiencies that permitted firms like the Riordan mills to continue operation as prices fell during the depression. Others, with the best of machinery, but with questionable financing, such as the New Brunswick Paper Manufacturing Company, were not in as secure a position. 'In 1878 and 1879,' wrote W.W. Johnson, 'of these thirty mills [in existence], *ten* had actually failed, with a resulting loss of $550,000; *seven*, representing a locked-up capital of $280,000, were idle, while *thirteen*, with an estimated capital of $1,190,000, were in operation.'[23]

Coal-mining, fishing, shipping, and shipbuilding were key industries in the Maritime provinces. The early years of the decade seemed to hold great promise for coal-mining. The price slope for bituminous coal (the basic product of the Nova Scotian mines) was upwards, and it sold for as high as $9 per ton in Ontario during the winter of 1872–73. Demand for Nova Scotian coal in the rest of British North America more than doubled to 337,983 tons from 1871 to 1873. Exports to the United States had slumped with the end of reciprocity and reached a low in 1872, but soared to 264,760 tons the year after, partly stimulated by the lowering of the American duty on coal. To contemporaries it must have seemed that both the internal Canadian and the American markets were opening up.[24]

Disappointing developments followed. Prices and sales dropped in 1874 and then even more sharply in 1875. The American market threatened to vanish; in 1875 a mere 89,746 tons were sent there. The rapid and effective integration of the American railway network after the Civil War permitted Pennsylvania and Ohio coal to dominate the seaboard American market. The same cheapening transportation rendered the central Canadian demand for the Nova Scotian product static; in contrast, imports of anthracite coal from Pennsylvania and Ohio expanded. Though the impact of these negative conditions was uneven, with mines supplying the American market being worst hit, the industry faced the erosion of both foreign and domestic markets. A few mines closed; others cut back on production; there was a corresponding fall in wages and a rise in unemployment.[25]

The fisheries suffered concurrent hardship. Cod prices fell somewhat, and so did exports from 1874 to 1878. The downturn in the mackerel fishery was much more severe; the decline in exports from Nova Scotia by one-half from 1873 to 1877 was evidence of considerable domestic difficulties, for the major part of the mackerel catch was consumed in the province. The introduction of new methods of fishing by the Americans was seen as at least partly responsible.[26]

Shipowners found the depression rough weather. Premier transoceanic shipping lines such as Cunard, Allan, and Inman slashed their freight rates in half. Wind-driven wooden vessels did not escape the gales of competition, as Robert Moran, one of a shipbuilding and shipping family of New Brunswick explained to his brother in 1878: 'With regard to the working of ships in all my experience I never knew things so bad. Freights to and from all parts low, and in most cases not sufficient to pay expenses. Unless some improvement takes place, it will be very difficult to work ships, especially wood ships – the rate of insurance is so much more and less rate for freight, so that it cuts two ways on wood ships.'[27] While Robert Moran's complaints were perhaps exaggerated, profits shrank enormously from the high levels of the early 1870s.[28]

The effect on the export-oriented wood shipbuilding industry was predictable. While the boom times of the early 1870s sent total tonnage of vessels built to heights never before reached, the glory days came to an end in Nova Scotia and New Brunswick in 1875–76.[29] At Quebec City, where shipbuilding employed thousands, already flagging construction fell yet more in the later 1870s, as the trade in timber to Britain continued to decline. Shipbuilders who began vessels in the expectation of good times continuing found conditions distinctly unappetizing by 1876.

The problems faced by shippers and shipbuilders seem again to have been the product of a juncture of depression and structural change. The rapid deployment of the iron hull and the compound steam-engine beginning in the 1860s were crucial developments, while the slump in the shipping of staples to Britain undercut the viability of that market for Maritimes vessels, and Maritimes shipowners sought more secure investments. Consequently, the drop in wooden-vessel construction that began after 1875 saw no further recovery in the industry. The British market for wooden ships rapidly declined, though the vessels remained in demand (especially in the Maritimes) for coastal trade, the fisheries, and increasingly marginal oceanic trade.[30] Capital investment in shipbuilding was low, and so while failures were limited in number – only nine shipbuilders and joiners assigned in fourteen months after January 1875 – breakup value was minimal. The failures did not even pay 10 cents to the dollar.[31]

To these conditions can be added the serious difficulties the New Brunswick lumber industry faced in common with that of central Canada. Though the economy of the Maritimes had many unique aspects, it shared with central Canada the essential consequences of the depression: economic uncertainty, increased competition, troubled or reduced markets, reduced income, and increased unemployment.

Seasonal unemployment in the urban centres of Canada was a chronic problem throughout the nineteenth century.[32] When worsened by the lay-offs, wage reductions, and factory closures of the depression, the situation disturbed even the hardened Victorian mind. It is, of course, impossible to reconstruct the exact extent of unemployment for that era, which had not fully discovered the wonders of bureaucracy and statistics, but it is not hard to gain a sense of changing relative conditions.

The time at which unemployment was most severe varied according to location and industry. The coal-miners of Nova Scotia had a hard time of it, especially in the winter of 1875–76, as the unemployed already had used up their credit and savings in the previous winter. In December 1875, a meeting called by the sheriff at Sydney petitioned the provincial government for aid: nine mines were seriously affected, and a total of 1198 families were in desperate need of assistance.[33]

Conditions were similar elsewhere in the Maritimes. The high rate of unemployment in Halifax was evidenced by the growing number seeking charity or needing the help of the dispensary.[34] Harbour labourers and sawmill workmen were unable to prevent the reduction of their wages in Saint John under the pressures of unemployment; there was a general exodus from the city to find work in autumn 1876. One journalist noted with a private bitterness the contrast between the fancy ball being thrown by the governor general in Ottawa and the poor in Saint John enduring the depression winter of 1875–76: 'Within a stone's throw of Mr. Burpee's [Isaac Burpee was minister of customs] Portland residence, people are nearly dying of starvation. And it is a notorious fact that while the great bulk of the laboring population are without work & hundreds of mechanics in the same case, – from the most extensive business firm to the humblest laborer who can secure work, in the City, it is with the utmost difficulty that any can make ends meet.'[35]

Similar conditions existed elsewhere in the country. At Quebec City, the volume of lumber shipped reached an extraordinary low in 1878–79; shipbuilding in the province fell to a mere 9099 tons that year (it had been three times larger in the poor 1875–76 season). This situation and the failure of major employers, such as the Woodley boot and shoe firm, left large numbers without jobs. In summer 1878, the president of the city's Board of Trade soberly estimated that 'three quarters of the working population of the city were idle.'[36] That, and large wage reductions, led to strikes and severe rioting during the year, and again in 1879.

The cycle of winter unemployment was always sharply pronounced in Montreal because of the length of time the port was frozen shut, and matters were, therefore, made much worse by unemployment in manufacturing. One major manufacturer stated that he had laid off half his hands in the summer of 1875. 'I suppose it is about the same in other factories,' he added, 'though I am told several are closed.'[37] By December that year, food and work riots nearly broke out in the city. In March 1876, the Protestant House of Industry and Refuge was distributing as much as 3563 quarts of soup and extra meals per week, compared with 1097 per week in the previous, already tough, winter.[38]

Matters were scarcely better in Ontario. Ottawa workmen sent deputations to the mayor and prime minister to request public works employment, and a special committee composed of all major charitable organizations held meetings to develop a coherent response to the emergency in the winter of 1876. Special meetings of a like sort were held in Kingston, Belleville, and elsewhere to consider 'means for the relief of the unemployed poor, who are numerous this winter [1875–76], owing to the stoppage of so many manufacturing concerns.'[39] There were wage reductions in Hamilton as elsewhere, and as one paper reported, 'there is not the slightest prospect of any *permanent* employment for a large section of our working men. Mechanics, in many establishments in this and other cities, have been working short time; and in several instances we have heard of working men being paid off in considerable numbers.'[40] The Great Western laid off 400 men in late spring 1878; the railway's workshop men were given the option of working a four-day week or taking a one-third wage cut. A major furniture manufacturer, Robert Hay, estimated that in his industry, half the jobs had disappeared by early 1876; certainly he had laid off a large number of workers. Toronto charities greatly expanded their activities in response to these conditions.[41]

Yet despite the many insolvencies and high unemployment, despite the crises in Canadian industry, manufacturing grew at more than 4 per cent per annum between 1870 and 1880. What is to be made of the apparent contradiction? First, the decade's high general rate of growth in manufacturing was not reflected in the growth of per capita value added in the same sector. Indeed, the annual compound rate of value added in manufacturing per unit of population was a poor 0.7 per cent – much poorer than the previous or following decade, and clearly a reflection of the depression.[42] Moreover, given the small size of the Canadian manufacturing base, major episodes of growth could be compressed into short periods of time. And there were parts of two major booms in the census decade 1870–80 that could account for much of the growth measured: that from 1870–74, and the second beginning in late 1879. The apparent growth can also be partly accounted for by the uneven impact of the depression. In every type of manufacturing there were efficient producers who continued to be profitable even in the worst of times. Moreover, not all parts of the economy suffered relapse: this and the nature of competition in a world undergoing rapid technological change provided structural reasons for the economy's resilience.

Significantly, agriculture continued to do relatively better than manufacturing in Ontario during the depression. 'Relatively' needs emphasis, because rural pursuits were undergoing challenge and transformation. Wheat remained the single most important agricultural crop, but the trade in the grain became increasingly domestic. From 1840 to the mid-1860s, the Maritimes and Lower Canada together rarely absorbed more than 40 per cent of the wheat and flour shipped out of Upper Canada. By 1870, that figure stood at 70 per cent. For most of the 1870s, Canada was a net importer of grain and flour, a situation that made agricultural protection attractive.[43]

Indeed, as the American market for Canadian wheat closed after the Civil War, as the productive capacities of the American midwest shot upward, as transportation costs for the movement of American wheat to the east slid, the Canadian staple came under challenge in its home market. Ontario millers were particularly sensitive to strong American competition in the Maritimes, which had proved such a growth area for them after Confederation. Added to this were several years of poor crops in the mid 1870s, and generally declining prices. Farmers in the Georgetown region of Ontario were unwilling to sell their wheat for $1 a bushel in March 1876, an understandable response in the light of the $1.20 to $1.40 prices offered that month in the years 1871 to 1874. Serious doubt was expressed about wheat's future. 'As far as Ontario is concerned, the end of exporting wheat is not far off,' one journal warned in 1878. 'We have sold wheat till in an average year we lose money by every bushel sold.'[44] Yet the gloom was exaggerated. When this dark prognosis was made in 1878, the grain price was at an extreme low. Only for seventeen months of the six disturbed years after 1873 was the monthly average wheat price below $1 a bushel. Indeed, prices were good beginning in late 1876 and for much of the following year, moderating the effects of the depression. Though a net importer in the decade after 1869, Canada still shipped out wheat and flour throughout the decade, so there remained an important export orientation for the grain commodity.

Wheat farmers were troubled, but agriculture in Ontario had been diversifying away from the grain since the 1850s. Many agriculturists moved to mixed farming. In the Ottawa valley lumbering required coarse grains, hay, and meat, which farmers were pleased to supply. Farming in the region was hard hit by the slump

TABLE 4
Imports of mowing, reaping, and threshing machines, 1869–79 (current dollars)

Year	Value	Quantity
1868–69	$39,415	566
1869–70	46,863	740
1870–71	56,684	1068
1871–72	52,186	1149
1872–73	63,250	1704
1873–74	49,783	1262
1874–75	43,416	975
1875–76	38,396	658
1876–77	40,483	640
1877–78	43,990	588
1878–79	39,666	563

SOURCE: *Sessional Papers* 1869–79, Trade and Navigation Returns

in the timber trade, though. Elsewhere, barley functioned as one substitute for wheat and a great deal was exported to the United States. Vegetable gardening and the growing of fruit were more profitable as the urban markets of the province expanded. Animals and animal products were exported more heavily after Confederation. Measured in turn-of-the-century dollars, prices for these items improved during the depression, so there is reason to believe that the mania for cheese factories that grew from the mid 1860s onwards was soundly based. Cheese exports grew from 4.5 million pounds in 1868–69 to 39.4 million pounds a decade later. There were fat years for some, while others faced the lean.[45]

The continuing strength of the agricultural sector had effects in other areas of the Canadian economy. Towns closely tied to a well-to-do agricultural region could be prosperous. Caledon East, a village not far from Toronto, boasted that 'while during the hard times the commercial atmosphere was resounding with the din of business collapses on every side, our merchants stood safe through it all and the wave of depression and hard times beat – perceptibly, perhaps, – but harmlessly on our village trade.'[46] So manufacturers who made agricultural implements and machinery were less troubled than others. Of course they had advantages, in the declining prices of iron and steel during the depression, in lower (as compared to American) labour costs, in the considerable expense transporting bulky machinery involved, and in the strong demand an expanding western American agriculture had for American machines.[47] Besides, diversification in farming meant diversification in equipment. Imports of agricultural implements remained limited, and import prices relatively high (see table 4). Though domestic (and at times American) competition was vigorous and a source of complaint, it wasn't debilitating. Demand was actually good enough for a large new farm-equipment factory to open in Toronto in 1878. The major failure among these manufacturers, the Joseph Hall firm in Oshawa, reopened for business after the dust settled.[48]

Positive effects had their limits, for wagon and carriage makers (with their considerable rural market) failed in signal numbers. Nor did millers fare well. American demand for Canadian flour had subsided, and the Maritimes began to turn to the cheaper American product. Competitors in the United States adopted advanced technology in the 1870s that greatly lowered costs; and they were not above dumping flour in the Atlantic region and even in Ontario.[49] With grain milling, as in other industries, the depression downturn was exacerbated by significant technological change. The relative health of the agricultural sector could not sustain the entire economy.

Whatever the experience of various sectors of the economy through the business cycle, competition generally intensified in the downturn. But it intensified not only because of slowing incremental increases in demand, but because the character of the Victorian market was undergoing alteration. The increasingly rapid movement of detailed business information, the extension of transportation systems and the enormous reduction of transportation costs, and the expansion of productive forces through technological and organizational advance brought with them the possibilities of much broader national and international markets; this integration meant yet greater competition. These forces rapidly compounded after the American Civil War and after Confederation; the depression imploded them.

Take the case of transportation. From 1870 to 1908, a long cycle of declining ocean-freight rates took hold. Yet rates fell with particular speed during 1873–84.[50] On land, something similar could be observed. The massive railway construction in North America during the 1840s and 1850s did much to lower transportation costs, but after 1865–67, the tangle of lines was rationalized, filled in, and further expanded. At least seven different varieties of rail gauges were slowly consolidated towards the 4-foot 8½-inch norm; railway companies linked lines and came to car-exchange agreements; fast-freight lines were set up to avoid the expense of breaking bulk. So, while in 1858 it cost 38.61 cents a bushel to ship grain from Chicago to New York by rail, by 1890 it cost 14.3 cents. The depression hastened this downward trend in freight rates. A harsh rate war broke out in 1876–77 between major American lines, including the Grand Trunk. Passenger fares fell by one-half on long east–west runs; fares on first-class freight going west dropped by one-third; eastbound goods obtained reductions of up to 85 per cent.[51] Freight-rate declines of this order integrated not only national but continental markets, and by reducing the prices of goods reduced tariff protection.

Technological innovation also had a marked impact. The 1874–88 period was actually one of widespread innovation. It has been tentatively labelled as one of 'maximum technical change' in the United States, measured against developments from 1869 to 1938.[52] Even in areas of established technology, such as railways, better engineered roadbeds and bridges reduced costs; the rapid advent of steel rails had a remarkable impact in lowering depreciation costs – just as they effectively drove a Toronto rolling mill, which remanufactured iron rails, out of business. The newspapers abounded with examples of new and useful inventions. The number of patent applications rose steadily, and then sharply, with 274 being issued in 1866, 570 in 1868, and over 600 or 700 from then until 1873, when a startling 1124 were made, and 1026 were granted. Nor did the depression reduce the flood of innovation.[53] It was the context of constant innovation that led Montreal sugar refiner George Drummond to calculate that technological obsolescence counted 10 per cent per year above actual depreciation in his industry. So essential did the rapid introduction of new technology become that many of the trade associations formed in the era had as one of their explicit purposes the sharing of information about improved machinery and inventions.[54]

While some manufacturers responded to the structurally based, depression-enhanced competition through curtailment of production, lay-offs, or closure and liquidation of plant,[55] aggressive businessmen expanded to take a larger market share. Improvements in machinery were seized upon avidly if they could be afforded. Financial stability in pursuit of growth was often sought through the injection of new capital from acquired partners – as in the woollens industry in the 1860s – or through the more modern though still suspect procedure of becoming a joint stock company.[56]

The same aggressive approach required the reduction of labour costs. Longer hours of work were demanded from employees, with no increase in pay. Wage reductions were obtained. James Smart, an iron founder, indicated that wage cuts for skilled workers in his industry had been in the order of 8 or 10 per cent in 1875 alone. Springhill coal-miners were informed that beginning in January 1876, the rent on their houses would increase, the price of their heating coal would double, and they would face a 12½ per cent reduction in wages.[57] Perhaps here we see the source of the company's 5 per cent dividend for the year.

Success was thus possible. As in a more devastating economic crisis sixty years later, many firms still made a profit or at least paid out dividends: the Montreal Saw Works, the Baylis-Wilkes Manufacturing Company, and the Springhill Coal Mining Company were a few in this group. With 1876 passed what seemed the most trying phase of the crisis. The Starr Manufacturing Company of Dartmouth, Nova Scotia, which had lost money in 1875 and had closed its skate factory for a time, declared a 10 per cent dividend on preferred stock in 1877. In the same year, increased sales were reported by the Dominion Type Company, 'the losses [from non-paying accounts], remarkable to say in these days, being very light.'[58] The partial recovery, stimulated by better agricultural prices for the 1876 grain crop, brought about plans for a number of new factories, especially ones that were to produce for the rural community of Ontario.[59] Throughout it all, driven by competition, drawn by the prospects of greater profit in a returning boom, other firms bolstered their place in the market. The McDonald Tobacco Company expanded plant in Montreal, while a rival closed his doors to wait out a glut, and yet another fled to the United States and thus disposed of his Canadian debts. Bankruptcy dogged sewing-machine companies, but the Wanzer firm of Hamilton kept up to date on innovations, sought overseas markets, established a presence in the Maritimes, bought out a rival, and built a plant in the United States to by-pass the American tariff wall. C.W. Williams of Montreal, also a sewing-machine firm, did well in the latter part of the depression: 'Much new machinery has been added each year, more particularly the year just expired [1878] and the sales of 1878 were nearly double those of 1877. The rapid growth and extension of the business was such as to necessitate the erection of ... very extensive premises ... Of course the company has capital to back it, its shareholders being all men of means.'[60] The great weight of capital (Sir Hugh Allan was president) encouraged the adoption of the latest machinery and fostered aggressive expansion. No better recipe for success could be concocted for an individual firm.

However, the very process of strengthening one firm through growth or innovation necessarily encouraged the industry-wide instability the individual businessman wished to escape. Risks inherent in the forced growth of commercial and industrial firms under competitive pressure find bountiful illustration in the depression of the 1870s. In an effort to keep his firm afloat, one junior partner of a foreign commercial house was advised to 'not pay the drafts [on the firm] until they are due, and if past due you must scrape up money be it through advances on stock or otherwise.'[61] His senior elaborated:

> According to my idea it will be best for you to buy there [Montreal] from $10,000 to $15,000 or more of leading articles, and sell them again at cost price or cheaper. You can then pay promptly ... A stoppage must not take place under any circumstances, for I am in hope to raise the business there considerably ... It is better to have $1000 less than to have on your shoulders the large stock and debts. Buy tea and other articles which you can dispose of at once ... Above all, buy largely there, that the old affairs get settled

... Heap up money and notes, and I quite agree to sell the stock at any price, only that we must not stop.[62]

The Moorehead Furniture Company of London, a major Ontario firm in that line, was by the mid 1870s in considerable debt and facing active rivals. An expanded market was seen as necessary. Physical plant was enlarged, production costs lowered through speedy construction, and the low-quality furniture was auctioned off in markets as distant as Montreal to gain desperately needed cash. Pressed to the wall, company officials misrepresented the firm's financial position and encouraged investment by local capitalists to obtain funds to cover debts. They were found out at the last moment. Failure followed.[63] J. & J. Woodley, the important boot and shoe manufacturers of Quebec City, proceeded along similar lines. The Woodley firm expanded rapidly and in order to develop a stronger hold on the market and to service the large debts created in its expansion, often sold at or below costs. As the depression stretched on, the policy led to compromise on debts, and finally insolvency.

A third and somewhat different example might be cited. The New Brunswick Paper Company was established in 1869, and in 1872 it enormously expanded its plant, purchasing the very latest and best of equipment in expectation of an ongoing boom. The equipment proved too heavy for its water-power source; the company then constructed a dam at considerable expense to improve power. Under debt and competitive pressure, forced sales of the product took place. In 1875, the company went bankrupt.[64]

Still, only a limited degree of concentration followed this ongoing bout of failures among businessmen and artisans of all ranks (one shoemaker accused the Liberal government of the mid 1870s of 'favoring the large manufacturing companies to kick us little Shoemakers & Blacksmiths etc. out of the country,' dating the problem to the beginning of the depression). Though published census data probably obscure the degree to which concentration took place because protection and economic recovery brought a large crop of small businesses to bloom from mid 1879 to 1881, it was clearly not a dominant tendency. In his examination of concentration in the late nineteenth century, which focuses on the period from 1890 to 1910, Tom Walkom generated some useful statistics on the degree of concentration in twenty-four selected consumer product industries in Ontario from 1870 to 1880. It is striking that concentration (which he defined as the number of plants required to produce 80 per cent of the industry product) took place in only eight of those industries.[65] Data on the average number of employees in some additional industries Canada wide lead to similar conclusions about the uncertainty of the process of concentration.

A variety of forces ran counter to any rapid concentration. In an era of rapidly

TABLE 5
Average number of workers per establishment in selected industries, 1870 and 1880

Industry	1870	1880
Foundries, machine shops	17.8	14.2
Fittings foundries	13	14
Wool cloth making	16.5	5.4
Cabinet and furniture	5.1	5
Carriage making	2.8	2.8
Sash, door, and blind	11.4	8.1
Edge tools	8.6	16
Paper manufacturers	36.2	42.2
Cotton manufacturers	93.1	186.6

SOURCE: Calculated from Canada, *Census of Canada* 1871, vol. 3; *Census of Canada* 1881, vol. 3

expanding markets and high prices, inefficient productive facilities can be sustained even though plants of great efficiency are being introduced. This was precisely the phenomenon of the early 1870s, and a return to prosperity by late 1879 did much to retain this aspect of the business world.

But even the depression did not encourage concentration as much as might be expected. Markets were only partially integrated; problems of transportation still stood in the way. Customers often preferred purchasing from local producers, as faulty goods could be more readily repaired and credit arrangements might be more flexible. The most obvious method of organizing industry in more concentrated form – through joint-stock companies – was viewed with some suspicion, especially as widespread corporate organization did not offer obvious advantages for businesses with limited markets and capital requirements. Moreover, the new technology transformed production unevenly, for high levels of human skills remained vital and capital equipment requirements were low in many industries. Water continued to be the major power source, and it both dictated the location and potential size of factories – a situation only reluctantly transcended by manufacturers going to more costly steam-power.[66]

The system of insolvency also helped to prevent concentration. Failure, after all, was supposed to thin the overcrowded ranks of businessmen, and allow a return to stability. However, many merchants and manufacturers were embedded in a structure of local investors, local creditors, and local debtors; social pressures to sustain a business could, therefore, be great. Selling off the assets of a company unable to meet its debt commitments often meant that creditors received very little. Compromising on the debt was consequently attractive to creditors. Better a smaller than a greater loss, they might reason, and the firm having written off a portion of its debts, would continue. This was hardly a vigorous thinning of the ranks.[67]

The openness of the Canadian economy to foreign competition also impeded concentration within the country. Canada imported a much higher volume of finished goods in relation to its population than did the United States, for example.[68] During the depression, and even earlier, many manufacturers stressed this factor as a reason for limited growth. Product specialization or plant expansion could not be financed, given the threat of foreign competition, they claimed.[69] While this argument was often worked up into pathetic melodrama – with unbearably cruel foreigners maltreating youthful Canadian industry – it was not strictly a matter of imagination. Despite reduced demand in the depression, imports in a number of areas rose. In iron and iron products, imports remained at levels roughly equal to those of 1871 through the period (though lower than the boom years of 1872 and 1873); in chemicals and like products they increased slightly; in animal products they rose somewhat; and in textiles and fibres, they leaped by a third from the boom year of 1873 to the depression year of 1875. As demand declined, imports took a larger share of the market in many areas, a tendency with disastrous implications for individual businesses.

Great Britain and the United States together accounted for roughly nine-tenths of Canada's imports from Confederation until 1880. Britain had long been British North America's major trading partner and remained the major source of imports till the turn of the century. However, the depression of the 1870s provided a foretaste of the long-run shift to American sources of supply. In 1870–71, Britain supplied 56.5 per cent of Canada's gross imports by value, the United States 33.5. The worsening economic times virtually reversed these positions by 1877–78, when the United States provided 53.3 per cent and Britain 41 per cent of total imports. The data shows that the Americans maintained almost the same level of exports to Canada during the depression as during the preceding boom (and this in current, deflating, dollars).[70] While American competition in Canada had been negligible during the Civil War and for a time thereafter, and the boom masked its growth, declining transport costs, efficiencies of scale and specialization, and an American avidity for technological progress brought it to a peak. 'The American manufacturers, with whom they now had to contend,' Donald McInnes informed a meeting of businessmen in Hamilton, 'have made extraordinary advances in producing great quantities of goods, and at greatly reduced cost, so that we cannot shut our eyes to the fact that the competition is likely to be greater, not less, and the consequence to the Canadian manufacturer will be a constantly demoralized market.'[71]

Certainly rapid deflation left manufacturers who failed to maintain productivity gains with falling levels of protection under the *ad valorem* tariff. The historical statistics are eloquent on the decline of prices in the late nineteenth century, a decline that began in 1873. The total import price index (1900 = 100) fell from an extraordinary high of 145.7 in 1872 to 104.4 in 1879. Iron and steel fell from 132.3 to 113.4; agricultural products from 133.3 to 116.1 in the same period. On fibres and textiles, the drop in import prices was from 177.7 to 90.8.[72] Contemporaries were only too aware of the devastating decline from the very high prices of the preceding boom. When the commissioner of customs, reflecting the finance minister's concern about revenue, asked his collectors to report on prices in late 1877, he was told that the previous year had witnessed wholesale price drops of 10 to 15 per cent on such goods as cottons, silk, clothing, sugar, glassware, oil, dried fruit, paper, heavy iron goods, and shelf hardware. Moreover, the collectors said, price declines were abrupt and uneven; prices fluctuated wildly.[73] That had a devastating competitive effect. The Americans could readily compete in the Canadian market; the American tariff, substantially higher than the Canadian, made returning the compliment difficult.

Where hard but fair competition shaded into American 'slaughtering' (as dumping was called at the time) of goods is not clear. But as Canadian manufacturers did not hesitate to sell goods below cost at home or abroad when in dire need, it cannot be doubted that the U.S. producers dumped goods north of the border. Once again, the much higher American tariff made retribution unlikely. Some Canadian manufacturers thought slaughtering was intended to drive them out of business and give the Americans the larger market – a classic element in the movement toward concentration. While such public views require cautious treatment, aggrieved manufacturers privately complained to the Department of Customs that goods as diverse as pianos, pipe and hydrants, silk thread, buggies, seed, cordage, car wheels, bridge iron, and hardware were being undervalued at the customs houses. Both the Liberal and Conservative governments attempted to devise methods of combating what seemed to be chronic undervaluation of goods.[74]

The spectrum of international competitive pressures likely fostered the concentration of industry south of the border at the expense of Canadian producers. The massive consuming public in the United States permitted great economies of scale, and American manufacturers could sell goods cheaply, could dump them out of desperation, could indulge in predatory marketing in Canada with limited fear of retaliation. The plight of Canadian carriage makers provides an excellent example of the possible consequences of an unequal rivalry. Carriages coming into Canada paid a 17½ per cent duty; the American duty was 35 per cent. During the depression, imports of ever cheaper buggies from the United States mounted, flooding a shrinking market, while exports declined (see table 6).

The declared value of an imported carriage fell from $72 in 1874 to an

TABLE 6
Carriage imports and exports, 1869–79
(current dollars)

Year	Imports value	Number	Exports value	Number
1868–69	$ 42,275	708	$25,157	506
1869–70	37,799	809	24,841	766
1870–71	52,304	894	25,262	531
1871–72	45,143	642	26,135	533
1872–73	66,384	967	25,262	468
1873–74	131,221	1815	20,050	333
1874–75	118,184	2213	14,203	234
1875–76	85,291	1918	17,945	405
1876–77	95,913	3253	14,942	219
1877–78	85,429	1812	58,409	626
1878–79	111,726	n.a.	43,984	612

SOURCE: *Sessional Papers* 1869–79, Trade and Navigation Returns

astonishing $29 in 1879. By then, Canadian manufacturers complained the valuation was only half of what it should have been. They ignored the general deflation in emphasizing undervaluation and dumping and they by-passed the fact that the American carriages were machine-made and 'not first class by a good deal.'[75] As one collector of customs explained in defending his acceptance of a low valuation Canadian carriage makers had challenged: 'Men who have been accustomed to making them by the old process of hand labour, knowing only what it would cost themselves to produce them, may be quite conscientious although sadly astray in appraising them at that [higher] price, whilst others who know the rates at which they are now turned out by machinery, and the prices at which such articles are daily sold under their own observation may be equally conscientious and more correct in putting a much lower value upon them.'[76] A combination of newly introduced machine manufacture, deflation, and slaughtering by American producers placed makers of carriages in Canada – who were capable of making most of the carriages required in the country – in a very poor position. In little more than a year in 1875–76, thirty Canadian carriage manufacturers assigned. Clearly, some of the Canadian market was being taken over by United States producers.

The carriage trade (to re-coin the phrase) was not an anomaly, although its artisanal emphasis may have been unusually heavy. Canadian boot and shoe manufacturers, even though some used a great deal of machinery, faced escalating imports at ever reduced costs in the 1870s (see table 7), a development which, combined with Canadian productive capacity, resulted in substantial domestic concentration. From 1875 to 1879 failures were frequent. Imports grew as prices

TABLE 7
Boot and shoe imports, 1869–79
(current dollars)

Year	Value	Quantity*
1868–69	$137,428	2546
1869–70	139,134	2122
1870–71	156,112	2208
1871–72	196,336	2797
1872–73	198,616	3089
1874–75	234,712	3913
1874–75	241,223	4774
1875–76	283,293	n.a.
1876–77	302,111	n.a.
1877–78	243,578	n.a.
1878–79	200,150	n.a.

SOURCE: *Sessional Papers* 1869–79, Trade and Navigation Returns
*The quantities are given in 'bundles' of unspecified size.

fell, and manufacturers made convulsive efforts to expand export markets. Some of the large Montreal firms were sustained only by means of liberal bank support. Even the major boot and shoe manufacturers in Montreal, much given to adopting the latest technical innovations and to a fair degree responsible for slowly driving the industry in the rest of the country under, complained about the economies of scale that their American competitors enjoyed. In the United States there were firms that specialized in cutting soles or uppers, and others that, for the most part, put together the finished product from purchased component parts.[77] The combination of American competition and a domestic industry that had expanded rapidly and recently led to the temporary closure, in summer 1875, of seven Montreal firms capable of producing 30,000 pairs of boots and shoes a week; at the same time in Hamilton, workers in the industry faced four-day weeks and in Toronto several firms halted production.[78] Not surprisingly even large firms such as M. Francis and Sons of Saint John, J. & J. Woodley of Quebec, Messrs Mullarkey & Co. of Montreal and Messrs Walter, Evans & Co. of Toronto failed during the depression. Though the industry seemed to be reaching a degree of equilibrium towards the end of the slump, it sacrificed sixty-five of its number to the two-faced god of success and failure in a little more than one depression year.[79]

The temporary shift to heavy importation of American goods in the 1870s not only damaged Canadian manufactures, but also had a highly negative impact on wholesale importers in the major urban centres, for it was combined with the beginnings of a major alteration in marketing methods. For most of the nineteenth century, the international marketing of goods had depended on a developing system of specialization in which wholesalers, independent commercial agents, and acceptance houses (banks financing international trade) acted as intermediaries between manufacturer and retailer. It was the structure of commerce under which much of Canadian economic life had become established. Starting in the 1860s, this system began to be assaulted by new methods that emphasized direct manufacturer/retailer connections. The beginnings of brand-name recognition by consumers, combined with cheaper transport, machine work, economies of scale, and a degree of business concentration, all facilitated this shift in marketing technique. Some manufacturers sold on very long credit; and yet others pushed direct-factory-to-consumer sales; the mass auctioning of goods became more common, especially as declining transportation charges made it more attractive than formerly.[80]

In this context, American suppliers were closer to the Canadian market than the British. Major Canadian cities had their entrepôt status challenged as retailers in smaller centres bought directly from American sources. The many commercial travellers representing American wholesalers and manufacturers effectively undercut the Canadian importer/wholesaler; this development would make major importers who obtained supplies in Britain sympathetic to the protectionist cause. Old Laurentian patterns reasserted themselves.[81]

Had Canadian industry penetrated the external markets that had been so tantalizing at the beginning of the 1870s, American and British competition in Canada would have been less daunting,[82] but only a handful of products found a secure export niche, such as cheese and butter in Great Britain. The depression, then, reduced potential expansion overseas, while at the same time opening further an already open Canadian economy to imports. From the viewpoint of domestic producers, as well as of some commercial elements, it became of the utmost importance to consolidate control over the main market.

Central Canadian interests made ongoing efforts to establish themselves in, and to dominate the markets of the Maritimes after the political union of the country. Nova Scotian and New Brunswick interests reciprocated.[83] Some aspects of this process are instructive, for they illuminate a depression-heightened development going on at all levels, and at the same time illustrate the economic tensions that formed an important part of the national experience.

The ever larger number of commercial travellers was prime evidence that market integration was taking place. These 'restless emissaries of trade' who ranged from small-time pedlars to representatives of prestigious wholesale houses or manufacturers, began to appear in such numbers after Confederation that by 1871 they organized into the Commercial Travellers' Association. Four years later, there were three such associations (two having national pretensions) with a total membership of 1679.[84] The salesmen were vital in expanding markets, and during the depression their operations became so pervasive as to be a bane. Sales were pushed hyper-aggressively as demand and prices declined. 'Speaking for ourselves, as manufacturers,' wrote one Maritimer, 'we find our greatest difficulty lies in meeting the Quebec and Ontario wholesale dealers in time and terms. They send a swarm of salesmen down here, who spread over the land like locusts, the most of them selling on Commission, and they sell to everybody who will buy, without much reference to their standing, and will give any time or terms asked for. It is not uncommon for your manufacturers of our lines of goods to give from six to eight months credit, and if cash is paid from 20 to 60 days, a discount from 6 to 10 per cent.'[85] The commercial travellers and their credit dumping met much local business resistance in the Maritimes, Quebec, and elsewhere, but the process of market integration, aggravated by the depression, could not be halted.[86]

Still, the integration at the national level was only partial, because the Canadian market was so accessible from the outside. The propensity to import products from abroad was especially strong in the Maritimes, despite the considerable growth of manufacturing there in the 1860s and early 1870s. If contemporary assertions are to be believed, a few central Canadian agricultural equipment manufacturers, among others, had established steady sales in Nova Scotia and New Brunswick, but even these men admitted that their products faced strong foreign competition there. Characteristic of the market penetration of the Maritimes by central Canada was the uneven sales a locust-like plague of central Canadian commercial travellers could make, or the purely speculative sales made by the Montrealer Mr Shaw in his Halifax furniture auctions.[87] The conquest of the domestic market by domestic producers was limited and under challenge, and a protective tariff could be just the device to make it secure and complete.

A comprehensive description of a dynamic economy enduring structural change in the context of depression is not possible or necessary here. Yet though the characteristics of change for a number of business activities have been only briefly explored in this chapter, the importance of the business cycle of the 1870s should be apparent. Richard Pomfret has implied that the depression of the 1870s was part of the first non-commercial business cycle in Canada and British North America significantly affected by industrial developments.[88] The idea is a useful one. Consequently, the depression set in place economic preconditions for a powerful protectionist reaction among manufacturers as well as others. Following as it did on a time of extraordinary growth, it precipitated intense competition in Canadian business life. Business failure was commonly viewed as the end product of immorality and personal dissipation, of poor business practices, and of speculation, and though the most notorious failures of the 1870s were built on a compound of these sins, everyone still knew that a virtuous personal and business life was no guarantee of success. The general outlook was one of insecurity, generated by a combination of structural change and a severe cyclical downturn. Gaining dominance in the market-place could offer some measure of stability, but the process was heavy with danger, and in the face of foreign and domestic competitors, dominance was at best uncertain and transitory. The foreign competitor was a far more powerful presence in the Canadian market than in the American or British. And if in a variety of industries, domestic manufacturers were capable of meeting the bulk of domestic demand, this did not reflect a mature national market dominated by national producers. It reflected fragmented markets that some large productive facilities were just beginning to transcend, but in which local demand was to a very great degree still supplied by small local workshops. In most industries, the ability to meet Canadian demand did not exist. Whatever the case, the reduction of foreign competition was a direct means of expanding the domestic market for at least some domestic producers, and could provide breathing room for the small shop, economically inefficient though this might be. The creation of a larger market through Confederation, the expansion of industrial capacity in Canada, and a depression that sharply limited export prospects while leaving the home market vulnerable to foreign producers: these formed the historical context in which the potential of protectionism increased and was ultimately realized.

As before, demands for high customs duties in the depression took individual, political, and associational paths, but the balance between these altered markedly. Political pressures became overwhelmingly partisan. The strength of narrow self-interest did not fade, and individuals continued to badger and cajole politicians for tariff concessions. The greater emphasis on association among businessmen – in order to collectively control competition, as a means of transcending petty interest and applying more effective pressure on government, and to provide a rationale for the aspirations of a business élite – was a key element of the new balance.

6
'An age of combination and association,' 1870–1879

Endless rivalry, businessmen well knew, could breed destructive instability. Collective control over competitive excesses had to be asserted, so even while competition rose to greater heights during the depression, pricing and production agreements were being made and broken. The approach was neither new nor limited to foul business weather. Nearly a century earlier, Adam Smith had written that 'people of the same trade seldom meet together, even for merriment and diversion, but the conversation ends in a conspiracy against the public, or in some contrivance to raise prices.'[1] But such informal and even customary local understandings were of a different order from the formal regional organizations which appeared frequently in the Canada of the 1870s.

Formal organizations occurred very early in situations where a large number of competitors were geographically concentrated. Over-production and declining prices in the lumber industry of the Ottawa valley brought about the formation of an Ottawa Lumber Association as early as 1836. It didn't last, but similar organizations were formed to stabilize the forest industry in later decades. The oil rush of 1861–62 in Canada West, which resulted in a multitude of crude producers crowding around Oil Springs and Petrolia, and a concurrent glut and price collapse, led to the formally constituted Canada Oil Association, the aim of which was to reduce risk. The proliferation of the variety and number of industries from the 1850s through the boom of the early 1870s and the widening geographic scope of competition combined to create a context that made formal collective business organization increasingly possible and probable.[2] The depression accelerated the trend: by 1874 it was reported that 'in larger cities almost every interest is in the habit of meeting for consultation.'[3]

Trade organizations could choose from a broad repertoire of mechanisms in their efforts to create a climate of stability and predictability. Sometimes employers found it convenient to deal with labour on an industry-wide basis, though the weakness of unions during the depression made this approach relatively unnecessary. Still, the Lumbermen's Association of Saint John, New Brunswick, was established in response to the mill men forming a union, and iron founders in Ontario and Quebec made efforts to reduce wages in a concerted manner.[4] Even in trades that lacked formal organization, leading men tried to set stabilizing trends. A circular sent out at the beginning of 1875 by George Stephen, dean of woollen manufacturers by virtue of wide investment in the industry, expressed the agreement he and other leading figures in the trade had reached about the undesirability of 'dating forward' on goods (selling goods on extremely long credit), as it extended too much credit to wholesalers and retailers. The stated objectives of the Shoe, Clothing and Fur Exchange of Montreal, formed in 1878, give some sense of the range of mechanisms used. To ensure the 'mutual benefit and protection of its members,' the exchange proposed to make information about dishonest traders available, to limit credit given to those of small means, to lessen losses of manufacturers and wholesale merchants by obstructing compromises at less than 75 cents to the dollar, to share information on the financial standing of buyers and on technological developments, and lastly, to gain protective legislation from the government.[5]

Pricing and production agreements formed one of the most common means of ordering a chaotic domestic market in Canada, as elsewhere. If the big British Atlantic shipping firms came to frequent conference agreements on freight rates beginning in 1869 and during the 1870s (agreements that just as frequently broke down), similar ideas were discussed among Great Lakes shippers. The Tug-Boat Union of Saint John, New Brunswick, shared out work between the boats on an equitable basis, which of necessity meant a common price.[6] There are innumerable examples of such associations. Montreal brewers came to a meeting of minds on price and production for the local market by 1873, and their example was followed elsewhere. Salt manufacturers combined in summer 1874 to limit production. The Montreal Hardware Exchange formed in 1874, the Tobacco Association of Canada, the Canadian Flax Manufacturers' Association, a paint and varnish association, and a marble dealers' group all had a concern with fixing prices. The Canadian Booksellers' Association, established in 1876, was intended in part to prevent slaughtering by American publishers and underselling by retailers. The metals trades displayed similar tendencies. 'During the last four or five years,' said Montreal spike and nail manufacturer Randolph Hersey in 1874, 'we have had a sort of union among ourselves not to "kill each other." ' Until the previous year, secondary producers of iron in Canada had been able to defy foreign competition, Hersey said, but the competitive struggle within the country had been so debilitating that a pricing agreement among rolling-mills operators had been necessary; he suggested that the scale had been moderate and well managed (well managed it was from Hersey's point of view: his firm garnered a 106 per cent profit on invested capital in 1871).[7] In 1878, paper manufacturers set up an association and a pricing agreement for newsprint, anticipating a higher tariff. The idea was to give 'tone and strength to the market,' to make sales easier and to reduce 'toadying to customers.'[8] Apparently the contemporary fear of manufacturers' rings or cabals had something to commend it.

One such ring that had a degree of public acceptance and met with relative success was the Refiners Association located at London and Petrolia. The success it met was based on its structure, the physical proximity of the refiners, the history of previous organization, and the favourable treatment that refined oil received in the tariff. The customs duty virtually excluded the refined American product, so that even the Maritimes were open to the Ontario producers. Pricing and production pacts in this field of endeavour could not be undermined by cheap imports, especially as the United States was a major export market for the Canadian producers until an 1873 upsurge in American crude production. These favourable market conditions stimulated competing refiners to build excess refining capacity before that year. This glut of productive capacity led to combination among refiners even before the advent of the depression.[9]

The Refiners' Association was a half-way house to merger; this encouraged success. The association took a bond for lease for all the refiners, and paid each of them a rental fee on a monthly basis in proportion to the demand for oil in that month. Production was controlled and satisfactory prices maintained. The arrangement was vulnerable to crude-oil producers' rings, but these in turn were extremely fragile because of the then low capital cost of drilling new wells. Most troublesome was the yearly renegotiation of the lease, when crisis regularly flared.[10]

Arrangements aiming at market stability or control were not easy to reach, though. Here the experience of the starch manufacturing industry is instructive, for with few competitors, an understanding should have been readily reached. George Foster & Co. of Brantford, the leading rival of the Edwardsburgh Starch Company, made pricing propositions to the Edwardsburgh firm during the depression. Upon having its advances rejected, the Brantford company took to price cutting and product imitation in order to improve its competitive position. After these presumably had time to take effect, new proposals for price-rigging were broached by Foster & Co., only to be again spurned by the Edwardsburgh people, who sought to establish market dominance strictly through competition.[11]

Enforcement of pricing arrangements was nearly impossible, of course. Under law the pacts had no force; and participants seemed to have few hesitations about going their own way, even after making the most solemn vows not to deviate. The iron founders' association set prices in 1873 or 1874, only to have its work sabotaged by the underselling practised by some members. When this came to public attention, the leading founder Edward Gurney Jr took to making the tautological claim that the agreement was not binding. Similar developments took place in the coal trade. The highly competitive Nova Scotian coal industry had an ephemeral association in the late 1860s that disappeared under the positive price conditions of the early 1870s. Caught in the sudden downturn of the market, the industry made a new effort to organize by September 1875. 'At the meeting,' reported the mines inspector for Nova Scotia, 'it was proposed to partially control the trade, if possible, by regulating the output, the prices and the rates of wages; and further to use any political influence they, as a body, might acquire for the interest of their trade.' To this the inspector gave his cautious approval, given the wretched state of the industry, and by February 1876 he felt that 'more than the rudiments of such an association now exist in Pictou County, but not in Cape Breton.'[12] More than that would have been necessary if the business was to have been successful; rivalry remained too stiff. Given the lack of adequate enforcement, pricing and production agreements rarely gave more than temporary respite from the rigours of competition. Every one of the numerous agreements recollected by the mercantile agent W.W. Johnson in his *Sketches of the Late Depression* (1882) was sustained for only the briefest of periods.[13]

Concurrent with the trade associations' efforts to police competition among their members was an effort to press the federal government to bring some order to their disordered industries; they used, as the coal association had promised to do, 'any political influence they, as a body, might acquire for the interests of their trade.' In this, they had significant examples before them. Boards of trade had recommended and criticized legislation on commercial matters for decades. The Dominion Board of Trade, the descendant of the mutuality of interest that British North American boards and chambers of commerce discovered at the great Detroit reciprocity convention of 1865, was founded for purposes of influencing legislation. A Dominion board was necessary, the formal letter that began the organizational effort indicated, 'for commercial purposes and to secure unity and harmony of action in reference to commercial usages, customs and laws; and especially, that a united opinion should be obtained so as to secure a proper and careful consideration in Parliament of questions pertaining to the financial, commercial and industrial interests of the Country at large, and to all public works calculated to cheapen and lessen costs of transport between one part of the Dominion and another.'[14] Indeed, for the first few years of its existence, the place of the Dominion Board of Trade within the political process found symbolic assertion in its annual meetings in the House of Commons Railway Committee Room.

Once established, the board had an institutional interest in encouraging the formation of constituent groups. As its secretary wrote the 1874 president, W.H. Howland, he 'would like very well to aid you in carrying out your idea of visiting certain places, for the purpose of stimulating the mercantile community to *organize*.' Perhaps this aim was a vital element in the decision of the board to hold a major meeting in Saint John in summer 1874, and then to unofficially tour the lower provinces. The campaign continued. The ever-active secretary, William J. Patterson, sent out a circular to all organizations that were, or could be, affiliated with the board. He 'urged that Local Boards of Trade, to be affiliated with the General Board should be multiplied; that existing Local Boards should be strengthened by an increase in membership; and that organizations not of a strictly trade character, such as Associations of Lumbermen, Dairymen, Mechanics, Manufacturers, etc., might derive benefit from connection with the Central Board.'[15]

A similar interest in greater organization resulted in a major expansion of the Montreal Board of Trade in 1874. At the 7 January meeting, consensus had it that a wider variety of members should be inducted. The membership as it stood was mostly among grain and flour exporters, and some major importers. Other interests in the city were organizing, and rather than a united business voice, the outside world would only hear a babble unless manufacturers and bankers took their rightful place on the city's board. A mass induction of new members followed in March.[16]

There was, then, a confluence of concern about the importance of organization and the need for parliamentary intervention, and it is no astounding revelation to find that many groups met with the intention of influencing tariff legislation. The foundrymen's association, the Montreal Shoe, Clothing and Fur Exchange, the marble dealers' group, the Dominion Millers' Association, the Ontario Fruit Growers' Association, the Refiners' Association, that of the coal owners, a combination of salt producers, and a cabinet makers' society were among those making recommendations on tariff matters to the Liberal government of 1874 to 1878. The more comprehensive organizations did their share as well: petitions and pleas for higher tariffs were received by the government from various boards of trade including the Dominion Board, from the Ontario Manufacturers' Association, the like Montreal association, the New Brunswick Manufacturers' and Mechanics' Association, and the short-lived Nova Scotia Association for the Encouragement of Industrial Interests.[17]

The existence of trade groups provided an underlying strength for, and in turn was encouraged by, the formation of a permanent Ontario Manufacturers' Association in 1874. It is suggestive that at one of its early meetings, those present were divided into subsections along trade lines for discussion of tariff matters.[18] The longevity of the association clearly reflects the weight manufacturing had gained in the province and the persistence of crisis conditions in the 1870s. Similar organizations of earlier vintage had been evanescent, tied to specific economic and political trauma. This parent of the Canadian Manufacturers' Association was the culminating development of businessmen's rush into organizations in the decade before 1879, for of all the formally constituted groups it had the most decisive influence in tariff matters.

How widespread and how representative it was cannot be accurately answered; there are no membership lists available. A count of those mentioned as attending its meetings before 1879 reveals more than 300 names, and more than that number were present at the founding, though at the important 1877 annual convention, as few as 50 assembled. The association constantly claimed 150 adherents for purposes of Dominion Board of Trade membership, a suspiciously arbitrary number. Evidently the membership was amorphous. If one can conclude that those listed as attending meetings were representative, the metals, textile, and clothing trades were crucially important in the make-up of the organization, with wood and wood products following closely behind. Food processing was poorly represented: only millers had any notable membership, though their numbers were not great because they had their own organization. The leather trades also had a surprisingly weak position within the manufacturers' group. Of course, busy men often could not waste a couple of days in unproductive bombast, and the timing of meetings to accompany fall fairs or, more important, in expectation of tariff changes, might have had something to do with the character of attendance.[19]

Despite the apparently skewed membership, the Ontario Manufacturers' Association blandly assumed it was representative of the larger industrial community. Only when the leaders undertook membership drives did they display any concern about this matter, and then only in terms of the size of the membership rather than in its specific character. Manufacturers who viewed the association with detachment, cynicism, or dislike generally had the unfortunate grace to keep their opinions private, so the organization's spokesmen could simply presume that they stood for all of industrial Ontario. Uncontradicted by their peers until the election of 1878 (and even then not widely), men such as W.H. Howland, W.H. Frazer, Donald McInnes, or the stove founder Edward Gurney Jr stated their protectionist truisms not only to meetings of manufacturers, but to parliamentary committees, in newspapers, interviews, or to public gatherings, and gained able assistance from pamphleteers. In conjunction with a select group of like-minded men in Quebec and the Maritimes, they expressed both a frame of mind and engaged in active propaganda in pursuing their organizational and tariff aims.[20]

Manufacturers' rings, cabals, and associations gave protectionism a conspiratorial air. Indeed, on the presumption that high tariffs were exclusively beneficial to the owners of the protected industries, the probability of conspiracy seemed self-evident to many observers. After all, a protectionist policy insured stable market size and growth potential associated with the upward movement of prices if domestic production did not equal domestic consumption. Yet businessmen regularly argued that they were attempting to benefit everyone. The whole associational impulse was justified on grounds that business organizations were in and of themselves means of negating narrow self-interest. Protectionist ideologues stressed that their ideals, once implemented, would provide rewards to every class of society, every region of the country. The nationalism that infused protectionism was vital to the high-tariff argument in the 1870s, as it had been earlier. Based on correct theory and correctly worked, high customs duties were a means of creating the near perfect nation-state. The usefulness of that goal was not questioned.

The protectionism expressed in the 1840s in British North America had been in large part a reaction to changing British policies; the mother country and the United States were the presumed external enemies against which the incipient nationalism of the colonies had to struggle. This protectionist viewpoint remained evident in the writings of Isaac Buchanan in the late 1850s and early 1860s. By the following decade, Britain no longer loomed high on the protectionist horizon. The United States did.

Vocal manufacturers regularly claimed that they were at important competitive disadvantages with the industrialized world and with the United States specifically. Whether the disadvantages were ephemeral or enduring, involving mere problems of marketing or ones of structural change, tariff protection was widely seen as the answer. There were some manufacturers who wanted reciprocity with the Americans, who felt they had some competitive advantage and found forty million American consumers an abiding lure. F.W. Glen, an agricultural implements manufacturer, thought in 1874 that a new reciprocity treaty would be 'the means of immensely developing the manufacturing interests of the Dominion,' and some of his peers agreed. Others made casual genuflection in the direction of reciprocity simply in order to favourably impress the Liberal government of the mid 1870s.[21] However after 1874, the possibility of reciprocity was recognized as virtually non-existent. As William Lukes, a major Ontario miller said, men in his line of business favoured protection because they had been closed out of the American market, but Americans still had access to the

Canadian market. Canadian iron founders 'have a very limited market,' William Buck of Brantford stated. He later added: 'I would hesitate to increase my works, in the present condition of affairs. I feel the American competition, I say, as a disturbing influence ... The American manufacturers have a vast market, and are building up enormous concerns. We have a small market, with few consumers, and they are easily got at; and it is not fair that the American manufacturers should come here and disarrange our market, while we are excluded from their market.'[22] Here, fused with nationalism, was a desire for retaliation, a not entirely reasoned wish to strike out against an opponent perceived as unfair.

It was obvious enough that the Americans and other foreign competitors had many very real advantages in terms of market size, integrated facilities and efficiencies of scale, cheaper (in Europe) labour, and cheaper credit.[23] But it was easy to inflate American competitive unfairness to mythical proportions. To the Americans was ascribed behaviour of the utmost ruthlessness – behaviour in which no self-respecting Canadian would indulge. The hidden assumption was that rivalry among Canadians was gentlemanly: only Americans sold goods below cost; only Americans hired unscrupulous agents; only Americans (and some Englishmen) produced mediocre goods and tried to palm them off as products of the highest quality. As one Hamilton furniture factory manager explained, 'Our goods are a better class than can be got in the States at the same price, and whenever goods are got cheaper there than in Canada they are defective, in the upholstery work, although the defect is so concealed that only people in the trade can discover it. The Americans have always special rates for Canada.'[24] And why special rates? The often repeated story was that the Americans were deliberately underpricing their goods in Canada to destroy competition in order to gobble up the market and charge monopoly prices.[25] While such intent undoubtedly existed in some cases, Canadian protectionists perceived it as a pervasive conspiracy. At some of the meetings of the Ontario Manufacturers' Association, speaker after speaker would rise to bring forth some variation on archetypal tales of woe concerning imports from the United States, steadily reinforcing commonly held perceptions. The erection of a high tariff wall was seen as of the utmost necessity.

Part of the problem, so protectionists felt, was simply that Canadian industries weren't long in place. 'Every person knows that the introduction of a new manufactory is very expensive,' pronounced Mr A. Watts, machinery manufacturer of Brantford, 'so much so that many a person has been obliged to sacrifice his whole property in establishing it. Our industries are young.' Outside competition could readily trample them, consensus had it. Not only did it cost a great deal to start up a factory, it took time to gain experience in efficient management and in training or obtaining experienced personnel. This 'infant industry' argument naturally shaded into one concerning Canada's 'infant nation' status, arising less from the country's brief years than from its lack of industry. The 'manufacturing interests still required fostering,' one Saint John man opined in tying the two themes together. 'To be brought into competition with older countries now might be ruinous.'[26]

Canada's fundamental economic problems were imported, not internal: this, then, was the idea that could be effectively presented and sustained with a selective use of evidence. Though it had some basis in reality, it served another function as well. The role that expanded capacity in Canada played in glutting the market and causing harsh competitive conditions was denied, an external economic enemy was created, and unity among producers both large and small was made possible. Had it been proved that domestic competition fostered the difficult economic climate, it would have followed that inefficient manufacturers had nothing to gain from protection. So despite the obvious role businessmen's associations played in reducing competition among domestic producers, when it was suggested that home competition was responsible for the problems of the depression, protectionists issued vehement denials. Economic nationalism was vital to the protectionist position.

Though the outside threat justified high tariffs, the actual duration or extent of the proposed protection varied. Tariff retaliation against the United States was sometimes urged as a necessary first step in bringing that country to renew reciprocity. Similarly, protection as a means of defeating the existing depression suggested that high tariffs were nothing more than a phase of a cycle. The infant-industry argument presumed a future adulthood; protectionists frequently cited the great free trade economist John Stuart Mill, who in his *Principles of Political Economy* admitted that the infant-industry position taken by John Rae had merit as a justification for a temporary protection.[27] A longer, though still limited, period of protection found a basis in the infant-nation argument. Friedrich List, who had fully propounded the theory by 1841, had asserted that in the developmental path of nations, protection was a necessary prelude to industrialization, which in turn permitted an era of free trade. Canadian protectionist propagandists often seemed unwilling to admit the last step in the process,[28] even though the limited duration of high tariffs in this and the other scenarios was useful in attracting theoretical free traders. In contrast, the famous American protectionist Henry C. Carey provided a theoretical rationale for a policy of permanent protection, and his perspective infused the thinking of some pamphleteers: free trade was nothing but an aberration caused by British crop failures in the 1840s; all progressive nations practised protection, even Great Britain; dependence on foreign trade resulted in loss of population and wealth.[29] To a significant number of manufacturers, a partial, time-limited protection was frankly insufficient. 'There should be no over-protection, but enough to secure perfect success and make capital invested safe – permanently so,' said one. 'Incidental protection is a perfect humbug,' snapped another. No confidence could be developed 'until it be settled, as a certainty ... that Canada has deliberately adopted a National Policy of Protection to home production and manufacture as the permanent policy of the Dominion.'[30]

The nationalism that was continually expressed was not, however, merely that of a siege mentality. Protection was needed to weld a fragmented Canada into a united one. High tariffs would force trade between the regions: central Canadian wheat and manufactures would be exchanged for Maritimes coal, shipping, and manufactures. This broader vision had been contained in Isaac Buchanan's argument for Confederation, and his Canada First heirs R.G. Haliburton and W.H. Howland continued to express it. Howland, a commercial man, an investor in manufacturers, the president of the Ontario Manufacturers' Association in 1877 and 1878 and the one-time president of the Dominion Board of Trade, passionately asserted the need for commercial and industrial protection for the purposes of national unity. He had little doubt 'that the theory of Confederation was to bring together these separate Provinces, to destroy the old provincial lines, to encourage trade and industry among them, and to increase communication between them until we should become one country.' But, he went on, 'the practice of Confederation has been very different ... I do not consider the Provinces to-day to be anything more than a bundle of sticks loosely tied together; and we can well afford to sacrifice money, if need be, to pay increased taxes, and have a fiscal policy which many may object to, if we can only accomplish the larger object of having one country and a united people. That is what I call a national policy, and I do not think it should be considered in a fiscal light at all.'[31]

However, protectionists had not lost sight of the conception that manufacturing was vital to national independence and greatness. Continuing staple production and export meant a political and economic life of subservience and relative poverty.[32] Diversification was the way out. The nub of the problem could be directly addressed by stressing the need for manufacturing growth in language laden with moral and economic imperatives: coal was a 'primary agent of national progress and power. This is the iron age. People who work iron partake of its strength and hardy nature ... National progress may be traced directly to the production of coal and iron.'[33] Another manufacturer's resolution before a large meeting of peers read: 'The development of a healthy manufacturing system is essential to the material prosperity of any country, and that, without it, neither true greatness nor independence can be achieved; that in opening new fields to industry, it promotes population for agriculture to feed; gives birth to invention, from whence follows intelligence; rewards labour, which begets progress, succeeded by wealth, and with wealth refinement and power.'[34]

The harmony of interests would emerge through the processes of diversification and expansion brought about by protection. Jobs would be created for those unable or unwilling to follow other lines of endeavour. Immigrants would fill urban manufacturing centres. The enlarged urban population would provide a remunerative market for a diversity of agricultural products, and the internal commerce of the nation would thrive as city traded with country, and region with region.[35] Material growth on a national scale, and conversely, the creation of a national community through the process of material growth was the aim. Self-consciously an élite, the protectionist manufacturers conveniently blurred distinctions between national and class or private interest in the rhetoric of national mission.

For the appeal to nationalism to be effective, both to attract the Canadian public to the cause of higher tariffs and in order to provide themselves as an élite with a sustaining mission, manufacturers had to struggle against the tyranny of selfish special interest. They were repeatedly accused of being involved in just such a tyranny, of course. The important Toronto distiller and banker J.G. Worts argued that the pressure for increased duties on grain in 1870 came from 'twelve or fifteen manufacturers.'[36] Not only did protectionists have to shield themselves from attacks like Worts's, they had to counter selfishness in their own ranks. At the 1876 Dominion Board of Trade meeting, W.H. Howland spoke acidly of those who were 'free traders when their interests are not affected, although protectionists' when those interests were at stake.[37] The ideologically committed did not hesitate to use mockery to pressure the recalcitrant self-seeking ones.

Organization was a means of asserting class over selfish or limited group interest. In the attempted revival of the Association for the Promotion of Canadian Industry in 1866, these issues were revealingly developed. There was much dispute over the proposed centralized structure of the association, commanded by a powerful executive located in Toronto. Some of the manufacturers viewed the proposal with profound suspicion, feeling that their interests would take second place to those of the Toronto men. After lengthy debate, it was agreed that some representation of locales outside the Queen City was necessary on the central committee, but special and localist interests none the less got the short end of the stick.

Whether the organization was to represent manufacturers exclusively was a matter of considerable dispute as well. Some of those present at the 1866 meeting felt the association should be for manufacturers only, unlike the unrestricted membership of the earlier organization on which it was being modelled. Isaac Buchanan publicly cautioned against this, warning those assembled that they would appear a 'mere conspiracy of manufacturers.'[38] Donald McInnes, the Hamilton dry-goods wholesaler and manufacturer, tried to conciliate Buchanan in private. He agreed that 'it would be well for the manufacturers to take your advice and not agitate what may be argued by their opponents is a "selfish one" [policy] & avoid giving it the appearance of the agitation of a "*class*." ' But, McInnes added, 'I am not quite clear how far it would be wise for those who are not manufacturers to take up the question at present.'[39] The dispute, as it turned out, had no immediate consequence, for the association quickly died out. But the need for manufacturers to have organizations exclusively their own was clear enough. When the case for the formation of a manufacturers' association in Saint John was presented in 1874, the justification was that it 'would develop a better feeling among a deserving class' that while benefiting the country, would also be 'advancing their own interests.' The local board of trade was insufficient; votes there on manufacturing issues 'would not be a fair idea of the feeling of the class especially concerned. A batch of lawyers might vote them down with impunity.'[40] The benefits manufacturers wished to derive from organization could not be obtained if the organizations they belonged to were too comprehensive in their membership.

Organizations, however, had a special role in mediating between conflicting interests. Compromise, say between pig-iron producers and secondary iron-product manufacturers, was vital if a united front to the world was to be presented. Mr Law of Tillsonburg, speaking to one of the early meetings of the Ontario Manufacturers' Association, 'was in favour of a congress of manufacturers, with committees of each separate industry who should report to the general body the amount of protection they each thought necessary.'[41] Exactly this approach was taken by the association in discussing the proposed reciprocity agreement of 1874, and it used a similar method in deciding what content was wanted in the tariff of 1879.

What functioned on a lower, worked on a higher level as well. Manufacturers' organizations were not incompatible with those of the business community in general. Both the Montreal Board of Trade and the Dominion Board actively encouraged the membership of manufacturers in bodies originally dominated by commercial men. Manufacturers hardly viewed merchants as mortal enemies; it was, however, recognized that their interests could differ. In discussing the expansion of the Montreal Board of Trade, one manufacturer member indicated that the problem could be overcome through the 'formation of distinct trade organizations, whose members should be members of the Board of Trade, and should be properly represented on its Council.'[42] In this fashion, the concerns of each trade could find expression, while a forum for reaching common ground existed.

The growing multiplicity of organizations was an expression of group and class concerns; the protectionists did not deny the place of interest in their activities or claim their stance to be a philanthropic one. Yet through the advocacy of the harmony of interests, these organizations assumed the role of a broader social leadership.[43] 'This seems to be an age of combination and association,' one editorial writer mused. It was all for the best. In words reminiscent of Henry C. Carey (though the argument was much twisted), it was asserted that human activity in combination and association transcended anything that many individuals each working on their own toward the same end could achieve. It followed that 'associations of men with similar purposes and occupations, managed in a way to direct combined skill and combined wisdom toward the legitimate work of the association, and to guard its members against evil, oblique motions which are coming from evil, selfish combinations, are productive of great good and are, in the present condition of society, the safeguard of an honest prosperity.'[44]

This was fine abstraction, but the various manufacturers' associations pursued harmony in ways more expeditious. Widespread public support for the idea of protection had to be gained, so spreading propaganda was one of the factors that made organization necessary. The existing political system responded to the weight of numbers, 'and in consequence it is requisite to endeavor to secure in favor of Protection the adhesion of the greatest possible number ... it is necessary to agitate unceasingly the question and keep it continually before the public.' That was a basic thrust behind the founding of the Montreal Manufacturers' and Mechanics' Association.[45] Members of the Ontario Manufacturers' Association agreed. Appeals were constantly directed toward the farming community on the basis of the harmony of interests; it was likewise vital to strengthen the protectionist resolve of the urban working class. Without question (at least from the high-tariff point of view), 'Manufacturing industries confer a benefit on the country for the employed are as much benefited as the employers, and a market is created for [agricultural] produce that cannot be exported.'[46]

As it was, from what was said as well as left unsaid, from what was done, the factory labourer was often identified as part of a broader manufacturing interest. Labour and capital created each other and were so bound up in this productive dialectic that the one's loss or gain was the other's. Speaking to a large audience of mill men in the process of forming a union in 1874, sawmill owner and operator Andre Cushing of Saint John admitted the element of self-interest in his opposition to the union, but claimed sympathy for the position of the working man having, he said, started out that way himself. Yet, as he saw it, 'every right minded man felt the same interest in the business and success of his employer as though it was his own. This was the ... normal condition of employer and employed, and this condition must be maintained in order that any business may prove profitable or successful ... Our interests are indissolubly bound up together. The prosperity of one is the prosperity and success of the other.'[47] Tied to him in this way, his employees were acting in a perverse and destructive fashion in setting up to oppose their interests to his. They should, he told them, give up this idea of a union; those who persisted, he warned, would be fired. The mill men, only a limited number of whom were his employees, listened respectfully, and at their next union meeting transformed their organization into a benevolent society. They were undoubtedly not only impressed by Cushing, but by the united anti-union stand of the employer Lumbermen's Association. Under an umbrella of interwoven coercion and paternalism, harmony was asserted. The same attitude prevailed, at least nominally, among protectionists. Higher tariffs provided more jobs; employees had a responsibility to act with their employers in the matter of agitating for protection. That certainly proved to be the most common position taken by active protectionist manufacturers in the election campaign of 1878. Harmony in the factory was a corollary to harmony in the nation.

Vocal high tariff manufacturers gave themselves a leadership role in the economic world and, not surprisingly, they posited a closer relationship between business and government. If manufacturing was the key to the future progress of the country, businessmen ought to have the primary say in directing the nation. Before the Parliamentary Committee on the Causes of the Present Depression in 1876, Guillaume Boivin had the temerity to announce that 'we had too many lawyers, doctors and importers in Parliament ... they do not know the wants of the country.' More manufacturers should be there.[48] The same perspective, though with a wider horizon, caused the protectionist newspaperman Thomas White to wax rhapsodic about the future of the Dominion Board of Trade:

> He was glad we were now united in one whole – one in interest, one in sentiment, with no narrow sectional prejudices to gratify. All this had been gained through Confederation – without it a Dominion Board of Trade could not exist. No Commercial Parliament could have been formed. It was a Parliament greater than the Political Parliament which meets in Ottawa. The great importance and influence of this body was felt and appreciated everywhere ... They secure not simply legislation for one party, but for the future well-being of the whole ... He hoped that through its influence men would be sent to seats in Parliament, to advocate the commercial interests of the nation. Then would the Board rise to its fullest influence and proper sphere.[49]

Due allowance being given for hyperbole, White's expansive views expressed the sense of purpose and power businessmen in organization could feel. It was all very clear. Businessmen should become the cutting edge of government decision making.

Organizations were a vital part of the changing relationship of business to government. Because petty interests were transcended in associations, it was only through that channel that advice should be funnelled to the country's rulers. While it was recognized that the government, especially the Liberal government, would only respond to intense, well-organized public pressure for protection, the high-tariff men felt certain that only through the mediation of organizations could the relationship between business and government move beyond individual and group interest to benefit the country as a whole. When tariff changes were being contemplated in early 1879, E.K. Greene, the Montreal fur manufacturer, somberly told Sir John A. Macdonald that the old system of individual manufacturers using their influence with a finance minister to gain desired tariff changes was unacceptable. It was not to the good of the nation, as the advice of business organizations would be.[50]

In speaking at the opening of the industrial exhibition in Saint John in autumn 1875, the president of the New Brunswick Manufacturers' and Mechanics' Association summed up for public consumption the fundamental organizational concerns of his members: 'This exhibition marks the beginning of an era in the industrial history of New Brunswick, and will, we hope, lift our manufacturers from the obscurity of private enterprize, in which they have struggled into existence, to a public and political recognition commensurate with their importance as a productive element ... It also shows that our manufacturers have united their hitherto isolated forces, and mean to work together in the future for the advancement of their common interests – an advancement,' he pointedly added, 'identical with the public weal.'

'When the people and the leading statesmen of the great political parties,' he said on the same occasion, 'learn to appreciate this fact, learn that there is a community of interests, not a diversity, between the different elements of the public economy – we may hope for such legislative enactments as will most effectually promote the growth of industries so necessary to the settlement of the country and the development of its manifold resources.' Perhaps these points were not lost on the once and future finance minister, Lieutenant-Governor Samuel Leonard Tilley, who shared the platform and opened the exhibition.[51]

The effort to reach business stability through associations was by no means exclusive to the 1870s; it had a history that stretched back to the 1860s and earlier. The diversification of the economy, and the increasing number of businessmen involved in each industry created a context in which such associations were useful and even necessary from the late 1850s onward. And after 1879, they became such dominant characteristics of business and economic life as to be the focus of substantial scholarly study.[52] But organizational developments were a vital part of the shift toward protection in other countries during the 1870s, so similar movements in a Canadian political economy experiencing integration and depression were not unusual.[53] *National* business organizations were, however, uncommon in the Canada of that decade, and the national articulation of protectionist business aspirations, as will be seen, required the active involvement of a political party.[54] This was a reflection of the still-fragmented nature of the Canadian market and the limited degree of economic concentration reached before 1879. It was possible for businessmen to obtain desired protection without joining an organization, partly because the many channels of contact with those in political power robbed protectionist organizations of full political legitimacy, and partly because businessmen could acquire – even if they were not members in an association – the benefit of any tariff change.[55] For all that, for all the petty self-interest voiced through associations, these groups were an expression of, and acted as a channel for, an élite's sense of collectivity and national mission. The structure of protectionist ideology so generally accepted and propounded in associations meant that the collective interest of the men involved was identified by them with the national good.[56]

Manufacturers' associations during the depression were protectionist. Where, one might ask, were the free traders? In Germany and France, where the bulk of politically active manufacturers were protectionist, there were still pockets of free-trade industrialists, both vocal and organized. Those who were heavily export dependent or who needed imported, partially manufactured input items had, in those countries, a free-trade orientation.[57] Export dependency was quite limited among Canadian manufacturers, though lumbermen tended to be free trade, as did the dairy industry with its large cheese and butter exports, and as did some mine operators with export markets.[58] While there remained a hope for an American market for Nova Scotian coal, there remained an important streak of free-trade feeling among colliery owners there. Some manufacturers closely tied to the farming community, in which a low-tariff outlook was frequently to be found because of export dependency, also held that view. Free-trade manufacturers in Canada, however, did not establish associations to foster free trade.

Nor were merchants successful in this regard. Segments of the commercial world had some reason to support protection, of course. The feebleness of the organized mercantile response reflected the threat American commercial penetration posed to importers oriented towards England. Still, importers in southwestern Ontario had a long-standing enmity to tariffs that interrupted the movement of goods from or through the United States. Montreal grain shippers, eager to exploit the continental hinterland, had a strong low-tariff interest, at least in their chosen products; a large number of merchants in Quebec and the Maritimes held the same perspective. Yet while in Europe in the 1870s, as in England earlier, mercantile interests developed organizations, set up newspapers, and published pamphlets in great number to do battle with the forces of protection, not so in Canada. In this country, free-trade merchants were content to take their stand in boards of trade, where they were often overwhelmed by high-tariff men.

Perhaps the problem with organizing a free-trade resistance to protectionist advances lay in the difficulties of organizing the farmers of Ontario, a fundamental source of free-trade sentiment. As chapter 8 shows, farmers were divided on the dispute over the tariff, and protectionists sometimes dominated rural organizations. The response of free traders was again to do battle within the existing structure of the Patrons of Husbandry (the Grange) to take one example, rather than setting up other, ideologically pure, groupings. Even more telling, the decision to do battle within the Grange came from the highest echelon of the free-trade oriented Liberal government.[59] Here lies an important clue: free trade was entrenched in the seats of power for much of the 1870s. The necessity of organizing for those who held to liberal ideology from interest or otherwise was undercut. The Liberal party, the Liberal government, provided the avenues through which free traders could find institutional expression.

7
The Liberal interregnum, 1874–1876

There was a break in Conservative hegemony over the federal government in 1873. The enormous flow of money from Sir Hugh Allan to the Conservative party during the election of 1872 in presumed exchange for the Pacific railway charter became public knowledge, and the ensuing scandal brought the Liberals into power. Just as a conjunction of economic developments and the formation of interest organizations signalled a crisis in Canadian business life, the Pacific Scandal precipitated suspicions about large concentrations of wealth and of the influence of such wealth on government. Just as the idea of a national policy of tariff protection was reaching a higher level of political acceptance, a Liberal party with an ideological leaning toward free trade gained power. The intersection proved crucial in defining the form of the movement toward the tariff policy of 1879.

Cynics might suggest that equally opportunistic Liberal or Conservative parties could have adopted protection or free trade in the mid 1870s.[1] However, though each party had its share of members advocating one or the other of the two nostrums, the drift toward protection among the Conservatives before 1873 was as evident as the free trade bias in the Liberal or Reform leadership. There was no room for easy opportunism even before 1876, though party viewpoints on the tariff issue conveniently blurred into each other.

That much was obvious in the way the protection issue was used during the federal election of early 1874. Cautious Conservatives in Toronto included a few sentences favouring Canadian interests and industries in their platform for example, but even Liberal Prime Minister Alexander Mackenzie could go further. He outlined a Liberal commitment to incidental protection at Hamilton, where the topic was of great importance. Revenue had to be garnered through customs duties,

> and the distribution of those duties should always be in such a way as to confer the greatest amount of benefit upon our own people ... [We] will be obliged, I fear, to increase it [the tariff] very materially at no distant day, unless the country becomes a great deal richer and more prosperous during years to come than we have any reason to expect ... So that the question of protection or free trade does not arise in this contest at all. Sir Francis Hincks stated last year ... that he was in favour of incidental protection. I said I was also in favour of it. It is a stupid phrase at best, but it means simply this, that so long as duties are levied upon articles imported, they should be levied upon articles produced by our own people.[2]

Neither would the Liberals reduce protection already granted, protection under which manufacturers had developed and on which they relied, Mackenzie added. The Liberal candidates in Hamilton were appropriately protectionists. This also was the case in some other urban ridings: the incumbent in Montreal East, L.A. Jetté, avoided a sharp contest with boot and shoe manufacturer Guillaume Boivin by agreeing to a protectionist stance.[3]

Any movement to higher tariff levels was none the less viewed with reluctance by the Liberal leadership. If Mackenzie's cautious pragmatism was an appropriate prime-ministerial stance, the restraining influence of George Brown, Luther Holton, A.G. Jones, David Mills, and other free traders just outside the charmed circle of the cabinet was strong. The Liberal free-trade penchant was nowhere more firmly expressed than in Mackenzie's own speeches during his Scottish tour of 1875. With blunt acuity, Sir John A. Macdonald had noted as early as 1872 that 'Manufacturers have no hope from the opposition should they come in. They are pledged through Brown and the Globe to a policy of Free Trade & would be obliged to carry that out.'[4]

The first real test of Liberal attitudes came with the tariff changes of 1874, made necessary by a growing government deficit. Knowing the tariff was to be changed, and conscious of deteriorating economic conditions, manufacturers in St Catharines, Toronto, Montreal, and Halifax held meetings to demand more protection. As many as 300 manufacturers were present at the Toronto meeting, where they demanded increases to 20, 25, and even 30 per cent.[5] As well, the Dominion Board of Trade came out for moderate protection, a change from earlier non-commitment. The January 1874 board convention resolved that 'the principle of protection to the manufacturing industries of the country be embodied in such revision of the tariff, so far as the same can be carried out consistently with the commerce and revenue requirements of the Country.'[6] This was not much in advance of Alexander Mackenzie's own position, but it did show that commercial and industrial interests were able to achieve concord within the board. Pilgrimages to Ottawa by protectionist delegations formed the next step of the campaign. There they were politely greeted and just as politely dismissed by Finance Minister Richard Cartwright after a lengthy interview. Cartwright's intentions could hardly be fathomed from his bland willingness to take their arguments into consideration.[7]

The consideration must have seemed rather skimpy when the tariff was announced in mid April. It was 'with the utmost reluctance' that the government was compelled to 'propose an augmentation' in the customs duties, Cartwright explained, but the projected deficit of over $2 million had to be met. There was no intention 'to disturb existing interests,' yet in a rough way the new tariff was supposed to bear evenly on all classes. Duties on a number of necessaries and luxuries – tea, coffee, wine, liquor and cigars – were to be increased, and excise on cigars and liquor was to be raised to negate any inadvertent protection.[8] Traditionally free materials used in constructing ships were now to pay 5 per cent, as were some types of raw iron. A variety of locomotive parts, factory machinery, textile threads, webbing, and felt were to pay 10 per cent; as these were necessary inputs of the country's manufacturing, they would generate revenue while reducing protection on finished goods. Sugar and dry-goods classifications were also altered, and the rate on goods not otherwise enumerated was to be marginally increased from 15 to $16^2/_3$ per cent. The primary aim of this first Liberal tariff was revenue. It nevertheless had protectionist elements in the form Cartwright first brought it forward. A limited protection was given to primary iron producers; the duties on felt, webbing, factory machinery, and shipbuilding materials were useful to a small number of manufacturers; the reclassification of sugar was intended to favour refiners; and the minor increase in the general rate was a protectionist titbit.[9] But at the same time, most of these items were fine revenue generators.

It was thin gruel not only for manufacturers but for merchants as well. Importers found the proposed dry-goods classification confusing, and the higher duties on tea, wine, and sugar unacceptable. Manufacturers had their share of complaints. One powerful group of Montreal industrialists returned to the attack and demanded 20 per cent. The Montreal Rolling Mills and an assortment of foundrymen were as displeased as they had been in 1859 with the duties imposed on pig-iron, while shipbuilders raised an outcry against the proposed duties on their input items. On the single busy day of 22 April, Cartwright faced a battery of eleven different deputations. 'Every interest which thinks Mr. Cartwright has not attached sufficient importance to its claims, is, of course, off to the seat of Government armed with statistics and brawling with a grievance,' the *Globe* editorialized with perverse satisfaction.[10] The newspaper spoke a little too soon, for Cartwright had to make some concessions. The classification of dry goods was reformulated, and the proposed rearrangement of the sugars was dropped.

The planned duties on tea and wine were lowered. Some materials used in shipbuilding regained their old place on the free list, as did pig-iron, steel, and copper. Some other planned duties were not imposed, and to make up revenue thus lost, the rate on unenumerated goods was raised to $17^1/_2$ per cent.[11] Many businessmen remained unhappy, however, and suspicious of Cartwright's high-handed ways. For the most part, the protectionist manufacturers' associations brought into being in expectation of tariff changes did not disband.

They were given good reason, for the tariff settlement soon appeared fleeting. A hint escaped when Cartwright (perhaps tongue in cheek) asked one protection-demanding manufacturers' delegation, 'would you be prepared to fight the United States manufacturers in their own market if it were thrown open? (A score of voices, "Yes, gladly!").'[12] The chance to exhibit the appropriate joy soon came, as the Liberal government undertook to gain reciprocity.

The new government was convinced that its Conservative predecessors had not pursued reciprocity with all vigour possible. It also felt that the circumstances in 1873–74 were more favourable to reciprocity than those immediately following the American Civil War and the creation of the new Canadian nation. Soon after the Liberals formed the government in 1873, they expressed their determination to reopen the matter. In hopeful coincidence, the British minister at Washington, Sir Edward Thornton, who was trying to settle the fisheries question left open by the Treaty of Washington, wrote that the Americans might accept reciprocity rather than giving monetary compensation for American access to Canadian inshore fisheries.[13] This was the avenue the Liberals chose to pursue, not being aware of how strenuously Sir John A. Macdonald had canvassed the matter in 1871. George Brown, supposedly beloved by the American government because of his pro-northern stance during the Civil War, thought he had a special competence concerning reciprocity and was commissioned to survey conditions in the United States in early 1874. His trip to Washington led him rapidly to a positive assessment. The American executive was favourable to a trade agreement, and so was the generally unpredictable legislative branch: Brown thought negotiations should be immediately opened. To do so took time, however, as the British government remained in charge and had to decide on the exact status of the necessary Canadian representative at such talks. It was late March by the time Brown received this prestigious appointment and arrived in Washington.[14]

The negotiations that followed pitted the energetic and eternally optimistic Brown against the wily and procrastinating American Secretary of State, Hamilton Fish, and the business dragged on despite Brown's impatience. By the time a treaty was formulated, the American Senate was only a few days away from adjournment and felt under no compulsion to deal with the proposals quickly, especially as the American administration did not officially endorse them. The Fish–Brown treaty, whatever its merits, had to be left over to the next session. In the minds of most historians, this sealed the fate of the agreement, but it remained a live business and political issue in Canada until the American Senate rejected the agreement in early 1875.[15]

Because the public debate in Canada was more about the treaty's substantive points than about the abstract principle of reciprocity, some of the details of the Fish–Brown agreement must be noted. The 1874 proposal, though it would have run twenty-one rather than eleven years, was patterned after the 1854 Reciprocity Treaty. The first three articles of both were alike, and the list of natural products to be allowed in free was, beyond a few additions and deletions, almost identical.

But the Fish–Brown agreement was much more extensive than its predecessor, including as it did a large list of manufactured goods: cotton and woollen textiles, books, shoes and other manufactured leather, various types of partially and fully manufactured metal and wooden goods, and a considerable selection of machinery. There were other complications not found in the earlier treaty, because the customs were now to be reduced in three annual instalments, leaving the very high American tariffs higher than the Canadian until the final instalment. Also a matter of some concern, though not mentioned in the draft treaty, was whether Canada could or should erect discriminatory customs duties against British manufactures. Britain had insisted that the Canadas allow in duty free all goods listed in the 1854 treaty regardless of the country of origin. The eager Liberal free traders would have accepted the same arrangement again, but the Americans feared the possibility of re-export from Canada. The British finally agreed that a Canadian tariff under reciprocity could discriminate against British manufacturers.[16] Then, too, the more expansive 1874 agreement allowed not only for the reciprocal use of canals, as had its predecessor, but also included an inland coasting trade clause, the mutual registration and ownership of vessels, and the provision that the Canadians enlarge the Welland and St Lawrence canals, and construct a Caughnawaga canal before 1880.[17] The accord was replete with new opportunities, dangers, and burdens.

Although a few manufacturers heartily approved of the proposed reciprocity and others like George Stephen could accept it with reservations, the reaction of manufacturers as a group was negative. George Brown had expected as much when he concluded his meetings with Fish.[18] The Ontario Manufacturers' Association stated that the proposed pact went counter to long-established policy, that the free admission of manufactured goods from both Britain and the United States would be disastrous, that the sliding scale was mortally unfair to Canada, and that the effect on labour supply and cost of living would be very much to the advantage of the United States. Their gloomy predictions went further: the revenue would be adversely affected and direct taxation would result; many Canadian manufacturers would be excluded from the American market because their products infringed on American patent rights; the Americans would interpret the wording to their own best advantage; and the Canadian canal improvements promised were excessive. All in all, the proposed treaty 'would cause great disturbance of business generally, weakening the manufacturing interests, and seriously injuring the farmers' home market, and bring loss upon merchants through the failure of accustomed markets ... It would cripple and diminish our direct trade with countries beyond the sea.[19] The manufacturers of Saint John were as disturbed as their Ontario counterparts by the treaty, and were stimulated to form the Manufacturers' and Mechanics' Association of New Brunswick. Their early meetings consisted largely of long denunciations of the proposed treaty as destructive of manufacturers and ultimately of the country, and resolutions of the same tenor were passed.[20]

The wider business community was rather more hesitant to condemn the Fish–Brown accord in such a sweeping fashion, or in the virulent language the manufacturers used. The resolutions passed by most boards of trade balanced disapproval of the treaty's specifics with a generalized approval of reciprocity. Only some of the boards were entirely hostile to George Brown's achievement.[21] These attitudes were reflected in the debate over reciprocity at the Saint John midsummer meeting of the Dominion Board of Trade in 1874: the struggle was sharp, but it was clear that those who opposed the treaty were the majority. The Americans were getting too good a deal, most businessmen at the meeting thought, and a committee was struck to report on how the proposed treaty might be made acceptable.[22]

The confidential report, sent to the government in November 1874, was extensively critical. Two major objections were raised. The idea of lowering duties over a period of years 'meets with the very general condemnation of the commercial community' because American duties were so much higher than Canadian, and annual percentage reductions could give Americans substantial tariff advantages for two years. Secondly, the time limitation on canal improvements was too close at hand, and the Americans might cancel the treaty if those deadlines were not met. These matters raised profound uncertainties about the impact of the potential treaty, for 'with our smaller population and more limited capital invested in the industrial enterprises of the country, any check ... would prove very disastrous.' The Canadian economy was a fragile thing; 'the results of the early years of the treaty are matters of infinitely greater moment to Canada than to the United States.'[23]

Amid furious infighting, the Dominion Board adopted the report in January 1875. The *Globe* waxed bitter in defence of its owner's work, claiming the report was the product of Tory conspiracy. Some businessmen shared the feeling: one 'regretted that the opposition to the draft Treaty had been largely, if not entirely, political, coming from the prominent men of one of the two great parties in the country. (no, no, and yes).'[24] The opinion was inaccurate, for condemnation of the Fish–Brown agreement was widespread. Few businessmen would have opposed a treaty that dealt only in natural products, but the inclusion of manufactures, the stringent canal requirements, and the way in which customs duties were to be lowered fostered a deep sense of disquiet at a time the economy was stagnant.

That the Fish–Brown treaty was not implemented is often passed off as inevitable because of American conditions.[25] This may be. But the furore caused by the proposal in Canada is too instructive to be ignored. A greater formal unity among manufacturers was fostered, and a wide-ranging discussion among different elements of the business world produced general agreement among manufacturers and merchants alike. A sense of common purpose developed, as businessmen asserted the vitality of their role in developing the nation.

Through the proposed treaty, the Liberals tried to solidify and extend their support among Ontario farmers who desired the American market, among export-oriented grain merchants, and among Ontario commercial men who wanted to buy from American sources. They also sought additional support in the coal interest, among fishermen, and among powerful shipping and trade interests in the Maritimes. The government readily accepted the inclusion of manufactures in the treaty (though Mackenzie was uncertain about the revenue implications of including iron and steel, which generated about $1.5 million of government income),[26] and expressed a willingness to allow British as well as American goods in free. The Liberals had a deeply rooted revenue-tariff, free-trade perspective. Governor General Lord Dufferin wrote, 'My Government advocate such a Policy [Reciprocity], in the first place, because it coincides with the abstract economical principles they are prepared to maintain, and in the next because they believe the proposed arrangements will be mutually advantageous to both countries.'[27] Stripped of its altruism and injected with a healthy dose of self-interest, the sentence would have captured the Liberal position.

The treatment of manufacturers in the making of the 1874 tariff and in the Fish–Brown agreement indicates that the Liberals had a somewhat different vision than the Conservatives of the place of manufacturers and other businessmen in the development of the country. Though rooted in their overall ideological stance, this vision received fresh coloration from the Pacific Scandal. Newspapers spilt much ink on the issues of personal and political morality involved in the Scandal, and inherently 'about the danger arising from a large concentration of wealth.'[28]

While chastising Sir Hugh Allan and his colleagues, and braying in shocked yet triumphant fashion about the ethical depravity of Conservative leaders, the *Globe* made a great deal out of the rejection of the norms of competition and the assertion of monopoly power that was implicit in the event. The scandal 'shows the people of the Dominion their rulers and a ring of speculators at work, the first selling and the other buying a charter.' The Conservative government had decided 'to crush out the least particle of competition' in the construction of the Pacific railway, and to create monopoly.[29]

In contrast, the Liberals promised to keep their government independent of these evil influences. The dangers of monopoly and government corruption and the necessity for personal and governmental rectitude were obvious. Combined with a Liberal anti-urban bias and a belief in the primacy of agricultural pursuits in both a moral and an economic sense,[30] this perspective made relations between large businesses and the Liberal government somewhat awkward. Business was no monolith, though, nor was the Liberal party. The Liberals had among them a representative group of businessmen, and the party depended, as did the Conservatives, upon the appeasement of various interests for a continuing existence. There is more than sufficient evidence to show that the Liberals indulged in petty pork-barrelling, and the party did not shy away from recruiting new combinations of interests.[31] Yet they were not an organized political hypocrisy, preaching against corruption on the one hand, while shamelessly indulging in the condemned sins on the other. Alexander Mackenzie's efforts to stem unwholesome patronage in the Department of Public Works testified to the rectitude at the heart of the party – though his work in this regard may have been the reason so many leading Liberals sought to have him resign the ministership of that department.[32] Concurrently, Richard Cartwright as minister of finance tried to limit the direct influence of special interests in the formation of commercial policy.

One method of doing so was to interpose bureaucracy between businessmen and the Liberal government. The contrast between the uses made of the Treasury Board by the Conservatives and Liberals is a notable case in point. The board adjudged all instances of requests for the removal of duty on raw materials, a power granted to the governor general in council in 1871. While the Tories were far more liberal in their treatment of requests from 1871 to 1873 than their Reform counterparts were in the following five years, the differences in procedure were even more striking. Under the Reformers, the Treasury Board saw civil servants present elaborately argued cases, demonstrating the agonizing character of the decisions being made. Under the Tories, the process was lax and arbitrary in comparison.[33]

The Liberals could make more stringent demands because the customs bureaucracy was growing and developing a degree of professionalism. Professionalization was a slow and uncertain process of course, especially in the patronage-ridden 'outside service' in the many ports of entry. Still, in the 1830s the lack of organization and system in the administration of the various collectors' offices came under reformist criticism, and a comprehensive review of the service in the Canadas was made in 1843. A more bureaucratic administrative structure slowly emerged, particularly at the busier ports of entry. By 1862 in Montreal, the Customs House had thirty officers, keeping a total of sixty-three books of records. Such assiduous effort could be misguided: the inspector who examined the operations of the Customs House that year estimated that one worker was 'a good and faithful officer, much attached to his book, and very unwilling to believe that his life has been lost in keeping a useless book.'[34] But professionalism came in many guises. By the 1860s and after, conflicts between customs men who had strong administrative ideas and wanted more rigid enforcement of the law and those of more lax perspective can be found.[35] The trends towards professionalism and bureaucratization were more obvious in the 'inside service,' made up of those working in the Department of Customs in Ottawa. While in 1867 there were only thirteen members of the 'inside service,' by 1875 there were twenty-five. Though the economical Liberals trimmed that number slightly to twenty-three by 1878, the growth in size of the central office reflected demands created by Confederation and by more complex tariff formulations. And the tasks of this growing administration became more specialized and subdivided.[36] Accompanying these developments was an ability to present sophisticated estimates of changes in customs duties, as we have seen in the case of the Treasury Board under the Liberals.

The Liberal approach seemed narrow and niggling for those who thought they saw an identity between manufacturers and the national good. But Cartwright was more at ease with raw statistical data than with the opinions and special pleadings of lobbying groups. To importuning deputations prior to the making of the 1874 tariff, Cartwright asked difficult questions about the number of manufacturers in the country, the number of hands employed, or the probable importations of a single trade in the coming year.[37] He was not merely attempting to embarrass, for the questions were a facet of Cartwright's methods of solving the problems of commercial policy. Expanding on the efforts of previous finance ministers, he tried to develop sources of information and statistics independent of manipulative interpretation by businessmen. A year after the imposition of the 1874 tariff, he confidentially canvassed the collectors of customs at thirty different ports of entry about the effects of the legislation: were any of the duties prohibitory? Had trade decreased in any single class of goods and was the general level of trade improving or declining? Had new factories started up recently? Were projected imports less or greater than those of the year previous? His concern with revenue was apparent. Later, Cartwright also requested the collectors to make estimates of the decline of prices during the depression, in order to better calculate means of raising revenue, and to counterbalance the claims of businessmen.[38]

Even in the finance minister's occasional attempts to mollify businessmen unhappy with his conduct, his desire to gather precise information was evident. Late in 1875, he told the collector at Quebec to inquire among manufacturers of the city as to the causes of the depression, as to the growth of business and factories, the size of existing inventories, the nature and location of their markets, and what remedies for the depression they had in mind. The manufacturers, the collector reported, were flattered at the attention the finance minister bestowed on them.[39] That inquiry was the van of the 1876 parliamentary Committee on the Causes of the Present Depression. Both were intended to allow manufacturers and others to fully express their views, thereby draining any reservoir of ill feeling toward the Liberals; at the same time, both were extensions of efforts to gather information on which Cartwright could base his financial calculations. Whatever its partisan functions, the committee was to be a 'thorough and exhaustive examination into the facts.'[40] In this way, Cartwright tried to escape the framework of lobbying within which information was usually gathered; thus he armed himself against the onslaught of the interests.

Despite Liberal low-tariff proclivities, pressure for higher customs duties continued to mount. Economic conditions worsened as growth became stagnation in 1873–74, followed by contraction. Demands for increased protection soon gained an urgency not earlier apparent. By summer 1875, Isaac Buchanan was once again sending wordy epistles to people in positions of power, though his loss of wealth greatly reduced his prestige ('I enclose you a fresh installment from Mr. Buchanan,' Edward Blake wrote Richard Cartwright. 'How much you owe me for providing the light reading for your journey!').[41] The ageing businessman also pressed the two Hamilton MPs for action to protect Canadian manufacturers. Those two were, along with Thomas Workman of Montreal and Paterson of Brant, among the most protection-minded of the Liberal MPs. The obvious interest labouring men had in keeping their jobs could lead to protectionism permeating urban communities, and the resultant demands readily penetrated to the government via parliamentary representatives.

The situation in Montreal in 1875–76 is instructive in this regard. Montreal manufacturers, more than most others in the country, had a national and something of an international market; they were badly hit when demand weakened and imports remained strong. The extremely high unemployment that resulted inevitably allied workingmen and their employers in the agitation for protection.

Liberal Montreal MP (and Parti national member) L.A. Jetté had in 1874 indicated some partiality for protection but only under duress, and a year later he was backsliding. The lengthy interview boot and shoe manufacturer Guillaume Boivin granted the Montreal *Gazette* showed that Jetté would have to perform in a more satisfactory fashion. 'We want petitions signed in favour of increased protection,' the blunt-spoken Boivin stated,

> and we are forming an Association of mechanics, which will have the accomplishment of this our principal object in view. We want these to be members who will agree to put the interests of the country, in all cases, above the interests of a party; that is what we want Jetté to do; and Jetté promised to do, last night, by pledging himself to work for protection, etc. and to-day he is somewhat in a fix ...
>
> The Government is against protection; and we want Jetté to decide whether he will assist us in this movement. We told him what was to be done, and we gave him a few days to consider the question; but at the first public meeting he will have to decide. He decided last night, but it was not very clear.[42]

The continual squeezing had an effect on the beleaguered MP. At a public meeting held some days later, he told an audience composed of labouring men – Boivin was there as well – that he was in favour of higher customs duties and swore to do his best to get them, particularly for the boot and shoe trade. Jetté was, by the beginning of September, a member of a Montreal committee pledged to publicly agitate for protection.[43]

Then in October 1875, a by-election took place in Montreal West, the major issue of which was tariff protection. The Conservative candidate, the newspaperman Thomas White Jr, tried to make the advocacy of higher customs duties exclusively his, painting the Liberals as deep-dyed free traders, and speechifying about the growth of employment, population, and the economy as the certain consequences of protection. Boivin and other Montreal manufacturers appeared on the platform with White. Running for the Liberals was the hardware importer and investor in industrial enterprises, Thomas Workman, who had no intention of allowing the Conservatives a monopoly on protection. In reply to a questionnaire from the Protective Association of Montreal, Workman stated he was 'in favor of and will advocate, if elected, a protective policy that will impose the same rate of duty on all manufactured articles coming into Canada from the United States that Americans charge on similar articles going into the United States from Canada.'[44] He promised independence from party lines on the issue. The association found this satisfactory, though it thought the response of Thomas White even more attractive. Workman's much publicized interview with Alexander Mackenzie, which the public presumed had involved concessions on the part of the prime minister to get the businessman to run, gave Workman' protectionist statements the ghost of an official imprimatur.[45] Workman won th election narrowly. Expectations of a tariff increase were great.

The widespread distress arising from unemployment in Montreal that winte made the issue even more vital. Workman was expected to produce immediatel he and the federal government were, however, not quick in their relief provision By December 1875, dissatisfaction had grown to such a degree that men wer gathering in groups in the public places of the city to demand work. Petition for public-works employment were sent to the mayor, and through him to th federal government, but Prime Minister Mackenzie refused to increase exper ditures. On the 17 December an explosive stage was reached: a crowd of ove 2000 workingmen gathered at City Hall while the City Council was in sessior demanding work or bread – one individual was heard to cry 'work or blood.' A number of men rushed into the main entrance of the City Hall where th mayor gave them a speech advising moderation. The crowd continued to mi outside; bread and beer wagons were raided; the police engaged in a mêlée wit parts of the crowd; finally police armed with rifles arrived. Under a state c siege, the City Council hurriedly developed a public works program.

Tariff protection was, in this context, not a matter of interest or class, but community demand. A monster meeting of late January 1876 expressed fur damental agreement between the industrial élite, the politicians, and a massiv audience containing 'several thousand workingmen' of the city. George Stephe sent a publicly read letter expressing his sympathy with the protectionist cause That set the tone of the meeting. Customs duties the equivalent of America ones were demanded, so Thomas Workman's cautious statement 'that while . the duties would be considerably raised ... they need not expect reciprocal dutie was met with groans.[47] The Montreal Industrial Association not long after ha an interview with Richard Cartwright, during which the deputation gained th impression that the tariff was to be raised from $17^{1}/_{2}$ to 20 per cent. It looke as if public pressure was going to make the Liberal government bend.

Such a prognosis was not the product of Montreal conditions alone. Unem ployment was high in many industrial areas in 1875 and 1876, and protectioni agitation was widespread. Newly established, the Ontario Millers' Associatio gathered in Toronto in October 1875, largely to complain to each other abou the hard times. Politicians, the millers advised each other, had to be pushe toward protection, and if MPs were hardened free traders, the solution was simpl to vote for someone else. The Liberals would respond, the millers agreed: th only difference between the parties was that one was in power, the other not. A month later, the Ontario Manufacturers' Association was even more optimisti At a well-attended two-day meeting in Toronto, the chairman W.H. Howlan waxed enthusiastic: 'Since the last meeting of manufacturers, there has been a great change of opinion throughout the country, and ... the free trade feeling had very much lessened ... extreme free trade views were not applicable to this country.' The meeting took on a revivalistic air, as manufacturer after manufacturer rose to witness to the evils of the existing depression and of free-trade policy, and declare the glories of the coming protectionist kingdom. The resolutions that passed were couched in moderate terms, with lip service being paid to 'incidental protection' and government revenue needs. The central resolution showed no such moderation, however. It requested a minimum 20 per cent tariff on a broad range of goods imported from Great Britain, and much higher rates on the same goods imported from elsewhere.[49]

Discontent with the existing state of affairs found expression in New Brunswick and Nova Scotia as well. The New Brunswick Manufacturers' and Mechanics' Association took up the question of tariff changes at two different meetings; practically everyone who spoke advocated protection from foreign manufactures. A lone free-trade voice came from a leather producer; he met with savage ridicule.[50] Matters were still more unsettled in Nova Scotia, as the situation in the coal-mining industry showed. Though the industry faced very serious difficulties arising out of falling prices, declining exports to the United States, and growing joblessness, the collective response was muted. The attempt to form a combination in September 1875 to control domestic output, wages and prices, and to garner government support for the industry was convulsive and without consequence. The interest's failure to press a coherent case on the federal government and its lack of unified action was to be seen in the letter columns of the newspapers. Some writers felt a duty on anthracite coal should be imposed but R.G. Haliburton had by this time concluded that opposition from central Canadian interests made that impossible; he advocated a bounty on coal exports. Others suggested preferential rates on the Intercolonial Railway for the mineral, or that the provincial royalty on coal should be removed. Wages could be reduced to an absolute minimum to allow for year-round employment, someone else asserted. The need for improved methods of mining and storage of coal was another line taken.[51] A united and effective voice was lacking.

Residual free-trade feeling was apparent in many of the solutions posed to meet the coal-trade's problems, but the failure of the interest to group together decisively was due partly to the failure of central Canadian interests and those involved in the coal industry to come to a meeting of minds. The understanding reached in 1870 – a customs duty on coal in return for one on breadstuffs – did not get much support from Ontario manufacturers or from Maritimes consumers, and was sabotaged the following year when Ontario MPs revolted against it. Neither the Ontario Manufacturers' Association resolutions nor those coming from the Montreal Industrial Association in 1875 and 1876 offered concession to the Maritimers on coal. Nor did the Dominion Board of Trade when R.G Haliburton approached it.[52] The industry was not encouraged to demand protection.

Low-tariff sentiment remained dominant in Nova Scotia. A small minorit voiced approval of protection in the Halifax Chamber of Commerce, but the were quickly drowned out. Protection would make the Maritimes shipbuilde suffer; it would ruin the shipping interest by reducing trade; Maritimers alread paid more tax than other Canadians on a per capita basis. Protection woul damage the revenue by encouraging smuggling and thus hurting the fair trader And it went counter to free-trade principles. So, at least, thought the Halifa Chamber of Commerce.[53] Several Maritimes interests had reasons to be suspicious of tariff increases as well. Richard Cartwright's proposed duties on ship building materials in 1874 had only been partially beaten back, and though h had been forced to retreat on tea duties that would have discriminated agains the Atlantic provinces, he remained suspect.[54] Also, the Liberal government' failure to mollify conflicting interests over sugar duties in 1874 and 1875 nc only upset central Canadian interests, but left Halifax men, represented by Libera A.G. Jones in the Commons, irate. Jones subsequently proved difficult on th 1876 tariff.

For, as Lord Dufferin was informed, the Liberal government intended to rais the tariff that year. Revenue needs made it necessary. Under the tariff of 1874 there had been a projected government income increase of $3 million; the actua increase had only been one-third of that, due to declining prices and imports.[5 Businessmen were aware of the situation, and Cartwright's inquiries of manufacturers may have made them believe that the finance minister was becomin more amenable to influence. He received a large protectionist correspondenc in early 1876.[56]

A similar upsurge of interest in high tariffs was apparent at the Dominio Board of Trade meeting of January 1876, where Liberals made a great effort t obtain a moderate incidental-protection resolution, hinting that a rise in th unenumerated rate to 20 per cent was likely. Cartwright made similar suggestion to others: a deputation of protectionist Liberal MPs was welcomed so cordiall by him that one of their number, John Macdonald of Toronto Centre, afterward wrote to the Toronto Board of Trade asking for tariff recommendations.[57]

There remained great uneasiness within the Liberal government about raisin the customs duties, though direct evidence about it is lacking. Richard Cartwrigh was of two minds, for when he had introduced the tariff of 1874, he took th trouble to explain that 'I do not think that any greater increase of the tariff tha we suggest now would be wise. I think we have gone to the limit beyond whic it would be impossible to pass without resorting to direct taxation [to increas the revenue].'[58] Further tariff hikes would bring about a decline in imports and an accompanying fall in total governmental income, a view that paralleled A.T. Galt's experience after 1859. A certain trepidation marked Cartwright's resolve to test the limit in 1876.

There were rumours of trouble within the Liberal party. A few days before the budget came down, the *Free Press* of Ottawa reported that the 'majority of the members from the Maritime Provinces, through Mr. Church, informed the Premier to-day that they would be compelled to vote against any change in the existing tariff.'[59] As the Maritime MPs who met with Cartwright at this time recalled the incident, not threats but cogent arguments were made, showing that many seats would be lost in the Maritimes at the next election if the tariff was adjusted upwards. Threat or rational argument aside, the government prudently altered its plans: there were no major changes announced in the tariff. Recalling this intraparty clash years later, and giving himself a prominent role as an Ontario Liberal protectionist, James Young wrote: 'In 1876 I had a special correspondence with him [Mackenzie] urging him to increase the tariff 2½%. My letters went into it fully, and I have one or two in reply. However, as you probably know, Holton & I took the question up when we met at Ottawa, and the Govt. finally decided to add 2½%. But as you also probably know, Jones, Carmichael [an MP for coal-producing Cape Breton] & the Maritime members spoiled that, and really ruined the party.'[60]

Richard Cartwright, largely responsible for both the promise of a higher tariff and for its non-realization, provided an analysis indicating the reasons for the government's dependence on the Maritimers. As he wrote to Edward Blake in 1875, 'I am every day more and more convinced that no stable govt. is possible except in one of two ways, i.e. either by securing a decisive majority in Ontario and Quebec taken together, or by deliberately purchasing the smaller provinces from time to time. The first is possible now but it certainly will not be long if there is any serious division in the ranks.'[61]

The rumoured tariff of 1876 had been intended to strengthen the grip of the Liberals on Ontario and Quebec; no tariff increase was, in Cartwright's cynical words, an act of 'deliberately purchasing the smaller provinces.' Central Canadian free-trade Liberals could for pragmatic reasons be persuaded to live with a modest tariff increase, and many urban Liberals and the Parti national would actually be pleased. However, the Quebec wing of the party was wracked with internal dissension that progressively weakened it and, in addition, faced an ultramontane spirit that dominated much of the politics of the province in the 1870s. By 1876, it seemed probable that the Liberals would not be able to repeat their 35-seat performance of 1874 in the province. Liberal domination of the Maritimes would consequently prove vital if the party was to maintain a comfortable majority. At the time, the logic was impeccable, especially as the Liberal hold on Nova Scotia was none too secure.[62] The need to hold the Maritimes was imperative because attempts to strengthen the Liberal party in Quebec had failed.

Certain changes in the tariff of 1874 had been aimed at gaining support among Montreal capitalists, with some modest success, given George Stephen's temporary partiality to the Liberal cause about this time. Subsequent Liberal moves had the same end in view, especially in the matter of the sugar duties. The Liberal government intended to change these duties to garner support in the Montreal and Halifax areas. Since Redpath's sugar refinery was built in Montreal in 1854, refining had received protection, much to the irritation of grocery wholesalers who imported raw and low-grade refined sugars. In 1874, the government intention had been to reclassify sugars to increase protection, which would have pleased prospective refining interests in Halifax represented by A.G. Jones, as well as the large Montreal refining interest. Strong counter-pressures made Cartwright back away from the reclassification project at that time. Nothing had been done on the matter during the parliamentary session of 1875, but in April that year, a deputation of employees of Redpath's met with Cartwright to tell him that the Montreal refinery would be closed if additional protection was not granted. Cartwright, shocked into action, persuaded the cabinet to pass an order in council reducing the duties on sugars going into refining, under the 1870 law that permitted the government to place raw materials on the free list.[63] Unfortunately, the manoeuvre, which Cartwright probably intended to be surreptitious, caused great moral indignation among grocery importers. Luther Holton, the Liberal MP considered to be the representative of the Montreal mercantile community, was placed in a highly embarrassing position. 'No one can appreciate the humiliation it [the order in council] has inflicted on me,' he bitterly informed Alexander Mackenzie, 'who does not understand the extent to which I am held responsible by the English speaking people especially the mercantile portion of this community for the acts of this present administration and the sting of the humiliation is in the fact that I cannot frame even a plausible defense for the actions of my friends without abandoning those constitutional views [responsible government] which as a public man I have always insisted upon and secondly the free trade principles on which I have had to vindicate some exceedingly unpopular acts of the administration.'[64]

The order in council actually went beyond the powers granted by the law, which permitted items to be placed on the *free list*, but not to have the duty merely *reduced* on them. Revocation of the offending order followed, compounding the embarrassment of the Liberals. Much unhappiness was then displayed in Halifax. A.G. Jones showed all of Holton's bitterness, but because the protection had been snatched back: if justice was not be granted to the

Maritimes, if the West Indies trade went to the United States, 'our people wont be slow to realize what we always assured them when we opposed Union that we had no interest in common with Canada & must only look to separation for relief.'[65] Support from the Maritimes had been shaken, the Liberal administration was viewed with suspicion by part of the central Canadian mercantile community, and the Redpath votes had not been won.

The Liberals also tried to recruit Sir Alexander Tilloch Galt. In the midsummer of 1875, Galt decided to re-enter active politics, but his party allegiance was in question. He had parted with the Conservatives in 1870 and sat as an independent, along with Richard Cartwright. The Pacific Scandal had caused him to voice disgust with the Conservatives. Moreover, he was on friendly terms with Cartwright and shared with the Liberal finance minister a belief in the necessity of retrenchment and a profound distrust of free-spending finance ministers like Francis Hincks. Galt's much-touted reputation for financial acumen and the leading position he held in the protestant and financial communities of Quebec made him a desirable commodity for the Liberals. With the intellectual Goldwin Smith, with Edward Blake and the Canada Firsters, with the Conservative but politically flexible Montreal financier George Stephen, Galt shared a belief in the necessary independence of Canada from Great Britain.[66] Thus it was that Stephen could give advice to George Brown on reciprocity in 1874 and suggest improvements in the tariff to Cartwright as late as January 1876; as well, Smith knew Stephen and visited with him in Montreal to discuss newspaper purchases and turned also to Edward Blake on similar matters. And finally, so it was that Stephen corresponded with Blake about the desirability of recruiting Galt into Liberal ranks.[67]

Protectionists saw Blake as the great hope for high-tariff nationalism in the Liberal party, and the addition of Galt would have strengthened the tendency in Liberal ranks. A political alliance to strengthen the Liberals in Quebec and to move them in a protectionist direction briefly shimmered in the heat of the late summer of 1875 – then receded and disappeared.

What exactly stood in the way of the Liberals gaining Galt is not clear. His open advocacy of incidental protection disturbed some Liberals, of course, but Galt also cherished himself as a political independent of a Conservative character. This was made clear to Liberals who approached him.[68] He possibly had designs on the finance ministership, which Cartwright jealously guarded. Galt was not gained at any rate, and the Liberals were left vulnerable to the demands of the Maritimers.

After the 1876 budget was made public and the Liberal administration reneged on what protectionists saw as a virtual promise to increase the tariff, outrage among Montreal manufacturers reached a pitch of intensity. A delegation of them had interviews with Mackenzie and Cartwright in order to press for changes, but though the prime minister was polite enough in refusing to give way, the delegation saw Cartwright as negative, harsh, and peremptory.[69] The evidence-gathering sessions of the parliamentary Committee on the Causes of the Present Depression turned into ugly confrontations between acidic free-trade MPs and tenaciously protectionist manufacturers, with a few individuals desperately trying to keep avenues of influence to the Liberals open. The debate in the House of Commons turned savage.

The Conservatives took full advantage of the sudden intransigence of the Liberals. Myth has it that Charles Tupper, who replied to Cartwright's budget speech, was prepared to defend either free trade or protection, depending on what Cartwright had to say, and that on this singular piece of opportunism depended the direction of Conservative economic policy.[70] The story is a pleasant perversity. A large number of Tories had already committed themselves to protection in the wrangling over the make-up and function of the Committee on the Causes of the Present Depression. Admittedly, so had many Liberals. But the matter can be taken further. Of course, the Conservatives would have attacked any policy brought forward by the government, and Tupper was apparently well prepared to attack an increase in the tariff, and ill prepared to do otherwise. Yet it was not necessary for him to proclaim the splendour of free trade in order to decry tariff increases by those who held power. Had the tariff been increased, he likely would have taken the stance presented by the Montreal *Gazette* before the budget came down: a Liberal increase would be of a blanket character, insensitive to the needs of Canadian industries – indeed by 1877 the Tory tack was that a 'scientific re-adjustment,' not necessarily an increase, was required. Richard Cartwright, who was partially responsible for perpetuating the myth that the Conservatives could have gone either way in 1876, none the less asserted that the customs alterations he had considered were 'not in the least' of a protective character. 'I had made up my mind on the question of protection,' he recalled, 'and was in no way inclined to give it any countenance. We intended to stand or fall on a revenue tariff.'[71] Easy enough to say in retrospect, but it would have perfectly suited the *Gazette* critique.

Rather than an issue muddied by compromise, however, the Conservatives were given an attractive half of a polarity. After an amiable meeting with the Montreal protectionists, Sir John A. Macdonald chortled that the government 'are between the Devil and the Deep Sea.'[72] In debate he casually tossed barbs into the sensitive hides of protectionist Liberals whose anguish over the inaction of the government was public spectacle. But he carefully avoided any personal or party commitment to full-fledged protectionism while allowing some of his followers to go that far, and he presented an amendment urging a 'fitting encouragement and protection' to manufacturing and agriculture though, interestingly, not to mining. He and other Tories rang changes on the protectionist argument: the nostrum would be retaliation against the United States and encourage a move to reciprocity; infant industries would be encouraged to grow; diversity of employment would be provided and emigration thus prevented; the depression would be brought to an end; trade between central Canada and the Maritimes would spring up; a harmony of interests and regions would result; indeed, Charles Colby went so far as to suggest that protection was crucial for the development of the great northwest.[73] The end of the session brought the pamphlet publication of the choicest protectionist Commons speeches, including a number from Liberals. The pamphlet was heavily subsidized by industrial advertising.[74] A fruitful subject for a summer of picnic and by-election speeches had been found.

The great error the Liberals had fallen into, if error it was, grew in part out of the difficulties faced by the Liberals in government. The cabinet contained few men of lengthy administrative experience.[75] Richard Cartwright, who fancied himself a political manipulator, proved more adept at alienating potential supporters. And while he probably had a more flexible political morality than either Edward Blake or Alexander Mackenzie, all three, and the government as a whole, were placed in the unenviable position of trying to limit influence peddling and venal patronage in a political system that could not otherwise adequately operate. So Cartwright vacillated between efforts at keeping business interests at arm's length and trying to ingratiate himself with them. The party was also fragmented and fractious along regional and other lines. Internal divisions on the issue of protection were obvious: some urban Liberal MPs in Ontario and Quebec were quite strongly protectionist and others, such as Halifax's A.G. Jones, had special interests they wanted protected while advocating free trade; low-tariff and free-trade sentiment dominated at the heart of the party, in the Maritime wing, and in parts of the Ontario section. The contemplated increase in the tariff of 1876 was to enlarge the revenue, but it was also intended to serve as a stroke of practical statesmanship in conciliating protectionists without giving offence to low-tariff protagonists. It was to have been an incidental protection of a largely accidental sort. In the event, even a 2½ per cent increase proved too much for low-tariff interests in the party and the Liberal government backtracked. The party leadership thereafter had to justify a more rigid revenue tariff or 'free trade' perspective to the electorate.

Overall, the choice did not seem to be a bad one in 1876. In the liberal intellectual Goldwin Smith's estimation, the government had not been wise to alienate the protectionists, but Smith thought the protectionists were few in number.[76] A return to good times had in the past quieted protectionist demands;

there was no evidence that the depression would linger for another three years. Advocates of high tariffs in Liberal ranks could be controlled. As long as the agricultural community in Ontario did well, and remained in the party fold along with the Maritimes, Liberal government could be maintained. Some Liberals boasted they could retain power without support from urban manufacturing centres.[77] The perspective was accurate as long as party strength was otherwise sustained. The inability to gain reciprocity was a symbolic failure of the first order in this context, whatever its actual consequences might have been.

8
The Liberal interregnum, 1876–1878

The events of 1876 were by no means decisive in fixing political alignments prior to the federal election of 1878. The Conservatives took care not to plunge heedlessly into high-tariff waters; and protectionists persisted in hoping the Liberal government could be forced to see the light. The Liberals assumed the leadership of low-tariff forces, undertook to reform protectionists in their own ranks, and struggled to prevent supporters from straying into the high-tariff heresy. Straying had at all costs to be prevented among the farmers of western Ontario, where the party had its traditional power base.

In the 1840s and 1850s, western Ontario had in part become a staple-producing hinterland to the eastern United States. Trade under the Reciprocity Treaty of 1854 had functioned to confirm a yearning for the American market in many farmers, that readily translated into a free-trade attitude constantly reinforced by the Toronto *Globe*'s liberal assertions. Good crops, good export markets, and good prices for the wheat staple left farmers pleased in their free-trade outlook, so it was unfortunate for the Liberals that wheat prices were poor for much of the depression (they slumped quite badly in September 1878, the month of the election), and that for several years crops were substandard.[1]

There were also significant protectionist streaks in the farming community of Ontario. Residual feelings of that character persisted from the 1840s and earlier, when the areas of upstate New York produced heavy wheat crops and provided competition in the markets of the Canadas. The net import position Canada held in wheat in the 1870s created a positive context for agrarian protectionism.[2] Canadian wool producers moved towards protection as well, as Canadian woollens manufacturers shifted to imported wool.[3] Even in southwestern Ontario, particularly in areas along the United States border, an agriculture that had diversified into fruit and vegetable growing favoured higher tariffs on such products because of American competition. The argument that protection to manufacturers fostered a larger urban market for diversified agriculture to serve was appealing.[4]

Yet protectionist sentiment among farmers also reflected a desire for reciprocity. With the abrogation of the treaty in 1866, Canadian farmers were confronted with high American duties that made U.S. markets less accessible, while Canada remained open to American agricultural products. The invidious contrast was made all the more pointed by the repeated failures to gain a new reciprocity and by the extraordinary growth of protection and competition from the rich wheat fields of the American midwest that forced prices down.

Tariff retaliation seemed a plausible alternative and an emotionally satisfying one. American farm products would be kept out and, with good fortune, the Americans might reconsider their ways. 'A great many farmers are narrowminded and selfish,' one Liberal wrote to Alexander Mackenzie, 'and when an appeal is made to them somewhat plausibly although unfairly, that the Americans have almost unrestricted access to our markets, while we are subjected to heavy duties on entering theirs, they are unable to view the matter in all its bearings and are ready to denounce any government that will not meet the Americans on their own grounds. In fact "retaliation" that is, treating them as they treat us, has such a *smack* of fairness about it, that do our best, we cannot prevent a serious loss of political support.'[5]

Hop growers in both Ontario and Quebec loudly proclaimed these views to the government of the day, for while Canada was a net exporter of hops, the country also imported a large quantity.[6] The brewer G.T. Labatt coached farmers to vote protectionist in 1878, arguing that excise duties on malt reduced demand for barley in Canada, and Canadian barley faced high American customs duties; at the same time, hard liquor made from *American* corn was capturing the Canadian market. Surely it was self-evident, Labatt concluded, that a duty should be imposed on American corn in order to expand the home market for barley.[7] Similar practical manifestations of the harmony of interests and the need to create a home market for agricultural products were routinely enunciated in the later 1870s.

Political expression of these views came through persistent petitioning, and through members of Parliament.[8] Grain millers also presumed that they had the right to speak for the agricultural community, and they were joined by some manufacturers having close contacts with farmers.[9] Still, free-trade views were dominant in western Ontario among the yeomen, though the dominance was severely threatened as the Patrons of Husbandry, otherwise known as the Grange, became established in Canada.

Founded in 1867 in the United States, the Grange first penetrated Canada in 1872; by 1874 it had expanded sufficiently to form an independent Dominion

Grange. Farmers were conscious of the rapid growth of interest organizations among workers, professionals, and businessmen. The lack of similar organization among agriculturists meant that they were 'fair game for all to prey on, and well they have been and still are being fleeced.' The only answer was the Grange: 'in union there is strength.'[10]

Although the organization was non-partisan, the leadership soon found agricultural protection an attractive cry. More than a third of the membership (some 5000 names) signed a petition in 1875–76 requesting higher customs duties on agricultural products. Never presented because a large portion of the membership and a number of the subordinate Granges disapproved of it, the petition nevertheless indicated the great extent of agricultural protectionism. Dissatisfaction with the tariff prior to 1876 was widespread among farmers, and retaliatory import duties were necessary, a parliamentary committee of that year was told by the master of the Dominion Grange.[11]

Admittedly the Select Committee on the Agricultural Interest was a protectionist vehicle, but farmers were supposed to be free-trade oriented. Yet witnesses favouring higher tariffs to farm products were numerous and in substantial majority before the committee. And they must have held representative views. After all, leaders of local farming communities such as masters of subordinate granges, reeves, presidents, and other officials of agricultural societies provided most of the replies. Nearly two-thirds of the replies came from Ontario, so at least an active minority of farmers in the province wanted high tariffs on agricultural commodities.[12]

The same feeling was well-rooted in Quebec. Tariff protection to farmers was popular in the Eastern Townships, where the Grange was well established.[13] The Parti national wing of the Liberals also advocated tariffs on farm products, and the leader of the wing, 'practical farmer' H.G. Joly, favoured protection to farm and factory in 1876 as a means of keeping French Canadians at home. Roughly a third of the respondents to the 1876 parliamentary committee questionnaire were from Quebec, with a fair proportion being French Canadians, among them two parish priests.[14] The clergy often guided or assisted French-Canadian farmers in petitioning to have import duties on raw tobacco imposed.[15] As for protection among Maritimes farmers, evidence seems limited. Other than Prince Edward Island, those provinces were heavy importers of foodstuffs, and resistance to the imposition of duties on grain was especially strong. Still, farmers who faced persistent American competition, as did those of Charlotte, New Brunswick, could demand protection in the same tones as their Ontario and Quebec brethren.[16]

Farmers did not automatically extend their advocacy of protective duties on farm products to manufactured goods. Only two-thirds of the respondents to the

Select Committee on the Agricultural Interest's circular chose to answer the queries on higher customs imposts on manufactured products.[17] The Grange reflected rural suspicion of the evils of business concentration: did not high customs tariffs on manufactures encourage trusts, rings, and monopolies? Would protection not increase prices?

These suspicions had to be overcome if a full protectionist system was ever to be implemented. High-tariff manufacturers responded with a basic rationale of protectionist nationalism: urban growth would be fostered by protection to industry, enlarging the market for a diversified agriculture. As a basic tenet of the 'harmony of interests,' this was repeated regularly at manufacturers' meetings, where it was supplemented by discussions of methods of spreading the word to farmers. The entreaties to agriculturists combined open reference to tariff retaliation against the United States (to obtain reciprocity if nothing else), a direct appeal to the interest of farmers in agricultural protection, the assertion that a trade-off with manufacturers would be necessary to gain the desired end, and the argument that the resulting protective system would be ideologically and nationally progressive.[18]

A basic method of bringing the message home to rural areas was through the influence of protectionist manufacturers, businessmen, and other notables. One flax manufacturer reported that in his area most farmers 'agreed that it was only fair that Canadian manufacturers should be placed on an even platform' with American ones.[19] Well they might agree, seeing they grew the flax he bought. With the election of 1878, protectionists found this work vital, as the circular to barley growers put out by the brewer Labatt shows. One Beauharnois businessman, Baker by name, eagerly pronounced that protection would be 'more beneficial to farmers than to Busines men.' He enthused over the advantages of protection to corn, oats, barley, butter, and wheat producers, and then triumphantly concluded that even in terms of protection to manufactured goods, the farmer came out ahead: 'If we would tax the American manufactured goods high enough so that they could not be sent here, we would manufacture them ourselves, we would employ a great many workman and all the money our farmers gives us would go back to them again, as our manufacturers would employ a great many hands, all those hands produce and return to them their own money.' Conservative politicians were then advised to follow Baker's example and 'din this thing in their [the farmers'] ears every opportunity they get.'[20] Isaac Buchanan would have been proud.

Dinning of this nature, from manufacturers, from other protectionist agencies, and from Conservative politicians was certain to have some effect, much to the dismay of the Liberals. Already in the by-elections of 1876, the Liberal party was scrambling. Well before the by-election there, one party stalwart in the constituency of Ontario South wrote Edward Blake urgently. 'The grangers are determined to have a duty imposed on American corn and other things. The tories are trying to make capital out of this among the farmers and I am afraid they will succeed with a great many as they think it will affect their pockets directly. 'How,' he asked Blake, 'would you answer that?'[21] The question remained, not only in Ontario South, but in the Wellington by-election where the Grangers and protectionists were 'causing some trouble,' as Alexander Mackenzie tersely noted.[22]

The summer of 1876 was the first great summer of Tory political picnics, with their easy campaigning over salads, sandwiches, and 'dubious lemonade,' followed by the heavier fare of speeches from the party leaders.[23] Protection was not the only matter of concern to the Tories: Macdonald, Tupper, and others spent much time in defusing the Pacific Scandal and attacking Liberal incompetence and corruption. But protection found its way in, emphatically with Tupper, and more cautiously with Macdonald, who asserted that he did not advocate 'Chinese Wall' protection, and tried to establish the historical validity of protection as a Conservative plank. Yet Macdonald was capable of bringing home the lesson sharply to the rural audiences, as he did in Cooksville. Dependence on a single staple product was dangerous to long-run prosperity, he told farmers who must have been well aware of the advantages of diversifying away from wheat. Canada needed a multitude of different pursuits, 'which would be the means of employing the people according to their various tastes and faculties.' Protection to manufactures was vital, 'so that they would soon be able to grow and walk along without the assistance of the State.' That had been the historical policy of the Conservatives, and would remain so.[24] The public response was sufficiently strong to force some Liberal by-election candidates, like J.D. Edgar in Ontario South, into an ambiguous advocacy of modestly higher tariffs,[25] even while they were being attacked for representing the party of free trade. The Liberals won Wellington and Glengarry (narrowly), but both Ontario North and South were lost and the key issue, the despondent Liberals agreed, had been protection.[26]

The tariff was developing into a major partisan issue, and though many Liberals remained soft on the matter, many of then now chose to do battle in ways both insidious and direct, rather than bowing to pressure as Edgar had done. David Mills was suspected of providing financial incentives to the *Farmer's Advocate* of London, in order to have it take a free-trade stance.[27] In the face of Granger protectionism, Edward Blake frankly suggested that the organization be infiltrated and redirected towards free trade. Public protectionist pronouncements of Grangers were vehemently attacked by Liberals, and the Grangers often felt obliged to back down.[28] Those in the van of the Liberal revenue tariff, free-trade army plunged into the battle with intensity. The Liberal candidate in Ontario North had refused to modify his free-trade stance, despite great pressure to do so. John Charlton, the lumberman MP and self-confessed convert from protectionism, took the Liberal message to his constituents in some seventy meetings in two years before the election of 1878.[29] David Mills took a similar position when he had to resign and run for a seat after becoming minister of justice. He boasted to Edward Blake of his tough free-trade position; his opponents were 'fairly squelched out' he chortled. On other occasions he steeled the wavering in Liberal ranks.[30]

Crying free trade was not the sum of Liberal rhetoric. Their rural appeal was also strengthened by assertions as to the centrality of agriculture in Canadian society, and by flattering reference to the unique characteristics of the farmer. As Alexander Mackenzie told the Commons in 1877, farmers had too much sense to be taken in by protection. Then, too, leading Liberals did not hesitate to express an anti-urban bias. Immediately after the 1876 tariff debacle, as Reform MPs saw the negative impact the event would have on their party's urban fortunes, some of them began declaring that they could rule the country without urban support. The bias showed itself in a more distinctive fashion in Richard Cartwright. The finance minister seemed to share an older vision of a conservative agrarian society that was rooted in the Upper Canadian gentry among whom his family had once a prominent place.[31] At one political picnic in the summer of 1877, he told an appreciative rural crowd: 'No man can desire more than I do to see our Canadian towns grow and thrive. But ... I have for a long time become convinced that a system or a policy which tended to promote the unhealthy growth of towns at the expense of the rural districts is most disastrous to the true interests of any country ... The cities of Canada are not what make Canada. They are the healthy outgrowth of our rural populations, and anything tending to injure the growth and demoralize the rural population will ultimately injure the growth and demoralize the population of the cities themselves.'[32] Speaking to workingmen in Toronto, another Liberal spokesman was equally explicit. 'Where there are large centres there also is great misery,' he counselled. 'To hold land was better than to engage in manufactures. Unless there was a great agricultural population, manufactures could not be consumed.'[33] The protectionist position about the value of urban growth was here inverted.

The Toronto *Globe* went on to enrich the contrast between urban and rural. The farmer had nearly complete independence while the workingman depended on others for food, clothes, shelter, and provision for old age; protection, in making things more expensive for farmers, would ultimately raise the cost of living for the urban dweller; enormous populations would be drawn to the cities by a high-tariff system, to endure the worst of any depression, to suffer through consequent illness, to become 'dependent upon capitalists and combinations of capitalists.'[34] In so cajoling and threatening the farmer, the newspaper revealed him to be more than just a voter. He was a symbol of the virtues of liberalism in his individuality and economic independence; he was a symbol, through the apparent economic homogeneity and egalitarianism of the farming community, a symbol of the relative absence of the harsh class distinctions and great disparities of wealth to be found in Britain.[35]

The leading figures of the party used rhetoric which magnified their fears and concerns, but they none the less doubted the survival of liberal society under a system of protective tariffs. Though the actual commercial policy of the party was a revenue tariff with an increasingly grudging acceptance of some incidental protection, the leaders used free-trade theory to explain why the tariff should not be increased to prohibitively protective levels. To point out the flaws of the protectionist argument, to indicate the dreadful consequences of protection by means of extrapolating liberal economic theory, was at one and the same time the best defence of the pedestrian policy of a revenue tariff and the best way to address the underlying issues.[36]

From the Liberal perspective, the depression was not the result of government inaction, of a failure to legislate palliative measures, as the Conservatives would have it. It followed from over-production and over-importation, which grew out of a system of excessively easy credit and too many people entering non-productive middlemen and service roles. Partially the depression was imported from a languishing outside world, for neither protectionist nor free-trade countries had escaped the economic downturn. A government could do little but keep taxation down and goods inexpensive through relatively low tariffs. In time, the business cycle would right itself.[37] The introduction of a protective system could not alleviate the distress; it could only make it worse. Canada was a staple-producing and exporting country and would remain so in the foreseeable future; prices for its most important products such as foodstuffs and lumber were set in international markets, so whatever the strength of the protectionist case, it did not hold for this country. Canada should be kept a cheap place to live, so that immigrants would be attracted to it. Liberal free traders identified as rank sophistry the arguments that protection would not raise prices, or that it was the foreign producer of imported goods that paid the customs duties on them, not the consumer.[38]

As the protectionist/free-trade debate reached a pitch of intensity between 1876 and 1879, the Liberals elaborated an economic morphology arising out of tariff protection that ended in disaster. The imposition of a protective tariff would reduce imports, damaging trade and the shipping industry and rendering useless Canada's railways and canals as the economy moved toward full self-dependence, toward autarky. Member firms of the protected industries might form rings to take full advantage of the potential for increasing prices. Profits in the favoured industries would rise rapidly, and a flood of new firms would enter the market place, eager to gain a share of the wealth. Then for a time, internal competition might reduce prices as protectionists predicted, but the situation would be unstable. The hot-house protection system produced sickly growth; too many competitors would arise, markets would become over-supplied, ruthless attitudes would prevail, and an economic crash would follow. All but the strongest firms would then be weeded out, and they would become luxurious monopolistic growths, feeding on monopoly prices. The only alternative to monopolies were the equally hideous price-fixing cabals. All consumers, urban and rural, would suffer from the much higher cost of living that resulted, and immigrants would shun the country.[39]

Liberal predictions about the social and political results of protection were equally gloomy. They were not able to envision the world of social harmony and national integration under a protective system for which its proponents yearned. Conflict and disunity, rather, would be assured. The British empire could only be damaged as daughter country was sundered from mother by unnatural trade restrictions and differing ideological perspectives. Conflicts between regions in Canada were foretold, as sectional advantage under the tariff became a prize. One social group would struggle with another to gain parliamentary favour, with bribery and corrupt politics following close behind. Under protection everyone would turn to the government. It would be paternalism with a vengeance. Ultimately, of course, only the owners of protected industries would benefit. These men, through the tariff, through their price-fixing rings and monopolies, could amass great wealth by means of a parliament-sanctioned robbery of the rest of the community. A protective system was thus class legislation that destroyed competition and bred monopoly, replaced man's independence with dependence, and brushed aside the potential of the individual to erect class interest in its place. Class conflict would then loom.[40]

The analysis was buttressed with copious historical and contemporary illustration, mostly from the experience of foreign countries. Great Britain was held up as the paradigm of what could be achieved under free trade; the evils of protection could be demonstrated from the example of the United States, where only bounteous natural resources and other advantages staved off economic and social degeneration, though not completely.[41]

Conscious collective control could not and should not be exercised over the economy, the more extreme free traders thought. Natural economic processes such as depression had an inevitable cyclical evolution, and any attempt to interfere could have no more effect than a fly could have on a turning wheel. The image was Richard Cartwright's, and for all its force it was unfortunate, because it made the Liberal position an essentially negative one.[42] The party was not offering a better world through *its* agency; it only offered to prevent the scenes of destruction that would accompany Tory protectionism.

The full Liberal critique was for the most part accumulated and fashioned from 1876 to 1879. However, even after the fierce parliamentary debate of 1876, the growing inflexibility of the government on tariff matters was not entirely appreciated, even within the party. Rhetoric was one thing, performance might be another. A variety of reasons were to be found for a continued protectionist hope that the Liberal administration might give way. Neither the depression nor the fiscal deficit showed signs of departing quickly, and the latter in particular was always a motive for increasing tariffs. Liberal leaders also did not entirely stop making quick bows in the direction of incidental protection. That was needed to maintain a hold on the protectionists in Liberal ranks, who at the parliamentary level included A. Irving and A.T. Wood of Hamilton, T. Workman and Devlin from Montreal, and W. Paterson from Brant South, as well as some of a milder stripe such as James Young or John Macdonald. Gentle protectionist urgings came from such stalwarts as Ontario Lieutenant Governor D.A. Macdonald who, in early 1877, dryly told Blake that there were problems in the way of the government adjusting the tariff, 'but as you had a whole year to think over what is best to be done, I have no doubt you will be able to get over the difficulty.'[43] Then also, protectionist forces had lacked sufficient organization and synchronized effort in the campaign of 1876. Had organization been better, one high-tariff man sagely noted, 'by this time enough pressure would have been brought to bear upon the Government to cause them to have done something to alleviate the present depressed state of trade in the country.'[44] Headway might yet be made with the stubborn Liberals.

Whatever the basis of such expectations, they were misplaced. Richard Cartwright showed great ability in denying interest-group demands. His apparent desire to consult with manufacturers prior to the possible tariff changes in 1876 was an exception to the rule. He had not paid much attention to the advice of deputations in 1874, and the abrupt treatment he gave in 1876 was further along the same path. In 1877, the Dominion Board of Trade's secretary found the way Cartwright dealt with the board's memorial on the tariff hypocritical: the finance minister said he had received the memorial too late for consideration for the budget, but the board's secretary had earlier been sent acknowledgment of the memorial's timely arrival![45] The apparent charmlessness of Cartwright's personality did nothing to ease the pain felt by petitioning businessmen. He was a 'vain, pedantic creature,' one embittered sugar refiner fulminated, '– as full of conceit as an egg is full of meat – altogether unable to understand a practical question connected with our trade and commerce.'[46]

Cartwright suffered the brunt of protectionist hostility, perhaps unfairly, as spokesman for the government on matters of economic policy. The revenue-tariff attitude he asserted had increasing support from the Liberal leadership group after 1874. The Conservative differential duty on tea imported from the United States, imposed in 1872 to encourage direct importation via the St Lawrence, was removed by the Liberals and replaced by a general duty on tea for revenue purposes in 1874. After the debacle over the sugar duties in 1874 and 1875, the Liberal government's attitude towards lobbying interests became tougher, and having offended major grocery importers already, the government refused to bend to heavy pressures to have the differential duties on tea reimposed.[47] Any differential duty would discriminate against the smaller importer who bought at New York and was unable to bear the costs of direct importation, and would increase the price of tea to the consumer, all to the profit of a few major Montreal, Toronto, and Halifax importers, the Liberals argued.[48] Similarly, when the salt industry pressed for a protective duty against American competition, the government refused to act though the salt region was in Liberal territory.[49] The liquor interest was offended by the government as well. Excise duties on malt and non-malt beers were raised in 1877, alienating maltsters, brewers, and other liquor interests, an alienation made nearly complete by the Scott Act of 1878 that allowed local prohibition.[50] Possibly in the petitions and deputations that reached the government, the Liberal leaders saw the rings and monopolies they professed to fear.

Even when the Liberals were tempted to deal generously with an interest, they turned niggardly. They only wanted to allow what they thought was legitimate appeasement, such as the equalization of business opportunities in the removal of the differential duties on tea. Maritimes shippers were wooed by the Liberals through plans to expand trade with the Caribbean, but Sir A.T. Galt refused to undertake the necessary trade mission, and the government did nothing but take the plan of subsidizing steamers for the trade under advisement.[51] A taste for caution and free trade also characterized the Liberal dealing with the oil-refining industry in southwestern Ontario. Both crude and refined oil had long received high protection, but on refined oil a high excise duty had been imposed by the Conservatives in 1868, negating some of the protection. The Liberals from the oil region were associated with the interest, and even Alexander Mackenzie had once lobbied in its favour. The public was very aware of the oil-refiners' ring, and the Conservative opposition made efforts to embarrass the government: here were the antimonopoly Liberals encouraging a manufacturers' cabal! The government then made changes that hardly endeared it to the interest. Cartwright reduced both the excise and the customs duties, lowering the protection enjoyed by the refiners. He argued this would eliminate smuggling, and so increase total revenue. But the multitude of small crude-oil producers did not have their protection reduced. Refiners were left dissatisfied by the Greek gift: in 1879 they pushed the Conservatives for a higher customs duty.[52] The lumbering industry, for which admittedly little could be done, secured a limited concession in 1875, when the export duty on stave bolts and oak logs was removed.[53] Again, that was in the direction of equalizing opportunity for the export lumberman or frontier settler with those who had combined lumbering and sawing facilities. The drift of Liberal policy was towards the encouragement of competition, and the equalization of opportunity. At the same time, some of the Liberal legislation was focused on southwestern Ontario, a party stronghold.

The Mackenzie administration's ability to say 'no' to the interests was most severely tested in 1877 in the matter of the coal industry. The lesson of 1876 to the industry was that a consistent and organized stand had to be taken and an understanding with central Canadian manufacturers reached if the government was to be forced to raise the tariff. A tremendous push took place in early 1877. Meetings were held by the colliery owners in Halifax in early January, when it was decided that the interest required either a bounty equivalent to the American tariff on coal exported to the United States, or a duty of 50 cents per ton on all coal imported. More than 100 men of standing in the industry signed a petition to the Dominion Board of Trade making these demands, and the colliery owners decided that they had to make a good showing at the board meeting, 'with a view to impressing upon the Board the necessity of its urging the Government to adopt measures to foster the Coal Trade.' Shortly after this, a Pictou Board of Trade was organized, and it sent a petition to the government asking for either bounty or duty. Though the Pictou Board of Trade was unable to send delegates to the Dominion Board meeting, the Cape Breton organization was represented. The coal interest was to be ignored no longer.[54]

Potential for an alliance with central Canadian protectionist interests had improved. W.H. Howland, who had long advocated reciprocal tariffs on Nova Scotian coal and central Canadian foodstuffs, was the leading protectionist figure at the Ottawa Dominion Board meeting. Intent on having a comprehensive protectionist position adopted, Howland read the Maritimers a quick lesson in the unacceptability of special interests being tariff-sheltered: 'He wished to say to the representatives of the Maritime Provinces, they would not have an opportunity of voting for protection to certain industries of Nova Scotia, and against the general principle of a protective tariff.'[55]

The several members of the Mackenzie administration watching must have been relieved to see the Dominion Board vote down the protectionist resolution Howland wanted by a single vote. A modest incidental-protection motion passed which, as has been noted, Cartwright chose to ignore. Despite the manoeuvring at the meeting, an understanding was being affirmed between coal and manufacturing interests, between region and region. Howland had moved his amendment so as to, in his words, 'show how entirely I sympathize with our friends from the Maritime Provinces, and to prove that our friends in the West are prepared to make a reasonable sacrifice on their behalf.'[56] The understanding was to be asserted more vigorously yet.

The coal industry's push had just begun. Assiduous writers to the Nova Scotian papers pressed for a unified position in the province on the coal question, or at least silence from those who did not agree with the colliery owners.[57] A flood of petitions advocating a bounty on, or tariff protection for, coal reached the House of Commons in February.[58] They precipitated the Parliamentary Select Committee on the Coal Trade. Though some observers thought that the coal issue was going to be whitewashed, the committee stimulated even more widespread concern in Nova Scotia.[59] Central Canadian interests proved anxious to tie the coal question into the issue of a general protective system: the Toronto and Hamilton boards of trade both passed resolutions favouring a duty on coal, but only in the event of a general revision of the tariff towards protection. The passage of those resolutions was a crucial development, for a major group of commercial men were now supporting protection. The changing character of trade and marketing was biting deep.[60]

George Stephen's letter to the newspapers in March 1877 brilliantly exemplified the attempt to make the coal question one involving a general developmental policy. The letter bore witness also to how far Stephen had removed himself from the party in power. After some contemptuous words for those who placed narrow self-interest above broad protectionist policy, the Montreal financier and industrialist came to coal. He had never met a Canadian manufacturer, he stated, 'who would object to a moderate duty of say seventy-five cents a ton, on bituminous coal, which is the only kind of coal Nova Scotia produces, *provided the impost formed a part of a general scheme of tariff reform* ... On the other hand, I have never met a manufacturer who would consent to a duty, either large or small, except on the condition stated. So it is, perhaps, just as well our Nova Scotian friends should understand this.' The businessman finished his missive by applying the lash to the Liberal government: they were incapable of giving 'themselves to the patriotic but difficult task of harmonising these various interests' in a general tariff reform.[61]

The Nova Scotian witnesses before the select committee echoed Stephen's position about a coal duty being part of a larger system of protection. Said

American Robert Belloni, part owner and manager of a coal-mine in Cow Bay, Cape Breton, 'Yes, I think we would' derive an advantage from 'increased protection to our own manufactures as well as protection to coal.' The manager of the Albion Mines at Pictou agreed a duty on coal would expand the market in central Canada for Nova Scotian coal. 'We would not object to a 25 cents duty on flour,' he added. Indeed, these and other enthusiastic men felt that increased coal production for central Canadian markets would lower coal prices, and that a market for Nova Scotian coal in Quebec and Ontario could enlarge Maritime demand for central Canadian goods.[62]

Conciliatory protectionist opinion in central Canada had come to accept at least the political usefulness of a duty on some types of coal, but many still rejected the idea. Low prices for American coal, and the high costs of transporting the Nova Scotian substitute to Ontario made a coal duty unappealing. Besides, Nova Scotian bituminous could not replace American anthracite for many industrial applications, and a duty on anthracite was unacceptable to many protectionists, as Stephen's letter made clear.[63] The Liberal government rejected the idea of protection to coal as well, a position for which it had at least some justification in the failure of the parliamentary committee to make any clear-cut recommendations. The entire exercise seemed futile.

Except that it had political ramifications. Unlike a year earlier, at least a superficial unity pervaded the Nova Scotian coal industry in 1877. Charles Tupper's sympathetic treatment of the Nova Scotian witnesses before the parliamentary committee indicated how carefully the Conservatives were cultivating the industry. Sir John A. Macdonald, among others in the Commons, expressed solicitude for the mining interest. The opposition leader took care to quote George Stephen's letter at length, and urged the necessity of 'united action with regard to all the great interests of the country ... to raise them out of the Slough of Despond into which all our industries had sunk.' If they were accused of encouraging a log-rolling action, he said, he could rightly point out that only by co-operative action could a heavy log be moved. The resolution he presented piously genuflected to fiscal restraint, but its heart lay in the demand for 'a readjustment of the tariff' to benefit agriculture and manufacturing – and mining as well.[64] If some Nova Scotian colliery owners felt an attachment to the American market (as shown by the demand for an export bounty to counteract the American coal duty) and still felt the urgency of reciprocity, as did both J.R. Lithgow and R.G. Haliburton, the events of 1877 shook them in their views, and directed them towards protection and the Conservatives. Lithgow, who even in 1879 was struggling to reconcile free-trade perspectives with the immediate interests of his industry, had moved into the Conservative camp by 1878.[65]

Prospective sugar refiners in Nova Scotia, who had good political reasons to hope for concessions from the Liberal government, must have been disappointed in the 1877 tariff, which literally ignored the industry. By 1880, if not before, the West Indies merchant W.J. Stairs was calling himself a political independent.[66] George Gordon Dustan, a tediously persistent correspondent on the matter of sugar duties (he hoped to operate a refinery at Dartmouth), found little sympathy in Richard Cartwright as early as 1875 and turned to Edward Blake and David Mills as figures of power within the Liberal party. Rejection by these men turned Dustan to the Conservatives with a commitment of despair and in splenetic fury against the Liberals. In the election campaign of 1878, the Halifax Conservative newspaper played on the connection between the West Indies trade and sugar refineries, between commercial and industrial protection, and Charles Tupper and Sir John A. Macdonald were both highly conscious of these issues as means of prying Liberal voters away from their allegiance.[67]

The tariff of 1877 repudiated protection for protection's sake in ways other than not providing for sugar refining and coal interests. Diminishing returns had not yet set in on tariff increases, Cartwright argued when he presented the budget, especially as prices and thus *ad valorem* revenue were dropping precipitately. More revenue was needed, and the tariff changes reflected this: the excise on malt and non-malt beers was increased, as were the customs duties on malt and imported beers; the excise and customs on oil was altered as previously noted; the customs duties on tea, cigars, and perfumes were raised; and those on various types of cotton and linen thread, and on iron, brass, and copper tubing were greatly increased.[68] The textile industry, and those who needed the drawn tubing that was integral to manufacturing boilers, gas lines, and piping and was not made in Canada, were affronted and others were upset, all in the name of revenue.

Many of the Montreal manufacturers had been alienated from the Liberals by 1876; by early 1877, if George Stephen was a good barometer, these figures were swinging into opposition. 'At present there is d – – – – d little encouragement to risk anything in Canadian enterprises, which are nearly all equally bad,' Stephen wrote to Sir John A. Macdonald, strengthening ties once nearly severed. 'I do not suppose this Govt. will deal with the depression which daily becomes deeper & darker.' Sir A.T. Galt, who had flirted with the idea of joining the Liberals, now harshly and publicly repudiated Justice Minister David Mills for the latter's interpretation of Galt as a rigid free trader.[69] These two men had never been more than in the attenuated periphery of the Liberal party, but the growing depression, an ever increasing supply of protectionist propaganda, and a more emphatic protectionist stance by the Conservatives began to weed protectionists and manufacturers out of Liberal ranks that no longer seemed anxious to hold them. A key loss for the Liberals was W.H. Howland, former president of the Toronto Board of Trade, one-time president of the Dominion Board, and president of the Ontario Manufacturers' Association. A Canada First nationalist, and a commercial and industrial protectionist, Howland had long made his views known. He had in 1874 financed the Canada First weekly, the *Nation*, which had taken a protectionist editorial position.[70] Family background and a powerful loyalty to Edward Blake, however, associated him with the Liberals. But by late 1876, he began to be assailed by doubts, asking Blake whether he should let the *Nation* expire rather than see it 'instrumental in making the moderates & independents side with the Tory Party.' If this was intended to press Blake and the Liberals toward protection, it failed, for Blake replied that the paper should die.[71] Without any real additional protection in the tariff changes of 1877, and with Blake's resignation from the government, Howland parted company with the Liberals. 'I cant stand it any longer,' he burst out to Blake. 'I do think the fiscal policy of the Govt. simply ruinous to the country and as you all seem to delight in being led by such lunatics as Cartwright ... I must give up my earnest and honest attempt to wait for yourself and the moderates to take control of affairs. I can assure you that I am just sick and miserable over the matter but as I said at first I know politically that the *fanatic* free trade policy is all wrong and I would do my best to assist you to get rid of such incubi.'[72]

Blake could no longer lead any struggle against Howland's free-trade nightmares. The only remaining hope was the Tories 'with whom,' Howland said, 'I may have to act for a time [though] I have little sympathy or liking [for them].'[73] Stephen, Galt, and Howland were crucial converts to the Tory cause because of the immense influence they wielded, but they were not the only ones to openly commit themselves to the Conservatives. Bennett Rosamond, the Almonte and Cornwall woollens manufacturer who was under Stephen's influence, had wavered in Conservative allegiance in the late 1860s and had for a time converted to the Liberal cause, but he was an active protectionist who campaigned for the Tories in 1878. James Goldie, the Guelph miller, broke with the Liberals in 1876, and stood for their opponents in the election of 1878. Robert Barber, a woollens manufacturer, Mr A. Paton, another, Robert Hay, a major Toronto furniture manufacturer who became a Conservative candidate, D. Ferguson, involved in manufacturing steam fire-engines, A.M. Ross, a London manufacturer John Haggart, an agricultural-implements manufacturer, and Wm Wilkie, a sewing-machine manufacturer of Guelph, all publicly moved from Liberal to Conservative ranks for the purpose of the 1878 election. Mr Mullarkey, the major shoe manufacturer of Montreal, confessed to having followed the same route. 'Here in Hamilton,' wrote one overly optimistic Conservative during the election campaign, 'I have talked with the proprietors of the extensive foundries in this city, and I can assure you that while one of them will be a supporter of the present Ministry, all condemn the policy of the Government, and all save that one will gave their strength to defeat them.' The same man could find only three foundrymen in Montreal who intended supporting the Liberals.[74]

Even manufacturers who had strong free-trade biases were not immune to conversion. Take, for example, the case of John Newton, a small Limehouse manufacturer of woollen blankets. Newton's business contracted sharply during 1876, and from his complaints, he was hurting as a creditor. Free-trade sentiments were expressed in his advertising circulars though he encouraged a 'buy Canadian' policy.[75] His analysis of the economic crisis followed standard liberal lines: it was a crisis of over-production and excessively easy credit. But in autumn 1876, Newton attended a Milton picnic at which Sir John A. Macdonald spoke. Shaken in his free-trade resolves, he took it upon himself to write to Macdonald affirming them. Newton feared that protective tariffs could not remove depression and would result in monopoly, the destruction of the middle class, and a consequent confrontation between rich and poor. There would be 'no community of feeling, because, I suppose, there is no common interest between employer and employed.'[76] Sir John took the trouble to reply, and though the politician passed over problems of class division, he indicated that he, too, was opposed to monopoly. However, the Canadian market had to be protected from slaughtering, and manufacturers had to be given a secure market. Native competition, the politician optimistically promised, would keep down prices. And though protection could not stop the roller-coaster effect of the business cycle, it would speedily correct the present depression.[77] Instead of confirming Newton in his free-trade views, the urbane exchange brought him to accept the necessity of tariff changes. 'A correct foreign commercial policy,' he later wrote Macdonald in a style reminiscent of a school-boy recitation, 'must rest on a friendly, fair & enlightened basis, neither desiring nor granting special favours. This meant equalization of our Tariffs in our dealings with the United States, as well as with all other nations.'[78] His advertising circulars took on a protectionist note, and though Newton did not reject all his earlier analysis, he grafted protectionism onto it.

If the picnic meetings of 1876 had won Macdonald the support of men like Newton, and the parliamentary struggle of 1877 brought new converts and the return of old allies once nearly lost, the campaigning of that summer brought him moments of political ecstasy. His tour of the Eastern Townships in Quebec during the picnic season was particularly rewarding: in Sherbrooke, for example, the proprietor of a large woollen mill assembled the workingmen and introduced Macdonald to them as the potential saviour of the country.[79] Remarkably sympathetic crowds graced his meetings, and thus stimulated, Macdonald made speeches that had a vehement protectionist edge, speeches that had great emotive force. At Bury in early July: 'We do not wish our young men to leave us. We do not want the power and strength of the country to go to the United States, to add to the wealth and strength of a foreign country. We want to keep Canada for the Canadians. We wish to see manufactories established in every town and village in the Dominion. We want to see the farmer sending his son, that does not take to farming, not to a foreign country, but to the neighbouring village, to become an artizan, a tradesman, a manufacturer.' The forceful sentences, with their appeal to a defensive nationalism and to an envisioned harmonious community then became explosive:

> Let the agriculturist and the manufacturer join together; let there be no selfish divergence of interest! I tell the manufacturer that unless he gives protection to the farmer, the farmer will not give protection to him. I say the same thing to the farmer ... It is only by the conjunction of interests, by saying if the whole world were shut out from us, if we did not receive a single article from abroad, we have such a soil, such a climate, and such resources, that we could, unaided, make this country great, rich, glorious, and educated, and develop it to the utmost extent by the skill, energy, and self-reliance of our people ... This is what I look for; this is what I pray for.[80]

The crowd cheered. Macdonald's tour was crowned and ended in Montreal where he was met by a vast assemblage optimistically estimated by the 9 July *Mail* at 75,000. The protectionist policy was forged; the Macdonald Conservatives had taken on the task of harmonizing the interests and persuading the nation of the righteousness of the cause.

The revenue tariff, free-trade outlook of the Liberal leadership hardened considerably in 1876 and thereafter, though it was rooted in perspectives held much earlier. Crucially important in the hardening process was wavering over the tariff in 1876, at which time the Liberal party committed itself to a basic electoral strategy. The low-tariff stance then taken, the leaders seemed convinced, could hold Ontario and the Maritimes and reduce dependency on the uncertain fortunes of the party's Quebec wing. The policy direction chosen also accorded with deeply held Liberal beliefs about the character of economic development in the new nation, and allowed Cartwright and other leaders to put aside half-hearted efforts to conciliate protectionist interests. Cartwright seemed to glory in a nearly unalloyed pursuit of revenue in his tariff changes of 1877. While those of 1874 were largely of the same character, they had included some concessions to special interests. Perhaps the rumoured changes would also have included concessions of this sort. These possibilities were never realized.

Coal was the crucial issue in 1877. If the Liberal government could be persuaded to foster this staple industry, protectionists reasoned, they could be forced to reconsider the whole tariff. No accommodations were reached, however, and protection-leaning industrialists moved into the ambit of the Conservative party in growing numbers. The hard conditions of depression made many of them desperate, the desire for market control eager. The Conservatives did their best to accommodate. Macdonald's treatment of the outraged Montreal manufacturers in 1876, his reasoned and friendly exchange with John Newton, his party's efforts in parliament in 1877 and his work on the campaign trail in that summer indicate some elements of the accommodation.

But only some, for these incidents portray manufacturers in a passive role, being shunted from party to party. Many businessmen pursued their own interests actively in an organizational framework, though in growing co-operation with the Conservatives. Some remained adherents of the Liberals.

9

The interests, the parties, and the election of 1878

A basic function of protectionist ideologues and organizations for twenty years prior to the election, had been to draw disparate interests into common political purpose and to combat the perception of protection as a class interest and prelude to monopoly. After 1876, as the political spectrum on the issue polarized, the task was increasingly shared with the Conservative party. The lines dividing party and interest associations became somewhat blurred. Though industrialists' and party organizations were both of importance in gaining the Conservative victory, the organizational principle had considerable limitations in practice. Had protectionist associations been widespread, sophisticated in action, and united in purpose, it is not likely that an alliance with the Conservatives would have been necessary.

After a slump of activity due to the disappointments of the parliamentary session of 1876, there were renewed organizational efforts among protectionist manufacturers. In the months before the annual meeting of the Ontario Manufacturers' Association in October 1877, secretary W.H. Frazer criss-crossed Ontario holding meetings to recruit businessmen.[1] The attendance at the meeting was, as a result, good though not as impressive as president W.H. Howland may have wished. While some 300 or more had attended the first major meeting of the association in 1874, around 50 were present in 1877.[2] However, when Howland asserted that those 50 were among the largest employers in Canada, he was not mistaken. Robert Hay, the furniture manufacturer of Toronto, employed some 500 hands; about 150 were employed by F.F. McArthur in the same line of business in Bowmanville; Edward Gurney and his father had roughly 1000 people dependent on the steady working of their two foundries; James Smart, a founder at Brockville, had 75 men in the depths of the depression and 175 in good times; Andrew Elliott and Bennett Rosamond each had some 300 hands in their Almonte mills; also in woollens, the Barber brothers of Georgetow gave work to over 120. The list could be greatly extended.[3]

There was little doubt that these powerful men were offended by the Libera government's attitude and found their relationship with it perverse. 'The Gov ernment,' the major dry-goods wholesaler and cottons manufacturer Donal McInnes flatly stated, 'ought to take the evidence of the people engaged in th business and be guided by it.' E.K. Greene, a fur hat and clothing manufacture of Montreal, agreed. 'He argued that the tariff should be remodelled by th Finance Minister, who, if he consulted with the leading manufacturers, coul not make a mistake.' W.H. Howland pointed out the central function of th convention: 'The meeting was an important one, because before parting the would come to the conclusion that the time was past for making vain appeal for alterations in the tariff, and that the time had come when they must divid the people of Canada at the polls on the question of free trade and protection.' The association's leaders were, however, too wise to commit their movemen overtly to one political party. That would place them in a difficult position wer the Liberals to retain power; even more worrisome was the inevitability of split in their own ranks if an open political alliance were made. The solution? Man ufacturers would be encouraged to support candidates of any political stripe wh supported protection.[5]

More thorough organization was advocated as well. Plans were made to widel distribute copies of the convention proceedings and to set up subsidiary protec tionist groups throughout the province. The major problem of convincing th public of the righteousness of the protectionist cause remained. Combined wit the need to keep the association's political partisanship in low profile, this mad another organization desirable.

In late March 1878, the Dominion National League was formed to fit the bi by combining protectionist mechanics, farmers, and manufacturers into a move ment and to convince the unconvinced to take up the cause. A concoction c the Ontario Manufacturers' Association and leading Conservatives, the leagu was supposed to seem independent. Its executive committee was composed c eight professed Reformers and five Conservatives, and the founding meeting a Hamilton was heavily attended by manufacturers of both political persuasions. Harmony of interests was to be pursued, though in a somewhat conspiratori way.

That the Dominion National League had the Manufacturers' Association a one parent is explicit in a printed circular sent out from the Hamilton office c the league in April; the circular tried to drum up financial support from manu facturers. Indeed, the organizer of the league and its main speaker was non other than W.H. Frazer, the secretary of the Ontario Manufacturers' Associatior

Ie held his position in the league as a favour to W.H. Howland, with whom e had associated in Canada First. Frazer proved unsatisfactory in rousing the nasses and the classes, however. A.W. Wright, a labour journalist and organizer, vas added as another speaker on the instigation of Sir John A. Macdonald and)onald McInnes, the Conservative vice-president of the Manufacturers' Asso- iation.[7] Further evidence of the collusion of the association and the Conser- 'atives over the league is to be found in Frazer's letter to Sir John, outlining ome of the basic strategy of the movement. 'It has been found expedient,' wrote 'razer stiffly a day after the league was formed, 'to construct a platform and orm an organization which will meet the views of a large number of Reformers vho will give their support and votes to candidates who will pledge themselves o support the National Policy as enunciated by you in Parliament.' Added Frazer, The formation of a Dominion National League was the subject on which I vished to consult with you personally' and he asked Macdonald to place his mprimatur on the policy resolution of the league.[8]

First Frazer alone, and then accompanied by Wright, toured the province, preading the gospel to all who cared to listen. A fair number did care – 200 ttended a Waterloo meeting, for example – and watched protection expounded, nd then in turn free trade. For in order to make the Dominion National League n effective recruiting agent for the protectionist cause, independents and Liberals ad to be attracted, and to attract them the League even requested speakers to lefend free trade. At each meeting, people were encouraged to join the league, n act that involved a pledge to vote only for candidates who advocated protection.[9]

As the campaign advanced through the summer, the league identified more nd more closely with the Conservatives. Frazer began to appear on the platform vith the party's candidates; he began to arrange meetings in tandem with them. Co-operating with the Toronto Conservative Workingmen's Union or Asso- iation, the league built an amphitheatre in the city at the end of July, where peakers could hold forth on protection before working-class audiences two or hree times a week. These meetings were superficially open to speakers advo- ating free trade, but such men were not welcomed. By August, the identification f the league with the Conservatives for all practical purposes was complete.[10]

How great was the league's impact? Its limitations were considerable. As a ne-shot electoral device, its organization was shallow, its program, leaders, nd itinerary hastily drawn together. Frazer was at best an uninspiring rote peaker, and he had a prickly sensitivity to criticism that could quickly place im on the defensive.[11] These weaknesses made it necessary to add A.W. Wright o the speaking team, which may have slanted the league toward an urban and vorking-class audience, limiting its usefulness in other contexts.

The weaknesses of the league were perhaps a reflection of the limits of the

Ontario Manufacturers' Association. Formidable on paper with 150 members claimed, the association had been enfeebled by its failure to achieve any increase in the tariff in 1876; in addition it was young and the product of an enthusiasm among manufacturers that might wane just as it had flared. Attendance at meetings was uneven, and the finances of the association were troubled. In 1877 and 1878 at least, bills went unpaid. The secretary of the Dominion Board of Trade was reduced to dunning Howland and Frazer in order to get the association to pay its dues to the board.[12] Pique may have been part of the reason for this in 1877 when the Dominion Board had not moved to the advanced protectionist position the association wanted; but Howland explained that he had been unable to collect the money from association members. The dues were finally dredged out of the manufacturers, but the next year, when the board proved more amenable to protection and the association was at a height of power, Frazer was again being dunned by the board for payment of dues. The Manufacturers' Association actually ran deficits in both 1877 and 1878 and may have in others years as well. Chronic under-financing drove Frazer on one occasion to the extreme of issuing drafts on the membership with hardly any notice.[13] The evident lethargy of the membership was not entirely surprising. The benefits of tariff alterations could accrue to non-members as well as members, of course, which did not encourage membership. But more strikingly, the association had not proved itself effective in gaining appropriate tariff changes. While the Liberal government granted a strong legitimacy to the Dominion Board of Trade through a variety of means, including the attendance of cabinet members at the board meetings, no such legitimacy was granted the Ontario Manufacturers' Association. It was not a fully effective channel for the expression and implementation of manufacturers' views in the context of Liberal rule.

Nowhere else in Canada did the manufacturers show the degree of organized effort in relation to the election as in Ontario. The Nova Scotia manufacturers' association, briefly organized in 1874 to demand protection, did not again appear, not even when the tariff of 1879 was being framed. The colliery owners had formed associations in the late 1860s, in 1875, and in 1877, but the association of 1877 rapidly faded away, as had its predecessors. There was hard competition in the coal trade; there was a tendency to focus demands through individual MPs and occasional outbursts of petitioning; such factors made a coal association difficult to maintain. For a time, a healthy Manufacturers' and Mechanics' Association had existed in Saint John, New Brunswick, but financial over-commitment in an industrial exhibition in 1875 was a problem that, compounded with the depression and the great fire of 1877, made the organization impossible to maintain. The generous hand of the federal government in aiding the city to its feet by various projects made opposition to the Liberals harder to justify.[14] Only when plans were being laid for tariff changes in 1879 did the Saint John association reappear.

The failure of the Quebec manufacturers to organize in the face of the election is particularly surprising. The Montreal Manufacturers' and Mechanics' Association remained quiescent from late 1875 until after the election of 1878. The manufacturers may have been wise not to agitate among workingmen who had been on the verge of riot in the winter of 1875–76, but a consideration of this character was unimportant in an election campaign where plenty of agitation was the norm. The industrialists may not have felt the need to convince each other or workingmen of the need for protection, for there was widespread agreement in Montreal on the matter. A number of the city's capitalists also had considerable investments in Ontario enterprises, and some attended the conventions of the Ontario Manufacturers' Association, finding organizational expression there.[15] The huge factories concentrated in the Montreal region represented investments by a limited body of industrialists and capitalists. Informal, non-organizational consultation was much more possible than in Ontario. Powerful Montreal manufacturers also had close links with Macdonald and other figures in the Conservative leadership,[16] so their opinions might receive more direct political expression.

The campaign mounted by the Ontario Manufacturers' Association and the Dominion National League was unusual, and some of its importance derives from this very fact. It provided a focus and stimulus for the protectionist activities of manufacturers, the urban working class, and to a lesser degree the farmers. Supplemented as it was by the writing and speaking of the journalist E.K. Dodds and other activities of the Canada Brewers' and Maltsters' Association and the Licensed Victuallers' Association (the liquor interest),[17] the campaign formed a basic element in the Conservative electoral victory.

Individual manufacturers, inspired by the association and league, often also gave a great deal of aid to the Conservative cause. Manufacturers and other businessmen could offer influence and money to the political parties. Influence was vital. Prestige in the general community and among peers counted a great deal for a businessman; the influence he had as an employer was of equally great importance in an election. It is impossible to define the nature and extent of this sort of influence with any precision; it varied from place to place, from employer to employer, from employee to employee. The upsurge of unionism in the early 1870s, which paralleled organizational activities among other social groups, showed that skilled workmen in major urban centres were making a sharp distinction between their interests and those of their employers.[18] Yet unions were few in number, their total membership was minuscule, and the depression destroyed most of their strength. Even those who formed unions did not necessarily think that their interests were constantly opposed to those of their employers.[19] In addition, the workingman knew the coercive power of his employer; the advantages of the secret ballot, used for the first time in a federal general election in 1878, were perhaps not immediately apparent. Finally, there were strong elements of paternalism and deference in many employer/employee relationships.

It makes some sense to examine the relationship between a work-force and an employer at the time of the election in brief detail. Most jobs in Almonte, a town in the Ottawa valley, were in a few large woollen mills located there to take advantage of the water-power. One major mill was run and largely owned by Bennett Rosamond, and another by Andrew Elliott, both figures of importance in the Ontario Manufacturers' Association. Elliott encouraged his employees to boycott merchants and mechanics in the area who did not support a higher tariff, it was alleged.[20] But it was Rosamond who gained the greater notoriety in his extension of paternalism to politics. Just two weeks before the election, Rosamond called his employees together and advised them to vote Conservative. There is no record of his precise words, but some of his listeners interpreted them to mean that those who did not vote Conservative would lose their jobs. Rosamond denied that there was anything wrong in his suggesting to his employees how they should vote, and denied that he used any threat. As he wrote to the *Globe*,

> 1. No voter in our employment stated that I told the hands 'if they did not vote for Mr. Jamieson they would lose their employment.' I have a certificate to this effect signed by all the voters ...
> 2. I did not admit that I had 'used words that certainly bore out that construction,' and
> 3. I did not tell our hands on the Monday following [Rosamond called a second meeting due to the rumours] that 'they had misunderstood me.' On the contrary, I said that certain statements were being made on the street, and I asked them if they understood me to have made use of words which would bear out these statements, and they could not say they thought I had. I then repeated my words of the previous Saturday, and several called out that I was correct.[21]

Rosamond's evident belief in the rectitude of his behavior and in the honesty of his employees is touching, but is undermined by the logical circularity created by the potential of intimidation in his dealings with them. His and Elliott's advice to their employees did have considerable effect: in Almonte the Conservative candidate received 262 votes, and the Liberal 152, which was all the more impressive as the Liberal won in the traditionally Liberal riding.[22]

The situation in Almonte was not unique. Employees were squeezable; they were deferential; they could be persuaded that their interests were as one with their employers'. Consider Donald Robb, the workingmen's candidate in the 1874 Halifax election, who was actually a 'boss mechanic' hiring and firing men.[23] And we can recall the massed troops of boot and shoe manufacturer Guillaume Boivin in confronting A.L. Jetté, the Montreal Liberal MP, or Boivin's repeated reference to 'we' in speaking of himself, his workers, and the industry: 'We are forming an association of mechanics.' Donald McInnes' treatment of his people at his Cornwall factory was frankly coercive according to his own suggestive statement: the people there 'are all under my *thumb*.'[24] The employees of the Dominion Paper Company all voted correctly, the manager of the firm boasted to Sir John A. Macdonald after the election.[25] One Quebec clothing manufacturer put his demand for protection in these suggestive words: 'It is not necessary for us to say how much influence women [his employees] have in political matters when they choose to make use of their influence.'[26] Speechifying by manufacturers carried the same message.[27] The lessons inherent in having major employers appear on the platform with Conservative candidates, or for that matter the candidatures of manufacturers such as Samuel Merner, Samuel Platt, James Goldie, Robert Hay, T.N. Gibbs, M.H. Gault, or James Domville were surely not lost to employees either. What worked at lower levels worked at higher levels, too. Donald McInnes, whose notions tended to the coercive, suggested that George Stephen use his powers to sway employers, 'but as Pres of the Bank of Montreal he must be discreet – and later can keep his axes in good condition.'[28]

Nevertheless, workingmen were not to be led or prodded like so many sheep. While it might be perfectly evident to them that their interests were allied with those of their employers, skilled workmen especially expected to be addressed as a separate interest. So the Dominion National League had A.W. Wright as a speaker, identified as he was with the working class. So, too, protectionist public meetings in the 1870s occasionally had labour leaders on the platform, to speak to their fellows in the audience.[29] The Conservatives who had appealed to working-class interests through the Trade Union Act of 1872 also encouraged the formation of the Workingmen's Liberal Conservative Union in Toronto, which then aided in the construction of the amphitheatre. Labourers there heard speeches not only from politicians and manufacturers, but frequently from fellow workingmen. And both parties had meetings held exclusively by and for the workingmen.[30] Here the unity of interests fostered by employers generally and protectionists especially entered ambiguous territory.

Despite the work of protectionist organizations and individual manufacturers, the weight of the campaign had to be carried by the Conservative party. The Pacific Scandal and the disastrous results of the election of 1874 badly dispirited Conservatives, and to boost morale in Ontario, a provincial party convention was held in the autumn of the year. Little policy making took place, but plans were laid to strengthen the party's organization. A steady stream of riding associations were set up in the four years that followed. The convention also planned to set up a Conservative club in Toronto, to combine social and political life, to provide an organizational heart for the party.

A name reminiscent of the long-time Tory loyalty cry was chosen: the United Empire Club. The details of the Toronto-based club's existence do not concern us here; what does is that it became a clearing house for the decisions of the Ontario Conservative élite. A political secretary for the club was appointed at the beginning of 1878, and the eager lawyer Jack Macdonell thus came to arrange a multitude of details relating to riding associations, pamphlet publication and distribution, advice to candidates, and the channelling of whatever funds the central party organization had.[31]

Of money Macdonell did not have an endless supply. Manufacturers only made up a limited portion of the United Empire Club's membership, and both they and the Conservative leaders were understandably anxious to avoid anything that smelled like the Pacific Scandal.[32] Charles Tupper was given the job of gathering the money that Macdonell required for his work as political secretary, and Tupper's notebook records a failure to reach the stated goal of $5000 to $10,000. Equally noteworthy, Tupper asked for contributions from his fellow Conservative MPs as often as from businessmen. There is evidence to show that Macdonell asked for funds from major Conservative businessmen, but how much the political secretary received is not at all clear.[33] It was certainly not enough, for he resorted to tactics like having third persons who provided a service for the party bill Tory stalwarts directly, rather than himself. One possible source of money for the central party organization was the selling of United Empire Club debentures to the Conservative wealthy,[34] a process that began in 1874 when money was being collected for the construction of the club building. But the club was in financial straits after the election, when a desperate membership drive was undertaken, and Sir John A. Macdonald authorized one or two back-room Conservatives to press supposedly grateful manufacturers for the funds to rescue the institution.[35] The manufacturers were insufficiently grateful: the club was forced to fold.

It seems fairly certain that the central Conservative organization in Ontario was not lavishly funded by manufacturers expecting appropriate rates of return in the tariff, insofar as few leading Liberals in the province thought that the Conservatives had used corrupt practices or large sums of money to gain votes, but had depended largely on the tariff issue.[36] Candidates of the party had to finance their campaigns through the usual traditional means – their own and a few friends' pockets. That, of course, was a useful avenue for manufacturers' money. Probably most of the funds collected through the United Empire Club went to finance the extensive pamphlet campaign, Macdonell's work, and that of Frazer and Wright, for the Dominion League failed to finance its own operations.[37]

The Conservative/protectionist alliance leading to the election, though loose, was a relatively sophisticated political device. Conservative party organizations, from the United Empire Club to the constituencies, also reached an advanced level. Campaign strategies, such as the political picnics of 1876 and 1877 or the amphitheatre for workingmen in Toronto reflected organizational strength. These were vital in the victory of the party in Ontario, as was the careful framing of a policy statement on the central issue of the tariff.

The Conservatives did not develop their final policy position for nearly two years after the important parliamentary session of 1876. The mature version of party tariff policy, decided upon at the Toronto Conservative Convention of January 1878 and presented to the House of Commons in the session, was modest and comprehensive. The word 'protection' nowhere appeared; rather, the Conservatives found they wanted 'a judicious readjustment of the Tariff' in order to 'benefit the agricultural, the mining, the manufacturing and other interests.' Collective fears and aspirations of Canadians were touched on. A 'National Policy' would prevent Canadians from emigrating, would renew prosperity for 'our struggling industries,' and would bring an expansion of trade between provinces. Finally, in one cunningly phrased clause, extreme protectionists, those who wanted tariff retaliation and those who desired reciprocity were offered hope, for the National Policy 'moving (as it ought to do) in the direction of a reciprocity of tariffs with our neighbours, so far as the varied interests of Canada may demand, will greatly tend to procure for this country, eventually, a reciprocity of trade.'[38] Appeals to the interests, to Canadian nationalism, and to the ambivalent feelings many Canadians had towards the United States had been carefully blended together. Room was allowed for those unwilling to go beyond incidental protection. The potential for progress had been implicitly contrasted with the existing depression and the negativism of the Liberals. And while the policy indicated a political direction, it contained no specific items that might offend special interests and its design was so open that it could be embroidered to enhance its local or regional appeal.

For all its awkwardness and length, the policy statement was, therefore, a splendid political stroke. How splendid could be appreciated by the Liberal free-trade MP and New Brunswick lumberman A.H. Gillmor, who had one friend enthusiastically tell him that the policy could achieve wide acceptance in the province, 'for as we understand it, it simply means a re-adjustment of the tariff, with a view of revenue mainly, but incidentally to protect such interests as are now suffering from the one-sided free trade that allows the U.S. to supply all our markets. And it is contended that this can be done without very much increasing the *aggregate of taxation*, as Protection sometimes [can] be had by *lowering* as well as by *raising* duties. At all events more taxation seems inevitable to meet the deficit, and a *re-adjustment* does not seem inadvisable.'[39] This was an interpretation Macdonald encouraged, though at times he could be much more vehemently protectionist.

But vehement protectionism could have devastating effects in areas where opinion was not settled. The Liberals in New Brunswick during the election campaign belaboured the possibility of a tax on breadstuffs and coal, much to Conservative distress. 'Protection does not seem to go down very well in N.B. [and so] will have to be dealt with very gingerly,' the New Brunswick capitalist and protectionist MP James Domville informed Sir John.[40] The Liberal papers reported in July 1878 that Macdonald was advocating a 35 per cent tariff, and the province's Conservatives were terror-stricken, telegraphing and writing the Tory leader pleading for denial. Macdonald obliged, but the apocryphal story did not die. The province, dependent on lumber exports, and requiring agricultural imports, could reap no advantage from a protective tariff, many inhabitants reasoned. Poor party organization in New Brunswick compounded Conservative problems, and the election saw a majority of Liberals returned there.

Nominally moderate Conservative tariff policy was thus accompanied by high-tariff overtones. The overtones were very much the responsibility of local Tory candidates and speakers such as Frazer and Wright, but Macdonald, too, could be quoted as favouring a high protective tariff: 'Let each manufacturer tell us what he wants, and we will try to give him what he needs.'[41] In light of this the Liberal attack on protection takes on additional meaning. The Conservatives had to be portrayed as unyielding high protectionists in order to prevent them from capturing moderate voters, and the moderates could then be wooed with the Liberal position of a revenue tariff and some incidental protection.

The Liberals did more than debate with the Conservatives. By the end of 1876, the worried leaders of the Ontario wing of the party had set up the Reform Association of Ontario, with an office in Toronto and with a full time secretary organizer. This was G.R. Pattullo, an energetic journalist who had great faith in the powers of organization. As the election drew nigh, Pattullo could be found charging from one local Liberal meeting to another, giving talks outlining how the riding association should be organized, and providing details about correct canvassing procedures. He put out a booklet containing advice for Liberal workers as well.[42] The party also issued huge numbers of pamphlets, the bulkiest of these being a collection of picnic speeches made by Mackenzie, Cartwright, and other leaders in 1877, of which some 50,000 were printed.[43] Frazer and Wright's protectionist tub-thumpings brought a Liberal reaction as well. The party obtained the services of an eloquent journeyman tailor, Alfred Jury, whose function it was to trail the two Dominion National League men and speak for free trade at the league's meetings when possible, or to hold his own when not. The league's effectiveness was evidently feared by the Liberals, just as Jury's powers disturbed the Tories. Jury was allowed to speak in the Toronto amphitheatre only once. The Liberals also tried to limit Tory inroads in the working-class vote by establishing the Workingmen's Reform Association, in which Jury was a leading figure.[44]

Nor did the Liberal party give up on manufacturers. Some sitting MPs like William Paterson of Brant South, a cigar manufacturer, and John Charlton, the lumberman, rejected their former protectionist inclinations. Others, such as F.T. Frost, an agricultural implements manufacturer, or F.W. Glen, in the same line of business, or the distiller J.P. Wiser, were convinced to run for the party toeing the free-trade-inspired revenue-tariff line. Other manufacturers like James Noxon of Ingersoll, a maker of agricultural implements, stumped for the Liberals denouncing protection, or at least arguing that the depression was of limited severity.[45] The notable incidence of agricultural-implements manufacturers and others dependent on the farming community in this group, and the tendency for such activities to take place in areas where agriculture kept the economy relatively buoyant, shows the material interest interwoven in the position taken.

But the vast common ground of incidental protection in which the bulk of manufacturers were to be found, and which had been more or less amiably shared by both parties for years, had increasingly become a no man's land as protection became a partisan issue. Openly free-trade Liberal manufacturers were something of an exotic breed in 1878, as the *Globe* was willing to admit. Protectionists whose strong party loyalty to the Liberals placed them in an agonizing position took to a variety of expedients. Some found the Manufacturers' Association position and the Dominion National League a solace. James Smart, the iron founder and Liberal protectionist, was requested by the party to stand for election in 1878. Unable to choose between party and interest, he found a tour of Europe an attractive third choice. In the last week or so of the campaign, the Liberal press even crowed when protectionist manufacturers stated they could not trust the Conservatives to act according to promise.[46]

Protectionist Liberal MPs or candidates unwilling to recant also faced difficulties. Thomas Workman, who felt a particular sense of betrayal in 1876, simply did not stand for election in 1878. Toronto Liberal MP John Macdonald, who had advocated a modest protection, stood in 1878, but did not campaign very hard. Fearful of the protectionist storm, or attracted to the idea, a fair number of candidates advocated higher tariffs in public or private. Isaac Burpee (well before the election was called), W. Darling in Montreal, D.B. McLennan at

Cornwall, and Liberal candidates in Peel and Essex Centre all made vague or specific protectionist promises.[47] Both sitting members for Hamilton were Liberal protectionists, and one apparently told manufacturers in the dying days of the election campaign that if the Liberals were returned with a firm base of power, increased tariffs would surely follow. Senator David Macpherson, financier and leading Conservative campaigner, wrote Sir John A. Macdonald worriedly: 'The Hamilton manufacturers are going to desert us I fear.'[48] Desperate Liberal candidates were driven to the expedient of repeating the old claim that the tariff had been increased more by the Mackenzie regime than the previous Conservative one.[49] Indeed, as we have seen, the Liberal government had increased the tariff, but not in a manner satisfactory to protectionists. And though it is likely that the Liberals would have increased the tariff had they been returned to office, such increases would have been focused on enlarging government revenue. That much Cartwright made clear to the governor general before the election.[50]

Protectionist pledges by Liberal candidates proved a poor road to victory. The party was devastated in the election, particularly in urban centres, where however they expected to do poorly. They lost both seats in Hamilton, they lost the two seats in Montreal, they lost in Saint John and Halifax. A.G. Jones complained that the Liberal government's treatment of the sugar question had done him harm in Halifax, and furthermore that the voters had turned on him because of 'the dull times & want of work among the labouring men & mechanics.'[51] In the thirty-two most urbanized ridings in Ontario (two of them double ridings) the Liberals had won 19 seats in 1872; in 1878, they won 9.[52] The enormous impact of the National Policy as an election issue in Ontario ridings where there was substantial industrial activity is made even clearer by correlation analysis. In the twenty-five Ontario seats with the highest level of manufacturing per capita, the higher the industrial value added per capita, the Conservatives obtained in comparison to the Liberals in 1878. The trend was strong (a Pearson correlation of .697). A number of these seats were won by acclamation in 1872; if the remaining 19 are analysed for the election of 1872, there is no observable trend, though the same 19 seats generate a correlation of .694 in the election of 1878. There had been a striking upsurge in voter support for the Conservatives in these ridings from 1872 to 1878. There was also, in the same ridings, a notable correlation between the percentage of the population involved in commercial activities and the tendency to vote Conservative. In Ontario, at least, the tariff issue mattered a great deal.[53] Liberal voters in Ontario were perhaps made confused and uncertain by the force of the Conservative campaign and Liberal negativism, for as G.R. Pattullo was aware, many of those voters did not come out to the polls.[54] The turnout was low in the towns and cities of the province, which in part reflected high levels of population mobility resulting from depression conditions. The Liberal leaders, however, were particularly distraught about the failure of farmers to vote for them in overwhelming numbers, a failure magnified by their ideological attachment to the agrarian community. In the 54 Ontario ridings where agricultural pursuits were dominant, thirty had gone Liberal in 1872. In 1878, the party won only seventeen.[55] Where they had believed themselves to be the strongest, they had proven weak.[56]

The losses sustained in Nova Scotia and Prince Edward Island were almost as upsetting, for the Liberals had hoped that free-trade sentiment would sustain them in some strength there as it had in New Brunswick. The party strategy had been to accept relative weakness in Quebec and to maintain a strong hold in Ontario and the Maritimes, and that failed. Perhaps the Liberal imposition of customs duties on material used in shipbuilding in 1874 still rankled in Nova Scotia. Certainly the Conservative capture of the coal interest, and Tory inroads in commercial circles left the Liberals with a more limited political base. Conservative organization had been very good in the province, and voter turnout, in ironic comparison with Ontario, had been extremely high.[57] In Prince Edward Island, the tariff question had been overshadowed by local tensions over education rooted in religious and ethnic differences, that had led to Liberal defeat.[58]

Party organization in Quebec was left in disarray by infighting and the absence of a strong leader. The temporary advantages offered by the provincial party's victory in the spring of 1878 had rapidly faded.[59] The fundamental obstruction in their way to success in that province, beyond mere organization, had been the anti-Liberalism of the clergy and the ultramontanism that made it acceptable for the clergy to direct the voting habits of the French Canadians. Though this electoral characteristic had been somewhat eroded by 1878, it had by no means disappeared. French-Canadian newspapers, such as *La Minerve* of Montreal, emphasized issues of ethnicity and religion throughout the 1870s, and though the paper turned to protection as the key issue of 1878,[60] a decade's harping on the dangers of Rouge anti-clericalism and the Protestant supremacist attitudes of the Ontario Liberals was not easily forgotten.

However, the matter of free trade and protection was vital in the province. Montreal grain merchants had long been opposed to tariffs that divided their Canadian-American staple-producing hinterland, but it is possible that their opposition to protection was to some degree neutralized by the potential for drawbacks on American grain exported. Moreover, importers whose position was being undercut by the increasing flow of American goods could find some comfort in the National Policy, as was made clear when the Conservatives implemented the 1879 tariff. The attractions of protection to Montreal manufacturers have already been amply illustrated, as has the appeal of protection on an ethnic basis, and its charms for the French-Canadian farmer. Israel Tarte, the master-mind of the Conservative campaign in the province, decided on protection as the key party plank. It proved of crucial importance especially in Montreal, in the Eastern Townships, and also in the Quebec City area. Conservative party organization was superior to that of its opponent. A product of Conservative organizational enthusiasm in 1874, the Club Cartier attracted large numbers of active young men in both Montreal and Quebec City, for example.[61] The Parti national element of the Liberals, its protectionist plank repudiated by the federal leadership, was troubled. L.A. Jetté, one of its leading figures, refused the post of minister of justice in 1877, and failed to run in the election of 1878. Later, some of the Parti national threatened to join the Conservatives.[62] By that point, the Liberals had 18 seats in the province, rather than the 35 of 1874.

The west was a region apart. Eastern politicians, businessmen, and protectionist ideologues generally spoke of the west and the tariff with an eloquent silence. Tariff policy had implications for interprovincial trade and immigration, it was commonly admitted. 'National Policy' implied the rejection of special interests in favour of the broad public good and the encouragement of nationality and collectivity over individual aggrandizement. But the west was almost entirely left out when businessmen discussed specific measures. The trade to be fostered was to be between the Maritimes and Quebec and Ontario; the immigration would be to the urban centres where manufacturing took place. Hardly ever did the opening of the west figure in the speeches at the numerous public protectionist meetings in the entire period under consideration.[63] The development of the northwest was, along with the tariff and immigration, an issue at the conventions of the Dominion Board of Trade, but the speakers there only feebly integrated these matters, and never into an over-arching, dynamic, development policy.[64]

It is reasonable to suppose that one of the functions of politicians – of statesmen to be more precise – is to provide architectonic vision, a perception of how disparate and conflicting interests in national life can be brought into a functional and dynamic whole. Yet even politicians did not effectively deal with the relationship of the west and the protective tariff. Politicians had many ideas about the growth of the west, of course, and stressed the economic opportunities the region would provide. But railways and immigration loomed large as the instrument of growth in the northwest during the Confederation Debates, not the tariff. In the following years, leading politicians could not help but be aware of the importance of revenue generated by customs duties for the construction of any publicly supported railway;[65] however, this did not provide a policy base for the development of an integrated economy.

Only during 1876–79 did a few individual politicians begin to explicitly tie together the elements of western expansion with the perceived positive dynamics of tariff protection. One MP argued in 1876 that a policy for the construction of public works was necessary to ease the depression, and suggested that a protective tariff would encourage transcontinental trade. Charles Colby, in a Commons speech of 6 March 1877, asserted that in connection with a policy of railway construction, 'a fiscal policy which should utilize those public works and make them as valuable as they possibly could be made to the country' should be instituted. The fiscal policy should be one of discriminating protection.[66] Yet it was only a handful of MPs who held this concept explicitly, some of whom like Colby, had visions of Montreal's metropolitan hegemony. In the tedious Commons debate of 1879 on the National Policy tariff, only John McLennan, the Ontario businessman MP associated with Montreal interests, tied together tariff protection for manufactures, railway construction in the northwest, immigration and western settlement, and trade between an agricultural west and a manufacturing east.[67] It was remarked that his speech was inaudible. No one else, least of all a minister of the crown, touched on the web of ideas he had presented. Protectionist politicians were rarely the visionaries of the new west.

Nor were westerners the visionaries of the new tariff. They never had tariffs uppermost in their political considerations in the decade of the 1870s. Manitoba and British Columbia shared not at all the complex pre-Confederation tariff history of the eastern provinces. Customs duties in British Columbia were standardized with those of the rest of Canada in 1872, which – given the size of the provincial debt assumed by the federal government, the great costs involved in the promised railway construction, and the province's ocean access – made good sense. Similar factors did not hold in Manitoba, where a special low tariff was in effect until 1874, when the full Canadian one was imposed.[68] The Liberal tariff increases of that year did not, however, attract a great deal of fire in the west. British Columbia newspapers gave their attention to railway negotiations with the federal government.[69] The potential changes of 1876 received similar, limited attention. Arthur Bunster, MP for Vancouver, did make a connection with the construction of the railway, the expansion of the west, and a higher tariff, but later he retreated from his high-tariff advocacy.[70] The citizens of the west, if their newspapers are any indication, made very little of the 1876 Commons debate on the tariff, as the New Westminster *Guardian* briefly advocated its pet hobby of agricultural protection on 8 March 1876, the Winnipeg *Standard* supported free trade on 11 March, and only the *Colonist* of Victoria took up Bunster's line in an editorial of 27 February.[71] Railways were the political economy of the west for the whole of the decade.

Even during the 1878 election campaign, the tariff issue stirred up relatively little political froth in Manitoba and British Columbia. Alexander Morris, the former lieutenant-governor of Manitoba and a Conservative candidate, practically defused the issue by promising that a special tariff would be given to Manitob by a Conservative government. He and Donald Smith then turned to the mor pressing question of railways.[72] Passionate squabbling over railway routes wa also key in British Columbia.[73] Even in the Thunder Bay region, which wa virtually part of the west, and where for reasons of geography a wider perspectiv might be expected, the incumbent MP Simon Dawson gave most of his time t calming tempers scraped raw over railway route disputes. As soon as the railwa was put through, these disagreements would no longer matter, he urged. 'W are at the head of navigation, at the port which must become the point of shipmen for the wide region of the West ... The merchandise of the East would here b exchanged for the agricultural products of the West.' Dawson did not mentio the tariff or the role it might play in fostering this scheme.[74]

Once the tariff was made public in March 1879, there was western concern however. The new law did not include the special tariff that some westerner had expected, and western public opinion was restive.[75] Conservative-leanin papers often did their best to minimize or ignore the burdensome new custom duties; a few others claimed positive benefits,[76] none more boldly than th Winnipeg *Daily Times*, which promised a glorious future for the west, th agricultural products of which 'will be exchanged for those of the industria pursuits of the older provinces ... [whose] extensive manufacturing establish ments will increase the population to five times that which it is now, thus creatin a market for all the products of the northwest ... Protection and the developme of our railways will certainly produce these results.'[77] A hard regional intere underlay any acceptance of the tariff, however. One British Columbia newspape succinctly presented the political equation: 'If no Railway, then no new Tariff.' The tariff came, the price was paid. Until the Laurier era, the west overwhelm ingly elected Conservatives.

The tariff issue was key to the election of 1878. Qualifications must be imme diately added, however. Ethnic and religious tensions remained powerful dete minants of voting behaviour. Organized labour may have felt residual gratefulne to the Conservatives for the Trade Union Act of 1872. Liquor interests, an perhaps a great many ordinary men, felt the annoyance of the Canada Temperanc Act of 1878. A handful of petty scandals, such as that of the Neebling Hote allowed the Conservatives to paint the Liberals with the tar of corruption; th Liberals made feeble efforts to revive the Pacific Scandal. Quebec Lieutenan Governor Letellier de St Just's dismissal of his provincial Conservative gover ment served to enrage that party's politicians.[79] In the west, as has been show railways were virtually all. Nevertheless, protection and free trade were th essential grist for the mill of public discussion in 1878. Debates in the Hous of Commons from 1876 to 1879 on tariff-related matters made the *Hansard* of those years incredibly bulky.

During 1878, the Conservatives pulled together the loose coalition of interests they had assiduously developed for several years previously. The party functioned as the means of uniting a variety of interests, which had not effectively coalesced on their own, in order to pursue common, interrelated goals that could find some expression in the tariff. From the evidence available, the party did not involve itself in extensive illegal electoral activities in Ontario. Nor did manufacturers provide vast sums for the centralized Conservative campaign in the province, as the practical bankruptcy of the United Empire Club after the event makes clear. Their greatest importance to the party lay in the influence they could wield, among the urban working class and farmers, as well as among their peers. The influence could be persuasive or coercive, could find expression through the harmony-of-interests argument, or the exercise of naked power: the people 'all are under my *thumb*,' McInnes had said. The role of manufacturers in the election, though in some ways limited, placed them in a strong position when the tariff was formulated in 1879.

10
'Reconciling a legion of conflicting interests'

The resounding Conservative victory in the election of 1878 brought in its wake a range of tariff-related problems. The fashion in which tariff changes would be decided upon was open to question, and the potential character of a readjusted tariff was even more obscure. Was there to be a blind pandering to protectionist influences? Or were the portentous yet ambiguous protectionist promises of the Conservative campaign to be realized, as some cynical Liberals suggested in the election aftermath, by only minor alterations?[1] The deficit the federal government faced would have to be addressed as well, and the balance between revenue and protection adjusted. The answers to these matters lay not only in the budget Samuel Leonard Tilley brought down on 14 March 1879, but in the processes which led to it.

Any move to tariff readjustment faced a fundamental difficulty because it had not been decided how the understanding between the interests – and the interests and the new government – was to be worked out. Industrialists and merchants alike were anxious on this point, some strictly for themselves, as Sir John A. Macdonald must have realized in reading letters that congratulated him for the Tory victory in one sentence and asked for specific tariff changes in the next. Yet a broader view prevailed that could accommodate self-interest.

Montreal manufacturer and elder statesman of protection E.K. Greene was one of a number who suggested comprehensive formulas to change the tariff. After presenting his ideas about a multi-tiered tariff in which primary, secondary and tertiary levels of manufacturing were to be awarded with ascending protection, and goods that could not be manufactured in Canada were to be taxed according to revenue needs, Greene went on to advise Sir John how specific procedures could be decided upon. A committee composed of importers and manufacturers should sit to hear deputations and individuals engaged in the different branches of importing & manufacturing throughout the country. By this means they would become familiar with the details of the various branches of business and from the information thus obtained they could privately prepare a scheme for the consideration of the Finance minister which he could adopt or modify as he might think best. The Committee to be *pledged to secrecy* in all that pertains to their work. Whatever plan be adopted the knowledge obtained would be of material assistance to the Finance Minister & greatly lessen his heavy labours in preparing a tariff.[3]

The same ideas were held by the leadership of the Ontario Manufacturers' Association. An October meeting of the association in Toronto set up twenty-eight committees (many others were later added), each concerned with a major industrial interest such as woollens, cottons, edged tools, or furniture. Manufacturers were to use the committees to consult among themselves on tariff matters. W.H. Frazer urged immediate action, announcing that committee rooms had been reserved at a Toronto hotel and special rates for room and board were available.[4]

Stimulated by the Toronto example, similar action was undertaken in Montreal. Edward Gurney Jr, the stove manufacturer, 'was delegated by Western manufacturers to confer with manufacturers here [Montreal], so that when the next session of Parliament begins they might present the demands of the manufacturers without the clashing of interests.' Gurney's attempts to bring the quiescent Montreal Manufacturers' and Industrial Association into action were successful, as an arrangement for copying the Toronto committee system was made. The association was re-formed with vaster ambitions, dropping 'Montreal' from its name, and calling itself 'of Quebec.'[5] The Quebec and Ontario groups then issued the same circular questionnaire, which the committees were to use as a basis for their work. Queries about the form of the tariff – whether the method of classification in use was acceptable, and whether *ad valorem*, or specific duties, or a mix of the two were favoured – were not the only ones asked. Nor were the obvious questions about the existing rate of duty on products and the desired future rate the only ones added. Information about the raw materials used, and the duties thought appropriate to encourage their production in Canada, was also requested.[6] Narrow self-interest was seemingly frowned upon.

As the time for the annual convention of the Ontario Manufacturers' Association drew close, the pressure for collecting and collating the information grew. The convention was to be the forum at which the committee reports could be synthesized and an alternative tariff formulated. E.K. Greene, president of the Quebec group, told its members that the completion of the reports was vital, 'so they could submit them to the meeting to be held at Toronto, to which they as a body were about to appoint delegates. One of the principal objects of selecting a delegation to meet the Toronto Association,' Greene went on, 'was to adopt as far as possible an harmonious policy ... it was necessary that the Quebec and Ontario delegations should be harmonious and agreed.'[7]

Agreement was supposed to reach beyond the confines of Ontario and Quebec. Also reorganized in the expectation of tariff changes was the Manufacturers' and Mechanics' Association of New Brunswick, which had been defunct for some time. The key element in its resurrection was a letter of 15 October 1878 from W.H. Frazer suggesting the formation of a Dominion manufacturers' association. As Frazer expounded it, manufacturers had an obvious community of interest and trust between them should be the order of the day. Assuming trust to be forthcoming, he issued an invitation to the Toronto convention, which was to start 13 November, and sent along a batch of the Ontario Association's questionnaires, to be returned in completed form by the first of the month. The lateness of the proposal reflected on his organizational abilities or on his arrogance. He evidently expected quick action.

The New Brunswickers dallied. The first meeting of their association was in early November, by which time they were already badly out of synchronization with their central Canadian confrères. Nor were they about to accede to Frazer's ideas as a whole. Too many of the New Brunswick manufacturers regarded the questionnaire as an invitation into the spider's parlour. Too many had suffered from central Canadian competition and had no desire to give out detailed information about their market position to major rivals. Modified questionnaires, it was decided, would be sent out under the authority of the New Brunswick Association, which would develop its own generalizations with its own committees.[8]

Harmony was an ideal easy to envision, and difficult to achieve. The Montreal group did not have all its reports ready in time for the convention at Toronto. One of its committees, eager to strike an early blow, had a delegate in Ottawa while the convention was sitting. The Montrealers did not see eye to eye with the Ontarians on all matters, and were separately represented in Ottawa during the making of the tariff in 1879.[9] Yet the beginnings of agreements were reached in Toronto, and strengthened in the month that followed. By the end of December, forty-four reports had been pieced together by as many committees, with 457 manufacturers probably contributing.[10] A multitude of compromises had been hammered out.

Almost as an afterthought, the Ontario Manufacturers' Association decided to approach Nova Scotian interests. No manufacturers' organization existed there, so the Ontario group contacted the Halifax Chamber of Commerce. At a late December meeting, the chamber heard the association's message, which first played for the sympathy of commercial interests by declaring that Halifax should become the nation's winter port, and then went on to inquire about the nature of trade there and the sort of protection required. The chamber, refusing to commit itself to the mercies of Ontario manufacturers, did not answer in a specific fashion, though in preparation for the Dominion Board of Trade meeting, it did pass motions supporting protection for sugar refining, coal, and the manufacture of iron. For the tariff discussions in Ottawa during January 1879, the chamber chose its own representative: John Stairs, protectionist rope manufacturer, investor in other industrial enterprises, active Conservative on the provincial scene, and son of W.J. Stairs.[11]

Like the interests represented on the Halifax Chamber, the coal-mining industry chose to press its case with the Conservative government independently. The industry had R.G. Haliburton and George Dobson to represent it at the Dominion Board of Trade meeting in 1879, and Dobson remained in Ottawa afterwards as the parliamentary session began, lobbying on behalf of the Pictou and Cape Breton boards of trade.[12] This, coupled with the use of memorials asking for favour, was the tack taken by the coal industry, rather than combination with central Canadian interests many of whom still opposed protection to coal.

While the Ontario Manufacturers' Association sought organizational hegemony as a basis for placing the protectionist case before the Conservatives, the government itself had not been idle. The years 1878–79 were a fine time to develop foreign markets because the prospect of a greatly increased tariff provided Canada with strong bargaining points. Sir A.T. Galt, who had long felt the need for Canada to develop trading partners to countervail the American gravitational pull, was commissioned by the new government to pursue trade agreements with France, Spain, and their colonies in the Caribbean.[13] The substance of these negotiations are beyond the scope of this book, but suffice it to say that they were undertaken under pressure from Canadian interests. The advantages of expanding Caribbean and South American trade lay in strengthening the Conservative hold on the Maritimes. An enlarged trade with France was sought not only by Montreal manufacturers hungry for export markets, but by the declining Quebec shipbuilding industry. As Finance Minister Tilley left for England to arrange a new government loan in November 1878, he was seen off by a group of shipbuilders who begged him to press the French to remove high customs duties on Canadian-built vessels.[14] Part of Galt's mission was to pursue this, and though his negotiations were unsuccessful, they show the new government was not bent on autarky.

The Conservative leaders also had to take into consideration the problems of government finance. Tilley determined that some $2,000,000 in additional revenue would have to be generated to meet the deficit account and to provide at least the appearance of government solvency vital to arranging new loans (Cartwright, prior to the election, had felt $2,000,000 in new revenue was necessary). Combining the aim of increased revenue with the demand from manufacturers that the tariff be adjusted to give encouragement to every industry made 'full and reliable information for the use of the new Dominion Government' of the utmost importance.[15]

The new tariff was to be carefully calculated. Sir John had promised as much to the manufacturers before the election. 'We will have a sufficient protection for every interest,' he had told one audience heavily laden with the interested; 'We will give a sufficient protection for every industry, and we will be governed by evidence which we will carefully collect and gather regarding every manufacture and every trade. We will make every manufacture, every industry, produce the evidence of what is necessary for the purpose of protecting them in their struggle into maturity; and gentlemen, that protection will be given them.'[16] Macdonald here touched on the administrative difficulties inherent in formulating a tariff. Interests conflicted; manufacturers disagreed with each other; their demands had to be weighed against the wishes of raw materials producers, importers, and exporters. The agricultural interest had to be taken into consideration; methods of favouring Great Britain over the United States had to be found, and governmental revenue had to be increased. Major statistical talents were required.

Rumours to the effect that the Conservative government intended to establish a bureau of statistics were circulating in late 1878. Tilley was negotiating with Edward Young, an Americanized Nova Scotian who had assisted David Wells on the United States Revenue Commission after the Civil War. Young had, after that, been the chief of the U.S. Bureau of Statistics and had provided data to George Brown during the reciprocity negotiations of 1874. Recognized as a figure of importance by European statisticians, Young had published works on labour in Europe and America and on immigration, which were to gain him an audience with Lord Lorne, the new Canadian governor general. For though the government chose not to set up a bureau of statistics, it did hire Young as a tariff expert in December 1878.[17]

Two other men eagerly offered their services to aid Young. The journalist, protectionist, and tariff expert John Maclean was utilized when the burden of deputations became heavy in January 1879. His claim to expertise was based on his 1878 handbook on tariffs, a summary of Canadian, American, and other tariffs that could be effectively used to make Canadians yearn for retaliation.[18] The third in what the Liberals must have considered an unholy trinity was the ubiquitous W.H. Frazer, who felt his place was in Ottawa, to carry on the task he had begun in Toronto. Frazer had pestered Sir John A. Macdonald for a position as an assistant to Young, but whether he was actually hired is unclear. He was, none the less, given an office in the Parliament buildings. Certainly a three-month 'expenditure of $2914 ... entailed for the services of Experts and copyists engaged in assisting in the preparation of the Tariff' gave ample leeway for the payment of Frazer as well as Maclean and Young.[19]

The labours of these men have been almost entirely obscured by time. Frazer's function was probably to act as intermediary between the interests and the government and to further foster a unified approach among manufacturers. Young huddled with delegations as they came to Ottawa,[20] likely to provide statistical know-how in mediating conflicts. After the tariff became public, the talents of Young or Maclean were employed in showing how the tariff favoured Great Britain over the United States. From the detail provided in the newspaper articles, much effort had gone into developing a tariff structure having this bias.[21] Again, one or both of these men authored, beyond doubt, a 'Review of the Trade and Commerce of the Dominion of Canada from 30th June 1872 to 30th June 1878,' which provided statistical breakdowns of foreign trade in wearying detail.[22] Whatever the tariff owed to the experts was not the product of personal bias. Frazer and Maclean were both thoroughgoing protectionists, but the Liberals never accused them of having special interests to flog. The hiring of Young, and the work of these men generally indicated an incipient bureaucratization of the tariff-making process, as did the organizational approach suggested by the Ontario Manufacturers' Association and other protectionists.

Indeed, the government actively encouraged such an approach. Committee reports generated by a manufacturers' group meant that a wide variety of disagreements would be smoothed out before government involvement, and that written justification of tariff demands on the part of interests had to be broadly based. Finance Minister Tilley had the wisdom to foster the resurrection of the New Brunswick Association, and he steered manufacturers to consult with the Ontario Association committees. He also suggested the formation of a Dominion manufacturers' organization. Here was the political legitimacy the manufacturers' associations had previously lacked.[23]

The confluence of organizational effort and government encouragement resulted in a series of meetings at the beginning of 1879 in Ottawa. Edward Gurney Jr, president of the Ontario group, arrived by 14 January, bringing in tow W.H. Frazer and the fat files of committee reports. Representatives of the Quebec (née Montreal) protectionist organization, J.H. Parks and others from the New Brunswick association, and John Stairs from Halifax soon joined him. A round of consultations among these men, and between them and Tilley and his experts, followed; reports were presented, preliminary conclusions reached. For a time, mutuality of interest was found; inspired by Tilley's suggestion and possibly intoxicated by a sense of collective influence, the men agreed to form a national organization in one late-night meeting.[24]

While this idea proved to be stillborn, there was another national business organization to press business concerns about tariff matters on the government: the Dominion Board of Trade. Its annual convention in Ottawa from 21 to 23 January followed closely on the arrival of the manufacturers' groups and gave businessmen in the organization one last opportunity to express themselves publicly on protection before the government acted. Sharp internal struggles on protection had troubled the board throughout the 1870s; this was no more. Certainly in 1876 and later, an increasing number of boards of trade and chambers of commerce had seen the wisdom of W.H. Howland's arguments about increasing the internal trade of the country; moreover, wholesalers, agents, and the like were hurting from the direct marketing American manufacturers were undertaking, and from the relative decline of imports from Britain, where many had strong business connections. And other member organizations of the Dominion Board evidently resigned themselves to the inevitability of higher tariffs, avoiding comment on the issue of protection in their early 1879 local meetings, while sending protectionist delegates to the Ottawa convention.[25] Consequently the discussion of tariff matters at the Dominion Board meeting proved something of a protectionist celebration. The delegates strove to outdo each other in the vigour of their protectionism: incidental protection was denounced as humbug; near-exclusionist policies were demanded. E.K. Greene, a strong protectionist if there ever was one, felt it necessary to apologize for the weakness of his high-tariff resolution of the previous year! Only one speaker, representing the Quebec Board of Trade, actually questioned the validity of protection, and he bemoaned the pointlessness of his statements. If Tilley's resolve to introduce a protectionist tariff needed any stiffening, it certainly received a great dose of starch as he listened to the discussion. The need for protection to foster the Canadian nationality, the importance of commercial protection to enhance the flow of trade between the Maritimes and central Canada and to encourage direct importation, the need to eliminate the slaughtering of goods, the importance of protection to staple-producing industries as well as manufactures – these and other topics received an airing. The delegates to the convention made great efforts to maintain unanimity on tariff matters: the only subject over which there was open disagreement was on the issue of coal duties, with a small minority of delegates from central Canada rejecting any duty on anthracite coal.[26]

But the organizational approach had its limits. Self-interest on the part of manufacturers, discord among broader interests, regional tensions, haphazard consultation, and the persistence of a wide variety of mechanisms for political decision making all militated against its smooth functioning. The manufacturers' groups, for all their committee reports, had some substantial disagreements. Nor were all major interests adequately represented in these Ottawa discussions (J. Stairs could hardly represent all Nova Scotian industrial concerns, to point out one obvious limitation). Broader consultation proved necessary for the government, with, for example, Tilley sending for individuals involved in the sugar trade.[27] Beyond that, groups flocked to Ottawa unasked, fearful that their wishes were unknown or were being ignored.

Still, the many deputations that came to badger Tilley in the first three months of the year showed how pervasive the organizational principle was. Tilley was 'worried to death by deputations' noted an obviously impressed neophyte observer, the new governor general, Lord Lorne.[28] Delegations of producers and consumers of pig-iron, manufacturers of woollens, cottons and clothing, paint and oil manufacturers, boot and shoe producers, producers and refiners of petroleum, and makers of glue, chemicals, cordage, and salt were among those who paid their respects to the finance minister. The formally organized Brewers' and Maltsters' Association had a deputation in the capital at the same time as the manufacturers' associations were meeting with Tilley, and as momentum built up, representatives of the Ontario Cement Manufacturers' Association, the Dominion (formerly Ontario) Millers' Association, and the Paper Manufacturers' Committee arrived to press their cases. These were only a few of the many delegations contemporary newspapers mentioned. And after the tariff was made public, the flow of delegations surged forward again.[29] While their number and persistence were beyond all calculation, they were part of the method the government and vocal businessmen had decided upon for tariff making.

But there was more, much more. The traditional methods of petitioning and applying pressure through MPs were much in evidence. Petitions from fruit and tobacco growers asked for protection, as did shipowners and shipbuilders; when the tariff came down there was a tremendous burst of petitioning from newspapermen and other proprietors of printing establishments praying that the proposed duty on type not be imposed. Petitions from manufacturers were, however, notable in their absence.[30] *They* had found better means of making their wishes known.

Associated with petitions were other pressures applied through MPs. The free-trade outlook of the Quebec Board of Trade, and the fact that the city had no manufacturers' association, meant that Adolph Caron, the Quebec County MP, was especially busy. Caron was a natural expediter of protectionist demands because of his widespread industrial investments. 'I intended calling upon you, as requested, before your leaving Quebec,' wrote one high-tariff man to Caron, 'but finding that there were so many people calling upon you and all evidently on ''Protection'' business,' he thought he would write Caron in Ottawa instead.[31] Perhaps Caron was unusual in the volume of tariff business he handled, but he was far from alone in his role of transmitting protectionist demands from constituents to the government.[32]

A more sophisticated operation through MPs was mounted by the Nova Scotian coal interest. George Dobson, the lobbyist representing the Pictou and Cape Breton boards of trade, prepared and distributed to all MPs a pamphlet advocating a coal duty, and he helped arrange a meeting of Ontario and Maritime MPs where a common stance on coal was sought. A few days later, 'a large number of Conservative members, principally from Nova Scotia and Ontario, waited on the Hon. Mr. Tilley ... and asked that the tax on coal imported into Canada be placed at 75 cents per ton.' The MPs brought with them a memorial heavily signed by their fellows.[33] Dobson's efforts were essentially an extension of a method that had been used from time immemorial in representative assemblies.

Worst of all for Tilley and his experts was the constant press of individual manufacturers and other businessmen, each setting up his own claim for recognition. The manufacturers' associations' approach fell short of success. 'Never during the annals of Ottawa have beds been in such demand as they were last night. Every hotel was crowded, and people were actually sleeping on the floor, round the stoves, on settees, and in fact every available space was occupied. Boarding and lodging houses report a rich harvest,' reported the correspondent of the Quebec *Mercury* on 14 February. A bemused Lord Lorne reported to England that 'everyone who has ever raised a pig or caught a smelt wants protection for his industry.'[34] From January to the end of April, Tilley answered most of the letters on tariff matters with a bare formularistic sentence or two, and from March to the end of April much of this correspondence remained unanswered. The finance minister, unfortunately, could not treat those waiting outside his office in such a cavalier fashion.

The letters, the written submissions from committees, deputations, and individuals, and the memorials all made up an enormous bulk of written material that the overburdened Tilley felt it necessary to read and pore over. Only a man obsessed with tariffs would have the will or desire to read a statistical statement providing the price per yard, the price per pound of weight, the *ad valorem* equivalents of specific duties of 5, 10, 15, and 20 cents per pound of weight, those rates as compared to the existing duty, and all for some twenty-four types of woollens: seal cloaking, naps, Presidents, Black Unions, Union Tweed, Beaver, Black Supers, Cobourgs, Thibets, Maramattas, and more.[35] Tilley had a multitude of such documents to peruse, and the manuscript 'Review of the Trade and Commerce of the Dominion of Canada' written by his experts only provided a general overview. So unstintingly did the finance minister work that he had a bout of eye trouble and had to rest in darkened rooms for a couple of days, thereby giving rise to the sly and apocryphal joke of Sir John's about Tilley having to go the budget blind. Alexander Mackenzie suspected that 'his sickness is largely of the mental type. Were he an honest politician and not a mere party hack,' Mackenzie pungently added, 'I would sympathize with him, for the work of reconciling a legion of conflicting interests all demanding to be enriched at some ones expense must be an immense task for the ablest man and the most suave character the country could produce, far more to a man not above mediocrity.[36] At least the former prime minister realized the character of Tilley's work.

The argument that Tilley wished to erect a balanced and calculated tariff contradicts the assumption that the tariff was little more than a series of quid pro quos with manufacturers to whom the Conservatives were particularly indebted. The assumption, promulgated by the Liberal press of the time, and strengthened by the secrecy surrounding the formation of the tariff, is false. Of course, the tariff could be used in a politically partial manner. The lumbermen had sided with the Liberals generally, and Tilley made his lack of sympathy for their complaints over the tariff plain: he told one powerful deputation that lumbering was a waning industry and implied that their concerns were not of great import.[37] Manufacturers of agricultural implements, many of whom had sided with the Liberals, also found reason to complain when the tariff came down. And the textile industry, which had provided such crucial men as George Stephen and Donald McInnes, received particularly generous treatment. Some specific examples can be cited. The rules were stretched to allow G.G. Dustan to import sugar-refining machinery without paying duty. The regulations about banks of deposit were altered to accommodate solid Conservative supporters such as the distiller and banker J.G. Worts, when the duties on spirits and malt were changed requiring massive bank deposits to the credit of the government.[38] But in each of these cases, no charges of actual wrongdoing could be levied at the Conservatives. Lumbering did appear to be a declining industry in the 1870s, and it was so export oriented that little could be done for it by means of the tariff except to keep duties on input items low, and that was difficult if agriculture, textile, and iron manufacturers were to be protected. Caught in the middle of the much disputed matter of iron and steel duties, and the Conservative desire to propitiate the farmers of the country, the agricultural-implements people were unfortunate, not the victims of retribution. Generally speaking, the tariff was not a sufficiently precise instrument to effectively discriminate between friends and political foes – especially when so many friends wanted conflicting things.

More than enough evidence exists to balance the equation, for many staunch Conservatives did not get want they wanted. Sir Hugh Allan, the man to whom the Conservatives owed both most and least, indicated a preference for heavy duties on India rubber goods, on sewing machines, on cotton and wool manufactures, and on coal. Needless to say Allan had investments in these areas. The duties imposed were notably lower than Allan wanted. On pig-iron, which Allan wanted free, a $2 per ton duty was imposed. Donald McInnes, a key Conservative supporter, was aghast at the latter duty, not because he agreed with Allan, but because he wanted $4 per ton. He and George Stephen were major shareholders in the Canada Steel Company at Londonderry in Nova Scotia, which was losing vast sums of money.[39] Samuel Platt, the Goderich salt maker who fought strenuously for the Tories in the election, was upset when he discovered that salt could still be imported free for purposes of the Atlantic fisheries. A.W. Ogilvie, one of the largest millers in the country, and a vigorous Conservative, was in company with his fellow millers, astounded by the duty on breadstuffs. 'The budget you may imagine has astonished us very much,' he wrote his business acquaintance, the shipper, banker, and MP John McLennan: '15¢ per bushell on wheat is 75 on a barrel of flour, as it now takes five bushells to make a barrel, and the duty on flour is only 50¢ making 25¢ more duty on the raw material than on the manufactured article. I still think there is some mistake ... Our case is exactly reversed from what it should be, and if not changed will close up all the large mills and in many ways do harm and *hurt our party* ... I have had a hard time of it from the grits today.'[40] Distillers, who had strongly supported the Conservatives in Ontario, were shocked to find the excise duty on spirits made retroactive. Tory, as well as Reform, newspaper proprietors and printers were upset by the high duty on type. Many a Conservative manufacturer and shipper reacted glumly to the duty imposed on coal. The duty would mean increased costs on coal from $750 to $1500 per annum, one manager of a shipping firm wrote to the Conservative John McLennan.[41]

A question far more important than that of specific favouritism concerns the extent to which the manufacturers' associations dictated levels of customs duties to the Conservative government. Nearly a quarter of a century after the fact, the secretary of the Canadian Manufacturers' Association bluntly claimed that the tariff proposed by the Ontario Association was the same as that implemented by Tilley.[42] The claim is in the realm of hyperbole: as we have seen, the manufacturers were not united in their demands, and in addition many interests not allied with the Ontario Association were importuning Tilley.

Demand for agricultural protection, for example, was considerable in the months prior to the tariff being brought down. Farmers' groups discussed the principle of protection and what benefits could be had, and resolutions were sent to Ottawa asking for protective duties on grain, vegetables, fruit, dairy products, poultry, cattle, pork, and wool.[43] Divisions within the Grange prevented the rganization from lobbying for protection (group lobbying in the fashion of the anufacturers did not seem to appeal to the agrarian community), so members f Parliament became the channels through which demand for agricultural pro- ction found expression. In early March, a delegation of MPs representing gricultural constituencies presented Tilley with a petition signed by thirty-four f their number. The demands they made were to a considerable degree met in e tariff: the one significant disparity from the farmers' perspective was that heat was placed at 15¢ rather than 20¢ per bushel.[44] The Tories did not intend) offend protectionist farmers. The duties on wheat and oats were galling to e powerful protectionist milling interest: Ogilvie closed one of his flour mills protest; oatmeal millers asserted that if their mills were to be run year-round, merican oats had to be imported and the closure of some of these mills was lanned.[45] Thus did the Millers' Association, which was closely tied with the ntario Manufacturers' group, impose its will on the government.

The conflict of interest over agricultural protection involved regional protest. he possibility of a duty on breadstuffs had created a furor in the Maritimes uring the election, for the effect of customs duties of this sort would be to liminate the movement of American breadstuffs into those provinces, leaving e market for central Canadian products priced at a premium. Maritime mer- hants were busy in the weeks before the tariff came down, stocking up in xpectation of windfall profits under a higher price regime.[46] The adversity etween the region's interests and those of the Canadian farmers and millers as made plain by Tilley to a Saint John merchant: 'I fear however that your iews will not be acceptable to the farmers of Canada. They say, give us Free ade, but as long as the U. States imposes a heavy duty on meal and breadstuffs . that U. States Farmers & millers should not have our own markets free.'[47]

The grain forwarders and merchants of Toronto, Montreal, and Quebec City ere similarly opposed to high duties on American breadstuffs. Like the Mari- mes, the province of Quebec was dependent on grain imports, and even more nportant to the shippers, there was considerable trade in American grain moving rough Montreal overseas. This trade, it was feared, was going to be destroyed. he Montreal Corn Exchange in late February 1879 voted overwhelmingly for removal of grain duties: 'This meeting hears with considerable alarm a report at it is the intention of the Government to put a protective duty on breadstuffs, nd sincerely hopes that in adjusting the tariff they will consider the great hardship at would thus be inflicted upon this Dominion, and earnestly hope that all grain nd flour from the United States be admitted free, as heretofore.'[48] The govern- ent was to meet these concerns in large part by allowing American grain tended for overseas to be shipped in bond.

Having seen how the government's favourable response to demands for agricultural protection impinged on regional, commercial, and industria interests, we can point to one further example of a somewhat different character Agricultural-implements manufacturers had the duty on their products raised t 25 per cent in 1879, but that was not considered high enough, because dutie on input items had risen much more sharply.[49] Further increases in the duty o agricultural implements were made impossible by the probable reaction of th farming community, so the manufacturers were left with issuing threats of wag reductions and similar nefarious deeds.

Conflict between a staple-producing industry, commercial, and manufacturin interests was also evident in the matter of coal. Though a certain understandin had been reached between coal and central Canadian manufacturing interests i 1877, it was far from complete. Nova Scotian MPs, under prodding from Georg Dobson, were demanding as much as $1.35 per ton on coal. The least the intere seemed willing to accept was $0.75 per ton on all forms of the mineral. Centra Canadian industrial interests were willing to accept a duty on bituminous coa only – which would do nothing for the Nova Scotian industry – and even the were not willing to go higher than $0.50 per ton. A duty on coal was unpopula in Quebec as well, for British coal was imported there as ballast on lumbe vessels.[50] Transportation interests in central Canada disliked the idea of a tax o anthracite. J. Hickson, general manager of the Grand Trunk Railway, pointe out in a submission to the government that Nova Scotian coal had never bee used west of Brockville by the railway, and 'it would require either a very larg reduction in the cost of that coal or a heavy increase in the price at whic American coal can be laid down, to permit of the former being carried beyon that point.' The railway demanded special relief if a coal duty was imposed. Other transportation interests agreed, as has been seen.

Despite the pressures from a coalition of Nova Scotian and central Canadia MPs for a high protective duty to coal, and those countervailing from centra Canada, the government chose to disappoint both parties. Tilley compromised and cleverly insured himself a greater revenue flow, by placing $0.50 per to duty on all kinds of coal. There was a great deal of dissatisfaction; the Nov Scotians found it especially difficult to contemplate the high duties on breadstuff that were considered the quid pro quo. Dobson agitated for an upward revisio on the coal duties, but in the end the Nova Scotians accepted Tilley' position.[52]

More complex was the case of iron and steel, in which the manufacturer associations had tried to foster agreement. Iron (other than charcoal) and ste production in Canada was as yet experimental, immature, or simply prospective There were hopes of erecting blast furnaces in Toronto, and efforts to start u a production centre in the Ottawa Valley had begun. By far the largest produc

Canada was the Canada Iron and Steel Company in Nova Scotia. But it was lagued with labour and start-up problems, and faced serious technical obstacles. oncurrently, the prices of iron and steel were dropping, making imports very :tractive. Donald McInnes, who along with George Stephen was a major investor the company, confessed its difficulties to Sir John A. Macdonald in pressing or associated tariff changes. The firm required relief, 'and – entre nous – we equire it soon. The company has lost about $60,000 ... on last year's operations nd are losing over $3 ... on every ton of pig iron they are selling at present rices. Our cash Capital is £320,000 sterling, all paid up, and we have borrowed 100,000 sterling in addition on security of the property, all of which is ex- ended!!'[53] For McInnes, and for all other raw-iron producers, the obvious olution was a hefty duty on pig-iron. Yet secondary iron manufacturers and a ide variety of founders liked to get their pig-iron free of duty, while wanting eir own products to have an adequate protection. Tertiary users, while wanting uty-free pig-iron, wanted secondary iron products as cheap as possible. The terest was divided against itself.

Agreement among the various manufacturers in the industry was not reached the Toronto convention, or at a special meeting in Ottawa in late February. illey imposed a solution that predictably satisfied no one. The duty on pig-iron as set at $2 per ton, which left McInnes complaining bitterly. Equally distressed ere the investors who were planning to set up blast furnaces in Toronto: 'Permit e to draw your attention to the item of Pig Iron $2 a ton now as it takes say vo tons of coal paying 50 cts. a ton duty pig iron is *protected* by $1 only which no protection at all and will not encourage the erection of a single blast furnace. ence all the duties levied on iron and steel in the different levels of manufacture e for *revenue* and so heavy as to kill *export* trade – producing dear Iron and eneral dissatisfaction in our foundries, Engine & machine shops – a *protective* riff say not less than $4 a ton' was absolutely vital to stimulate competition Canada and produce cheap iron.[54] The Montreal Rolling Mills were unhappy ith $2 per ton on pig-iron and on blooms and billets: if nothing could be done lower the duty imposed on pig-iron, they cried, surely that on blooms and llets could be reduced.[55] Bridge fabricators complained (they received some inor concessions); the Kingston Locomotive Company found that despite the arp increase of duty on its final product, the increased duty on input items left e firm behind, rather than ahead.[56] No one was happy, with the exception of e government which, as the potential blast furnace investors from Toronto cognized, had arranged duties so as to increase revenue very considerably.

Still, even if these examples undermine any assertion that the manufacturers' sociations dictated the particulars of the tariff, it might be argued that an dustry that had no apparent adversary relationship with others, and was united in its perspective, could enforce its views on the federal government. An industr in this general situation was that represented by the Ontario Manufacturers Association committee on copper, brass, and other metals, excluding iron. Th committee offered a unified front in recommending that manufactures of copper brass, tin, and zinc pay a 30 per cent duty with gas and kerosene fixtures to pa 35 per cent. The tariff as enacted provided 30 per cent on manufactures of tin lead, and zinc. The lighting fixtures were set at 35 per cent. This appears to b substantially what the committee asked for, and the increase from the previou $17\frac{1}{2}$ per cent seems enormous. But when the qualifications are added, it n longer appears that the committee simply got what they asked for. The rav metals had formerly all been free of duty, and while the patriotic metals me were willing to admit a 5 per cent duty on them for revenue purposes, Tille imposed 10 per cent. The tariff calculations of manufacturers in that era wer generally not complex: in cases such as this, the manufacturer simply subtracte the duty on input items from the customs duty on the final product in order t come up with the amount of 'real' protection. Using that simple calculus, w find that the level of protection on manufactures of tin, lead, and zinc woul have seemed to decline $2\frac{1}{2}$ per cent, that on copper and brass finished good would have appeared to increase $2\frac{1}{2}$ per cent, and that on lighting fixtures $7\frac{1}{}$ per cent. These results were a considerable remove from those requested. Th gains had been limited in another fashion. The committee had declared itsel willing to accept a \$0.50 per ton duty on bituminous coal *only*; the anthracit they used for smelting they wanted duty free. They had a signal lack of succes in this regard. The report represented a high degree of compromise among on group of manufacturers; the rates desired were not as high as the American an were presumably based on adequate evidence about the state of the industry; th revenue requirements of the government and the market needs of the coal industr had been taken into some account. On these grounds the committee might hav considered its reports reasonable; on these grounds Tilley partly accommodate them. The mechanism represented what the finance minister likely wanted fror the manufacturers' associations, for it eased his work-load.

The tariff was not exclusively concerned with manufactured goods and agri cultural products, however. Canadian tariffs always had elements of commercia protection in them, and that of 1879 was no exception. The tariff, many mer chants felt, would maintain established lines of trade leading back to England c other countries; it would help prevent American wholesalers and manufacture wholesalers from circumventing the Canadian commercial structure to sell di rectly to retailers or consumers. Some of the commercial protection was carefull blended with industrial protection, as was the case with the duty on sugars. A George Dustan repeatedly argued: 'A fair Tariff would give the people of thi country cheaper and better sugar than they are now importing from Great Britain and the United States, and enable us to get every pound consumed in the country directly from the sugar-growing countries, in the shape of raw sugar, to be refined in our own country, and *as a return for our own produce of fish, lumber, coal, etc., etc.*'[57] A similar trade gambit was part of the argument for a duty on coal and breadstuffs – it would increase interprovincial trade. The whole concept of expanded national markets demanded the growth of commerce within the country. And the pursuit of external markets for Canadian products, an undertaking in which the Conservative government did not stint, involved the expansion of trade. An interweaving of commercial and industrial protection was also apparent in the matter of shipbuilding. The industry was export oriented, but many shipbuilders were shipowners as well. Builders were given a special consideration in the 1879 tariff, for they provided a loophole: there was a drawback on or rebate of duties paid on iron used in constructing vessels for sale abroad.[58]

The tariff also provided some purely commercial protection of a kind long familiar to Canadians, a system of differential duties to encourage direct importation. The tea importers were finally requited. A written babble of joy on the matter was sent to Macdonald soon after the victory of 1878 by one expectant importer: 'As you perhaps know my vocation is "Direct Trade" with the East Indies, China, Japan & [I] begin to feel "out of the wood" now that we are to have the 10% Differential Duty reimposed against the U.S. & in favour of (Direct) Eastern Produce & hope your Govt will include "*all Produce*" same as the American except Raw Silk & Wool then our Importers will be encouraged to bring vessels direct to our Harbor, with better assorted Cargoes than only all Tea Coffee or Sugar.'[59] The direct importer was granted part of his desire, for the differential duty on tea was reimposed. Direct importers from countries other than the United States were pleased with the forceful imposition of the last-port-of-shipment *ad valorem* system, which had pleased them in earlier tariffs as well. There remained a continuing hostility to the system by importers who did their shopping in the United States.[60]

The tariff that resulted from the web of interlocking considerations here partly examined reflected the implications inherent in the Conservative campaign phrase 'judicious readjustment of the tariff.' The readjustment had promised to take into account agricultural, mining and manufacturing interests. It had, and more. 'Judicious readjustment' was not only an ingeniously ambiguous phrase needed to sedate those fearful of tariff increases, though for the election it had done good service in that way. A more complex tariff framework was implied, to befit the growing complexity of the Canadian economy.

A number of clauses in the tariff act were intended to plug loopholes that unscrupulous traders might use to advantage: containers of goods imported would pay the same rate as the good contained; goods that had drawbacks applied to them by foreign governments would have the amount of drawback considered as part of the cost of the good; refunds of duties because of breakage or perishability would be limited by time and quantity; and refunds of duty on goods of inferior quality or goods having been discounted were strictly limited. Two clauses allowed for improved trade relations. One on trade with France and Spain permitted the lowering of duties on wine if agreement was reached, and the second included an option for orders in council to permit a reciprocity of trade with the United States on a limited number of natural products, if the Americans made moves to lower the duties on like Canadian products. The list was somewhat more limited than that of the 1854 Reciprocity Treaty.[61]

The system of rates in the new tariff was much more complex. To help prevent slaughtering, to provide revenue stability in a period of price decline, and to continue the encouragement of direct importation, a wide range of goods were given duties that were part specific and part *ad valorem*. Most cotton and woollen goods, sugars and molasses, some iron items, and a scattering of other products were placed under such a regime. It was a major departure from former tariffs in this respect. Further complexity followed. While the previous tariff had only four different levels of *ad valorem* rates, the new tariff had more than ten. On items where *ad valorem* rates applied, increases included not only the 2½ per cent increase on the unenumerated list to 20 per cent, but common increases of 7½, 10, and 12½ per cent.

Rates of 20, 25, and 30 per cent were thus common, with some rates going much higher than that. Yet a comparison with the American tariff shows considerable differences between the two, with the American tariff generally higher. Americans placed $7 per ton on pig-iron; the Canadian rate of 1879 was $2. Customs duties on iron partially manufactured were in Canada from 10 to 17½ per cent, and on finished iron products, rates were generally set at 25 or 30 per cent. The American rates on partially manufactured to finished iron goods were from 30 to 70 per cent. The differences between the two tariffs reflected, first, the relative weakness of the Canadian industrial establishment and a continuing dependence on imported manufactures and secondly, a considerable concern with revenue on the part of the Canadian government. The 1879 tariff could not raise to excessive levels tariffs on goods which were major revenue producers. The leading revenue producers of earlier years remained so, though the balance among them altered. Textiles remained the chief revenue producer, generating over 28 per cent of all customs revenue in 1879–80 (cottons provided some 12 per cent, woollens just under 12 per cent; the rest was provided primarily by silks). Sugar generated 15.4 per cent of total customs revenue; iron and steel goods roughly 9 per cent, non-alcoholic beverages 5 per cent and alcoholic beverages 7.7 per cent of such revenue. These government income generators provided almost the same percentages of customs revenue in 1879–80 as they had ten and twenty years earlier, though the structure of the tariff had visibly altered.[62]

The tariff's structure followed well-accepted principles. Businessmen wanted tiered tariffs, as they had wanted since at least the late 1840s. One of the most objectionable facets of tariff making by the Liberals was that they did not recognize this principle; the 'judicious readjustment' of the tariff the Conservatives promised involved this all-important fine tuning. The 1879 duties reflected a careful hierarchy. Thus, raw materials (especially those Canada did not produce) tended to be free, but each stage of manufacturing was reflected in higher customs duties. If one examines the various materials required by the boot and shoe industry, this thinking becomes quite evident. Leather that was untanned was duty free. Tanned but otherwise unmanufactured sole leather paid 10 per cent, a common rate in the tariff on partly processed input goods produced in Canada (cotton prunella, a cloth out of which uppers for light shoes was made, paid 10 per cent; so did woollen boot and shoe felt). Sole leather that had received a further level of treatment – waxing – paid 15 per cent, as did undressed leather for shoe uppers. Dressed leathers, both sole and upper, paid 20 per cent. Finished boots and shoes paid 25 per cent. Boot and shoe counters, which were stiff leather heel inlays, paid a specific duty equivalent to 28.9 per cent. At first glance, this would seem to be an anomaly, but in fact was not. Canada could produce virtually all of the counters the boot and shoe industry required, which meant that a high duty would not increase their price sharply, and counters made up only a limited portion of the final cost of shoes.[63]

The tariff was deeply protective. The depression and the business reaction to it, the adamant anti-protectionist stance of the Liberals, the character of the Conservative election campaign, and the fashion in which the tariff was formulated make this clear, if the high customs duties imposed on 14 March 1879 do not succeed in convincing. Yet there was room for vocal disenchantment among manufacturers, both protectionist and not. As Richard Cartwright pointed out to Alexander Mackenzie: 'A great many manufacturers are suffering seriously from the N.P., and that fact can hardly be brought out too prominently.'[64] And there were many who stood warily on the sidelines while the struggle to change the tariff was under way. But the manufacturers, whatever the role of commercial, agricultural and other staple-producing interests, were crucial in making the tariff. Broadly speaking, they had wanted more protection, and they received it. In the autumn of 1879, as the farmers gathered their crops and held their thanksgiving, the prospects of manufacturing began to revive, employment picked up, and business confidence grew. Whether this was the fruit of the tariff is hardly clear, but it seems the manufacturers thought so. They, too, held thanksgiving: Tilley was invited on tours of their factories and fêted at banquets.[65] Unhappy men do not act this way.

Conclusion

The 1879 tariff was not a mere political incident, for the substance of tariffs and the methods by which they were formed reflected the growth and integration of British North American societies. On an economic level, this meant the relative and temporary decline in the importance of some key staple exports, and the rise of an uneven industrialization in an era of expanding internal markets. On a political plane, it involved growing independence from Great Britain, the rejection of American hegemony, and Confederation. In the most reductive social terms, it meant an incipient collectivization.

The shift of tariff-policy emphasis from external trade considerations revolving around staple exports to internal production and commerce was far from complete, of course, for in a country heavily dependent on foreign trade and tariff revenue, a blanket exclusionist protectionism was impossible. A need for external trade marked Canadian policy even in 1879; none the less, a profound change in outlook had occurred. The country's commercial policy no longer had the free-trade characteristics induced in many Western economies by the prosperity of the 1850s.

The international economic context altered, especially after 1873. International demand grew more slowly, and this, combined with heightening international industrial productivity, made internal national markets very attractive to many Canadian businessmen. Depression intensified the attraction. Canadian industry had grown from the 1850s onward in several major bursts: in the 1850s, during the American Civil War, and in the boom of 1870–73. By the time of the depression, there was a very broad spectrum in plant size in many industries; there also appears to have been a great range in productive efficiencies and in the rate at which individual operators adopted new technology. These were characteristics that reflected significant structural changes in a number of industries and, in turn, the instabilities associated with industrialization. While many evolving industries were sheltered from extremes of competition during the 1860s and the boom at the beginning of the following decade, and so could accept the process of change with some equanimity, the depression that followed intensified the changes in some ways; in other ways slowed them down. It was a juncture of importance. Businessmen often responded to greater competition with production and pricing agreements, evanescent though most of these were, and undertook campaigns to limit foreign competition through the erection of tariff walls. Such campaigns required major organizational drives in the Canadian business world, a phenomenon evident in many Western national economies.[1]

There was, however, more to the making of protection in Canada than strictly economic pressures. The National Policy was, from a certain ideological perspective, an effort to construct a nationality that would avoid the social conflicts which wracked Great Britain, the chief industrial nation of the day. Harmony of interests smacks of corporatism; the role of the Conservatives in framing the relationship of the interests and the government suggests élite accommodation, even though the events of 1879 might better fit a pluralistic interest-group theory.[2] That aside, the pursuit of harmony was a dominant theme in the social history of mid and late nineteenth-century Canada.[3] In the context of protectionist ideology, harmony was premised on a romantic vision of pre-industrial and early industrial society with local or regional markets, small shop-factories, close employer/employee relations, and a perceived easy integration between town and country. With its nostalgic purity, it provided an intellectual bridge to the large-scale industrialization and integrated markets of an emerging mass society.

One of the chief methods of pursuing the ideal of harmony in an increasingly complex society was through organization and the institutionalization of conflict.[4] As contemporaries were well aware, it was an age of 'association and combination' – in labour, among farmers, in politics, and in business. Outside the purview of government, businessmen pursued this course not only because of competition, but because the structure of government did not formally represent or readily accommodate vested interests on a regional or national basis. The broad interests in the business community, and nationalist leaders among businessmen, wanted the relationship between business and government to move towards policies that met the needs of whole sectors of the economy. From their perspective, such an alteration of approach meant that self-interest could be subsumed under national purpose, especially if staple-producing, commercial, and urban working-class interests could be seen zto benefit. The emerging capitalist and manufacturing élite provided itself with a sustaining mission within the nation-state and asserted that only if the government responded to the demands of *organizations* could proper policies be developed.

Yet the protectionists' nationalism and advocacy of the ideal of harmony were quite properly open to profound scepticism. For

> protectionists, like others, must give and take – taking as much as possible and giving as little as possible – so they unite for the common weal. Individually they cannot make headway against the gross ignorance of society or of parliamentary bodies. A brutal outcry would be raised were one individual, or one branch of industry, to demand the exclusion from the country of foreign goods competing with theirs, because they were sold too cheap; but when a great number of widely different interests, spread all over the country, unite in asking for the same thing, and do it in the name of their destitute work-people, the effect is very different, the demand savours less of monopoly, and it can easily be made to appear that the welfare of the whole Dominion is identified with that of her manufacturers.[5]

There was a profound tension among the interests of the community as a whole, interest groups generally, and the self-interest of various protectionists – a tension clearly discernible in the political arena, though more obscure in economic terms.[6]

The impact of such organizations and their restrictive business practices on the progress of economic life remains unclear in Canada. Cartels in late nineteenth-century Germany did not inhibit rapid industrial growth or innovation in technique and business structures; similar practices in twentieth-century Britain evidently did. Was there a continuing predominance of the smaller firm in late Victorian Canada that reflected tariff-induced inefficiencies? And did the many combinations which operated from the 1870s to 1914 and beyond significantly stall managerial innovation and business reorganization? Or did they hasten such innovation? The historical study of the firm in Canada is insufficiently advanced to answer questions of this order, though the tariff obviously made restrictive practices more effective.[7]

Tariff politics lend themselves to discussion in terms of interest groups. Yet in the small colonial societies of the 1830s and well beyond, the modification of tariffs in a protectionist direction was clearly the result of personal relationships, patronage, and pork-barrelling.[8] Such special pleading was increasingly replaced by mass petitioning and then by vigorous group lobbying. In turn, governments tentatively sought methods of rationalizing the tariff-making process. Galt's polling of the boards of trade for their views on tariff changes in 1859 was a case in point. Later, after Confederation, the Liberals wanted to develop a tariff decision-making process divorced from lobbying, while the Conservatives were willing to tie the two together: both were attempting to erect a formal system under which tariff changes could be instituted in an equitable way – equitable at least to those whose voices were heard. In some degree, the political system was beginning to respond to groups and classes rather than individuals and cliques: to speak reductively, policy was replacing patronage.[9]

The lobbying that took place in 1879 had as an implicit premise that it was not Parliament that made basic decisions, but the government through the party it controlled. Hardening party lines made the assumption plausible. The rapid evolution of business interest groups from the 1850s to 1879 that produced some organizations evocative of the modern 'peak association' made the application of pressure by petitioning relatively unattractive, because too loose and discontinuous. The lobbying of 1879, given a certain order by the committee system of the Ontario Manufacturers' Association and by the role of men such as the statistical experts Maclean and Young, were uncertain early steps in the bureaucratization of the policy-making process.

Whatever the power of protectionist interest groups, it was insufficient to dominate the political system. Business and manufacturers' organizations remained fragmented on regional lines and, moreover, did not fully represent their claimed constituencies. Canadian industrialization, business concentration, and economic integration were incipient rather than realized, as the institutions of business life showed. The weaknesses of these interest groups made it possible for the Liberals to maintain not only their attachment to an idealized rural community, but to follow their bent toward low tariffs, despite the demand for protection that mounted in the years before 1879. While the Liberals gave political legitimacy to organizations such as boards of trade and the Grange, they did not to protectionist manufacturers' associations. Thus the Conservative party and then government became a chief means for the compromises between business interests at the national level; the interests themselves could not manage the task. The Conservative government, as governments before it, was able to pursue its own aims in this context.

Still, the National Policy and the interest groups contributed significantly to the development of political parties after Confederation. The policy, in theory at least, was supposed to create a nationality through growth, economic integration, and through a veritable manna of benefits for all interests and regions. Protection was, however, a national political issue that allowed federal electoral candidates of either party to stress at one and the same time their nationalism, their party allegiance, and their awareness of their constituents' needs.

The 1879 tariff was intended to foster economic growth on a broad front, and was the product of a wide range of understandings. On this basis, the tariff's name was suitable. But because of the very process by which it was formulated, it rested on serious ambiguities and contained potential imbalances. The government did not perform a predictive function; it only responded to existing demands and even that not perfectly. For example, though the political campaign of 1878 partly recognized labour as a separate group, in the making of the tariff it was presumed that labour's interests would be served through the growth of manufacturing, an attitude admittedly shared by many working-class voters. It also seems that the periphery of the country did not progress as rapidly as the centre while the National Policy was in effect. The degree to which this was due to the tariff is uncertain, but from the perspective of 1879, criticism mounted on this basis is not justified. Contemporary interests in Nova Scotia thought the policy would be beneficial, and so did agricultural interests in British Columbia. The largely prospective wheat-exporting interests of the Canadian west were ignored in the tariff. Had it been feasible, a special, low schedule of customs duties would have been best for the region, at least until the completion of the Canadian Pacific Railway. Ironically, the promised rapid construction of the railway limited western protest for some time after 1879. To businessmen and to the general run of politicians, the potential market of the west was at best a minor concern in the 1870s. Even in 1883, when the potential of the prairie west should have been far more evident than it had been five or ten years earlier, a parliamentary committee on interprovincial trade flogged the tired horse of Nova Scotian coal in exchange for Ontario wheat, with only bare mentions of the possibilities of trade with an agricultural west.[10]

From the perspective of contemporaries, the tariff did have many positive effects. The depression came to an end. Imports from the United States fell as the tariff imposed higher duties on American-made goods, including many goods formerly duty free; trade resumed more traditional paths as Great Britain returned to its role as Canada's major trading partner, with obvious benefits to importing Laurentian wholesalers.[11] Manufacturing expanded. Agricultural prices improved, and central Canadian agriculture continued to diversify. Whether these attractive economic developments were stimulated by policy changes or not, Macdonald's Conservatives, always eager to score political points, did their best to find their source in the National Policy. High-tariff politicians were quite willing to use the resources of the government to support their case. In 1882, a parliamentary committee stressed the positive effects of the tariff on agriculture (the struggle for the political soul of agrarian Canada continued); in 1884, the government financed a haphazard inter-census survey of manufacturing in Ontario and Quebec as a means of displaying the material benefits of protection.[12] The survey presented masses of statistical material, interspersed with apparently objective description of this suspect data, and supplemented by many *Maritimes* manufacturers' ringing endorsements of the National Policy. Presumably the opinions of their central Canadian counterparts were too well known to require exploration, even in a time of recession. This type of response, combined with vigorous election campaigning, proved effective in the face Liberal hopes for better trade relations with the United States and of ongoing Liberal denunciations that the tariff induced lower living standards, monopoly, and class conflict. The National Policy was entrenched. Whether it was for the good of the country remains open to debate.

Notes

ANQ	Archives Nationale du Québec
DUA	Dalhousie University Archives
PAC	Public Archives of Canada
PAO	Provincial Archives of Ontario
PANB	Provincial Archives of New Brunswick
PANS	Provincial Archives of Nova Scotia
QUA	Queen's University Archives
UNBA	University of New Brunswick Archives
UWO	University of Western Ontario
DFR	Department of Finance Records
DNNR	Department of National Revenue Records
ECO	Executive Council Office
PCO	Privy Council Office
SP	Canada, House of Commons *Sessional Papers*
CHR	*Canadian Historical Review*
CJE	*Canadian Journal of Economics*
CJEPS	*Canadian Journal of Economics and Political Science*
DCB	*Dictionary of Canadian Biography*
JEH	*Journal of Economic History*
JCS	*Journal of Canadian Studies*
JPS	*Journal of Political Science*
MT	*Monetary Times*
OH	*Ontario History*

INTRODUCTION

1 M.C. Urquhart and K.A.H. Buckley, eds, *Historical Statistics of Canada* (Toronto 1965) 141. 'Manufacturing' could include selling functions, however.

2 E.E. Rich and C.H. Wilson, eds, *The Cambridge Economic History of Europe*, vol. 4 (Cambridge 1967) 523–4

3 G. Stolper, K.H. Häuser, and K. Borchardt, *The German Economy, 1870 to the Present* (New York 1967) 35. For an analysis of the origins of the European movement to free trade, see C.P. Kindleberger's sophisticated 'The Rise of Free Trade in Western Europe, 1820–1875,' *JEH* 35 (1975): 20–55.

4 S.B. Clough, *France: A History of National Economics, 1789–1939* (New York 1939) 184–8

5 F.W. Taussig, *The Tariff History of the United States*, 8th ed. (New York 1931) 115

6 Ibid., 158–68, 192

7 M.S. Smith, *Tariff Reform in France 1860–1900: The Politics of Economic Interest* (Ithaca 1980)

8 I.N. Lambi, *Free Trade and Protection in Germany 1868–1879* (Wiesbaden 1963). H. Böhme, 'Big Business Pressure Groups and Bismark's Turn to Protectionism, 1873–79,' *The Historical Journal* 10 (1967): 218–36. For further parallels, see F.J. Coppa, 'The Italian Tariff and the Conflict between Agriculture and Industry: The Commercial Policy of Liberal Italy, 1860–1922,' *JEH* 30 (1970): 742–69. For a perceptive article examining similarities and differences in the Canadian and German experiences, see S. Zeller, 'Nationalism as a Function of Utility. The Protective Tariff of 1879 in Canada and Germany,' *Canadian Review of Studies in Nationalism*, 9 (1982): 225–45. For a detailed summary of tariff policy alterations in Canada, see the classic O.J. McDiarmid, *Commercial Policy in the Canadian Economy* (Cambridge, MA 1946). Less comprehensive though livelier is E. Porritt, *Sixty Years of Protection in Canada, 1846–1912* (Winnipeg 1913). W.L. Marr and D.G. Paterson, *Canada: An Economic History* (Toronto 1980) 117–48, 375–80 proffer theory and a compact, balanced presentation without much political content.

9 Canada, House of Commons *Debates* [hereafter *Debates*], 18 March 1879, 517

10 Urquhart and Buckley, *Historical Statistics*, 14. For the importance of population growth, see A.H. Hansen, 'Economic Progress and Declining Population Growth,' *American Economic Review* 29 (1939): 1–15.

11 Andrew Hill Clark, 'Contributions of Its Southern Neighbors to the Underdevelopment of the Maritime Provinces Area, 1710–1867,' in R.A. Preston, ed., *The Influence of the United States on Canadian Development: Eleven Case Studies* (Durham, NC 1972) 164–84. L.D. McCann, 'Staples and the New Industrialism in

the Growth of Post-Confederation Halifax,' *Acadiensis* 8–2 (1979): 47–79. J.M.S. Careless, 'Aspects of Metropolitanism in Atlantic Canada,' in M. Wade, ed., *Regionalism in the Canadian Community* (Toronto 1969) 117–29. See M.H. Watkins' important 'A Staple Theory of Economic Growth,' *CJEPS* 29 (1963): 141–58 for theoretical considerations.

2 F.W. Remiggi, 'La Lutte du Clerge contre Le Marchard de Poisson: A Study of Power Structures on the Gaspé North Coast in the Nineteenth Century,' in L.R. Fischer and W.W. Sager, eds, *The Enterprising Canadians: Entrepreneurs and Economic Development in Eastern Canada, 1820–1914* (St John's 1979) 188–9

3 A. Faucher, 'The Decline of Shipbuilding at Quebec in the Nineteenth Century,' *CJEPS* 23 (1957): 195–215. A.G. Finley, 'The Morans of St. Martin, N.B., 1850–1880: Toward an Understanding of Family Participation in Maritime Enterprise,' in Fischer and Sager, *Enterprising Canadians*, 49–51. C.K. Harley, 'On the Persistence of Old Techniques: The Case of North American Wooden Shipbuilding,' *JEH* 33 (1973): 372–98

4 In New Brunswick during the 1860s when there were considerable foundry operations, and fittings might be expected to loom rather less high in imports, shipbuilders imported fittings to the value of at least half a dollar per ton of shipping built. It was likely more, as this amount did not include spikes, nails, water tanks and other iron fittings (New Brunswick, House of Assembly *Journals* [hereafter NB *Journals*], 1865–1866, app., Trade and Navigation Return Report, 21).

5 D. Campbell, *Nova Scotia, in Its Historical, Mercantile and Industrial Relations* (Montreal 1873) 486, 493–5. S.A. Saunders, 'The Maritime Provinces and the Reciprocity Treaty,' in G.A. Rawlyk, ed., *Historical Essays on the Atlantic Provinces* (Toronto 1967) 173–4

6 A.R.M. Lower, *Great Britain's Woodyard: British America and the Timber Trade, 1763–1867* (Montreal 1973) 117–22. For the extent and nature of New Brunswick lumbering, see Lower, *The North American Assault on the Canadian Forest* (Toronto 1938) 165–6. G. Wynn, *Timber Colony: A Historical Geography of Early Nineteenth Century New Brunswick* (Toronto 1981) 72–5, 78–84, views the linkages between lumbering and farming in a positive light.

7 The saw mills of the city employed 2260 hands in 1871 out a total number of industrial hands of 6684 (Canada, *Census of Canada 1871*, vol. 3). R.H. Babcock, 'Economic Development in Portland Me., and Saint John N.B. during the Age of Iron and Steam 1850–1914,' *The American Review of Canadian Studies* 9 (1979): 3–37

8 Calculated from *Census 1871*, vol. 3

9 Campbell, 506

10 Calculated from *Census 1871*, vol. 3

21 Campbell, 506–9

22 *Citizen* (Halifax), 5 Jan. 1870

23 Lower, *North American Assault*, 137–47. Lower's analysis of the lumbering industry suggests the 'staple trap' thesis. For an approach which emphasizes indus trial linkages for the industry see L. Deschêne, 'William Price,' *Dictionary of Canadian Biography* [hereafter DCB], vol. 9 (Toronto 1976) 638–42. For associate theory, see Watkins, 'Staple Theory,' and also his 'The Staple Theory Revisited,' JCS 12 (1977) 83–95. T. Naylor, *The History of Canadian Business 1867–1914*, vols (Toronto 1975), has developed a controversial extension of the staple-trap thesis. The Naylorian thesis has come under sustained attack beginning with L.R. MacDonald, 'Merchants against Industry: An Idea and its Origins,' CHR 56 (1975): 263–81. K. Inwood, 'The Decline and Rise of Charcoal Iron: The Case of Canada' (PH D thesis, University of Toronto 1984), chapters 5 and 6, provides a substantial critique. The literature on the issue is extensive.

24 R.L. Jones, *History of Agriculture in Ontario* (Toronto 1946) 197–203

25 Ibid., 208–12, 250–60. J. McCallum, *Unequal Beginnings: Agriculture and Economic Development in Quebec and Ontario until 1870* (Toronto 1980) 45–9. The argument here owes a great deal to McCallum.

26 Calculated from *Census 1871*, vol. 3

27 J.M. Gilmour, *Spatial Evolution of Manufacturing: Southern Ontario 1851–1891* (Toronto 1972) 121–4, 157, 169, maps 54 and 60. W.R. Bland, 'The Location of Manufacturing in Southern Ontario in 1881,' *Ontario Geography* 8 (1974): 23–5. J.E. MacNab, 'Toronto's Industrial Growth to 1891,' OH 47–2 (1955): 67–80

28 *Globe* (Toronto), 5 April 1860. G.S. Kealey, *Toronto Workers Respond to Industrial Capitalism 1867–1892* (Toronto 1980) 20–3

29 For Smart, see *The Canadian Biographical Dictionary and Portrait Gallery of Eminent and Self-Made Men*, vol. 1, Ontario (Toronto 1881) 420–2. And see MacDonald, 'Merchants against Industry.'

30 G. Tulchinsky, *The River Barons: Montreal Businessmen and the Growth of Industry and Transportation 1837–53* (Toronto 1977) 222–3. McCallum, *Unequal Beginnings*, 97

31 J. Hamelin and Y. Roby, *Histoire économique du Québec 1851–1896* (Montreal 1971) 262

32 Tulchinsky, *River Barons*, 220–8. H.A. Innis and A.R.M. Lower, eds, *Select Documents in Canadian Economic History 1783–1885* (Toronto 1933) 597–8, 612–13

33 Calculated from *Census 1871*, vol. 3. With population differences factored out, th ratios become rather interesting, with Saint John at 2.1, Montreal at 1.3, and Toronto at 1.4. If sawmilling and the shipyards (the two major employers in Sain John) are excluded, the ratios are Saint John 1.3, Montreal 1.5, Toronto 1.6.

CHAPTER 1

1 For an analysis of changing British ideas about commercial policy see C.A. Bodelson's *Studies in Mid-Victorian Imperialism* (Copenhagen 1924). McDiarmid, *Commercial Policy* 32–3, indicates the impact of colonial desires on imperial commercial policy.
2 Lower, *Great Britain's Woodyard*, quoted, 88
3 D.A. Sutherland, 'The Merchants of Halifax, 1815–1850. A Commercial Class in Pursuit of Metropolitan Status' (PH D thesis, University of Toronto 1975) 189–97
4 Elizabeth Nish [Gibbs], ed., *Debates of the Legislative Assembly of United Canada* (Montreal, various dates) [hereafter Gibbs, ed., *Debates*] 18 Oct. 1843, 344. See also *Colonist* (Toronto), 20 Apr. 1847. For a full, though now somewhat dated discussion of the Laurentian commercial system, see D. Creighton, *The Empire of the St. Lawrence* 2nd ed. (Toronto 1956). G.N. Tucker, *The Canadian Commercial Revolution, 1845–1851* 2nd ed. (Toronto 1964), provides a substantial discussion of commercial policy from a mercantile and Laurentian perspective. For some valuable correctives, see Tulchinsky, *River Barons*.
5 Debates, in *Novascotian* (Halifax), 17 Feb. 1842. For early examples, see *Acadian Recorder* (Halifax), 24 Feb. 1821 and 26 Jan. 1822. Sutherland, 'Merchants of Halifax,' 23. The phrase 'hewers of wood and drawers of water' was frequently used in public debates over tariffs, though without subtlety. The phrase comes from Joshua 9:23 in the King James version of the Bible. Ironically, those who used it as a metaphor for Canada's relationships to Britain and the United States failed to note that in the original tale the subservient social economy is sheltered from its enemies, and thus is privileged in comparison to outsiders. Moreover, the sheltered position is obtained through base trickery. Indeed, Isaiah 12:3 admonishes readers to 'draw water out of the wells of salvation' with 'joy'. Protectionists did not explore these intellectual avenues.
6 F. Ouellet, *Histoire économique et social du Québec, 1760–1850* (Montreal 1971) 609
7 McDiarmid, *Commercial Policy*, 45–6, 49. Jones, *Agriculture*, 44–5. These authors discuss the conflict between grain exporters and farmers, though they do not place that conflict within the spectrum of policy choices available to the colonials.
8 L.F. Gates, 'The Decided Policy of William Lyon Mackenzie,' *CHR* 40 (1959): 204. The interpretation of Mackenzie's views on protection offered here differs from that of Gates. *Colonial Advocate* (Toronto), 19 Aug. 1824
9 *Colonial Advocate* (Toronto), 18 May and 18 Nov. 1824; 31 Jan. 1828
10 Upper Canada, House of Assembly *Journals* [hereafter UC *Journals*] 1836–37, app. (no. 7) 10

11 UC *Journals* 1836, 14 Jan., 6–8; 10 Feb. 135. *Colonial Advocate* (Toronto), 18 May and 1 July 1824; 17 Jan. 1828

12 UC *Journals* 1835, app., 'First Report from the Select Committee Appointed to inquire into the State of the Trade and Commerce of Upper Canada.' Debates, 15 Mar. 1835, in *Patriot* (Toronto), 3 Apr. 1835

13 UC *Journals* 1835, 145. See also 32, 33, 83–4, 100, 106, 145, 164

14 Ibid., 131. See also 71, 107, 218, 247, 298

15 Gibbs, ed., *Debates*, 27 Sept. 1842, 189

16 Lower Canada, House of Assembly *Journals* 1823–24, 176; 1825, 64–5; 1830, 207–8. UC *Journals* 1831, 18, 21, 29, 32; app. 'Second Report of the Committee on Trade,' and see items cited in n. 13 above.

17 *Colonial Advocate* (Toronto), 1 July 1824; 8 Mar. 1827. Rae, a Scottish-educated school teacher and economist, saw the necessity of moving towards a more independent economic policy in the two Canadas. See, for example, his essay of 1825, 'Sketches of the origin and progress of manufactures' in R. Warren James, *John Rae, Political Economist*, vol. 1 (Toronto 1965). While his ideas concerning the social context necessary for the accumulation of capital owed little to the New World, his assertion of the importance of the active involvement of the state in economic planning and his articulation of the infant-industry argument for protection did. The original publication of his *New Principles on the Subject of Political Economy* (1834, but more recently republished in James, *John Rae*) in Boston sold poorly and received little critical attention. Rae's thinking did not influence the assessment of protectionism in the 1835 report of the Upper Canadian Assembly's Committee on Trade.

18 UC *Journals* 1935, app. (no. 11)

19 Ibid., app. (no. 32)

20 Gibbs, ed., *Debates*, 27 Sept. 1842, 184

21 UC *Journals* 1836–37, app. (no. 7). Gibbs, ed., *Debates*, 3 Mar. 1845, 1873–5. *Patriot* (Toronto), 31 Mar. 1835

22 Jones, *Agriculture*, 124–35. Province of Canada, *Statutes* [hereafter Prov. Canada *Statutes*], 6 Vict. c. 31; and 7 Vict. c. 1 & 2

23 Province of Canada, Assembly *Journals* [hereafter Prov. Canada *Journals*] 1843, app. (B.B.); Gibbs, ed., *Debates*, 18 Oct. 1843, 344. UC *Journals* 1836, Report of the Committee on Agriculture, 331. *Gazette* (Montreal), 2 Apr. 1842

24 *News* (Saint John), 10 Nov. 1843; 22 Jan. 1844

25 Ibid., 15, 22, and 31 Jan.; 15 Feb. 1844. A.B. to the editor, *Courier* (Saint John), 22 Jan. 1844. T.W. Acheson ('The Great Merchant and Economic Development in St. John, 1820–1850,' *Acadiensis* 8–2 [1979]: 3–27) provides a valuable discussion of these developments from a restrained staple-trap perspective.

26 H. Greeley, ed., *The American Laborer*, modern edition (New York 1974). The

word 'proto-nationalist' is taken from E. Genovese, *Roll, Jordon Roll: The World the Slaves Made* (New York 1974). No implicit comparison between slaves and British North American colonials is intended.

27 *News* (Saint John), 16 Feb. 1844. NB *Journals* 1844, 12, 31, 57, 70, 71, 81, 82, 85, 88, 89, 93, 105, 106, 107, 111, 112, 114. *News* (Saint John), 15 Apr. 1844

28 'This subject has been lately much discussed,' began the *Colonist* (Toronto) of 19 April 1843, in an editorial attacking Horace Greeley and his protectionism. For petitions, see Province of Canada, Legislative Assembly, *General Index to the Journals* 1841–1851, 209–9.

29 Province of Canada *Statutes*, 8 Vict. c. 3. McDiarmid, *Commercial Policy*, 65. For Upper Canadian opposition, see the *Colonist* (Toronto), 25 Mar. 1845.

30 *Times* (Halifax), 29 Sept. 1846, quoted in the *Colonist* (Toronto), 27 Oct. 1846. The most dramatic statement of the crisis of the late 1840s is in Creighton, *Commercial Empire*, in which the crisis performs as the dénouement to a three-act tragedy. Tucker, *Commercial Revolution*, provides a more restrained approach.

31 *News* (Saint John), 28 June 1848

32 Ibid., 11, 13, 15, 20, and 27 Dec. 1848

33 *Gazette* (Montreal), 30 Mar. 1846. Porritt, *Protection*, 62–3. On the careers of two prominent members of the association, see H.C. Klassen, 'Luther Hamilton Holton,' *DCB*, vol. 10 (Toronto 1972) 354–8 and G. Tulchinsky and Brian Young, 'John Young,' ibid., 720–7.

34 Debates, 22 June 1847, in *Colonist* (Toronto), 29 June 1847. Prov. Canada *Statutes*, 10 & 11 Vict. c. 31. Prov. Canada *Journals* 1842, app. N

35 Prov. Canada *Journals* 1847, app. K. Nova Scotia, House of Assembly *Journals* [hereafter NS *Journals*] 1849, app. no. 13. W.M. Whitelaw, *The Maritimes and Canada before Confederation* (Toronto 1966) 85–7. McCallum, *Unequal Beginnings*, 17

36 PAC, Toronto Board of Trade Papers [hereafter Toronto B of T Papers], MG 28 III 56, meeting of 2 Jan. 1851, Council Minute Book 1850–71, 17. Jones, *Agriculture*, 190–5

37 Tucker, *Commercial Revolution* 31–45

38 PAC, Toronto B of T Papers, meeting 26 Jan. 1852, Council Minute Book 1850–71, 43. ANQ, Quebec Board of Trade Papers [hereafter Quebec B of T Papers], meeting 5 Apr. 1852, and 3 Apr. 1854, Minute Book 1852–78, 4–5, 89–90

39 M.J. Piva ('Continuity and Crisis: Francis Hincks and Canadian Economic Policy,' *CHR* 66 [1985]: 185–210) correctly emphasizes transportation and agricultural policies, but ignores the place of commercial policy and so passes over an important congruence: the 'commercial revolution' took place *because* of the colony's commitment to continuity in its economic life.

40 D.C. Masters, *The Reciprocity Treaty of 1854*, 2nd ed. (Toronto 1963) 8–9. This book provides the fullest account of the background to the treaty.
41 R.H. McDonald's 'Nova Scotia Views the United States, 1784–1854' (PH D thesis, Queen's University 1974) 285–305, provides a full discussion of this point.
42 Debates, 9 Feb. 1848, in *News* (Saint John), 14 Feb. 1848
43 *Colonist* (Toronto), 30 Jan. 1849. Debates, in *News* (Saint John), 6 Mar. 1848
44 C.D. Everett & Son to the editor, *News* (Saint John), 14 Apr. 1849
45 New Brunswick, *Statutes* [hereafter NB *Statutes*], 12 Vict. c. 18
46 McDiarmid, *Commercial Policy*, 116–17. Sutherland, 'Merchants of Halifax,' 413. Nova Scotia. *Statutes* [hereafter NS *Statutes*], 8 Vict. c. 3; 12 Vict. c. 10; 13 Vict. c. 3. *Colonist* (Halifax), 10 Oct. 1848
47 *Colonist* (Toronto), 30 Mar. 1847. Scobie's argument presumed that the great mercantile interests were responsible for the development of much large-scale British industry, and that these mercantile interests lacked paternalistic attitudes that otherwise existed between capital and labour.
48 R.B. Sullivan, *Lecture, Delivered before the Mechanics' Institute of Hamilton, on Wednesday Evening, November 17, 1847, on the Connection between Agriculture and Manufactures of Canada* (Hamilton 1848). Existing accounts of protectionism usually date the movement to the Canadas in the late 1840s, and stress Sullivan's lecture as seminal. Porritt, *Protection*, 166ff provides an early statement of this view. Its weaknesses should be apparent.
49 *Gazette* (Montreal), 15 Dec. 1847. *Colonist* (Toronto), 17 Dec. 1847. These contain a sampling of notices to the electors from hopeful candidates. For the revenue problem, see Prov. Canada *Journals* 1857, app. (62).
50 *Colonist* (Toronto), 12 Dec. 1848; 26 Jan. and 20 Feb. 1849
51 W. Weir, *Sixty Years in Canada* (Montreal 1903) 98–104. *Colonist* (Toronto), 9 Feb. 1849. *Gazette* (Montreal), 9 Feb. 1849. On Workman, see G. Tulchinsky, 'William Workman,' *DCB*, vol. 10 (Toronto 1972) 717–18.
52 *Gazette* (Montreal), 29 and 31 Jan. 1849
53 *La Minerve* (Montreal), José to the editor, 26 Oct., 9 and 30 Nov., 1, 14, 28 Dec. 1848; 4 and 11 Jan. 1849. See also 21 Dec. 1848; 8 Jan. 1849. Prov. Canada *Journals* 1849, app. AAAAA
54 *Gazette* (Montreal), 19 Feb. 1849
55 Prov. Canada *Statutes*, Vict. 12 c. 1. *Gazette* (Montreal), 11 Apr. 1849
56 C.C. Tansill, *The Canadian Reciprocity Treaty of 1854* (Baltimore 1922) 36
57 Prov. Canada *Statutes*, 16 Vict. c. 85. Gibbs, ed., *Debates*, 7 Apr. 1849, 1760; 10 Apr. 1849, 1814
58 But the economy was actually beginning the upturn. D. McCalla, *The Upper Canada Trade 1834–1872: A Study of the Buchanans' Business* (Toronto 1979)

71–2, provides a fine summary of the economic conditions of the depression of the late 1840s.

59 Compare *Gazette* (Montreal), 23 Mar. 1846 and 9 Feb. 1849 to the list of manifesto signatures in Weir, *Sixty Years*, 63–79.

60 Weir, *Sixty Years*, 41–63

61 C.D. Allin and G.M. Jones, *Annexation, Preferential Trade and Reciprocity* (Westport, CT 1912) 91–4, 224, 324, 361–2. W.S. MacNutt, *The Atlantic Provinces: The Emergence of Colonial Society 1712–1857* (Toronto 1965) 239–41

62 Allin and Jones, *Annexation*, 142–3, 208–12

63 *Minutes of the Proceedings of the Second Convention of the Delegates of the British American League* (Toronto 1849). J.M.S. Careless, *The Union of the Canadas: The Growth of Canadian Institutions 1841–1857* (Toronto 1967) 127–31. For a useful summary of the league's protectionist attitudes, see G.S. Kealey, *Toronto Workers Respond to Industrial Capitalism 1867–1892* (Toronto 1980) 6–7.

64 Despite Creighton, there is general agreement that annexationism in 1849 was a passing phenomenon, as Allin and Jones (*Annexation*) conclude in the only full-length treatment of the movement. Careless, *Union of the Canadas*, reaches the same conclusion through examining a broader context, 122–35. See also D.F. Warner, *The Idea of Continental Union* (Lexington 1963) 22–8.

65 R.S. Longley, *Sir Francis Hincks: A Study of Canadian Politics, Railways and Finance in the Nineteenth Century* (Toronto 1943) 249–50

66 Ibid., 259–60

67 *Gazette* (Montreal), 3 Sept. 1852. ANQ, Quebec B of T Papers, meeting of 1–4 Sept. 1852, Minute Book 1852–1878, 25–6

68 *Gazette* (Montreal), 14 Mar. 1853

69 Debates, 26 Aug. and 20 Sept. 1852, in *Gazette* (Montreal), 30 Aug. and 23 Sept. 1852. Debates, 28 Oct. 1852, in *Globe* (Toronto), 9 Nov. 1852. For opposition, see *Colonist* (Toronto), 28 Sept. and 19 Oct. 1852, and *Gazette* (Montreal), 19 Oct. 1852. *The Honble. Francis Hincks' Views of the Commercial Policy of Canada, in 1846 and 1847 and in 1852* (Montreal 1853) On Gamble, see B. Dyster, 'John William Gamble,' *DCB*, vol. 10 (Toronto 1972) 299–300.

70 L.B. Shippee, *Canadian-American Relations 1849–1874* (Toronto 1939), 41–3

71 L. Oliphant, *Episodes in a Life of Adventure: or Moss from a Rolling Stone* (Edinburgh 1896). For some hint of the lengths to which Francis Hincks might go, see PAC, Department of Finance Records [hereafter PAC, DFR], RG 19, vol. 3378, 166–76, Hincks to J.L. Hayes, 1 July 1871. For some differing views on the role of lobbying in these developments, see W.D. Overman, 'I.D. Andrews and Reciprocity in 1854: An Episode in Dollar Diplomacy,' *CHR* 15 (1934): 248–63; D.C. Masters, 'A Further Word on I.D. Andrews and the Reciprocity Treaty

of 1854,' *CHR* 17 (1936): 159–67; and I.W.D. Hecht, 'Israel D. Andrews and the Reciprocity Treaty of 1854: A Reappraisal,' *CHR* 44 (1963): 313–29.

72 Whitelaw, *Maritimes*, 87n. McDiarmid, *Commercial Policy*, 73

73 J.M.S. Careless, 'Mid-Victorian Liberalism in Central Canadian Newspapers, 1850–1867,' *CHR* 31 (1950): 221–36

CHAPTER 2

1 Debates, 4 Mar. 1859, in *News* (Saint John), 9 Mar. 1859

2 NB *Statutes*, 12 Vict. c. 18; 19 Vict. c. 18; 25 Vict. c. 9

3 NB *Journals* 1862, Report, Trade and Navigation Returns 3

4 W. Cayley, *Finances and Trade of Canada at the Beginning of the Year 1855* (London 1855)

5 *Montreal in 1856: A Sketch Prepared for the Opening of the Grand Trunk Railway of Canada* (Montreal 1856)

6 *Gazette* (Montreal), 21 and 23 Apr. 1856

7 Debates, 11 Apr. 1856, in *Gazette* (Montreal), 15 Apr. 1856

8 *Gazette* (Montreal), 21 and 23 Apr. 1856

9 McCalla, *Upper Canada Trade*, 96. M.J. Doucet, 'Working Class Housing in a Small Nineteenth-Century Canadian City: Hamilton, Ontario 1852–1881' in G.S. Kealey and P. Warrian, eds, *Essays in Canadian Working Class History* (Toronto, 1976) 84–5, 90, table 3

10 *New Era* (Montreal), 18 Feb. 1858. *Colonist* (Toronto), 26 Mar. 1858. PAC, DFR, vol. 3367, proposed tariff, signed by William Rodden, n.d.

11 ANQ, Quebec B of T Papers, Minute Books 1857–76, meetings of 11 Feb. and 17 Mar. 1858, 9, 11

12 *Colonist* (Toronto), 26 Mar. 1858. PAC, Buchanan Papers, vol. 117, 75864, memorial

13 *Colonist* (Toronto), 3 Mar. 1858. *Gazette* (Montreal), 10 and 17 Apr. 1858. QUA, Kingston Board of Trade Papers, City of Kingston Archives [hereafter QUA, Kingston B of T Papers], box 1120, Minute Book 1851–1910, meeting of 7 Apr. 1858

14 *Gazette* (Montreal), 17 Apr. 1858

15 I. Buchanan, *The Relations of the Industry of Canada* (Montreal 1864) 459

16 Ibid., 257–67, 429–30. See also 369–77 in which Buchanan's concern with his status as honorary lieutenant-colonel of a militia battalion is evident. See also McCalla, *Upper Canada Trade*, 11. Such identification with the landed gentry was common in Britain. See R.G. Wilson, *Gentlemen Merchants: The Merchant Community in Leeds, 1700–1830* (Manchester 1971) 2, 220–32

17 Buchanan, *Industry of Canada*, 186

18 Ibid., 185, 197–8, 438–40, 497
19 [John Barnard Byles], *Sophisms of Free-Trade*, 9th ed. (Manchester 1870)
20 Buchanan, *Industry of Canada*, 73–4, 88–9
21 Ibid., 13, 14–15, 75n., 134, 161–2, 499. For his associated monetary views, see ibid., 496–516.
22 S.D. Chapman, 'British Marketing Enterprise: The Changing Roles of Merchants, Manufacturers and Financiers, 1700–1860,' *Business History Review* 53 (1979): 205–33
23 H.C. Carey, *Harmony of Interests* (Philadelphia 1851), passim; Carey, *Principles of Social Science*, vol. 1 (Philadelphia 1888; originally 1858) 271–3, 289, 305, 411–30. Carey became the single most widely known protectionist of the mid and later nineteenth century: he was translated into German; the Italians took note of him; even J.S. Mill found him sufficiently dangerous a threat to liberalism to merit attention – attention Mill paid no other protectionist except John Rae. See U. Rabbeno, *The American Commercial Policy: Three Historical Essays* (London 1895) 355, 357n. J.S. Mill, *Principles of Political Economy*, 7th ed. (London 1871) 538–42. For a vigorous though compressed argument for the intellectual importance of 19th-century American protectionist theorists, see 'Introduction,' M. Hudson, ed., *Economics and Technology in 19th-Century American Thought: The Neglected American Economists* (New York 1975). See also R.J. Morrison, 'Henry C. Carey and American Economic Development,' *Explorations in Economic History* 5 (1968):132–44.
24 Friedrich List, *The National System of Political Economy* (London 1885), passim. J. Dorfman, *The Economic Mind in American Civilization 1606–1865*, vol. 2 (New York 1949) 575–84
25 Buchanan, *Industry of Canada*, 12–21, 145–6, 160–2
26 Alexander Hamilton, 'Report on the Subject of Manufactures,' in F.W. Taussig, ed., *State Papers and Speeches on the Tariff* (Cambridge, MA 1893) 1–107
27 See D.G. Rohr, *The Origins of Social Liberalism in Germany* (Chicago 1963) 104–9.
28 See also Carey's *Prospects of the Farmer under the Tariff of 1846* (New York 1852) and *Letters to the President* (Philadelphia 1858).
29 Buchanan, *Industry of Canada*, 507, 14. Buchanan has received considerable attention. McCalla (*Upper Canada Trade*) explores his business career; Bryan Palmer (*A Culture in Conflict: Skilled Workers and Industrial Capitalism in Hamilton, Ontario, 1860–1914* [Montreal 1979] chapter 4) and especially Steven Langdon ('The Political Economy of Capitalist Transformation: Central Canada from the 1840's to the 1870's' [MA thesis, Carleton University 1972] 174–82) have over-emphasized his intellectual achievements. Palmer's 'producer ideology' is similar to what I have called protectionist ideology; Palmer's tag presumes working-

class origins for this type of thinking; mine asserts the ideology's functional place within an industrializing society.

30 Buchanan, *Industry of Canada*, 483–7. Weir, *Sixty Years*, 105–18

31 *New Era* (Montreal), 24 Apr. 1858. *Gazette* (Montreal), 10 and 17 Apr. 1858. Cayley in Debates, 5 Mar. 1858, *Globe* (Toronto), 6 Mar. 1858

32 Debates, 17 June 1858, in *Globe* (Toronto), 19 June 1858

33 D.G. Creighton, *John A. Macdonald, the Young Politician* (Toronto 1952) 251. J.E. Hodgetts, *Pioneer Public Service: An Administrative History of the United Canadas, 1841–1867* (Toronto 1955) 103

34 *Spectator* (Hamilton), 23 June 1858. *Globe* (Toronto), 25 June 1858

35 PAC, DFR, vol. 3367, copy, J. Langton to W. Cayley, 27 June 1858. Substantial analysis of the fiscal position of the union of the Canadas remains to see the light of day. But see Piva, 'Francis Hincks' and A. Faucher, 'Some Aspects of the Financial Difficulties of the Province of Canada,' *CJEPS* 26 (1960): 617–24.

36 *Globe* (Toronto), 2 July 1858

37 *Spectator* (Hamilton), 7 and 8 July 1858. *Globe* (Toronto), 23 July 1858. Debates, 9 July 1858, in *Globe* (Toronto), 12 July 1858

38 Debates, 9, 13, 15, 23 July, in *Globe* (Toronto), 12, 15, 16, 27 July 1858

39 J.M.S. Careless, *Brown of the Globe*, vol. 1 (Toronto 1959) 263–80

40 *Globe* (Toronto), 12 and 14 Mar. 1859

41 The deficit of 1857 was equivalent to over half the total net revenue of the most productive revenue in the province to that point, 1854. Prov. Canada, *Journals* 1857, app. (no. 62). The distress caused by the poor crops is dramatically pictured in PAC, DFR, vol. 3367, R. Armour to A.T. Galt, 2 Feb. 1859.

42 PAC, Galt Papers, vol. 1, 47, A.T. Galt to T. Baring, 16 Aug. 1858

43 Debates, 14 and 16 Mar. 1859 in *Globe* (Toronto), 16 and 17 Mar. 1859

44 PAC, Ellice Family Papers, vol. 34, 11249–53, J. Rose to E. Ellice, 3 Jan. 1858 [sic]

45 Faucher, 'Financial Difficulties.' PAC, Glyn, Mills Papers, letterbook 4, 52, G.C. Glyn to A.T. Galt, 23 Nov. 1857

46 PAC, Galt Papers, vol. 1, 28–31, A.T. Galt to T. Brassey, 13 Feb. 1859

47 Debates, 11 Mar. 1859, in *Globe* (Toronto), 12 Mar. 1859

48 PAC, Galt Papers, vol. 1, 4–7, A.T. Galt to T. Baring, 16 Aug. 1858

49 PAC, DFR, vol. 3376, A.T. Galt to the presidents of the boards of trade of Hamilton, Toronto, Kingston, Montreal, London, Ottawa, and Quebec, 16 Jan. 1859

50 PAC, DFR, vol. 3368: J.G. Dinning to A.T. Galt, 19 Jan. 1859; J. Shannon to A.T. Galt, 27 Jan. 1859; London Board of Trade to A.T. Galt, 1 Feb. 1859; C. Robertson to A.T. Galt, 3 Feb. 1859. QUA, Kingston B of T Papers, box 1120, Minute Book 1851–1910, meeting of 14 Feb. 1860. PAC, Toronto B of T Papers, Council Minute Book 1850–71, 188, meeting of 28 Jan. 1859

51 PAC, Macdonald Papers, MG 26 A, vol. 216, 92106–8, Memorandum of A.T. Galt, 20 Aug. 1860. Galt's position was a continuation of his insistence on greater colonial independence on commercial policy matters. D.C. Masters, 'A.T. Galt and Canadian Fiscal Autonomy,' *CHR* 15 (1934): 276–82. D.L.M. Farr (*The Colonial Office and Canada 1867–1887* [Toronto 1955], 170) takes a more restrained view of Galt's accomplishments.

52 The note, in Galt's handwriting, is undated and unsigned, in PAC vol. 3368, Department of Finance, undated 1859. Echoes of the note found their way into Galt's public statements. In justifying the protective aspects of the tariff in his *Canada, 1849 to 1859* (Quebec 1860) 31, Galt asserted that the protective element of the tariff would, at the utmost, encourage 'the establishment of works requiring comparatively unskilled labour.' In his note, the third category that he believed should be protected was 'those in which unskilled labour can be employed most fully.' Some of the analytical distinctions made here are derived from J.H. Dales, 'Canada's National Policies,' in his *The Protective Tariff in Canada's Development* (Toronto 1966) 143–58.

53 For a perceptive discussion of Galt's interest in the West, see A.A. den Otter, *Civilizing the West: The Galts and the Development of Western Canada* (Edmonton, 1982).

54 PAC, Galt Papers vol. 8, 2917–25, Sir A.T. Galt to Hon. James Ferrier, 3 Sept. 1875. For a somewhat different assessment of Galt's conceptions, see den Otter, 'Alexander Galt, the 1859 Tariff and Canadian Economic Nationalism,' *CHR* 63 (1982): 151–78.

55 Prov. Canada *Statutes*, 22 Vict. c. 2

56 British North American Association, *Speech of Hon. A.T. Galt, at the Chamber of Commerce, Manchester, September 25, 1862* (London 1862) 4. PAC, DFR, vol. 3368: J.B. Forsyth to A.T. Galt, 31 Jan. 1859; J.G. Dinning to A.T. Galt, 19 Jan. 1859; Frothingham & Workman and others to A.T. Galt, 11 Mar. 1859. For a penetrating discussion of the tiered structure of the tariff for which I am greatly indebted, see D.F. Barnett, 'The Galt Tariff: Incidental or Effective Protection?' *CJE* 9 (1976): 389–407. The literature on the Galt tariff focuses on whether it was a tariff for revenue or protection. Barnett rejected O.D. Skelton's assertion (*The Life and Times of Sir Alexander Tilloch Galt*, 2nd ed. [Toronto, 1966] 115–23) that Galt's was a revenue tariff, and unfortunately does not assess the financial position of the government at all; den Otter ('Alexander Galt') accepts Barnett's position. For yet further references on this point, see den Otter, 'Alexander Galt,' 152. Galt's conception of incidental protection was rather more sophisticated than Barnett recognizes, as this study shows. Recently Marr and Paterson, *Economic History*, 147, have dissented from Barnett, and I owe something to the clarity of their theoretical conceptions. See their presentation of revenue considerations

in tariff structure, figure 5:1 and 119–21. Marr and Paterson do not derive a revenue curve to show first increasing, then decreasing, revenue as tariffs increase, a curve which would capture the essence of the conception of incidental protection. Incidental protection consists of all tariff levels that do not bring about declining revenue, and thus is a theoretically precise concept; Galt evidently was shooting for the maximum revenue level.

57 PAC, DFR, vol. 3368: J. Law to A.T. Galt, 19 Mar. 859; J.G. Dinning to A.T. Galt, 15 Mar. 1859; George Hall Lane Gibbs & Co. and nineteen others to A.T. Galt, 1 Mar. 1859; Gillet King & Co. and others, memorial to the governor general, 8 Mar. 1859. PAC, Department of National Revenue Records [hereafter DNNR], series A–1, vol. 204: J. & Greene & Sons to J. Rose, 10 Mar. 1859; J. Mitchell to A.T. Galt, 10 Mar. 1859

58 *Spectator* (Hamilton), 12 Mar. 1859

59 PAC, Province of Canada, Executive Council Office [hereafter Prov. Canada ECO], State Minute Book V, 38–47, Minute of 16 March 1860

60 Weir, *Sixty Years*, 115–17

61 PAC, DFR, vol. 3368, W. Rodden to J. Rose, 7 Feb. 1859

62 *Globe* (Toronto), 10 Mar. 1859. *Times* (Hamilton), 15 Mar. 1859. PAC, DFR, vol. 3368, Frothingham & Workman and others to A.T. Galt, 11 Mar. 1859

63 PAC, DFR, vol. 3368, J.G. Dinning to A.T. Galt, 15 Mar. 1859

64 *Globe* (Toronto), 9, 12, and 19 Mar. 1859. Debates, 15, 16 Mar. 1859, in *Globe* (Toronto), 16 and 17 Mar. 1859

65 *The Effects of the New Tariff on the Upper Canada Trade* (Toronto 1859). Debates, 14 Mar. 1859, in *Globe* (Toronto), 15 Mar. 1859

66 Debates, 16 Mar. 1859, in *Globe* (Toronto), 17 Mar. 1859

67 Ibid.

68 PAC, Buchanan Papers: vol. 27, 22912–14, I. Buchanan to A.T. Galt, 10 Mar. 1859; vol. 54, 43309–12, I. Buchanan to L.V. Sicotte, 12 Mar. 1859; vol. 118, 76425, 'Amendment to be moved on Mr. Galt's motion that the Speaker leave the Chair, and the House go into Committee on the Tariff'; vol. 46, 32920–3 J.A. Macdonald to I. Buchanan, 12 Mar. 1859

69 *Globe* (Toronto), 5 and 19 Mar. 1859. Debates, 18 Mar. 1859, in *Globe* (Toronto), 19 Mar. 1859

70 Debates, 11 Mar. 1859, in *Globe* (Toronto), 14 Mar. 1859

71 W.M. Samuel to the editor, *Globe* (Toronto), 21 Mar. 1859

72 *Times* (Hamilton), 9 Mar. 1859

73 During the 1859 agitation, there was no newspaper mention of the association. On the finances of the association, see PAC, Buchanan Papers vol. 58, 46633, W. Weir to I. Buchanan, 29 July 1858; vol. 58, 46656–8, circular signed I. Buchanan, 12 Mar. 1860

74 W.T. Easterbrook and H.G.J. Aitken, *Canadian Economic History* (Toronto 1956) 376

75 PAC, Glyn, Mills Papers, letterbooks, 19, G.C. Glyn to A.T. Galt, 4 June 1862

CHAPTER 3

1 See Saunders, 'Maritime Provinces' for a cautious statement of this position. For a more uninhibited position, see L.H. Officer and L.B. Smith, 'The Canadian-American Reciprocity Treaty of 1855 to 1866,' *JEH* 28 (1969): 598–603, and R. Ankli, 'The Reciprocity Treaty of 1854,' *CJE* 4 (1971): 1–20. See also Ankli, 'Canadian-American Reciprocity: A Comment,' *JEH* 30 (1970): 427–31 and Officer and Smith, 'Canadian-American Reciprocity: A Reply,' *JEH* 30 (1970): 432–4.

2 M. Cross, ed., *Free Trade, Annexation and Reciprocity, 1846–54* (Toronto 1971), introduction. Warner, *Continental Union* 34

3 While the railway system to and in the midwest was substantially complete by 1858, it cost 38.61 cents per bushel to move wheat from Chicago to New York; by 1890 the cost had declined to 14.3 cents (G.R. Taylor and I.D. Neu, *The American Railroad Network 1861–1890* [Cambridge, MA 1956] 2, 3–7). Wheat production in Illinois, Indiana, and Wisconsin rose from 7,384,000 bushels in 1839 to 19,914,000 in 1849, to 56,342,000 in 1859. New York production fell by nearly one-third in the same period (P.W. Gates, *The Farmer's Age: Agriculture 1815–1860* [New York 1960] 159–65, 183–5). Despite their assertions to the contrary, some suggestion of potential price improvements under reciprocity is found in Officer and Smith, 'Reciprocity,' 613–14. See also PAC, Merritt Papers, MG 24 E I vol. 20, 3245–50, I. Buchanan to W.H. Merritt, 28 Feb. 1846. As to coal, see Saunders, 'Maritime Provinces,' 173–4. Also, NS *Journals* 1876, app. no. 6, mines report, 5–11. For coal prices, see K.W. Taylor and H. Michell, *Statistical Contributions to Canadian Economic History*, vol. 2 (Toronto 1931) 82–3. Lower (*Great Britain's Woodyard*, 132) indicates the American market for lumber took any quality of lumber for a price, whereas the British was a premium market.

4 PAC, DFR, vol. 3370, J. Langton to A.T. Galt, 21 May 1860

5 Jones, *Agriculture*, 190–5. PAC, Buchanan Papers vol. 36, 29593–6, I. Buchanan to F. Jones, 27 Apr. 1872

6 PAC, Buchanan Papers vol. 48, 38344–8, E. Miall to I. Buchanan, 16 May 1864. PAC, DNNR, series A–1, vol. 210, T. Workman to A.T. Galt, 28 Mar. 1862

7 PAC, Macdonald Papers, vol. 297, 136159–62, printed open letter, W. Barber & Barber, 11 May 1860, with appended memorandum from Isaac Buchanan

8 PAC, Buchanan Papers vol. 58, 46645–50, W. Weir to I. Buchanan, 19 Jan. 1860. Skelton, *Galt*, 129–30

9 Debates, 2 Apr. 1861, in *Globe* (Toronto), 3 Apr. 1861. PAC, Macdonald Papers, vol. 216, 92110–15, A.T. Galt to J.A. Macdonald, 3 Oct. 1862

10 Debates, 16 May 1862, in *Globe* (Toronto), 23 May 1862

11 PAC, Buchanan Papers: vol. 22, 18607, I. Buchanan to D. Crawford, 19 May 1862; vol. 26, 22243, I. Buchanan to Messrs. Fraser & Co., 19 May 1862; vol. 58, 46685 I. Buchanan to W. Weir, 19 May 1862. PAO, Kirby Papers, vol. 4, J. Simpson to W. Kirby, 20 May 1862

12 Debates, 26 May 1862, in *Times* (Hamilton), 27 May 1862

13 PAC, Mackenzie Papers, MG 26 B, 92–5, G. Brown to L. Holton, 26 June 1863. PAC, Brown Papers, MG 24 B 40, vol. 5, 833–8, Sandfield Macdonald to Brown, 21 Jan. 1864. PAC, J.S. Macdonald Papers, MG 24 B 30, vol. 2, 1041–3, G. Brown to J.S. Macdonald, 25 Jan. 1864. PAC, DFR, vol. 3376, 342, L.H. Holton to J. Young, 3 Feb. 1864

14 R. Winks, *Canada and the United States: The Civil War Years* (Baltimore 1960) 347–8. PAC, Buchanan Papers vol. 39, 31754–7, 'Report of a Committee of ... Executive Council.'

15 Winks, *Canada and the United States*, 137–9. PAC, Buchanan Papers: vol. 4, 2400, Adam Brown to I. Buchanan, 4 Feb. 1864; vol. 3, 1384–5, J.G. Beard & Co. to I. Buchanan, 6 May 1864; vol. 18, 14962, Butler and Jackson to I. Buchanan, 8 June 1864. PAC, DFR, vol. 3376, 360–6, L.H. Holton to Lord Monck, 9 Mar. 1864

16 PAC, ECO, Submissions to Council, vol. 63, 31 Mar. 1864. Note that the inclusion of the Maritime provinces is an afterthought on Galt's part. PAC, J.W. Taylor Papers, A.T. Galt to C.J. Brydges, 9 June 1864. Masters, *Reciprocity* 90–2

17 PAC, Howe Papers, MG 24 B 29, vol. 8, 546–8, J. Howe to Lord Lyons, 2 Mar. 1864. PAC, DFR, vol. 3376: 408–9, A.T. Galt to L. Bloodgood, 23 Aug. 1864; 450–2, A.T. Galt to D. Stewart, 16 Dec. 1864

18 PAC, Prov. Canada, ECO, State Minute Book AB, 197–8, Minute of 24 Mar. 1865. PAC, Macdonald Papers, vol. 100, 39465–7

19 PAC, Buchanan Papers vol. 1, 520–4, I.D. Andrews to I. Buchanan, 9 Mar. 1865

20 PAC, DFR, vol. 3376, 396–7, A.T. Galt to C.J. Brydges, 9 June 1864. PAC, Buchanan Papers vol. 56, 45000–1, J.W. Taylor to T. Swinyard, 16 Mar. 1866. PAC, Taylor Papers, MG 27 I H2, I. Buchanan to J.W. Taylor, 24 Feb. 1866. PAC, DFR, vol. 3376, 528–9, A.T. Galt to M.P. Fessenden, 2 Sept. 1865. PAC, Galt Papers vol. 3, 1066–8, D.A. Wells to A.T. Galt, 31 Oct. 1865

21 PAC, Galt Papers vol. 3, 993–6, P. Redpath to A.T. Galt, 28 Apr. 1865. PAC, Macdonald Papers, vol. 246, 110641–3, G. McMicken to J.A. Macdonald, 28 Aug. 1865

22 It has been shown that Americans had genuine annexationist aims concerning the Red River and the northwest (A.C. Gluek, *Minnesota and the Manifest Destiny of the Canadian North West* [Toronto 1965]). In addition, there existed an annexa-

tionist sentiment generally associated with a belief in manifest destiny that affected the perspectives and actions of leading American politicians. A. Nevins, *Hamilton Fish: The Inner History of the Grant Administration* (New York 1936), 216–20. Some American consuls in Canada continued to encourage such annexationist sentiment in the American Department of State throughout the 1870s. United States Consular Records, [Toronto] dispatch 148, A.D. Shaw to Assistant Secretary of State, 3 April 1875

23 PAC, Toronto B of T Papers Council Meeting of 19 April and 19 May, 1865, Council Minute Book 1850–1871, vol. 2. ANQ, Quebec B of T Papers, meeting of 27 June 1865, Minute Book, 1857–76, 197–9

24 *Report of the Chamber of Commerce, Saint John,* N.B., *of Their Delegates to the Commercial Convention, Held in Detroit Mich., July 1865* (Saint John 1865), 10

25 PAC, Macdonald Papers, vol. 191, 79465–73, C.J. Brydges to J.A. Macdonald, 17 July 1865

26 PAC, Prov. Canada, ECO, State Minute Book AB, 488–9, Minute of 14 July 1865. PAC, Brown Papers, vol. 6, 1402–17, G. Brown to Lord Monck, 25 Dec. 1865, draft letter. PAC, Galt Papers, vol. 5, 2213–19, draft memorandum, A.T. Galt, Dec. 1865. D.G. Creighton, *The Road to Confederation* (Toronto 1964) 307

27 Farr, *Colonial Office and Canada*, 218

28 PAC, ECO, Submissions to Council, vol. 66, Minutes of the Proceedings of the Confederate Council

29 PAC, DFR, vol. 3376, 66–9, A.T. Galt to Baron de Boilleau, 21 Apr. 1860

30 For the personality clash between Galt and Brown, see Creighton, *Confederation*, 306, 335–6, and especially, Careless, *Brown*, vol. 2, 208–20

31 PAC, Brown Papers, vol. 6, 1402–17, Brown to Monck, 25 Dec. 1865

32 PAC, Watkin Papers, MG 24 E 17, item 83, C.J. Brydges to Sir E. Watkin, 11 Dec. 1865

33 PAC, DFR, vol. 3372, Minute in Council, 22 Dec. 1865

34 PAC, Galt Papers, vol. 3, 1100–2, D.A. Wells to A.T. Galt, 19 Jan. 1866; vol. 3, 1107–9, D.A. Wells to A.T. Galt, 23 Jan. 1866; vol. 3, 1085–8, E.H. Derby to A.T. Galt, 29 Dec. 1865; vol. 3, 1093–5, J. Aspinall to A.T. Galt, 13 Jan. 1865 [sic]. PAC, DFR, vol. 3376, 589–90, A.T. Galt to G. Sheppard, 27 Feb. 1866

35 Creighton, *Confederation*, 344

36 George Sheppard, for example, continued to be paid. PAC, Galt Papers vol. 10, 190, A.T. Galt to G. Sheppard, 6 July 1866. PAC, DFR: vol. 3375, 557–8, A.T. Galt to H.D. Southby, 27 Feb. 1866; vol. 3376, 595–6, A.T. Galt to E.H. Derby, 7 Mar. 1866; vol. 3375, 665–7, A.T. Galt to D. Wells, 19 May 1866. PAC, Galt Papers vol. 3, 1130–3, D. Wells to A.T. Galt, 16 July 1866

37 Province of Canada, *Statutes*, 29 & 30 Vict. c. 6. Debates, 26 June 1866, in *Globe*, 27 June 1866. Debates, 9 Aug. 1865, in *Globe*, 11 Aug. 1865

38 Careless, *Brown*, vol. 2, 230. Skelton, *Galt*, 180. Whitelaw, *Maritimes* 274, asserts

the compromise with the Maritimes. G.K. Pryke (*Nova Scotia and Confederation* [Toronto 1979], 63–4) takes the view that the tariff of 1866 was no compromise but simply a central Canadian imposition on the Maritimes.

39 Pryke, *Nova Scotia*, 14. For New Brunswick, see A.G. Bailey, 'The Basis and Persistence of Opposition to Confederation in New Brunswick,' *CHR* 23 (1942): 374–97. *Citizen* (Halifax), 31 Dec. 1874. PAC, Tilley Papers, MG 27 I D 15, vol. 17, J.D. Robertson to L. Tilley, 2 Feb. 1865. PAC, Buchanan Papers vol. 45, 36011–13, D. McInnes to I. Buchanan 4 Oct. 1866

40 Careless, 'Aspects of Metropolitanism.' D. Muise, 'Parties and Constituencies: Federal Elections in Nova Scotia, 1867–1896,' Canadian Historical Association *Historical Papers* (1971): 183–202 and 'The Federal Election of 1867 in Nova Scotia: An Economic Interpretation,' Nova Scotia Historical Society *Collections* 36 (1968): 327–51. Muise's important interpretation has altered the traditional emphasis on a blanket hostility to Confederation in Nova Scotia.

41 PANS, A.G. Jones Papers, vol. 523, item 3

42 Buchanan's ideas were well known to the Fathers of Confederation. Early in 1864 his *Industry of Canada* had been published, and supplied free to every member of the provincial assembly (*Globe* [Toronto], 7 May 1864). He was a cabinet member at the time. At the Quebec Conference at which the details of the confederation agreement were hammered out, this was widely distributed, and had a modest vogue (PAC, Buchanan Papers, vol. 48: 38918–21, H.J. Morgan to Buchanan, 12 Oct. 1864; 38942–5, Morgan to Buchanan, 24 Oct. 1864; 38939–41, Morgan to Buchanan, 18 Oct. 1864).

43 UNBA, James Brown Papers, A.J. Gilmour to J. Brown, 3 Jan. 1866

44 Brown was eager to firm the Liberals in opposition, and financial issues and government budgets were always a favourite ground for united opposition action (PAC, Brown Papers, vol. 7, 1462–3, G. Brown to A. Brown, 4 July 1866. *Times* [Ottawa], 17 July 1866).

45 PAC, Macdonald Papers, vol. 247, 111089–90, D. Macpherson to J.A. Macdonald, 14 Feb. 1866

46 I. Unger, *The Greenback Era: A Social and Political History of American Finance, 1865–1879* (Princeton 1964)

47 PAC, DNNR, series A–I: vol. 292, M. Dunscombe to R.S.M. Bouchette 21 Aug. 1865; vol. 217, Mr Lewis to R.S.M. Bouchette, 22 Aug. 1865; vol. 164, J.P. Masby to commissioner of customs, 24 Aug. 1865

48 Galt denied the tariff had any retaliatory purpose in one breath and asserted it in another (Debates, 10 July 1866 in *Globe* [Toronto], 12 July 1866). PAC, DFR, vol. 3375, 29–30, Galt to J.K. Moorehead, 27 July 1866

49 Debates, 10 July 1866, in *Globe* (Toronto), 12 July 1866

50 Pryke, *Nova Scotia*, 62–4, 69

51 ANQ, Quebec B of T Papers, Meeting of 7 Mar. 1860, Minute Book 1857–76, 55. PAC, DFR, vol. 3370: J. Lovell to A.T. Galt, 29 Mar. 1860; A. Fraser to A.T. Galt, 8 Mar. 1860. PAC, DNNR, series A–1, vol. 288, J. Hassock & Co. to A.T. Galt, 13 Mar. 1860. PAC, Buchanan Papers: vol. 28, 23916, W.W. Grant to I. Buchanan, 13 Mar. 1860; vol. 58, 46661, off-print from the *Gazette* (Montreal), W. Weir to the editor, 30 Apr. 1860
52 PAC, DNNR, series A–1, vol. 61: R.K. Bullock to R.S.M. Bouchette, 27 June 1862; A. Begg to R.S.M. Bouchette, 15 and 24 July 1862
53 Ibid., vol. 220, G. Stephen to A.T. Galt, 28 May 1866; vol. 116, J. Hespeler to R.S.M. Bouchette, 19 Dec. 1861; vol. 210, J.A. Converse petition to governor general in council, 25 Mar. 1862; vol. 377, A. Donaldson to L.H. Holton, 12 Nov. 1863; vol. 312, W. Arnold to W. McGivern, 4 Dec. 1863; vol. 377, Gordon & McKay to R.S.M. Bouchette, 4 Dec. 1863
54 *Gazette* (Montreal), 2 July 1866
55 *Globe* (Toronto), 2, 3, 4, and 6 July 1866
56 Ibid., 4 July 1866
57 Ibid., 3 and 6 July 1866
58 *Gazette* (Montreal), 2 July 1866
59 *Globe* (Toronto), 3 July 1866
60 Ibid., 5 July 1866
61 *Gazette* (Montreal), 28 June and 3 July 1866
62 Ibid., 7 July 1866
63 Ibid., 3 and 13 July 1866
64 Debates, 10 and 12 July 1866, in *Globe* (Toronto), 11, 12 and 14 July 1866
65 Debates, 17 July 1866, in *Globe* (Toronto), 18 July 1866. *Globe* (Toronto), 10 and 14 July 1866. J. Redpath & Son and J.H.R. Molson & Bros., open letter, *Gazette* (Montreal), 14 July 1866. PAC, DNNR, series A–1, vol. 272, W. Shanly to provincial secretary, 4 July 1866
66 *Gazette* (Montreal), 11 July 1866
67 *Herald* (Montreal), 27 Oct. 1866. PAC, Buchanan Papers, vol. 112, 73426, newspaper clipping dated 27 Sept. 1866
68 PAC, Buchanan Papers, vol. 45, 36015–18, I. Buchanan to D. McInnes, 4 Oct. 1866

CHAPTER 4

1 PAC, Brown Papers, vol. 6, 1402–17, G. Brown to Lord Monck, 25 Dec. 1865, draft letter
2 I.D. Andrews was decrepit; George Sheppard's opinion that the refusal of reciprocity would lead to annexation limited his usefulness as a lobbyist. Galt's efforts

to enlist the help of the American boards of trade was impulsive rather than carefull planned. The aid of the BNA boards was not obtained at all. PAC, Taylor Papers, G. Sheppard to G.L. Becker, 30 June 1865. PAC, Galt Papers, vol. 3, 1093–5, J. Aspinall to A.T. Galt, 13 Jan. 1865 [sic]

3 PAC, Macdonald Papers, vol. 224, 96005–8, W.P. Howland to J.A. Macdonald, 5 Feb. 1866

4 Ibid., vol. 516, 791–2, Sir John A. Macdonald to J.H. Cameron, 24 Dec. 1869

5 *Debates*, 29 Apr. 1869, 123–35; 16 Mar. 1870, 449–75; 21 Mar. 1870, 534–632

6 PAC, Macdonald Papers, vol. 146, 59563–6, G.W. Brega to Sir J.A. Macdonald, 1 Feb. 1869

7 Ibid., vol. 187, 77696–702, A.G. Archibald to Sir J.A. Macdonald, 26 June 1868

8 Ibid., vol. 146, contains the greater part of Brega's correspondence to Sir J.A. Macdonald. On Brega, see J. Snell, 'A Foreign Agent in Washington: George W. Brega, Canada's Lobbyist, 1867–1870,' *Civil War History* 26 (1980): 53–70.

9 *Debates* 7 May 1869, 211. PAC, Macdonald Papers, vol. 146, 59603–10, G.W. Brega to Sir John A. Macdonald, 10 May 1869

10 PAC, Macdonald Papers, vol. 516, 372, Sir J.A. Macdonald to J.S. McCuaig, 4 Nov. 1869

11 Ibid., vol. 191, 79627–32, C.J. Brydges to Sir J.A. Macdonald, 19 Nov. 1869; vol. 102, 41071–4, J. Taylor to C.J. Brydges, 6 Jan. 1870

12 F.L. Israel, ed., *The State of the Union Messages of the Presidents, 1790–1966*, vol. II, *1861–1904* (New York 1966) 1195

13 PAC, Macdonald Papers, vol. 516, 740, Sir J.A. Macdonald to G.W. Brega, 15 Dec. 1869; vol. 146, 59736–42, G.W. Brega to Sir J.A. Macdonald, 15 Dec. 186

14 PAC, Privy Council Office (herafter PCO), RG 2 series 1, OC, PC1179, 22 Feb. 1870

15 *Globe* (Toronto), 17 Jan. 1868. PAC, Macdonald Papers, vol. 281, 128843–4, Tupper to Duke of Buckingham and Chandos, copy, 8 Apr. 1868

16 PAC, PCO, series 1, OC, PC1006, 8 Jan. 1870. [P. Mitchell], *Review of President Grant's Recent Message* (Ottawa 1870). For Mitchell and the fisheries, see R. Tallman, 'Peter Mitchell and the Genesis of a National Fisheries Policy,' *Acadiensi* 4–2 (1975) 66–78; and R.S. Longley, 'Peter Mitchell, Guardian of the North Atlantic Fisheries, 1867–1871,' *CHR* 22 (1941): 389–402.

17 *Globe* (Toronto), 4 and 7 May 1868. *Herald* (Montreal), 3 and 6 Dec. 1867

18 D.M. McDougall, 'The Domestic Availability of Manufactured Commodity Output Canada, 1870–1915,' *CJE* 6 (1973): 194

19 For the American case, see A. Dawley, *Class and Community: The Industrial Revolution in Lynn* (Cambridge, MA 1976) 77–94.

20 J. Burgess ('L'industrie de la chaussure à Montréal: 1840–1870: le passage de l'artisanat à la fabrique,' *Revue d'histoire l'Amérique français* 31 [1977]: 187–210) provides a good overview of the changes in the industry in that city. Also see

her MA thesis of the same name (Université du Québec à Montréal, 1978). See also Langdon, 'Central Canada,' 84–5.

21 *St. John and Its Business* (Saint John 1875), 111. *Census* 1871, vol. 3

22 Babcock ('Economic Development,' 20–3) makes clear the mixed character of enterprise in shoemaking in the city.

23 Calculated from *Census* 1871, vol. 3

24 Although there are problems in matching Trade and Navigation Returns data and census data, calculations indicate that domestic production was the equivalent of 99 per cent of boots and shoes available for domestic use in 1870. *Census* 1871, vol. 3; *SP*, 1870, 1871, Trade and Navigation Returns. Figures on domestic capacity are calculated from the same sources.

25 *St. John and Its Business*, 118

26 *Globe* (Toronto) 19 Mar. 1870

27 PAC, PCO, series 3, vol. 3, petition of the Municipal Council of the Township of South Norwich, 5 Mar. 1870. Some of the many petitions to Parliament are noted in Canada, House of Commons *Journals* [hereafter *Journals*], 1870, 17, 26, 39, 51, 66, 97, 129, 166, 286.

28 R.G. Haliburton, *Intercolonial Trade Our Only Safeguard against Disunion* (Ottawa 1968). PAC, Macdonald Papers: vol. 116, 47661–8, R.G. Haliburton to Sir J.A. Macdonald, 29 Jan. 1870; vol. 516, 996, Sir J.A. Macdonald to R.G. Haliburton, 3 Feb. 1870. For a succinct and instructive discussion of the role of coal that parallels this one, see John N. McDougall, *Fuels and the National Policy* (Toronto 1982), 18–23.

29 *Citizen* (Halifax), 26 Feb. 1870

30 Ibid., 14 Mar. 1870

31 *Herald* (Montreal), 26 Mar. 1870

32 Canada, *Statutes* [hereafter *Statutes*], 33 Vict. c. 9. For Hincks' revenue pursuits, see *Debates*, 7 Apr. 1870, 916–40.

33 PAC, DFR, vol. 3377, 185–6, Sir F. Hincks to Sir J. Rose, 13 May 1870

34 *Globe* (Toronto), 11 Apr. 1870

35 PAC, Montreal Board of Trade Papers [hereafter Montreal B of T Papers], MG 28 III 44, General Meetings 1863–84, 143–50, annual meeting, 3 Apr. 1871. QUA, Kingston B of T Papers, Minute Book 1851–1910, vol. 1120, meeting of 25 Mar. 1870. *Globe* (Toronto), 22 Feb. and 14 Apr. 1870

36 *Globe* (Toronto), 26 Mar. 1870

37 *Debates*, 21 Feb. 1870, 107; 26 Apr. 1870, 1194–206; 27 Apr. 1870, 1221–43

38 PAC, Macdonald Papers, vol. 247, 11394, D. Macpherson to Sir J.A. Macdonald, 5 May 1870

39 *Correspondence with the Government of Canada in Connection with the Appointment of the Joint High Commission and the Treaty of Washington* (London 1872).

The Canadian initiative has generally been by-passed in the literature. See C.P. Stacey, *Canada and the Age of Conflict: A History of Canadian External Policies*, vol. 1: *1867–1921* (Toronto 1977) 20.

40 Israel, *State of the Union Messages*, 1210–13

41 Stacey, *Canada and the Age of Conflict*, 17–30

42 For the Macdonald-centred perspective, which has dominated Canadian historiography, and which downplays the reciprocity issue in favour of a railway-loan interpretation of the negotiations, see D.G. Creighton, *John A. Macdonald: The Old Chieftain* (Toronto 1955) 71–102.

43 PAC, Macdonald Papers, vol. 167, 68447–56, Sir F. Hincks to Sir J.A. Macdonald, 15 Feb. 1871

44 Ibid., vol. 518, 427–37, Sir J.A. Macdonald to Lord de Grey, 15 Mar. 1871

45 Ibid., vol. 167: 68175–211, Sir J.A. Macdonald to C. Tupper 29 Mar. 1871; 68293–308, same to same, 18 Apr. 1871. Also C. Tupper, in *Debates*, 20 Feb. 1877, 150

46 PAC, Macdonald Papers, vol. 224, 95776–7, Sir F. Hincks to Sir J.A. Macdonald, 5 Mar. 1871

47 Sir C. Tupper, *Recollections of Sixty Years in Canada* (London 1914) 153

48 Urquhart and Buckley, eds, *Historical Statistics*, 528. R.M. Breckenridge, 'Canadian Banking System, 1817–1890,' *Journal of the Canadian Bankers' Association* 2 (1894–95): 431–7

49 *Journals* 1876, app. (no. 3) 63. D.G. Burley ('The Politics of Business: Frederic Nicholls and the National Policy, 1874–1895' [MA thesis, Trent University 1974] 17–28) sees the Canada First protectionists as vital to the cause.

50 J.I. Cooper, 'Some Early French Canadian Advocacy of Protection: 1871–1873,' *CJEPS* 3 (1937): 530–40. PAC, Montreal B of T Papers, General Meetings 1863–84, 156–60, 184–7, meetings of 3 Oct. 1871 and 1 Oct. 1872

51 PAC, Macdonald Papers, vol. 344, 157430–1, S. Bellingham to Sir J.A. Macdonald, 30 Jan. 1872. Cartier Papers, MG 27 I D 4, vol. 4, 1539–41, J. Maclean to Sir G. Cartier, 18 Jan. 1872

52 PAC, Montreal B of T Papers, Dominion Board of Trade Minute Book 1870–80, 59–86, second annual meeting, 17–20 Jan. 1872. *Journals*, 1872, app. (no. 1, no. 3)

53 *Statutes*, 34 Vict. c. 10

54 Requests for the free importation of machinery were so frequent that regulations were passed making the process of admission purely administrative, not requiring the consideration of the Treasury Board and the Privy Council. PAC, PCO, series 1, OC, PC1079, 7 June 1871; PC892, 5 May 1871; PC1307, 29 July 1871

55 PAC, Macdonald Papers, vol. 519, 555–6, Sir J.A. Macdonald to A. Brown, 2 Dec. 1871

6 Ibid., vol. 520, 199–202, Sir J.A. Macdonald to G. Stephen, 20 Feb. 1872
7 Ibid., 192–3, Sir J.A. Macdonald to D.L. Macpherson, Feb. 20, 1872
8 *Colonist* (Halifax), 10 Aug. 1872. Pryke, *Confederation*, 141
9 PAC, Macdonald Papers, vol. 520, 672–5, Sir J.A. Macdonald to D. McInnes, 17 June 1872
0 *Globe* (Toronto), 25 and 27 July 1872
1 *Globe* (Toronto), 15, 16, and 25 July 1872. *Gazette* (Montreal), 12 July 1872
2 PAC, Howe Papers, vol. 4, 794–8, H. McDonald to J. Howe, 7 Sept. 1871. PAC, Macdonald Papers, vol. 521, 319–22, Sir J.A. Macdonald to Lord Dufferin, 2 Sept. 1872
3 D. Muise, 'Elections and Constituencies: Federal Politics in Nova Scotia, 1867–1878' (PH D thesis, University of Western Ontario 1971) 165, 206–8

HAPTER 5

1 E.J. Chambers, 'Late Nineteenth Century Business Cycles in Canada.' *CJEPS* 47 (1964): 391–412. A monetarist approach to Canadian business cycles is provided by K.A.J. Hay, 'Money and Cycles in Post-Confederation Canada,' *Journal of Political Economy* 75 (1967): 263–73. For survey examinations of the 1870s depression, now of limited usefulness, see J.C. Ingram, 'The Financial Depression of 1873 and Its Effects upon Canadian Industry' (MA thesis, Queen's University 1929) and S. Common, 'A History of Business Conditions in Canada, 1870–1890' (MA thesis, Queen's University 1930). For a brief discussion of the impact of the depression on a specific region see Hamelin and Roby's excellent *Histoire économique*, 88–91. More generally on Quebec, see Paul-André Linteau, R. Durocher, and J.-C. Robert, *Quebec: A History, 1867–1929* (Toronto 1982) 57–138. A contemporary and informed view of the 1873–96 period as one of virtually continuous depression is to be found in UNBA, Sir George Eulas Foster Papers, notebooks, book 10. Then examine O.J. Firestone, 'Canada's Economic Development, 1867–1952,' mimeograph, n.p. 1953, 117, 152–4 and S.B. Saul, *The Myth of the Great Depression 1873–1896* (London 1969). Firestone was the pioneer in what has proved to be an ongoing cliometric assault on the late nineteenth-century Canadian economy; no one involved in this assault accepts the traditional argument that the late nineteenth century was a period of continuous depression, though there is disagreement not only about the specifics of growth, but whether it was discontinuous. For some of the literature, see O.D. Skelton (*General Economic History of the Dominion, 1867–1912* [Toronto 1913] 139–91) which is an early narrative account stressing the impact of the business cycle; G.W. Bertram, 'Historical Statistics on Growth and Structure of Manufacturing in Canada, 1870–1957,' and J.H. Dales, 'Estimates of Canadian Manufacturing Output by Markets,

1870–1915,' both in Canadian Political Science Association, *Conference on Statistics, 1962 & 1963* (Toronto 1964); McDougall, 'Domestic Availability'; R. Pomfret, 'Capital Formation in Canada 1870–1900,' *Explorations in Economic History* 18 (1981): 84–96; J. Pickett, 'Residential Capital Formation in Canada, 1871–1921,' *CJEPS* 29 (1963): 40–58; Gilmour, *Spatial Evolution*. An interesting attempt to actually measure the impact of the tariff on economic growth is H.M. Pinchin, 'Canadian Tariff Levels 1870–1959' (PH D diss., Yale 1970). M.C. Urquhart and others have been undertaking a thorough revision of Firestone's data. See his photocopied typescript, 'New Estimates of Gross National Product Canada 1870 to 1926: Some Implications for Canadian Development' (Kingston 1984).

2 *Monetary Times* [hereafter *MT*], 21 May 1875

3 *MT*, 21 July 1876

4 *Journals* 1876, app. (no. 3) 265–6. *Year Book and Almanac of Canada for 1879* (Ottawa 1879) 145

5 Taylor and Michell, *Statistical Contributions*, 79. W. Kilbourn, *The Elements Combined: A History of The Steel Company of Canada* (Toronto 1960) 15

6 W.J.A. Donald, *The Canadian Iron and Steel Industry: A Study in the Economic History of a Protected Industry* (Boston 1915) 48–9, 58–9, 62. *MT*, 29 Oct. 1875. *Globe* (Toronto), 6 July 1874; 18 Jan. 1876. See G. Mainer, 'William Hamilton,' *DCB*, vol. 10 (Toronto 1972) 330–1 for some insight into impact of the depression on the capitalization practices of an iron founder. On the Moisie firm, see A. Dubuc, 'William Molson,' *DCB*, vol. 10 (Toronto 1972) 524–5.

7 Inwood, 'Charcoal Iron,' 299, 312–13, 345–6, 350

8 D. McDowall, *Steel at the Sault: Francis H. Clergue, Sir James Dunn, and the Algoma Steel Corporation 1901–1956* (Toronto 1984) 10–12

9 Donald, *Iron and Steel*, 63. *Citizen* (Halifax), 3 Jan. 1874. *MT* 10 July, 18 Sept., 30 Oct., and 11 Dec. 1874; 7 Jan., 17 Mar., and 25 Aug. 1876; 30 Nov. 1877

10 W.W. Johnson, *Sketches of the Late Depression* (Montreal 1882) 168. M.J.E. Brent, 'A Study of the Sewing Machine Industry of Ontario 1860–1897' (MA thesis University of Toronto 1977), indicates the upsurge of new firms in the early 1870s, followed by collapse.

11 *Journals* 1874, app. (no. 3) 20–2. PAC, DFR, vol. 3373, G. Stephen to R. Cartwright, 20 Jan. 1876. For a discussion of the long-term development of the industry in Canada, see R. Reid, 'The Rosamond Woolen Company of Almonte: Industrial Development in a Rural Setting,' *OH* 75 (1983): 266–89. Domestic production in 1870 was equivalent to between 60 and 85 per cent of domestic product availability. My calculations based on Trade and Navigation Returns 1870–71 and 1871–72, compared to *Census* 1871, vol. 3, and *Journals* 1876, app. (no. 3) 268–9.

12 *MT*, 24 Sept. 1875. *Mail* (Toronto), 19 July and 12 Aug. 1878

13 *MT*, 16 Jan. and 30 Oct. 1874; 16 Mar., 13 Apr., 3 and 15 June, and 10 Aug.

1877; 9 Feb. and 17 May 1878. Reid (Rosamond Woolen Company) concludes that by the end of the century, the industry was uncompetitive internationally and had only been sustained by protective tariffs (277–82).

14 For an effective revisionist argument about the early history of the industry, see M.N.A. Hinton, 'The Growth of the Canadian Cotton Textile Industry 1844–1873: "A New Industrial Career,"' unpublished paper presented to the Workshop in Economic History, University of Toronto, 1981.

15 J.A. Coote, *A Graphical Survey of the Canadian Textile Industries* (Montreal 1936) 66–7. Taylor and Michell, *Statistical Contributions*, 22–4. *Journals* 1876, app. (no.3), 128–42. *Mail* (Toronto), 12 Sept. 1878. *Gazette* (Montreal), 9 Feb. 1876

16 PAC, Macdonald Papers, vol. 347, 159439, D. McInnes to Sir J.A. Macdonald, 23 Nov. 1877

17 'Starting about 1860 and lasting until 1873, earnings rose on a deflated as well undeflated basis ... After 1873, profits sagged again; ground lost in the 1874–78 recession was only partially made up during the subsequent recovery.' P.F. McGouldrick, *New England Textiles in the Nineteenth Century: Profits and Investment* (Cambridge, MA 1968) 75

18 A.W. Cowan, 'The Canadian White Pine Trade with the United Kingdom, 1867–1914' (MA thesis, Carleton University 1966) 45–92, provides a persuasive discussion of these changes.

19 Cowan, 'White Pine Trade,' 53

20 Lower, *North American Assault*, 158. *MT*, 15 Oct. 1875; 8 Dec. 1876. *Globe* (Toronto), 10 Feb. 1876. *Journals* 1876, app. (no. 3), 266

21 *MT*, 21 Jan. 1876. *Speeches of the Hon. Alexander Mackenzie during his Recent Visit to Scotland* (Toronto 1876) 164

22 *MT*, 9 June 1876, provides a culling of a week or two of failures.

23 Johnson, *Depression*, 157. G. Carruthers, *Paper in the Making* (Toronto 1947) 463–6. J.A. Blyth, 'The Development of the Paper Industry in Old Ontario, 1824–1867,' *OH* 62 (1970): 119–33. *News* (Saint John), 13 Nov. 1874; 10 June 1875; 7 Jan. 1876. See also R.I.K. Davidson, 'John Taylor,' *DCB*, vol. 10 (Toronto 1972) 671–2.

24 NS *Journals* 1876, app. (no. 6) 2, 7, 8. Taylor and Michell, *Statistical Contributions*, 83

25 *MT*, 31 Mar. 1876

26 *Citizen* (Halifax), 20 Sept. 1875. *MT*, 15 June 1877. H.A. Innis, *The Cod Fisheries*, rev. ed. (Toronto 1954) 327–8. Shannon Ryan ('The Newfoundland Salt Cod Trade in the Nineteenth Century,' in J. Hiller and P. Neary, eds, *Newfoundland in the Nineteenth and Twentieth Centuries* [Toronto 1980] 54) notes the slump in Newfoundland's cod exports in the later 1870s, especially to the premium European markets.

27 Quoted in Finley, 'The Morans of St. Martins,' in Fischer and Sager, *Enterprising Canadians*, 51. F.E. Hyde, *Cunard and the North Atlantic 1840–1973* (London 1975) 96, 98

28 E.W. Sager, L.R. Fischer, and R.E. Ommer have asserted the continuing profitability of the shipping industry after 1874, though other economic historians have remained sceptical. See their 'Landward and Seaward Opportunities in Canada's Age of Sail,' and also their 'The Shipping Industry and Regional Economic Development in Atlantic Canada, 1871–1891: Saint John as a Case Study,' both in L.R. Fischer and E.W. Sager, eds, *Merchant Shipping and Economic Development in Atlantic Canada* (St John's 1982) 9–59; and Sager and Fischer, 'Atlantic Canada and the Age of Sail Revisited,' *CHR* 63 (1982): 144. For doubts see *Merchant Shipping*, 61–3, and L.R. Fischer and G.E. Panting, eds, *Change and Adaptation in Maritime History: The North Atlantic Fleets in the Nineteenth Century* (St John's 1985) 47–9.

29 It is probable that the early part of the depression of the 1870s provided a temporary reprieve for wooden sailing vessels, despite their rapid depreciation, because cheapness of construction could make them a preferred capital investment in depression conditions. See A. Slaven, 'The Shipbuilding Industry,' in R. Church, ed., *The Dynamics of Victorian Business: Problems and Perspectives to the 1870's* (London 1980) 114.

30 While no one disputes that the shipping and shipbuilding industries suffered decline in the late nineteenth century, there is disagreement among historians as to the timing of the decline and its causes. For some aspects of the debate, see R. Rice, 'Measuring British Dominance of Shipbuilding in the "Maritimes," 1787–1890,' in K. Matthews and G. Panting, eds, *Ships and Shipbuilding in the North Atlantic Region* (St John's 1978) 109–55; Harley, 'Persistence of Old Techniques'; Faucher, 'Decline of Shipbuilding'; and articles cited above.

31 *Journals* 1876, app. (no. 3) 266

32 J. Fingard, 'The Winter's Tale: The Seasonal Contours of Pre-industrial Poverty in British North America 1815–1860,' Canadian Historical Association *Historical Papers* (1974) 65–94

33 *Citizen* (Halifax), 4 Dec. 1875. *News* (Saint John), 17 Dec. 1875; 8 Jan. 1876

34 Halifax dispensary patients rose dramatically in number from 1602 in 1874 to 2769 in 1878. (*Chronicle* [Halifax] 18 Jan. 1876; 9 Jan. 1877; 14 Jan. 1879)

35 PAC, Macdonald Papers, vol. 346, 15881–4, J. Livingston to Sir J.A. Macdonald, 23 Feb. 1876

36 *Chronicle* (Quebec), 8 Aug. 1878. Hamelin and Roby, *Histoire économique*, 311–12

37 *Gazette* (Montreal), 26 July 1875

38 *Citizen* (Halifax), 18 Dec. 1875. *Gazette* (Montreal), 21 Mar. 1876

39 *MT*, 24 Dec. 1875
40 *Spectator* (Hamilton), 29 July 1878
41 *Times* (Hamilton), 5 June 1878. *Journals* 1876, app. (no. 3), 174–83. *Mail* (Toronto) 8 Dec. 1875
42 Bertram ('Historical Statistics,' 103) provides an estimate of 4.4 per cent compound annual growth in manufacturing during the 1870s. Pinchin ('Canadian Tariff Levels,' 160) estimated an annual compound rate of per capita value added in manufacturing of 4 per cent for the 1880s and 4.4 per cent in the 1860s. The data from these different sources are not strictly compatible; the text treats them as merely suggestive. Urquhart and Buckley (eds, *Historical Statistics*, 22) provide some figures on population expansion which may explain some of the difference between the growth of manufacturing and the low increase in per capita value added in manufacturing of the decade.
43 McCallum, *Unequal Beginnings*, 17, 126. Urquhart and Buckley, eds, *Historical Statistics*, 364
44 Quoted in Jones, *Agriculture*, 248. Taylor and Michell, *Statistical Contributions*, 65. UWO Regional Collection, John Newton Papers, journal 20, entry 26 Mar. 1876
45 M. McInnis ('The Changing Structure of Canadian Agriculture 1867–1897,' *JEH* 42 [1982]: 191–8) confirms and enhances this analysis. See also Marr and Paterson, *Economic History*, 108–16. D.A. Lawr, 'The Development of Ontario Farming, 1870–1914: Patterns of Growth and Change,' *OH* 44 (1972): 239–51. Jones, *Agriculture*, 206–7, 318–23, 254–60. Taylor and Michell, *Statistical Contributions*, *18*. *SP* 1870, 1880, Trade and Navigation Returns
46 *Conservator* (Brampton), 28 June 1878
47 W.G. Phillips, *The Agricultural Implement Industry in Canada: A Study of Competition* (Toronto 1956) 10
48 *Journals* 1876, app. (no. 3), 115–16, 118–20. *Mail* (Toronto), 13 Apr. 1878. M. Denison, *Harvest Triumphant* (Toronto 1955) 63
49 *Journals* 1876, app. (no. 3) 70–3, 75–8, 265–6
50 D.C. North, 'Ocean Freight Rates and Economic Development 1750–1913,' *JEH* 18 (1958): 537–55
51 Taylor and Neu, *Railroad Network*, 2 and passim. E.C. Kirkland, *Industry Comes of Age: Business, Labor and Public Policy 1860–1897* (New York 1961) 79–80
52 J. Schmookler, *Patents, Invention and Economic Change: Data and Selected Essays* (Cambridge, MA 1972) 35
53 Langdon, 'Political Economy,' 106. Naylor, *Business History*, vol. 2, 46–9. Naylor views the level of imported patents in Canada as unfortunate.
54 *News* (Saint John), 20 Nov. 1874; *Citizen* (Halifax), 9 July 1877; *Gazette* (Montreal), 26 and 29 July 1875; *Witness* (Montreal), 28 Aug. 1878. Carruthers, *Paper*,

504–5. *Journals* 1876, app. (no. 3), 37. For the American case, see L. Galombos, *Competition and Cooperation: the Emergence of a National Trade Association* (Baltimore 1966).

55 MT, 23 July and 15 Oct. 1875; 21 June 1878

56 *Journals* 1874, app. (no. 3) 52. For an examination of the origins of the business corporation in part of British North America, see R.C.B. Risk, 'The Nineteenth-Century Foundations of the Business Corporation in Ontario,' *University of Toronto Law Journal* 23 (1973): 270–306.

57 *News* (Saint John), 8 Jan. 1876. *Journals* 1876, app. (no. 3) 177

58 MT, 1 June and 6 Apr. 1877; 15 and 22 Feb. 1878

59 MT, 6 and 20 Oct. 1876; 9 Mar. and 27 July 1877

60 *Witness* (Montreal), 15 Feb. 1879. *Globe* (Toronto), 3 July 1878

61 MT, 11 Sept. 1874

62 MT, 15 Mar. and 21 June 1878. *Globe* (Toronto), 4 June and 2 July 1878

63 MT, 8, 22 Feb. and 2 Apr. 1878

64 *News* (Saint John), 13 Nov. 1874; 10 and 30 June 1875

65 PAO, Blake Papers, vol. 22, D. Cornish to E. Blake, 24 Aug. 1875. *Conservator* (Brampton), 28 June 1878. Gilmour (*Spatial Evolution*, 153–88) indicates that locational concentration advanced perceptibly but slowly from the 1850s to 1891. Alan Wilson, *A John Northway, Blue Serge Canadian* (Toronto 1963) 38. T.L. Walkom, 'The Daily Newspaper Industry in Ontario's Developing Capitalist Economy: Toronto and Ottawa, 1871–1911' (PH D thesis, University of Toronto) 1983, table 8–1.

66 Carruthers, *Paper*, 415. D.F. Walker, 'The Energy Sources of Manufacturing Industry in Southern Ontario, 1871–1921,' *Ontario Geography* 6 (1971): 56–66

67 MT, 23 Feb. and 13 Apr. 1877; 8 Feb. and 12 Apr. 1878

68 McDougall, 'Domestic Availability,' 195–6

69 *Journals* 1874, app. (no. 3), 40, 41, 51; 1876, app. (no. 3), 140–1

70 Calculated from SP, Trade and Navigation Returns, 1870–82

71 *Globe* (Toronto), 19 Dec. 1977

72 Urquhart and Buckley, *Historical Statistics*, 300

73 PAC, DNNR, series A–1: vol. 220-A, W.A. Simpson to J. Johnson, 8 Dec. 1877; vol. 151, W.R. Mingaye to J. Johnson, 29 Nov. 1877; vol. 293, M. Dunscombe to commissioner of customs, 24 Dec. 1877; vol. 19, H.B. Leeming to J. Johnson, 4 Dec. 1877

74 Phillips, *Agricultural Implement Industry* 10, 167. PAC, DNNR, series A–1: vol. 15, T.C. Newburn to commissioner of customs, 7 May 1879; vol. 46, Wm. Legget to same, 30 Nov. 1877; vol. 164, Cowan and Britton to same, 4 Feb. 1879

75 PAC, DNNR, series A–1, vol. 312, J. Rose to commissioner of customs, 24 May 1877. For an exploration of the rapid mechanization of the American industry in

this period, see E.P. Duggan, 'Machines, Markets and Labor: The Carriage and Wagon Industry in Late-Nineteenth-Century Cincinnati,' *Business History Review* 51 (1977): 308–25.

Ibid., vol. 393, Mr. Benson to J. Johnson, 5 June 1879

Journals 1876, app. (no. 3) 93, 95, 96–9

MT, 23 July 1875. PAC, Macdonald Papers, vol. 356, 164397, S.R. Wickett to Sir John A. Macdonald, 10 Mar. 1879. PAC, Tilley Papers, vol. 23, 571, S. Tilley to I.J. Christie, 28 Oct. 1879

Johnson, *Depression*, 160–70. Kealey (*Toronto Workers*, 51–2) and Babcock, ('Economic Development,' 20) provide some idea of the impact of domestic competition in this industry. *News* (Saint John), 28 June 1875. MT, 23 July and 24 Sept. 1875; 4 Feb. and 29 Dec. 1876; 2 Feb. 1877; 11 Jan., 22 Feb., and 8 Mar. 1878

For the analysis of alterations in marketing, see Chapman, 'British Marketing Enterprise.' Businessmen of the day were becoming keenly aware of the importance of brand-name recognition and product differentiation. E. Benson, *Historical Record of the Edwardsburgh and Canada Starch Companies* (Montreal 1959), 46, 50, 51. *Witness* (Montreal), 28 Aug. 1878. *Journals* 1876, app. (no. 3), 218. MT, 28 Apr. 1876

T. Houston to the editor, *Mail* (Toronto), 20 July 1876

Urquhart and Buckley, *Historical Statistics*, 174–7. MT, 8 Dec. 1876. *Dominion of Canada. The Province of Ontario as it is* (Toronto 1877)

Such efforts to develop wider markets by manufacturers in the Maritimes apparently met with less success than the attempts by their central Canadian counterparts. Under considerable debt pressure, the New Brunswick Paper Company managed some large sales at Quebec City and Montreal, and the Coldbrook Rolling Mills sold iron to the federal government for railway construction, as well as to shipbuilders in Quebec. The most determined effort to gain access to the central Canadian market came from Nova Scotian coal interests, and there were sales as far west as Montreal, the Ottawa valley, and Brockville. *News* (Saint John), 15 Feb. 1877. *Free Press* (Ottawa), 6 July 1878. *Journals* 1877, app. (no. 4) 18, 92–5

MT, 2 Jan. 1874; 4 and 11 Jan. 1878

MT, 20 Apr. 1877

Citizen (Halifax), 24 Nov. 1874. *News* (Saint John), 25 Apr. 1877. MT, 4 June, 9 July, and 26 Nov. 1875

Citizen (Halifax), 3 Feb. 1877. *Journals* 1876, app. (no. 3) 70–1. P.B. Waite (*Arduous Destiny*, 76) suggests that the Maritimes market was conquered by central Canadian interests by 1874. But W. Acheson ('The National Policy and the Industrialization of the Maritimes, 1880–1910,' *Acadiensis* 1 [1972]: 3–28) sees the National Policy as the crucial dividing line. L.D. McCann ('Metropolitanism and Branch Businesses in the Maritimes, 1881–1931,' *Acadiensis* 13 [1983]: 112–25) provides substantial additional evidence.

88 R. Pomfret, *The Economic Development of Canada* (Toronto 1981) 179

CHAPTER 6

1 A. Smith, *Wealth of Nations* (New York 1937, originally 1776) 128

2 S.D. Clark ('The Canadian Manufacturers' Association: A Political Pressure Group,' *CJEPS* 4 [1938]; 505) notes these preconditions for interest-group formation; he adds wider literacy, the existence of government intervention, and an organizational chain reaction as causes for the development of interest associations. Clark does not devote much space to predecessor associations to the CMA, and attributes an unrealistic strength to the Ontario manufacturers' group. See his 'The Canadian Manufacturers' Association and the Tariff,' *CJEPS* 5 (1939): 19–39, and his important though very compressed *The Canadian Manufacturers' Association: A Study in Collective Bargaining and Political Pressure* (Toronto 1939). Interest groups and interest-group politics have received substantial attention from economists, political scientists, and historians in terms of both theory and specific discussion. So innocent did Canadians seem of interest groups that Richard Presthus felt the need to prove their existence and activity in 1971 ('Interest Groups and the Canadian Parliament: Activities, Interaction, Legitimacy and Influence.' *JPS* 4 [1971]: 444–60). An introduction to the Canadian literature on interest groups is to be found in A.P. Pross, ed., *Pressure Group Behavior in Canadian Politics* (Toronto 1975). See also R. Presthus, *Elite Accommodation in Canadian Politics* (Toronto 1973), and Hugh G. Thorburn, *Interest Groups in the Canadian Federal System* (Toronto 1985). Classic theoretical statements include D. Truman, *The Governmental Process* (New York 1951) and M. Olson, *The Logic of Collective Action* (Cambridge, MA 1965). Mancur Olson's work has focused attention on the internal dynamics of interest groups, rather than on relations with governments. For a study that expresses concern over the predominance of business interests in tariff formulation in the United States, see E.E. Schattscheider, *Politics, Pressures and the Tariff: A Study of Free Private Enterprise in Pressure Politics, as Shown in the 1929–1930 Revision of the Tariff* (New York 1935).

3 *MT*, 20 Mar. 1874. Lower, *Great Britain's Woodyard*, 164–6. E. Phelps, 'The Canada Oil Association – An Early Business Combination,' *Western Historical Notes* 19 (1963): 31–9. And, of course, the various boards of trade functioned as interest groups from an early date. D. McCalla, 'The Commercial Politics of the Toronto Board of Trade, 1850–1860,' *CHR* 50 (1969): 51–66

4 *News* (Saint John) 11 Sept. 1874; 1 May 1875. *Journals* 1876, app. (no. 3), 177

5 PAC, Macdonald Papers, vol. 346, 158722, printed circular, 'To the Manufacturers of Canadian Woollens,' 1 Jan. 1875. *Witness* (Montreal), 28 Aug. 1878
6 Hyde, *Cunard*, 90–8; P.N. Davies, 'The Development of the Liner Trades,' in K. Matthews and G. Panting, eds, *Ships and Shipbuilding* (St John's 1978) 189–91. *MT*, 9 June 1876. *Citizen* (Halifax), 30 June 1875
7 *Journals*, 1874, app. (no. 3) 67–8. M. Denison, *The Barley and the Stream: The Molson Story* (Toronto 1955) 260. *MT*, 14 Aug. 1874; 23 Feb. and 27 July 1877. *Mail* (Toronto) 1 Feb., 4 and 9 Mar. 1876. *Citizen* (Ottawa), 1 May 1874. *Gazette* (Montreal), 3 Apr. 1874
8 Carruthers, *Paper*, 506
9 Edward C.H. Phelps ('John Henry Fairbanks of Petrolia (1831–1914): A Canadian Entrepreneur' [MA thesis, University of Western Ontario 1965] 91–9, 122–5) provides a fine discussion of the oil industry in Canada in the 1870s.
10 *MT*, 4 Sept. and 6 Nov. 1874; 5 and 16 Apr. and 31 Dec. 1875; 14 July, 25 Aug., and 1 Sept. 1876; 8 June 1877; 4 Jan. and 26 Apr. 1878
11 Benson, *Historical Record*, 39, 46, 50–1
12 NS *Journals* 1876, app. no. 6, 11–15. *Journals* 1876, app. (no. 3) 177, 182
13 Johnson, *Depression*
14 PAC, Montreal B of T Papers, Dominion Board of Trade Minute Book 1870–80, 1
15 Ibid., 443, W.J. Patterson to W.H. Howland, 24 Oct. 1874. *News* (Saint John), 11 Oct. 1875
16 PAC, Montreal B of T Papers, General Meetings 1864–84, 213–17
17 *Globe* (Toronto), 25 Feb. 1874; 31 Jan. 1875. *Mail* (Toronto), 4 Mar. 1876. *MT*, 17 Apr. and 14 Aug. 1874. *Citizen* (Halifax), 11 Apr. 1874. *Gazette* (Montreal), 26 July 1875. *Chronicle* (Halifax), 10 Apr. 1874. Pross, *Pressure Group Behavior* 133, provides an analytical distinction between institutional and issue-oriented groups. Though there is insufficient information on the internal organization of most of the groups discussed here to easily impose this distinction, many of them seem to have been involved with a range of activities that made them more than just issue oriented.
18 *Globe* (Toronto), 13 Aug. 1874. Clark, 'Tariff,' 27, suggests that later such subgroups could prove divisive.
19 Names are culled from the *Globe* (Toronto), 25 Feb., 18 and 24 Apr., and 13 Aug. 1874; 28 May 1875; 26 and 27 Oct. and 19 Dec. 1877; 24 Oct. and 14 and 15 Nov. 1878. Also from the *Mail* (Toronto), 25 Feb. and 7 Mar. 1874; 11 Mar. and 26 and 27 Nov. 1875; 26 Oct. 1877; 14 Nov. 1878. Also *Meeting of the Manufacturers' Association of Ontario Held in St. Lawrence Hall, Toronto Nov. 25, 26, 1875* (n.p., n.d.) and *Ontario Manufacturers' Association, Proceedings of Annual Convention, 1877* (Toronto 1877)
20 Robert H. Salisbury, 'An Exchange Theory of Interest Groups,' *Midwest Journal of Political Science* 13 (1969): 1–32. Salisbury argues that the core organizational

issue for a successful interest group is entrepreneurial leadership. W.H. Frazer had significant weaknesses in this regard.

21 *Globe* (Toronto), 29 July and 13 Aug. 1874. *News* (Saint John), 29 Dec. 1874. *Journals* 1876, app. (no. 3) 107–8, 134, 158, 161–2
22 *Journals* 1876, app. (no. 3) 185–7, 139, 147
23 Ibid., 1874, app. (no. 3) 25, 37–8, 45, 47, 49; 1876, app. (no. 3) 190–2
24 *Spectator* (Hamilton), 7 Sept. 1876. *Journals* 1874, app. (no. 3) 53. PAC, Macdonald Papers, vol. 353, 162580–7, A.R. Morrison, to Sir J.A. Macdonald, 14 Nov. 1878
25 *Globe* (Toronto), 19 Mar. 1870. *Spectator* (Hamilton), 7 Sept. 1878
26 *News* (Saint John), 20 July 1874; 21 Jan. 1875. J.H. Dales ('Canada's National Policies,' in his *The Protective Tariff in Canada's Development* [Toronto 1966] 143) provides a perceptive discussion of the 'infant' arguments.
27 Dominion Board of Trade, *Proceedings* 1876 (Montreal 1876) 134
28 See W. Dewart's letters in *Meeting of the Manufacturer's Association of Ontario ... 1875* (n.p., n.d.) 24–5, 33–4.
29 J.B. Hurlbert, *Field and Factory Side by Side* (Montreal 1870) 27–31, 35–9, 51–6
30 *Proceedings* 1876, 110. *Globe* (Toronto), 27 Oct. 1877
31 *Proceedings* 1876, 137
32 C. Beausoliel, *Système Protecteur ou de la nécessité d'une Reforme du tariff Canadien* (Montreal 1871) 1–11, 19–21
33 *Journals* 1877, app. (no. 4), 120
34 *Globe* (Toronto), 26 Sept. 1866. *News* (Saint John), 3 Sept. 1874
35 Hurlbert, *Field and Factory*, 19–22. Beausoleil, *Système Protecteur*, 36–7
36 *Globe* (Toronto), 26 Mar. 1870
37 *Proceedings* 1876, 84; 1877, 81, 88–90
38 PAC, Buchanan Papers, vol. 112, 73426, newspaper clipping, 27 Sept 1866
39 Ibid., vol. 45, 36011–13, D. McInnes to I. Buchanan, 5 Oct. 1866. Such a conflict over the character of membership was not unusual. *Chronicle* (Quebec), 3 Mar. 1870
40 *News* (Saint John), 3 Sept. 1874
41 *Mail* (Toronto), 25 Feb. 1874
42 PAC, Montreal B of T Papers, General Meetings 1863–84, 213–17, meeting of 7 Jan. 1874
43 Clark, 'Tariff,' 19, says that support for the tariff did not come out of 'any broad economic movement,' though his meaning is unclear.
44 *Gazette* (Montreal), 20 Mar. 1874. Carey himself did not have in mind the kind of collectivized action that business organizations or labour unions represented in his frequent discussions of combination and association. Rather, he conceived of individuals specialized in different ways co-operating in a 'harmony of interests' fashion. Carey, *Principles*, vol 1, 42, 52–3, 57 and throughout.

45 *Gazette* (Montreal), 2 Sept. 1875
46 *Globe* (Toronto), 27 Oct. 1877; 15 Nov. 1878. *Mail* (Toronto), 25 Feb. 1874; 26 Nov. 1875
47 *News* (Saint John), 28 and 29 Apr. 1874. Euramen to the editor, *Chronicle* (Halifax), 25 Feb. 1875
48 *Journals* 1876, app. (no. 3) 102
49 *News* (Saint John), 17 July 1874
50 B. Forster, 'The Coming of the National Policy: Business, Government and the Tariff, 1876–1879,' *JCS* 14–3 (1979): 39, 44
51 *News* (Saint John) 28 Sept. 1875
52 J.W.M. Bliss, 'A Living Profit: Studies in the Social History of Canadian Business, 1883–1911' (PH D thesis, University of Toronto 1972) 12–48. See also Bliss's book of the same name (Toronto 1974).
53 Lambi, *Free Trade and Protection*, 113–30. Smith, *Tariff Reform*, 63–150
54 For a useful comparative discussion of the evolution of the modern 'peak association' in business and its relationship to political parties, see A.J. Heidenheimer and F.C. Langdon, *Business Associations and the Financing of Political Parties: A Comparative Study of the Evolution of Practices in Germany, Norway and Japan* (The Hague 1968).
55 Mancur Olson (*Collective Action*) has argued that a successful organization has to offer substantial 'selective' benefits, which accrue only to members. If the only benefits offered are 'collective' ones accruing to non-members as well as members, people feel no compulsion to join, members are inactive, and the organization is weak.
56 Protectionist organizations thus offered members material benefits (in the form of potential tariff increases), solidary benefits, which allowed members to develop and assert a sense of collectivity, and purposive benefits in the form of protectionist ideology. See Peter B. Clark and James Q. Wilson, 'Incentive Systems: A Theory of Organizations,' *Administrative Science Quarterly* 6 (1961): 129–66.
57 Lambi, *Free Trade and Protection*, 3, 16, 17, 27. Smith, *Tariff Reform*, 65–89
58 *Free Press* (Ottawa), 29 Jan. 1876; 27 Feb. 1879
59 PAO Blake Papers, vol. 31, 427–8, E. Blake to R. Cartwright, 19 July 1876

CHAPTER 7

1 F.H. Underhill, from whom such attitudes sometimes are derived, in fact argued that the Liberals from Confederation to the 1890s had rather strong ideological beliefs ('The Development of National Parties in Canada,' *CHR* 16 [1935]: 367–87).
2 *Globe* (Toronto), 19 Jan. 1874
3 *Gazette* (Montreal), 23 Jan. 1874
4 PAC, Macdonald Papers, vol. 520, 672–5, Sir J.A. Macdonald to D. McInnes, 17

June 1874. *Speeches of the Hon. Alexander Mackenzie, during His Recent Visit to Scotland* (Toronto 1876)

5 *Globe* (Toronto), 25 Feb. and 16 and 19 Mar. 1874. *Mail* (Toronto), 7 Mar. 1874. *Chronicle* (Halifax), 25 and 27 Mar. 1874

6 PAC, Montreal B of T Papers, Dominion Board of Trade Minute Book 1870–80, 155

7 *Citizen* (Ottawa), 18 Mar. 1874

8 Debates, 14 Apr. 1874, in *Globe* (Toronto), 16 Apr. 1874

9 The intended (though unimplemented) duties on iron and steel would have generated considerable revenue, but would also have favoured the small number of primary producers, George Stephen being among the capitalists interested. But there were Stephen's investments in locomotive manufacture. Stephen, along with other Montreal capitalists, did win a struggle on the matter of felt. PAC, Treasury Board Records, RG 55, series A–3, vol. 294, 182–7

10 *Globe* (Toronto), 24 Apr. 1874. *Citizen* (Ottawa), 16, 18, 20, 21, 22, and 23 Apr. 1874

11 Canada, *Statutes*, 37 Vict. c. 6

12 *Citizen* (Ottawa), 22 Apr. 1874

13 PAC, Dufferin Papers, MG 27 I B 3, Dufferin to Prime Minister, 20–1, Lord Dufferin to A. Mackenzie, 21 Jan. 1874

14 PAC, Mackenzie Papers, 302–3, G. Brown to A. Mackenzie, 9 Feb. 1874. PAC, Brown Papers, vol. 9, 1997–8, A. Mackenzie to G. Brown, 27 Feb. 1874

15 For a good account of the negotiations and a sense of the indeterminacy of the outcome, see Careless, *Brown*, vol. 2, 312–24.

16 PAC, Mackenzie Papers, 473, Lord Carnarvon to Lord Dufferin, n.d. (but probably June 1874). Waite, *Arduous Destiny*, 285

17 *Commercial Reciprocity between the United States and the British North American Provinces* (n.p., n.d.)

18 PAC, Brown Papers, vol. 9, 2180–7, G. Stephen to G. Brown, 15 Dec. 1874. PAC, Mackenzie Papers, 584–7, G. Brown to A. Mackenzie, 24 June 1874

19 *Globe* (Toronto), 14 Aug. 1874. The U.S. consul in Toronto, A.D. Shaw, reported the extreme hostility of manufacturers to the proposed treaty, adding that he had 'no doubt whatever but that the effect of the proposed Treaty, if adopted ... will be to utterly ruin a large majority of the smaller manufacturing companies all over the Dominion.' He viewed a treaty as a useful first step in the ultimate annexation of Canada. United States Consular Records, [Toronto] dispatch 116, A.D. Shaw to the Assistant Secretary of State, 4 Dec. 1874

20 *News* (Saint John), 3 Sept. 1874; 21 Jan. 1875

21 *Globe* (Toronto), 11 Aug. 1874. *News* (Saint John), 4 July and 24 and 29 Dec. 1874. PAC, Montreal B of T Papers, General Meetings 1863–84, 238–40 meeting,

15 Sept. 1874. PAC, Toronto B of T Papers, meeting, 28 Sept. 1874, Council Minute Book 1871–87, vol. 3, 80–3

22 *News* (Saint John), 20 July 1874

23 PAC, Montreal B of T Papers, Dominion Board of Trade General Meetings and Executive Council Minute Book 227–30, printed confidential memorial to Lord Dufferin

24 *Globe* (Toronto), 21 Jan. 1875

25 Stacey, *Canadian External Policies*, 30–1

26 PAC, Brown Papers, vol. 9, 2025–9, A. Mackenzie to G. Brown, 22 Apr. 1874

27 PAC, Dufferin Papers, miscellaneous memoranda, Lord Dufferin to Sir E. Thornton, 19 Mar. 1874

28 Pryke, *Nova Scotia*, 158

29 *Globe* (Toronto), 5 and 21 July 1873. Frank Underhill gave attention to the ideas of the Liberals (see his *In Search of Canadian Liberalism* [Toronto 1960]); an instructive analysis of perspectives of the post-Mackenzie Liberals is B. Beaven, 'A Last Hurrah: Studies in Liberal Party Development and Ideology in Ontario 1878–1893' (PH D thesis, University of Toronto 1981).

30 Underhill, 'National Parties'

31 D. Swainson, 'The Personnel of Politics: A Study of the Ontario Members of the Second Federal Parliament' (PH D thesis, University of Toronto 1968) 516–18. P. Berton, *The National Dream* (Toronto 1970) 229–48

32 D. Thomson, *Alexander Mackenzie, Clear Grit* (Toronto 1960) 279

33 PAC, Treasury Board Records: vol. 294, 560, Report of the commissioner of customs, 20 May 1875; vol. 295, 113–14, 22 Apr. 1876; vol. 297, 113–14 5 July 1878

34 Gordon Blake, *Customs Administration in Canada: An Essay in Tariff Technology* (Toronto 1957) quoted, 59, see also 57–8. Prov. Canada *Journals* 1843, app. (B.B.)

35 PAC, DNNR, series A–1, vol. 61: R.K. Bullock to R.S.M. Bouchette, 27 June 1862; A. Begg to R.S.M. Bouchette, 15 and 24 July 1862

36 *SP* 1867, no. 2, 44; 1875, no. 1, 37–8; 1879, no.1, 37. It should be noted that the various sources on the size of the department disagree: *SP* 1870, no.7, 55 gives us a total of 16; *SP* 1870, no. 64, 9 gives us a total of 22; *SP* 1870, no. 52, 8, gives us a total of 20. The numbers of preference used here are from the public accounts and presumably consistent.

37 *Citizen* (Ottawa), 18 Mar. and 22 Apr. 1874

38 PAC, Treasury Board Records, series A–3, vol. 294, 498–515, abstract of collectors' reports, I.W. Courtney to R.J. Cartwright, 12 May 1875. PAC, DNNR, series A-1: vol. 151, W.R. Mingaye to J. Johnson, 29 Nov. 1877; vol. 332, C.E. Percey to commissioner of customs, 1 Dec. 1877; vol. 19, H.B. Leeming to J. Johnson, 4 Dec. 1877

39 PAC, DFR, vol. 3373, W. Dunscombe to R.J. Cartwright 25 Jan. 1876
40 PAO, Blake Papers, vol. 28, 882–3, E. Blake to D. Mills, 12 Jan. 1876
41 Ibid., vol. 26, 543, E. Blake to R.J. Cartwright, 21 Sept. 1875
42 *Gazette* (Montreal), 26 July 1875
43 Ibid., 28 Aug. and 2 Sept. 1875
44 Ibid., 15 and 11 Oct. 1875
45 Ibid., 12, 16, 18 Oct. and 1 Nov. 1875. Protection was also an issue in the Toronto West by-election of November 1875, though in a more subdued form. *Mail* (Toronto), 4 and 8 Nov. 1875
46 *Gazette* (Montreal), 8 Dec. 1875. *Citizen* (Ottawa), 17 and 18 Dec. 1875. For an assessment of the conditions of labour in Montreal during the decade, see B. Bradbury, 'The Family Economy and Work in an Industrializing City: Montreal in the 1870s,' Canadian Historical Association, *Historical Papers* (1979): 71–96.
47 *Gazette* (Montreal), 28 Jan.and 18 Feb. 1876
48 *Mail* (Toronto), 21 Oct. 1875
49 Ibid., 26 and 27 Nov. 1875. The Toronto Board of Trade passed a strongly worded protectionist resolution. *Globe* (Toronto), 26 Feb. 1876. For agitation in St Catharines, see *Gazette* (Montreal), 11 Mar. 1876. For protectionist petitions, see, for example, *Journals* 1876, 58, 76, 86, 92, 107, 121, 130, 139, 236, 289.
50 *News* (Saint John), 2 and 5 Feb. 1876
51 R.G. Haliburton attested to the lack of unity. *Proceedings* 1876, 142. *Citizen* (Halifax), 4 Jan. 1876. *Chronicle* (Halifax), 5, 8, 14 Jan. and 4 Feb. 1876
52 *Proceedings* 1876, 142–3. American anthracite was the fuel used for transportation and industrial purposes from Montreal westward. Manufacturers therefore opposed duty on it.
53 *Chronicle* (Halifax), 19 and 21 Feb. 1876
54 *News* (Saint John), 5 May 1874
55 PAC, Dufferin Papers, Dufferin to Mackenzie Letterbook, 31–3, Lord Dufferin to A. Mackenzie, 31 Jan. 1876. Urquhart and Buckley, *Historical Statistics*, 198
56 PAC, DFR, vol. 3373. The bulk of the letters came from Montreal, a number from Toronto, and a few others from centres such as Hamilton and Waterloo. Almost all asked for more protection, often for *ad valorem* rates of 20 or 25 per cent and even more.
57 *Gazette* (Montreal), 17 and 24 Feb. 1876. PAC, Toronto B of T Papers, meeting 23 Feb. 1876, Council Minute Book 1871–87, vol. 3, 108. W.R. Graham, 'Sir Richard Cartwright and the Liberal Party,' (PH D thesis, University of Toronto 1950) 86
58 Debates, 14 Apr. 1874, in *Globe* (Toronto), 16 Apr. 1874
59 24 Feb. 1876. *Debates*, 29 Feb. 1876, 327–8, 329–30; 3 Mar. 1876, 394–5
60 PAC, Buckingham Papers, MG 27 I I 3, J. Young to W.E. Buckingham, 25 May 1892

61 PAO, Blake Papers, vol. 19, R.J. Cartwright to E. Blake, 12 May 1875

62 Pryke, *Nova Scotia*, 173–5. In 1874, 35 Liberals were elected in the Maritimes, and the same in Quebec, along with 66 in Ontario and 2 in Manitoba.

63 *Globe* (Toronto), 6 and 13 Apr. 1875. PAC, PCO, series 1, OC, PC361, 12 Apr. 1875

64 PAC, Mackenzie Papers, 761–4, L. Holton to A. Mackenzie, 24 Apr. 1875

65 Ibid.: 788–90, A.G. Jones to A. Mackenzie, 27 Apr. 1875; 809–10, same to same, 7 May 1875

66 Debates, 14 Apr. 1874, in *Globe* (Toronto), 15 Apr. 1874. Sir F. Hincks to the editor, *Gazette* (Montreal), 21 Apr. 1874. PAC, Macdonald Papers, vol. 267, 121015–25, G. Stephen to Sir J.A. Macdonald, 22 Feb. 1872. For Galt's perspective, see *Debates*, 21 Mar. 1870, 534–51.

67 PAC, Brown Papers, vol. 9, 2180–7, Stephen to Brown, 14 Dec. 1874. PAO, Patteson Papers, vol. 1, G. Stephen to T.C. Patteson, 7 Nov. 1872 [sic]. PAC, Goldwin Smith Papers, G. Smith to E. Blake, 25 July 1875. PAO, Blake Papers: vol. 22, G. Stephen to E. Blake, 3 Sept. 1875; vol. 28, 708–9, E. Blake to G. Stephen 9 Oct. 1875

68 PAO, Blake Papers, vol. 22, E.G. Penny to E. Blake, 7 Sept. 1875. PAC, Galt Papers, vol. 8, 2908–12, L.H. Holton to Sir A.T. Galt, 2 Sept. 1875

69 *Gazette* (Montreal), 28 Feb. 1876. *Mail* (Toronto), 28 Feb. 1876

70 Porritt, *Protection*, 242

71 R.J. Cartwright, *Reminiscences* (Toronto 1912) 156–7. *Gazette* (Montreal), 24 Feb. 1876

72 PAO, Patteson Papers, vol. 2, Sir J.A. Macdonald to T.C. Patteson, 1 Mar. 1876

73 *Debates*, 10 Mar. 1876, 568–76; 15 Mar. 1876, 641–4

74 *Home Industries. Canada's National Policy* (n.p. 1876)

75 Thomson, *Mackenzie*, 213–15, 233–6, 251–4 outlines the great difficulties Mackenzie faced in forming and reforming his cabinet.

76 PAC, Goldwin Smith Papers, G. Smith to E. Blake, 10 Mar. 1876

77 *Gazette* (Montreal), 28 Feb. 1876

CHAPTER 8

1 Jones, *Agriculture*, 325. H. Michell 'Notes on Prices of Agricultural Commodities in the United States and Canada, 1850–1934,' *CJEPS* 1 (1935): 269–79

2 Urquhart and Buckley, *Historical Statistics*, 364

3 Jones, *Agriculture*, 276–7

4 PAC, DNNR, series A–1: vol. 164, printed petitions dated June 1866; vol. 312 D.W. Beadle to R.S.M. Bouchette, 17 Aug. 1866. PAC, PCO, series 3, vol. 3, no. 1237, Petition of the Municipal Council of the Township of South Norwich, County Oxford, 5 Mar. 1870. PAC, DFR, vol. 3374, petition from H. Wigle and others,

Essex Co. through J.C. Patterson. *MT*, 3 Apr. 1879. PAC, Macdonald Papers, vol. 356, 1643890–1, G. Durand to Sir John A. Macdonald, 10 Mar. 1879. *Globe* (Toronto) 25 Jan. and 7 Feb. 1879. R.E. Ankli and W. Millar ('Ontario Agriculture in Transition: The Switch from Wheat to Cheese,' *JEH* 42 [1982]: 207–15) suggest some economic bases for the attractions of diversified agriculture.

5 PAC, Mackenzie Papers, 1470–1, G. Ross to A. Mackenzie, 18 Dec. 1876. Debates, 1 May 1874, in *Globe* (Toronto), 2 May 1874. 'True Reciprocity,' to the editor, *Free Press* (Ottawa), 29 Jan. 1876

6 PAC, DFR: vol. 3377, 248–50, J. Rose to Mr Colby MP, 12 May 1868; vol. 3373, Jardine & Sons to A.J. Wood, 18 Feb. 1876

7 *Citizen* (Ottawa) 18 Aug. 1878

8 *Journals* 1867–68, 148, 170, 179, 182, 187, 198, 205, 214, 217; 1869, 46, 49, 79, 123, 138, 208; 1870, 59; 1874, 20; 1879, 21, 29, 31, 32, 36, 57, 140

9 See, for example, the number of millers who replied to the inquiries of the 1876 Parliamentary Committee on the Agricultural Interest (*Debates*, 1876, 1168–9).

10 The same sense of institutionalization is present in the *History of the Grange in Canada, with a List of Division and Subordinate Granges & Their Executive Officers* (Toronto 1876) 13. Also H. Michell, 'The Grange in Canada,' *Queen's Quarterly* 22 (1914–15): 164–83. L.A. Wood, *A History of Farmers' Movements in Canada*, 2nd ed. (Toronto 1975) 10, 41–9. *Farmer's Advocate* (London), Feb. 1874

11 *Journals* 1876, app. (no. 7). See P. Craven and T. Traves, 'The Class Politics of the National Policy, 1872–1933,' *JCS* 14–3 (1979): 19–20, 26–7, which provides an overview of the relationship of organized farmers in organization to the tariff issue.

12 Ibid. *Debates*, 1876, 1168–9

13 Wood, *Farmer's Movements*, 30–3, 65. *Mail* (Toronto), 18 Jun. 1878. *Witness* (Montreal), 14 Aug. 1878

14 *Debates* 1876, 1167–9

15 *Journals* 1873, 384; 1878, 150, 186, 187, 217; 1879, 65, 140. PAC, DFR, vol. 3374, Mr Casgrain to A. Mackenzie 22 Apr. 1878

16 PANB, A.H. Gillmor Papers, group II, C.E. Mowat to A.H. Gillmor, 10 Mar. 1877

17 *Debates* 1876, 1167–9

18 *Globe* (Toronto), 26 Sept. 1866; 22 Dec. 1870. *Gazette* (Montreal), 25 Mar. 1874. *Mail* (Toronto), 26 Nov. 1875

19 *Mail* (Toronto) 26 Nov. 1875. See also the circular enclosed in PAC, Macdonald Papers, vol. 352, 1622071–5, J. Newton to Sir John A. Macdonald, 20 Oct. 1878, which is an appeal from a woollens manufacturer to farmers to support protection.

20 PAC, Caron Papers, MG 27 I D 3, vol. 189, 1315–20, enclosed in J.H. Sullivan to A.P. Caron, 18 Aug. 1878

21 PAO, Blake Papers, vol. 23, J.C. Smith to E. Blake, 15 May 1876

22 Ibid., vol. 20, Mackenzie to E. Blake, 9 June 1876

23 The charmingly ambiguous 'dubious lemonade' is from the *Canadian Monthly and National Review*, October 1876, quoted in Waite, *Arduous Destiny*, *84*.

24 *Mail* (Toronto), 29 and 30 June, 3 and 28 July, 11 and Aug. 1876

25 Ibid., 4 July 1876

26 PAO, Blake Papers, vol. 19, R.J. Cartwright to E. Blake, 6 July 1876. Cartwright noted, in his acerbic manner, that 'we owe our defeat [in the Ontarios] to those absurd idiots the grangers who have apparently taken up the cry of "protection to the farmer." It would almost serve them right to give the blockheads what they ask.' As for Wellington, see PAO, Blake Papers, vol. 23, J. Young to E. Blake, 6 Oct. 1876.

27 Mills denied that he undertook such financing (UWO Regional Collection, D. Mills Papers, Letterbook 1875–77, 264–5, D. Mills to W.L. Brown, 24 Jan. 1877).

28 *Herald* (Halifax), 2 July 1877. *MT*, *12* Oct. 1877

29 PAC, Mackenzie Papers, 2189–90, J. Charlton to A. Mackenzie, 14 Dec. 1878

30 PAO, Blake Papers, vol. 20, D. Mills to E. Blake, 20 Nov. 1876

31 R.L. Fraser, 'Like Eden in Her Summer Dress: Gentry, Economy and Society: Upper Canada, 1812–1840' (PH D thesis, University of Toronto 1979)

32 *Reform Government in the Dominion* (Toronto 1878) 87–8, and also 35. Also *Speeches of the Hon. Alexander Mackenzie* 46, 47, 95. *The Trade Question. Fallacies of Protection or the So-Called 'National Policy*' (Toronto 1878) 3, 13. UWO Regional Collection, D. Mills Papers, Letterbook 1877–78, 174–6, D. Mills to J. Smith, 18 Aug. 1878. W.R. Graham ('The Alexander Mackenzie Administration, 1873–1878: A Study of Liberal Tenets and Tactics' [MA thesis, University of Toronto 1944] 211–28) offers a useful account of Liberal beliefs on tariff matters in the 1870s.

33 *Globe* (Toronto), 3 Aug 1878

34 *Globe* (Toronto), 7 Aug 1878; 7 Dec. 1877. *Witness* (Montreal), 25 Nov. 1878

35 *Speeches of … Alex. Mackenzie*, *23*, *44*, *46*, *47*, *97*. *Address of the Hon. Alexander Mackenzie to the Workingmen on the 'National Policy*' (Toronto 1878)

36 For the revenue tariff see Mackenzie's Sarnia speech of 1875 in *Speeches of … Alex. Mackenzie*, *150–3*. The assertion of the revenue-tariff policy, followed by an attack on protection on free-trade principles, is well illustrated by R.J. Cartwright's speech of 7 July 1877, in *Reform Government in the Dominion*, *82–3*. Cartwright, *Reminiscences*, *159*. Also *Debates*, *25* Feb. 1876, 253 (Cartwright); 3 Mar. 1876, 369 (J. Young); 20 Feb. 1877, 140 (Cartwright); 20 Feb. 1877, 174 (Mackenzie)

37 *Debates*, *16* Feb. 1876, 65 (D. Mills), 70 (Young), 82 (Macdonald, Toronto Centre); 17 Feb. 1876, 112–13 (Oliver)

38 The Liberals opposed not incidental protection but a tariff, the primary purpose of which was protection or near prohibition of imported goods. *Debates*, 3 Mar. 1876, 389 (Appleby); 7 Mar. 1876, 480 (Palmer); 17 Feb. 1876, 115 (Gordon); 18 Feb. 1876, 139 (Bertram); 24 Feb. 1876, 228 (Carmichael). *Political Points and Pencillings. Being Selections from Various Addresses Delivered by Hon. Alex. Mackenzie* (Toronto 1878)

39 *Debates*, 16 Feb. 1876, 72 (J. Young); 25 Feb. 1876, 253 (Cartwright); 18 Mar. 1879, 528–9 (Charlton); 21 Mar. 1879, 637 (Ross); 4 Apr. 1879, 1002 (Guthrie), 1025 (Fleming); 8 Apr. 1879, 1116 (Trow). *Globe* (Toronto), 13 Aug. 1878. Fear of monopoly was a constant theme of the Liberals in the late nineteenth century. See Beaven, 'A Last Hurrah.'

40 *Debates*, 17 Feb. 1876, 114 (Oliver), 117 (McDougall, Elgin); 29 Feb. 1876, 324–5 (A.G. Jones); 3 Mar. 1876, 389 (Appleby); 3 Mar. 1876, 370 (Young); 7 Mar 1876, 487 (Sinclair); 14 Mar. 1879, 440, 442, 451–2 (Cartwright); 18 Mar. 1879, 510–14 (Flynn); 21 Mar. 1879, 633–5, 643 (Ross); 26 Mar. 1879, 691, (Casey), 707–9 (Oliver); 27 Mar. 1879, 756 (Cameron), 766–9 (Robertson, Shelburne), 778 (King); 28 Mar. 1879, 812–13 (Paterson); 1 Apr. 1879, 880–1 (Mills); 4 April 1879, 990 (Burpee); 7 Apr. 1879, 1064 (Burpee); 8 Apr. 1879, 1112 (Rogers). *Reform Government in the Dominion*, 42, 83

41 *Debates*, 3 Mar. 1876, 389 (Appleby); 7 Mar. 1876, 487 (Sinclair); 20 Feb. 1877, 145 (Cartwright); 14 Mar. 1879, 468 (Mackenzie). *Reform Government in the Dominion*, 74–5. *Free Trade for the People. Protection for the Favoured Few* (Toronto 1878)

42 *Debates*, 28 Feb. 1877, 336

43 Blake Papers, PAO, vol. 22, D.A. Macdonald to E. Blake, 9 Feb. 1877. For the protectionist and mild protectionists in Liberal ranks, see *Debates* 1876, 72–3, 84, 110–11, 122, 130.

44 J. Mck. to the editor, *Gazette* (Montreal), 18 Mar. 1876

45 PAC, Montreal B of T Papers, Dominion Board of Trade Letterbook, 379–82, W.J. Patterson to A. Brown, 7 Mar. 1877

46 PAC, Macdonald Papers, vol. 348, 159954–7, G. Dustan to Sir J.A. Macdonald, 2 Mar. 1878

47 Canada. *Statutes* 35 Vict. c. 12. PAC, DFR, vol. 3378, 44, F. Hincks memorandum to governor in council, 10 Dec. 1872. *Globe* (Toronto), 14 July 1874; 20 Jan. 1875. PAC, DFR, vol. 3373, minutes of a meeting of the Grocery Trade, Mar. 9, 1876. *Proceedings* 1876, 81–90

48 *Debates*, 11 June 1872, 1102–3; 16 Mar. 1875, 763–4

49 PAO, Blake Papers, vol. 22, M.P. Hayes to W. McMaster, 6 Feb. 1875. *Debates*, 8 Mar. 1876, 507. *Journals* 1876, app. (no. 3) 160–4

50 *Statutes*, 40 Vict. c. 11 imposed the excise duties. PAC, DFR, vol. 3373, 'Brewer'

to R.J. Cartwright, 21 Feb. 1877, in which the nameless brewer states the duty will destroy his trade. He points out that he worked for the Liberals at the last election and suggests his potential desertion. Also brewers' deputation material to Cartwright, 28 Feb. 1877. PAC, Buckingham Papers, R.J. Cartwright to A. Mackenzie, 7 June 1878

51 Skelton, *Galt*, 247. *Proceedings* 1877, 171–83. *Debates*, 28 Feb. 1876, 299

52 Phelps, 'Canada Oil Association,' 31–3. PAC, DNNR, series A–I vol. 329, memorial, E. Folis, 17 Dec. 1863, with covering letter, A. Mackenzie to L.H. Holton, 24 Dec. 1863. For the excise duty, see *Statutes*, 31 Vict. c. 50. *Globe* (Toronto), 10 Mar. 1870

53 *Statutes*, 38 Vict. c 35. *Journals* 1874, 140–1

54 *Citizen* (Halifax), 6 and 8 Jan. 1877. *Chronicle* (Halifax), 4 Jan. 1877. For a useful account that stresses the struggle in the House of Commons, see McDougall, *Fuels*, 23–9.

55 *Proceedings*, 1877, 81

56 Ibid., 117–21. There is evidence to show that the Liberals were ready to do battle at the Dominion Board meetings. UWO Regional Collection, D. Mills Papers, letterbook 1877–78, 420–1, D. Mills to J. Cameron, 15 Nov. 1877

57 J.R. Lithgow to the editor, *Chronicle* (Halifax), 9 Feb. 1877. J.R. Lithgow to the editor, *Citizen* (Halifax), 16 Feb. and 8 Mar. 1877

58 *Journals* 1877, 27, 37, 54, 58, 61, 70, 92, 106, 158

59 *Chronicle* (Halifax), 15 and 22 Mar. 1877. *Citizen* (Halifax), 17 Mar. 1877

60 *Citizen* (Halifax), 24 Mar. 1877

61 *Chronicle* (Halifax), 16 Mar. 1877

62 *Journals* 1877, app. (no. 4), 26, 28, 40, 41, 47–8, 52–4, 72–4, 82–3

63 PAC, Toronto B of T Papers, meeting of 16 Mar. 1877, Council Minutebook 1871–87, vol. 3, 125–6. PAC, Macdonald Papers, vol. 223, 95306–17, J. Hickson to Sir J.A. Macdonald, 15 Jan. 1879. A.D. Chandler Jr ('Anthracite Coal and the Beginnings of the Industrial Revolution in the United States,' *Business History Review* 46 [1972]: 141–81) indicates the importance of coal in the American process of industrialization. For some idea of American coal's penetration in Ontario, see D.F. Walker, 'Transportation of Coal into Southern Ontario, 1871–1921,' *OH* 63 (1971): 15–30.

64 *Debates*, 2 Mar. 1877, 405; 6 Mar. 1877, 519

65 PAC, Macdonald Papers, vol. 350, 160983–5, J.R. Lithgow to Sir J.A. Macdonald, 9 July 1878. *Chronicle* (Halifax), 8 Feb. and 24 Mar. 1879

66 *Canadian Biographical Dictionary*, vol. 2, 528–9

67 PAO, Blake Papers, vol. 27, 467, E. Blake to G.G. Dustan, 14 Dec. 1875. UWO Regional Collection, D. Mills Papers, letterbook 1875–77, 3, D. Mills to G.G. Dustan, 29 Nov. 1876. PAC, Macdonald Papers: vol. 349, 160560–1, G.G. Dustan

to Sir J.A. Macdonald, 7 May 1878; vol. 282, 129334–47, C. Tupper to Sir J.A. Macdonald, 6 Jan. 1878

68 *Statutes*, 40 Vict. c. 11

69 PAC, Macdonald Papers, vol. 267, 1211035–8, G. Stephen to Sir J.A. Macdonald, 7 Feb. 1877. This letter is incorrectly identified as dating from 1871 in the Macdonald Papers. *Mail* (Toronto), 2 Apr. 1877

70 *News* (Saint John), 25 July 1874. *Mail* (Toronto), 26 Mar. 1874

71 PAO, Blake Papers: vol. 23, W.H. Howland to E. Blake, 19 Sept. 1876; vol. 33, 136–7, E. Blake to W.H. Howland, 19 Sept. 1876

72 Ibid., vol. 24, W.H. Howland to E. Blake, 11 Mar. 1877

73 Ibid., vol. 24, W.H. Howland to E. Blake, 16 Mar. 1877

74 PAC, Macdonald Papers, vol. 267, 121026–9, G. Stephen to Sir J.A. Macdonald, 26 Feb. 1872. 'Ramsay' to the editor, *Globe* (Toronto), 11 Sept. 1878. *Mail* (Toronto), 16 Apr., 6 and 14 May, 4 and 14 June, 13 July, and 3 Aug. 1878. *Gazette* (Montreal), 23 Aug. and 14 Sept. 1878. For the quote, see *Mail* (Toronto), 15 Aug. 1878.

75 UWO Regional Collection, John Newton Papers, journal 20, end papers

76 Ibid., copy entered after 8 Oct. 1876, J. Newton to Sir J.A. Macdonald, 1 Sept. 1876

77 Ibid., copy entered after 8 Oct. 1876, Sir J.A. Macdonald to J. Newton, 17 Sept. 1876

78 Ibid., journal 21, draft, J. Newton to Sir J.A. Macdonald, 21 Feb. 1877

79 *Mail* (Toronto), 7 July 1877

80 *Mail* (Toronto), 10 July 1877

CHAPTER 9

1 *Mail* (Toronto), 25 Sept. and 1 Oct. 1877

2 *Globe* (Toronto), 26 Oct. 1877

3 *Canadian Biographical Dictionary*, vol. 1, 420, 476–7, 614–18. *Journals* 1874, app. (no. 3) 34; *Journals* 1876, app. (no. 3) 174. *Mail* (Toronto), 3 Nov. 1877. Others who might be mentioned: Robert McKechnie employed 140 to 160 men in a machine-tool factory at Dundas; Samuel Merner had two sons each running a foundry, was a silent partner in a furniture factory in Berlin, and ran a grist mill at New Hamburg where he owned several town blocks; T.T. Coleman manufactured lumber to the extent of 2.5 million feet a year and his salt works produced 65,000 to 75,000 barrels. For these, see *Canadian Biographical Dictionary*, vol. 1, 145–6, 647–8, 724–5.

4 *Globe* (Toronto), 26 and 27 Oct. 1877

5 Ibid., 27 Oct. 1877

6 *Mail* (Toronto), 28 Mar. 1878
7 PAC, Buchanan Papers, vol. 26, 22366, Circular from W.H. Frazer, Apr. 1878. PAC, Macdonald Papers, vol. 350, 160863–6, D. McInnes to Sir J.A. Macdonald, 18 June 1878
8 PAC, Macdonald Papers, vol. 348, 166062–3, W.H. Frazer to Sir J.A. Macdonald, 28 Mar. 1878. Similar mechanisms were later undertaken. See R.C. Brown, *Robert Laird Borden: A Biography*, vol. 1 (Toronto 1975) 190–1.
9 *Globe* (Toronto), 6 May and 6, 11, 13 July 1878
10 Ibid., 28 May, 1 Jun., and 30 July 1878
11 Ibid., 20 Oct. 1877. PAC, Macdonald Papers, vol. 350, 160863–6, D. McInnes to Sir J.A. Macdonald, 18 June 1878
12 PAC, Montreal B of T Papers, Dominion Board of Trade Letterbook, 347, W.J. Patterson to W.H. Howland, 9 Feb. 1877
13 Ibid., 101, W.J. Patterson to W.H. Frazer, 7 Jan. 1879. *Globe* (Toronto) 26 Oct. 1877; 15 Nov. 1878; 8 Jan. 1879
14 *News* (Saint John), 2 Feb. 1876. K.J. Donovan, 'New Brunswick and the Federal Election of 1878' (MA thesis, University of New Brunswick 1973) 20
15 *Gazette* (Montreal), 4 Jan 1879
16 George Stephen had such contacts, for example; so did E.K. Greene. PAC, Macdonald Papers: vol. 348, 159660, E.K. Greene to Sir J.A. Macdonald, 5 Jan. 1878; vol. 348, 159882, same to same, 16 Feb. 1878
17 *Mail* (Toronto), 1 Feb. 1876. *Free Press* (Ottawa), 10 Aug. 1878
18 Kealey, *Toronto Workers*, 37–63
19 L.E. Wismer (ed., *Proceedings of the Canadian Labour Union Congress: 1873–77* [Ottawa 1951] 31, 36, 80, 85–7) shows that while labour leaders were anxious for the independent organization of labour, strikes were not viewed as the best method of solving labour disputes.
20 *Globe* (Toronto), 12 Sept. 1878
21 Ibid., 12, 14, 16, and 19, Sept. 1878. On Rosamond's paternalism, see Reid, 'Rosamond Woolen Company,' 279–80.
22 The Liberal candidate, Daniel Galbraith, won the riding by 43 votes (*SP* 1879, no. 88). Galbraith was the incumbent, and had been acclaimed in 1874; the riding was considered Liberal. PAC, Macdonald Papers, vol. 267, 121026–9, G. Stephen to Sir J.A. Macdonald, 26 Feb. 1872
23 *Citizen* (Halifax), 3 Feb. 1874
24 PAC, Macdonald Papers, vol. 349, 160189, D. McInnes to Sir J.A. Macdonald, 3 Apr. 1878
25 PAC, Macdonald Papers, vol. 351, 161809–14, J. Livingstone to Sir J.A. Macdonald, 27 Sept. 1878

26 PAC, Caron Papers, vol. 190, 2906–7, Glover, Fry & Co. to A.P. Caron, 5 Apr. 1879
27 *Globe* (Toronto), 12 and 14 Aug. and 3 Sept. 1878
28 PAC, Macdonald Papers, vol. 349, 1610189, D. McInnes to Sir J.A. Macdonald, 3 Apr. 1878. *Canadian Biographical Dictionary*, vol. 1, 295–6, 724–5. G.M. Rose, *A Cyclopedia of Canadian Biography* (Toronto 1886), 431. *Journals* 1876, app. (no. 3), 160–4. B.D. Palmer (*Working Class Experience: The Rise and Reconstitution of Canadian Labour, 1800–1980* [Toronto 1983]) provides an insightful discussion of paternalism, but places it in the context of 'stages' of labour relations, and foreshortens its chronological life.
29 *Gazette* (Montreal), 2 July and 18 Oct. 1875
30 *Mail* (Toronto), 30 July 1878. D.G. Creighton ('George Brown, Sir John Macdonald and the "Workingman,"' *CHR* 24 [1943]: 362–76) provided one of the earliest accounts of the place of the labouring classes in nineteenth-century politics. B. Ostry ('Conservatives, Liberals and Labour in the 1870's,' *CHR* 41 [1960]: 93–127, and 'Conservatives, Liberals, and Labour in the 1880's,' *CJEPS* 27 [1961]: 141–161), like Creighton, viewed workingmen as a battlefield over which the two major parties fought; F.W. Watt ('The National Policy, the Workingman and Proletarian Ideas in Victorian Canada,' *CHR* 60 [1959]: 1–26), while ignoring the role of the tariff of 1879 in attracting labour to the Conservatives, was more sensitive to the emergence of an independent labour political interest, a point of view Kealey (*Toronto Working Class*) treats exhaustively while accepting the central importance of the tariff in defining labour's political alignments.
31 See PAC, Tupper Papers, vol. 25, 14970–1, undated, untitled sheet, 'We agree to pay the amount opposite our respective names.' PAC, McLennan Papers, vol. 1: 484–99, J.A. Macdonell to J. McLennan, 24 Apr. 1878; 524–7, same to same, 29 July 1878
32 Sir John A. Macdonald indicated that one of the functions of the United Empire Club was to gather party financing; money then would not have to go through his hands as in 1872 (*Mail* [Toronto], 3 July 1876). For a fuller discussion of the club and the nature of late nineteenth-century political organization, see B. Forster, 'A Conservative Heart: The United Empire Club 1874–1882,' *OH* 78 (1986).
33 PAC, Macdonald Papers: vol. 348, 149734–7, J. Macdonell to Sir John A. Macdonald, 21 Jan. 1878; vol. 350, 161219, same to same, 23 Aug. 1878. PAC, Tupper Papers, vol. 25, 14962–9, 'Private & Confidential,' dated 1 Feb. 1878
34 PAC, McLennan Papers, vol. 1, 69, D. Creighton to J. McLennan, 16 July 1878. PAO, Patteson Papers, vol. 1, Sir J.A. Macdonald to T.C. Patteson, 29 Oct. 1874
35 *Free Press* (Ottawa), 11 Dec. 1878. PAC, A.B. Campbell Papers, Sir J.A. Macdonald to A.B. Campbell, 27 Jan. 1879. PAC, Scarth Papers, Sir J.A. Macdonald to W.B. Scarth, 2 Apr. 1880.

6 Metropolitan Toronto Library, Pattullo Papers, replies to Pattullo's questionnaire

7 PAC, McLennan Papers, vol. 1, 532–5, J. Macdonell to J. McLennan, 13 Aug. 1878

8 PAC, Progressive Conservative Party Papers, MG 28 IV, 2 vol. 7, 'Resolution of the Liberal Conservative Convention,' Jan. 1878. *Debates*, 12 Mar. 1878, 1071

9 PANB, Gillmor Papers, group II, W.H. Venning to A.H. Gillmor, 26 Mar. 1878

0 PAC, Macdonald Papers: vol. 350, 160914–17, J. Domville to Sir J.A. Macdonald, 23 June 1878; vol. 350, 16010–11, S.J. King to Sir J.A. Macdonald, 18 July 1878; vol. 276, 126303–13, S.L. Tilley to Sir J.A. Macdonald, 2 Sept. 1876

1 Quoted in Porritt, *Protection*, 260. Yet see the *Globe* ([Toronto], 27 July 1878), which provides a more sympathetic interpretation.

2 *Globe* (Toronto), 24 Nov. and 4 Dec. 1877; 28 and 30 Jan. 1878. *Mail* (Toronto), 17 Aug. 1878

3 *Reform Government in the Dominion* (Toronto 1878). UWO Regional Collection, D. Mills Papers, letterbook 1877–78, 397–401, D. Mills to Dr McCully, 13 Nov. 1877. For pamphlets, see in addition to those cited above, *Address by David Glass, Q.C., to the Electors of East Middlesex* (London 1878) and J.D. Edgar, *A Protest against the Increased Taxation advocated by the Canadian Opposition* (Toronto 1878)

4 *Globe* (Toronto), 5, 13 July and 1, 14 Aug. 1878

5 *Free Press* (Ottawa), 28 June and 29 Aug 1878. *Globe* (Toronto), 29 Apr. and 6 and 9 Sept. 1878

6 *Globe* (Toronto), 11 Apr., 2 Aug., and 6 and 11 Sept. 1878. *Mail* (Toronto), 14 June and 26 Aug 1878. *Canadian Biographical Dictionary* vol. 1, 420–2

7 PAC, Macdonald Papers: vol. 347, 159469–72, J. Domville to Sir J.A. Macdonald, Dec. 1877; vol. 350, 16112–15, G. Orton to Sir J.A. Macdonald, 10 Aug. 1878; vol. 348, 160095–8, J.C. Patterson to Sir J.A. Macdonald, 27 Mar. 1878. *Gazette* (Montreal), 11 Sept. 1878

8 PAC, Macdonald Papers, vol. 247, 111516–21, D.L. Macpherson to Sir J.A. Macdonald, 11 Sept. 1878

9 *Address by David Glass* …

0 PAC, Dufferin Papers, miscellaneous memoranda, 'Confidential Memorandum on the financial position of Canada,' R. Cartwright, 25 July 1878

1 PAC, Mackenzie Papers, 2084–7, A.G. Jones to A. Mackenzie, 18 Sept. 1878

2 The urban and rural ridings were calculated by R.C. Brown, Malcolm Davidson, and myself from *Census 1871*, vol. 2, 'Occupations,' and *Census 1881*, vol. 2, 'Occupations.' This research was undertaken to provide material for the *Historical Atlas of Canada*, vol. 2 (forthcoming) and I am grateful to the atlas for allowing its use. See *SP* 1879, no. 88 for the election results.

3 The inspiration for this statistical analysis came from work for the *Historical Atlas*

of Canada. For the 39 seats with the highest level of manufacturing (this includes an additional group of 14 seats in which wages for workers tended to be good, and value added per worker was high, but in which workers in manufacturing made up a more modest proportion of the work-force than in the 25 seats first analysed), a correlation of .574 was derived. Taking all Ontario seats, there was no observable trend. Though more distant in time, the 1871 census data are preferable to those from the 1881 census because the latter reflect the early material impact of the National Policy, rather than the potential for defensive reaction in ridings already having substantial manufacturing.

54 One of the questions Pattullo asked in his circular to Liberal notables after the election was 'What proportion of the Reform vote was unpolled?' Answers to the questionnaire often complained of low turnouts (Metropolitan Toronto Library, Pattullo Papers).

55 B. Forster, M. Davidson, and R.C. Brown, 'The Franchise, Personators and Dead Men: An Inquiry into the Voters' Lists and the Election of 1891,' *CHR* (forthcoming 1986), shows the impact on the electoral process such population movement could have. The Liberals won 26 seats of the 88 in Ontario. For those ridings in which turnout exceeded 75%, the Liberals gained 42.9%; for those in which the turnout was less than 65%, they won 15.8%. Of the towns and cities identified as such in the returns, over two-thirds went to the Conservatives, with extremely low turnouts. The lower the turnout the more likely a Conservative victory *in the towns* (*SP* 1879, no. 88).

56 'All of us underrated the power of humbug and believed that the rural mind could comprehend more fully than it did, what was so plain to us,' wrote John Charlton (PAC, Mackenzie Papers, 2189–90, Charlton to Mackenzie, 14 Dec. 1878). For a very useful analysis of the 1878 election in Ontario, see D. Lee, 'The Dominion General Election of 1878 in Ontario,' *OH* 51 (1959): 172–90. Lee makes clear the importance of the protection issue.

57 Muise, 'Elections and Constituencies,' 288ff, 419. *SP* 1879, no. 88

58 PAC, Tupper Papers, vol. 5, 2092–3, J.C. Pope to Sir J.A. Macdonald, 22 Oct. 1876. PAC, Macdonald Papers, vol. 276, 126353–59, S.L. Tilley to Sir J.A. Macdonald, 3 Aug. 1878. *Globe* (Toronto), 28 May 1878

59 UWO Regional Collection, Mills Papers, letterbook 1877–78, 315–18, D. Mills to G.A. Fye, 3 Nov. 1877. Cartwright, *Reminiscenses*, 183–6

60 A reading of *La Minerve* (Montreal) from January to the end of April 1870 indicates an obsessive concern with the Guibord affair, church-state relations, and the Riel rebellion – and hardly any concern with the tariff. Though the same paper reported on the tariff of 1874 (4 Mar. and 23 Apr. 1874), the paper was generally much more concerned with the Riel amnesty. Liberal anti-Catholicism

was given great play in 1876 (e.g. 21 Feb. 1876), but the protectionist reaction in the city was discussed (2 Feb. 1876).

61 R. Rumilly, *Histoire de la Province de Québec* vol. 2, 3rd ed. (Montreal 1941) 227–30. *La Minerve* (Montreal), 17, 26, 30, 31, Aug. and 16 Sept. 1878. *Le Nouveau Monde* (Montreal), 1 Oct. 1878. L.G. Desjardins (*De l'idée Conservatrice dans l'ordre politique* [Quebec, 1879]) provides an indication of the intellectual enthusiasms of the club.

62 *Répertoire des parlementaires québecois 1867–1978* (Quebec 1980) 291. *Globe* (Toronto), 29 Oct. 1878. *La Minerve* (Montreal), 3 Feb. 1879

63 A meeting reported in the *Gazette* ([Montreal], 18 Oct. 1875) provides one of the few significant instances I have found. The speaker who brought the matter up noted considerable disagreement about it.

64 A.W.C. Hale, 'The National Policies of Canada: Myth and Reality, 1867–1900' (PH D thesis, Wales 1979), ch. 4

65 PAC, Macdonald Papers, vol. 520, 636, Sir J.A. Macdonald to A. Brown, 30 May 1872. D. Owram, *Promise of Eden: The Canadian Expansionist Movement and the Idea of the West, 1856–1900* (Toronto 1980) 38–78. D.G. Creighton, *British North America at Confederation* (Ottawa 1963) 41–3. Some time ago, J.H. Dales (*Protective Tariff in Canada's Development*) launched a sharp attack on the 'national policy' as an explicit and integrated tripartite policy, one of the most powerful expositions of which is to be found in D.G. Creighton ('Economic Nationalism and Confederation,' Canadian Historical Association *Report* [1942]: 44–51). Owram, as well as Hale ('National Policies'), shows that politicians and businessmen had an interest in developing the west through immigration and railway construction, but fails to deal with Dales. More recently, A.A. den Otter ('Alexander Galt') tried to revivify the Creightonian perspective, dating its historical origins to the late 1850s. Creighton in his 'Economic Nationalism' had some difficulty fitting the tariff into his construct, which is precisely the point at issue. Though a number of observers conceived of a dynamic transcontinental economy based on western agriculture, railways, and eastern manufacturing by the mid and later 1870s, the conception is not a policy. V.C. Fowke implicitly assumes that the tripartite national policy of which Creighton spoke was an analytical construct used by observers, not stated government policy ('The National Policy – Old and New,' *CJEPS* 18 [1952]: 271–86)

66 *Debates*, 15 Mar. 1876, 678–9 (Casey); 6 Mar. 1877, 515 (Colby). See also G. Orton, 9 Mar. 1877, 607

67 Ibid., 18 Mar. 1879, 517–26

68 Canada, *Statutes*, 35 Vict. c. 37; 36 Vict. c. 39

69 *Guardian* (New Westminster), Jan.-Apr. 1874. *Colonist* (Victoria), Jan.-Apr. 1874

70 *Debates*, 18 Feb. 1876, 128–9; 3 Mar. 1876, 375–6; 7 Mar. 1877, 532–3
71 *Guardian* (New Westminster) Jan.-Apr. 1874. *Colonist* (Victoria) Jan.-Apr. 1874
72 *Free Press* (Winnipeg), 20 and 22 Aug. 1878
73 *Guardian* (New Westminster), 4 and 25 Sept. 1878. *Colonist* (Victoria), Jan.-Mar. 1879
74 *Sentinel* (Thunder Bay), 13 June 1878
75 PAC, Mackenzie Papers, 2112–13, A.N. Richards to A. Mackenzie, 30 Sept. 1878. PAC, Macdonald Papers, vol. 294, 134403–4, G.A. Walkem to Sir J.A. Macdonald, 24 Apr. 1879 (telegram), reported, 'If railway policy longer withheld general serious row is certain and feeling increased by new tariff which is severe.'
76 *Colonist* (Victoria), 29 Mar. 1879 offers one of the few editorials on the tariff from 1 Jan. to 30 Mar. and defends it in the fashion indicated. See also *Standard* (Winnipeg) 19 Apr. 1879.
77 *Daily Times* (Winnipeg), 9 June 1879, quoted in Hale, 'National Policies,' 186
78 *Guardian* (New Westminster), 29 Mar. 1879
79 Waite, *Arduous Destiny*, 86–90, 98

CHAPTER 10

1 PAC, Mackenzie Papers, 2094–5, A. Hope to A. Mackenzie, 20 Sept. 1878
2 PAC, Macdonald Papers: vol. 351, 161773–80, M. Heward to Sir J.A. Macdonald, 26 Sept. 1878; vol. 352, 162106–8, E.R. Steinhardt to Macdonald, 21 Oct. 1878; vol. 353, 162580–7, S. Dawson to Macdonald, 14 Nov. 1878
3 Ibid., vol. 350, 161905–6, E.K. Greene to Sir J.A. Macdonald, 7 Oct. 1878; vol. 351, 161809–14, J. Livingstone to Macdonald
4 PAC, Buchanan Papers vol. 115, 74633, W.H. Howland, circular letter, 30 Sept. 1878. *Globe* (Toronto) 24 Oct. 1878
5 *Witness* (Montreal), 17 Oct. 1878. *Gazette* (Montreal), 26 Oct., 12 Nov. 1878
6 *Globe* (Toronto) 24 Oct. 1878
7 *Gazette* (Montreal), 12 Nov. 1878
8 *Sun* (Saint John) Nov. 13, 20, 1878
9 PAC, Macdonald Papers, vol. 353, 162580–7, A.R. Morrison to Sir J.A. Macdonald, Nov. 14, 1878. *Witness* (Montreal), 4 Jan. 1879. *Globe* (Toronto) 14 Jan. 1879
10 Ibid., vol. 353, 163031–2, W.H. Frazer to Sir J.A. Macdonald, 23 Dec. 1878. *Globe* (Toronto), 8 Jan. 1879
11 *Gazette* (Montreal), 28 Dec. 1878; 6 Jan. 1879. *Canadian Biographical Dictionary*, vol. 2, 425–6
12 *Proceedings* 1879, 4. For some of Dobson's activities, see *Free Press* (Ottawa),

20 Jan. 1879. Also *Globe* (Toronto), 28 Jan., 25 Mar. 1879. And see Dobson's *A Pamphlet Compiled and Issued under the Auspices of the Boards of Trade of Pictou and Cape Breton on the Coal and Iron Industries* (Ottawa 1879)

13 PAC, Macdonald Papers, vol. 216, 92353–9, Sir A.T. Galt to Sir J.A. Macdonald, 26 Feb. 1879. PAC, DFR, vol. 3845, 'Documents relating to the visit of A. Galt and Lt. Col. Bernard to Spain 1878–1879'

14 PAC, Montreal B of T Papers, Dominion Board of Trade Letterbook, 111–13, J. Patterson to S.S. Lloyd, 16 Jan. 1879. PAC, Tilley Papers, vol.22: 263, S.L. Tilley to R.S. Hawlins, 17 Jan. 1879; 319, S.L. Tilley to J. Harris, 21 Jan. 1879

15 *Debates*, 14 Mar. 1879, 409–15. *Sun* (Saint John), 13 Nov. 1878

16 *Globe* (Toronto), 27 July 1878

17 PAC, Tilley Papers, vol. 20, E. Young to Sir J.A. Macdonald, 16 Oct. 1878; E. Young to S.L. Tilley, 1 Nov. 1878. E. Young to J.T. Bulmer, 5 Sept. 1881, in Public Archives of Nova Scotia *Report* (1945) 24–9

18 PAC, Macdonald Papers, vol. 353, 163161–6, J. Maclean to Sir J.A. Macdonald, 1 Jan. 1879. J. Maclean, *The Complete Tariff Hand-Book*, 2nd ed. (Toronto 1879). J. Maclean, *Protection and Free Trade* (Montreal 1867)

19 PAC, Macdonald Papers, vol. 353, 163034–5, W.H. Frazer to Sir J.A. Macdonald, 23 Dec. 1878. *Free Press* (Ottawa), 15 Jan. 1879. PAC, PCO, series 1, OC, PC1474, 24 Oct. 1879

20 *Globe* (Toronto), 16 Jan. 1879

21 *Free Press* (Ottawa), 31 Mar. 1879. *Citizen* (Ottawa), 7 Apr. 1879. J. Maclean, *Protection in Canada* (Ottawa 1879)

22 PAC, 'Review of the Trade and Commerce of the Dominion of Canada from 30th June 1872 to 30th June 1878,' MG 29 A 13. *Globe* (Toronto), 25 Feb. 1879

23 PAC, Tilley Papers, vol. 22: 308–9, S.L. Tilley to I.T. Harris, 20 Jan. 1879; 83, Tilley to J. Laidlaw, 7 Jan. 1879. *Sun* (Saint John), 13 Nov. 1878. *Globe* (Toronto), 18 Jan. 1879

24 *Globe* (Toronto), 18 Jan. 1879

25 See the mild comments made in the Montreal Board of Trade (PAC, Montreal B of T Papers, General Meetings 325, meeting of 14 Jan. 1879). The Toronto Board of Trade made some specific criticisms while supporting the tariff generally (PAC, Toronto B of T Papers, Council Minute Book, 1871–87, 174).

26 *Proceedings* 1879, 73–125

27 *Citizen* (Ottawa) 18 Mar. 1879

28 PAC, Lorne Papers, part 2, 975–9, Lorne to Sir M. Hicks Beach, 10 Mar. 1879

29 *Citizen* (Ottawa), 14 Jan., 26 Feb. and 26 and 29 Mar. 1879. *Chronicle* (Quebec), 7, 21, 28 Feb. and 17, 18, 19, 26 Mar. 1879. Free Press (Ottawa), 5, 12, 27 Feb. and 1, 18, 19, 21, 22 Mar. 1879. *Globe* (Toronto) 7, 8, 10, 12, 26 Feb. and 3, 8, 21, 22, 26, 28 Mar. 1879

30 *Journals* 1879, 18, 21, 29, 31, 36, 55, 65, 140, 144, 154, 161, 165, 178, 183, 185, 187, 224, 245, 251, 300

31 PAC, Caron Papers, vol. 189, 2417–20, A. Walsh to A. Caron, 24 Feb. 1879

32 PAO, Wallace Family Papers, J. Speight to N. Wallace, 2 Apr. 1879. PAC, Tilley Papers, vol. 22, 610, S.L. Tilley to M.A. Gault, 6 Feb. 1879. PANB, Gillmor Papers, group II, J.N. Clarke to A.H. Gillmor, 28 Mar. 1879

33 *Sun* (Saint John), 6 Mar. 1879. *Citizen* (Ottawa), 8 Mar. 1879. *Globe* (Toronto), 8 Mar. 1879

34 PAC, Lorne Papers, MG 27 IB 2, part 2, 975–9, Lorne to Sir Michael Hicks Beach, 10 Mar. 1879

35 New Brunswick Museum, Tilley Family Papers, shelf 75, box 6, nos 42 & 43

36 PAC, Mackenzie Papers, 2252–3, A. Mackenzie to M. Thompson, 6 Mar. 1879

37 *Free Press* (Ottawa), 12 Feb. 1879

38 PAC, Treasury Board Records, series A-3, vol. 300, 408–10. PAC, Macdonald Papers: vol. 355, 163690–3, J.B. Robinson to Sir J.A. Macdonald, 1 Feb. 1879; vol. 362, 167621, Gooderham & Worts to Macdonald, 14 Nov. 1879

39 PAC, Macdonald Papers: vol. 353, 162895–9, Sir H. Allan to Sir J.A. Macdonald, 16 Dec. 1878; vol. 365, 169413–20, D. McInnes to Macdonald, 11 Feb. 1880

40 PAC, McLennan Papers, vol. 2, 715–16, W.W. Ogilvie to J. McLennan, 15 Mar. 1879

41 Ibid., vol. 1, 319, J.R. Henderson, to J. McLennan, 17 Mar. 1879

42 Clark, 'Tariff,' 23 accepts the claim.

43 *Journals* 1879, 18, 21, 36, 65. *Globe* (Toronto), 25 Jan. 1879. PAO, Wallace Family Papers, J. Langstaff to N. Wallace, 2 Apr. 1879. PAC, Tilley Papers, vol. 22, 545, S.L. Tilley to S.C. Rykert, 20 Feb. 1879

44 *Globe* (Toronto), 6 Mar. 1879. *Witness* (Montreal), 17 Mar. 1879. Canada, *Statutes*, 42 Vict. c. 15

45 *Free Press* (Ottawa), 17 Mar 1879. *Globe* (Toronto), 10 Feb., 19, 20, 26 Mar. and 2 Apr. 1879

46 DUA, Parker Eakins Papers, letterbook 1879–80, 39–43, Parker Eakins Co. to F. Killam 19 Mar. 1879. DUA, Dickie Papers, Gourlie & Co. to J. Dickie, 15 Mar. 1879

47 PAC, Tilley Papers, vol. 22, 247–8, S.L. Tilley to A. Moffitt, 15 Jan. 1879

48 *Gazette* (Montreal), 1 Mar. 1879. *Witness* (Montreal), 17 Mar. 1879. *Globe* (Toronto), 27 Feb. 1879. The continuing importance of Laurentian access to the American hinterland is made clear in S. McKee, Jr, 'Canada's Bid for the Traffic of the Middle West: A Quarter Century of the History of the St. Lawrence, 1849–1874,' Canadian Historical Association *Report* (1940): 26–35.

49 *Free Press* (Ottawa), 25 and 26 Mar. 1879. *Globe* (Toronto), 21 and 27 Mar. 1879

50 *Globe* (Toronto), 3 and 4 Mar. 1879. Macdonald Papers, vol. 353, 162605–8, E. Redpath to Sir J.A. Macdonald, 15 Nov. 1878
51 PAC, Macdonald Papers, vol. 223, 162605–8, J. Hickson to Sir J.A. Macdonald, 15 Jan 1879
52 *Globe* (Toronto), 20 Jan. and 8 Mar. 1879. *Citizen* (Ottawa), 8 Mar. 1879. *Gazette* (Montreal), 11 Mar. 1879. *Free Press* (Ottawa), 15 and 17 Mar. 1879. *Sun* (Saint John), 6 Mar. 1879
53 PAC, Macdonald Papers, vol. 357, 164935–8, D. McInnes to Sir J.A. Macdonald, 17 Apr. 1879
54 PAC, Macdonald Papers, vol. 356, 164645, C. Martin to Sir J.A. Macdonald, 18 Mar. 1879
55 *Sun* (Saint John), 19 Mar. 1879
56 *Globe* (Toronto), 22 Mar. 1879
57 PAC, Macdonald Papers, vol. 303, part 2, 138405–52, G.G. Dustan to Sir J.A. Macdonald, 23 Feb. 1875. *Proceedings* 1879, 74, 104–22
58 PAC, PCO, series 1, OC, PC1557, 12 Nov. 1879
59 PAC, Macdonald Papers, vol. 351, 161773–80, M. Heward to Sir J.A. Macdonald, 23 Feb. 1875
60 PAC, Toronto B of T Papers, Council Minute Book 1871–87, vol. 3, 174
61 *Statutes*, 42 Vict. c. 15
62 Maclean, *Tariff Hand-book*, 170
63 Rates on counters are based on 'effective protection' (C. Barber, 'Canadian Tariff Policy,' *CJEPS* 21 [1955]: 513–30, and Barnett, 'Galt Tariff'). Tariff rates calculated from *SP* 1880, Trade and Navigation Returns.
64 PAC, Mackenzie Papers, 2308–9, R. Cartwright to A. Mackenzie, 29 Nov. 1879
65 PAC, Tilley Papers: vol. 23, 632–4, Sir S.L. Tilley to D.L. Herrington, 6 Nov. 1879; vol. 24, 24, Sir S.L. Tilley to G. Guillet, 25 Nov. 1879

CONCLUSION

1 For a discussion of the European context, see D. Landes, *The Unbound Prometheus* (Cambridge 1969) 231–47.
2 L. Panitch, 'Corporatism in Canada,' *Studies in Political Economy: A Socialist Review* 1 (1979): 43–92. P. Schmitter and G. Lehmbruch, eds, *Trends toward Corporatist Intermediation* (Beverly Hills 1979). Suzanne Berger, ed., *Organizing Interests in Western Europe: Pluralism, Corporatism and the Transformation of Politics* (Cambridge 1981). Pross, *Pressure Group Behavior* 132–3, argues that social and economic rigidities are produced through an élite accommodation process of interest-group politics, because this process is not accessible to non-élite groups. This is not quite the argument made here.

3 P. Rutherford, *A Victorian Authority: The Daily Press in Late Nineteenth-Century Canada* (Toronto 1982) 176–81

4 L. Galambos, 'The Emerging Organizational Synthesis in Modern American History,' *Business History Review* 44 (1970): 279–90. Also see D. Truman, *The Governmental Process* (New York 1951)

5 [A. Skaife], *The Comedy of Trade* (Montreal 1876) 5–6. Smith, *Wealth of Nations*, 127–8, notes that 'the clamour and sophistry of merchants and manufacturers can easily persuade them [landlords, farmers, and labourers] that the private interest of a part, and of a subordinate part of the society, is the general interest of the whole.'

6 For a theoretical view of interest-group politics that emphasizes narrow interest, see Olson, *Collective Action*.

7 For a brief suggestive discussion of these matters, see L. Hannah, ed., *Management Strategy and Business Development* (London 1976), 13.

8 NS *Statutes*. 7 Will. c. 9, for the example of a single chocolate manufacturer being granted tariff protection and a bounty. For considerably later examples, see NB *Journals*, 1856, index head 'Petitions.'

9 R. Whitaker (*The Government Party: Organizing and Financing the Liberal Party of Canada 1930–58* [Toronto 1977] 407–8) provides suggestions as to how the same process continued in the twentieth century. In the modern context, there is considerable debate about the place of such groups in the political process – whether they are created under government incentive or co-opted by government in order to play an advisory role in the policy-making process, or whether they are independent and forceful representatives of interests imposing their will on government. See Thorburn, *Interest Groups*, 9–14.

10 *Debates*, 5 Mar. 5 1883, 113–15. *Journals* 1883, app. (no. 4)

11 Pinchin, 'Canadian Tariff Levels,' Chart II-C-III

12 *Journals* 1882, app. (no. 2) and *SP* 1885 (no. 37)

Bibliography

ARCHIVAL SOURCES

Public Archives of Canada

Records of Foreign Governments	
United States Consular Records	RG 10 A 1
Government Records, Canada	
Department of Finance Records	RG 19
Department of National Revenue Records	RG 16
Privy Council Office	RG 2
Treasury Board Minutes	RG 55
Government Records, Province of Canada	
Province of Canada Executive Council Office	RG 1
Private Manuscripts	
James Cox Aikins Papers	MG 27 I D 1
Baring Brothers and Company Papers	MG 24 D 21
Sidney Robert Bellingham Papers	MG 24 B 25
Mackenzie Bowell Papers	MG 26 E
George Brown Papers	MG 24 B 40
Isaac Buchanan Papers	MG 24 D 16
William E. Buckingham Papers	MG 27 I I 3
A.B. Campbell Papers	MG 27 I I 63
Sir Alexander Campbell Papers	MG 27 I C 2
Sir Adolphe Philippe Caron Papers	MG 27 I D 3

Sir George Etienne Cartier Papers	MG 27 I D 4
Brown Chamberlin Papers	MG 24 B 19
S.A. Crowell Co. Papers	MG 28 III 3
Thomas Mayne Daly Jr. Papers	MG 27 I D 6
Marquess of Dufferin Papers	MG 27 I B 3
Ellice Family Papers	MG 24 A 2
Sir Alexander Tilloch Galt Papers	MG 27 I D 8
Hon. Sir James Robert Gowan Papers	MG 27 I E 17
Hon. T.N. Gibbs Papers	MG 27 I D 9
William Grey Papers	MG 27 I I 33
Glyn Mills & Co. Papers	MG 24 D 36
Joseph Howe Papers	MG 24 B 29
Jonas Jones Family Papers	MG 24 B 154
William Loch [Stuart] Papers	MG 24 D 82
Marquess of Lorne Papers	MG 27 I B 2
John Lowe Papers	MG 29 E 18
Sir John A. Macdonald Papers	MG 26 A
John Sandfield Macdonald Papers	MG 24 B 30
John Alexander Macdonell Papers	MG 27 I I 15
Alexander Mackenzie Papers	MG 26 B
John McLennan Papers	MG 27 I E 8
Merritt Papers	MG 24 E I
Montreal Board of Trade Papers	MG 28 III 44
Viscount Monck Papers	MG 27 I B I
H.J. Morgan Papers	MG 29 D 61
Progressive Conservative Party Papers	MG 28 IV 2
William Bain Scarth Papers	MG 27 I E 19
Goldwin Smith Papers	MG 29 D 69
James Wicks Taylor Papers [originals held by The Minnesota Historical Society]	MG 27 I H 2
Sir Samuel Leonard Tilley Papers	MG 27 I D 15
Toronto Board of Trade Papers	MG 28 III 56
Sir Charles Tupper Papers	MG 26 F
Sir Edward William Watkin Papers	MG 24 E 17
The United Empire Club of Canada	MG 55/28, no. 6

Archives nationales du Québec

Chambre de Commerce de Lévis, Papers
Quebec Board of Trade Papers

Dalhousie University Library

James Dickie Papers
Parker Eakins Papers

Metropolitan Toronto Library

Pattullo Papers

New Brunswick Museum Archives

Tilley Papers

Provincial Archives of New Brunswick

Arthur Hill Gillmor Papers

Provincial Archives of Nova Scotia

A.G. Jones Papers
Alexander Mackenzie Papers
Young Family (Falmouth) Papers

Provincial Archives of Ontario

Blake Papers
Cartwright Papers
William Kirby Papers
T.C. Patteson Papers
Wallace Family Papers

Queen's University Archives

Kingston Board of Trade Papers

Regional Collection, University of Western Ontario

David Mills Papers
John Newton Papers

University of New Brunswick Archives

James Brown Papers
Sir George Eulas Foster Papers

University of Toronto Library

John Charlton Papers

NEWSPAPERS

Chronicle, Halifax
Chronicle, Quebec City
Citizen, Ottawa
Citizen, Halifax
Colonial Advocate, Toronto
Colonist, Halifax
Colonist, Toronto
Le Courrier du Canada, Quebec City
Daily Colonist, Victoria
Era, Newmarket
Examiner, Toronto
Free Press, Ottawa
Free Press, Winnipeg
Gazette, Montreal
Globe, Toronto
Herald, Montreal
Mail, Toronto
Mainland Guardian, New Westminster
Mercury, Quebec City
La Minerve, Montreal
Monetary Times, Toronto
News, Saint John
New Era, Montreal
Nova Scotian, Halifax
Patriot, Toronto
Pilot, Montreal
Sentinel, Thunder Bay
Spectator, Hamilton
Standard, Winnipeg
Sun, Saint John

imes, Hamilton
Vitness, Montreal

GOVERNMENT DOCUMENTS

Canada

House of Commons
Debates, 1867-1872, 1875-1879
Journals, 1867-1888
– 1867-69, app. (no. 11), 'Third and Fourth Reports of the Select Committee Appointed to Inquire into the General Condition of the Building of Merchant Vessels in the Dominion of Canada, and as to the Means of Promoting Its Development'
– 1872, app. (no. 1), 'Second Report of the Select Committee Appointed to Enquire into the Manufacturing Interests of the Dominion'
– app. (no. 3), 'First Report of the Select Committee on the Agricultural Interest'
– 1874, app. (no. 2), 'Report. Agricultural Interests'
– app. (no. 3), 'Report of the Select Committee on the Extent and Condition of the Manufacturing Interests of the Dominion'
– 1876, app. (no. 3), 'Report of the Select Committee on the Causes of the Present Depression of the Manufacturing, Mining, Shipping, Lumber and Fishing Interests'
– 'Report of the Select Committee on the Agricultural Interests of the Dominion'
– 1877, app. (no. 4), 'Report of the Select Committee on the State of the Coal Trade, and the Promoting of Inter-Provincial Trade'
– 1882, app. (no. 2), 'Report of the Select Committee to Enquire into the Operation of the Tariff on the Agricultural Interests of the Dominion'
– 1883, app. (no. 4), 'Evidence Taken before the Select Committiee on Inter-Provincial Trade'
– 1888, app. (no. 3), 'Report of the Select Committee to Investigate and Report upon Alleged Combinations in Manufactures, Trade and Insurance in Canada'
Sessional Papers, 1869-1879
– Trade and Navigation Returns, 1869-80
– 1879, no. 80
– 1885, no. 37
Statutes, 1867-1879

Canada, Province

Legislative Assembly
Debates, 1841-1851

General Index to the Journals, 1841-1852
General Index to the Journals, 1853-1866
Journals, 1841-1866
– 1843, app. (B.B.), 'Report of Malcolm Carmeron into the State and Management of Customs'
– 1847, app. (K.)
– 1849, app. (AAAAA), 'Report of the Select Committee into the Causes and Importance of Emigration from Lower Canada to the United States'
– 1854-5, app. (DDDD), 'Report on Trade and Commerce'
– 1857, app. (no. 47), 'Report of the Special Committee on Emigration'
– 1858, app. (no. 2), 'Report of William Hamilton Merritt'
Statutes, 1841-1866

New Brunswick

House of Assembly
Journals, 1833-1866
– 1865, app., 'Trade and Navigation Returns'
– 1865-66, app., 'Trade and Navigation Returns'
Statutes 1841-1866

Nova Scotia

House of Assembly
Journals, 1832-1866
– 1853, app. (no. 45), 'Report of the Committee on Manufactures'
Journals and Proceedings, *1867*-1879
– 1870, app. (no. 15), 'Mines Report'
– 1875, app. (no. 4), 'Mines Report'
– 1876, app. (no. 6), 'Mines Report'
– 1878, app. (no. 6), 'Report on the Inspection of Mines in Nova Scotia'
Statutes, 1837-1866

Prince Edward Island

House of Assembly
Journals, 1835-1866

Lower Canada

House of Assembly
Journals, 1823-1836

Upper Canada

House of Assembly
Journals, 1827-1841
– 1835, app. (no. 11), 'Appendix to the Report on Trade'
– 1836-37, app. (no. 7), 'Report of the Select Committee on the Subject of Trade & Commerce'

CONTEMPORARY PRINTED SOURCES

Address by David Glass, Q.C., to the Electors of East Middlesex. London 1878
Address of the Hon. Alexander Mackenzie to the Workingmen on the 'National Policy.' Toronto 1878
Address of the Hon. John A. Macdonald to the Electors of Kingston. N.p., n.d.
Beausoliel, C. *Système Protecteur ou de la nécessité d'une Reforme du tariff Canadien*. Montreal 1871
British North American Association, *Speech of Hon. A.T. Galt, at the Chamber of Commerce, Manchester, September 25, 1862*. London 1862
Buchanan, I. *The Relations of the Industry of Canada*. Montreal 1864
[Byles, John Barnard]. *Sophisms of Free Trade*. 9th ed. Manchester 1870
Campbell, D. *Nova Scotia, in Its Historical, Mercantile and Industrial Relations*. Montreal 1873
Carey, H.C. *Harmony of Interests*. Philadelphia 1851
– *Prospects of the Farmer under the Tariff of 1846*. New York 1852
– *Letters to the President*. Philadelphia 1858
– *Principles of Social Science*. Philadelphia 1888
Cartwright, R.J. *Reminiscences*. Toronto 1912
Cayley, W. *Finances and Trade of Canada at the Beginning of the Year 1855*. London 1855
Commercial Reciprocity between the United States and the British North American Provinces. N.p., n.d.
Desjardins, L.G. *De l'idée Conservatrice dans l'ordre politique*. Quebec 1879
Dominion Board of Trade. *Proceedings* 1876. Montreal 1876
– *Proceedings* 1877. Montreal 1877

– *Proceedings* 1878. Montreal 1878
– *Proceedings* 1879. Montreal 1879
Dominion of Canada. The Province of Ontario as It Is. Toronto 1877
Free Trade for the People. Protection for the Favoured Few. Toronto 1878
Greeley, H., ed. *The American Laborer.* Modern edition. New York 1974
Haliburton, R.G. 'The Coal Trade of the New Dominion,' article X. Nova Scotia Institute of Natural Science *Transactions* (1866-67)
Hamilton, Alexander. 'Report on the Subject of Manufactures.' In F.W. Taussig, ed., *State Papers and Speeches on the Tariff.* Cambridge, MA 1893
History of the Grange in Canada, with a List of Division and Subordinate Granges & Their Executive Officers. Toronto 1876
Home Industries. Canada's National Policy. 1876
The Honble. Francis Hincks' Views of the Commercial Policy of Canada, in 1846 and 1847 and in 1852. Montreal 1853
Hurlbert, J.B. *Field and Factory Side by Side.* Montreal 1870
Johnson, W.W. *Sketches of the Late Depression.* Montreal 1882
List, Friedrich. *The National System of Political Economy.* London 1885
Maclean, John. *Protection and Free Trade.* Montreal 1867
– *Protection in Canada.* Ottawa 1979
Meeting of the Manufacturers' Association of Ontario Held in St. Lawrence Hall, Toronto Nov. 25, 26, 1875. N.p., n.d.
Mill, J.S. *Principles of Political Economy.* 7th ed. London 1871
Minutes of the Proceedings of the Second Convention of the Delegates of the British American League. Toronto 1849
[Mitchell, P.] *Review of President Grant's Recent Message.* Ottawa 1870
Montreal in 1856: A Sketch Prepared for the Opening of the Grand Trunk Railway of Canada. Montreal 1856
Oliphant, L. *Episodes in a Life of Adventure: or Moss from a Rolling Stone.* Edinburgh 1896
Ontario Manufacturers' Association, Proceedings of Annual Convention, 1877. Toronto 1877
Political Points and Pencillings. Being Selections from Various Addresses Delivered by the Hon. Alex Mackenzie. Toronto 1878
Reform Government in the Dominion. Toronto 1878
Report of the Chamber of Commerce, Saint John, N.B., *of Their Delegates to the Commercial Convention, Held in Detroit Mich., July 1865.* Saint John 1865
St. John and Its Business. Saint John 1875
[Skaife, A.]. *The Comedy of Trade.* Montreal 1876
Smith, A. *Wealth of Nations.* New York 1937. Orig. pub. 1776

Speeches of the Hon Alexander Mackenzie during His Recent Visit to Scotland. Toronto 1876

Sullivan, R.B. *Lecture, Delivered before the Mechanics' Institute of Hamilton, on Wednesday Evening, November 17, 1847, On the Connection between Agriculture and Manufactures of Canada.* Hamilton 1848

The Canadian Biographical Dictionary and Portrait Gallery of Eminent and Self-Made Men, vol. 1, Ontario. Toronto 1881

The Complete Tariff Hand-Book, 2nd ed. Toronto 1879

The Effects of the New Tariff on the Upper Canada Trade. Toronto 1859

The Trade Question. Fallacies Protection, or the So-Called 'National Policy.' Toronto 1878

Weir, W. *Sixty Years in Canada.* Montreal 1903

Year Book and Almanac of Canada for 1879. Ottawa 1879

BOOKS

Allin, C.D., and G.M. Jones. *Annexation, Preferential Trade and Reciprocity.* Westport, CT 1912

Benson, E. *Historical Record of the Edwardsburgh and Canada Starch Companies.* Montreal 1959

Berg, M. *The Age of Manufactures, 1700-1820.* London 1985

Berger, C. *The Sense of Power: Studies in the Ideas of Canadian Imperialism, 1867-1914.* Toronto 1970

Berger, Suzanne, ed. *Organizing Interests in Western Europe: Pluralism, Corporatism and the Transformation of Politics.* Cambridge 1981

Berton, P. *The National Dream.* Toronto 1970

Blake, Gordon. *Customs Administration in Canada: An Essay in Tariff Technology.* Toronto 1957

Bliss, M. *A Living Profit: Studies in the Social History of Canadian Business, 1883-1911.* Toronto 1974

Bodelson, C.A. *Studies in Mid-Victorian Imperialism.* Copenhagen 1924

Böhme, H. *An Introduction to the Social and Economic History of Germany: Politics and Economic Change in the Nineteenth and Twentieth Centuries.* Oxford 1978

Brown, R.C. *Robert Laird Borden: A Biography*, vol. 1. Toronto 1975

Careless, J.M.S. *Brown of the Globe*, vol. 1. Toronto 1959

– *Brown of the Globe*, vol. 2. Toronto 1963

– *The Union of the Canadas: The Growth of Canadian Institutions 1841-1857.* Toronto 1967

Carruthers, G. *Paper in the Making.* Toronto 1947

Clough, S.B. *France: A History of National Economics, 1789-1939*. New York 1939
Coote, J.A. *A Graphical Survey of the Canadian Textile Industries*. Montreal 1936
Creighton, D.G. *The Commercial Empire of the St. Lawrence*. Toronto 1937
– *John A. Macdonald, The Young Politician*. Toronto 1952
– *British North America at Confederation*. Ottawa 1963
– *The Road to Confederation*. Toronto 1964
Cross, M., ed. *Free Trade, Annexation and Reciprocity, 1846-54*. Toronto 1971
Dales, J.H. *The Protective Tariff in Canada's Development*. Toronto 1966
Dawley, A. *Class and Community: The Industrial Revolution in Lynn*. Cambridge, MA 1976
Denison, M. *The Barley and the Stream*. Toronto 1955
– *Harvest Triumphant*. Toronto 1955
Donald, W.J.A. *The Canadian Iron and Steel Industry: A Study in the Economic History of a Protected Industry*. Boston 1915
Dorfman, J. *The Economic Mind in American Civilization 1606-1865*. New York 1949
Easterbrook, W.T., and H.G.J. Aitken. *Canadian Economic History*. Toronto 1956
Farr, D.L.M. *The Colonial Office and Canada, 1867-1887*. Toronto 1855
Firestone, O.J. *Canada's Economic Development, 1867-1972*. Mimeograph. n.p. 1953
Fischer, L.R., and G.E. Panting, eds. *Change and Adaptation in Maritime History: The North Atlantic Fleets in the Nineteenth Century*. St. John's 1985
Galombos, L. *Competition and Cooperation: The Emergence of a National Trade Association*. Baltimore 1966
Gates, P.W. *The Farmer's Age: Agriculture 1815-1860*. New York 1960
Genovese, E. *Roll, Jordon Roll: The World the Slaves Made*. New York 1974
Gilmour, J.M. *Spatial Evolution of Manufacturing: Southern Ontario 1851-1891*. Toronto 1972
Gluek, A.C. *Minnesota and the Manifest Destiny of the Canadian North West*. Toronto 1965
Hamelin, J., and Y. Roby. *Histoire économique du Québec 1851-1896*. Montreal 1971
Heidenheimer, A.J., and F.C. Langdon. *Business Associations and the Financing of Political Parties: A Comparative Study of the Evolution of Practices in Germany, Norway and Japan*. The Hague 1968
Hodgetts, J.E. *Pioneer Public Service: An Administrative History of the United Canadas, 1841-1867*. Toronto 1955
Hudson, M. 'Introduction,' *Economics and Technology in 19th-Century American Thought: The Neglected American Economists*. New York 1975
Hyde, F.E. *Cunard and the North Atlantic 1840-1973*. London 1975
Innis, H.A. *The Cod Fisheries*. Rev. ed. Toronto 1954
Innis, H.A., and A.R.M. Lower, eds. *Select Documents in Canadian Economic History 1773-1885*. Toronto 1933
James, R. Warren. *John Rae, Political Economist*. Toronto 1965

Jones, R.L. *History of Agriculture in Ontario*. Toronto 1946
Kealey, G.S. *Toronto Workers Respond to Industrial Capitalism 1867-1892*. Toronto 1980
Kilbourn, W. *The Elements Combined: A History of the Steel Company of Canada*. Toronto 1960
Kirkland, E.C. *Industry Comes of Age: Business, Labor and Public Policy 1860-1897*. Chicago 1961
Lambi, I.N. *Free Trade and Protection in Germany 1868-1879*. Wiesbaden 1963
Landes, D. *The Unbound Prometheus*. Cambridge 1969
Longley, R.S. *Sir Francis Hincks: A Study of Canadian Politics, Railways and Finance in the Nineteenth Century*. Toronto 1943
Lower, A.R.M. *The North American Assault on the Canadian Forest*. Toronto 1938
– *Great Britain's Woodyard: British America and the Timber Trade, 1763-1867*. Montreal 1973
McCalla, D. *The Upper Canada Trade 1834-1872: A Study of the Buchanans' Business*. Toronto 1979
McCallum, J. *Unequal Beginnings: Agriculture and Economic Development in Quebec and Ontario until 1870*. Toronto 1980
McDowall, D. *Steel at the Sault: Francis H. Clergue, Sir James Dunn, and the Algoma Steel Corporation 1901-1956*. Toronto 1984
McGouldrick, P.F. *New England Textiles in the Nineteenth Century: Profits and Investment*. Cambridge, MA 1968
MacNutt, W.S. *The Atlantic Provinces: The Emergence of Colonial Society 1712-1857*. Toronto 1965
Marr, W.L., and D.G. Paterson. *Canada: An Economic History*. Toronto 1980
Masters, D.C. *The Reciprocity Treaty of 1854*, 2nd ed. Toronto 1963
Naylor, T. *The History of Canadian Business 1867-1914*. 2 vols. Toronto 1975
Nevins, A. *Hamilton Fish: The Inner History of the Grant Administration*. New York 1936
Olson, Mancur. *The Logic of Collective Action*. Cambridge, MA 1965
Ouellet, F., *Histoire économique et social du Québec, 1760-1850*. Montreal 1971
Owram, D. *Promise of Eden: The Canadian Expansionist Movement and the Idea of the West, 1856-1900*. Toronto 1980
Palmer, B. *A Culture in Conflict: Skilled Workers and Industrial Capitalism in Hamilton, Ontario, 1860-1914*. Montreal 1979
– *Working-Class Experience: The Rise and Reconstitution of Canadian Labour, 1800-1980*. Toronto 1983
Phillips, W.G. *The Agricultural Implement Industry in Canada: A Study of Competition*. Toronto 1956
Presthus, Robert. *Elite Accommodation in Canadian Politics*. Toronto 1973
Pross, A. Paul, ed. *Pressure Group Behavior in Canadian Politics*. Toronto 1975

Pryke, G.K. *Nova Scotia and Confederation*. Toronto 1974
Rabbeno, U. *The American Commercial Policy: Three Historical Essays*. London 1895
Répertoire des parlementaires québecois 1867-1978. Quebec 1980
Rich, E.E., and C.H. Wilson, eds. *The Cambridge Economic History of Europe*, vol. 4. Cambridge 1967
Rohr, D.G. *The Origins of Social Liberalism in Germany*. Chicago 1963
Rumilly, R. *Histoire de la Province de Québec*, vol. 2. 3rd ed. Montreal 1941
Rutherford, Paul. *A Victorian Authority: The Daily Press in Late Nineteenth-Century Canada*. Toronto 1982
Saul, S.B. *The Myth of the Great Depression 1873-1896*. London 1969
Schmitter, P., and G. Lehmbruch, eds. *Trends toward Corporatist Intermediation*. Beverly Hills 1979
Schmookler, J. *Patents, Invention and Economic Change: Data and Selected Essays*. Cambridge, Ma 1972
Shippee, L.B. *Canadian-American Relations 1849-1874*. Toronto 1939
Skelton, O.D. *The Life and Times of Sir Alexander Tilloch Galt*, 2nd ed. Toronto 1966
– *General Economic History of the Dominion, 1867-1912*. Toronto 1913
Smith, M.S. *Tariff Reform in France 1860-1900: The Politics of Economic Interest*. Ithaca 1980
Spelt, Jacob. *Urban Development in South Central Ontario*. Toronto 1972
Stolper, G.; K.H. Häuser; and K. Borchardt. *The German Economy, 1870 to the Present*. New York 1967
Tansill, C.C. *The Canadian Reciprocity Treaty of 1854*. Baltimore 1922
Taussig, F.W. *The Tariff History of the United States*, 8th ed. New York 1931
Taylor, G.R., and I.D. Neu. *The American Railroad Network 1861-1890*. Cambridge, MA 1956
Taylor, K.W., and H. Michell. *Statistical Contributions to Canadian Economic History*, vol. 2. Toronto 1931
Thomson, D. *Alexander Mackenzie, Clear Grit*. Toronto 1960
Thorburn, Hugh G. *Interest Groups in the Canadian Federal System*. Toronto 1985
Truman, D. *The Governmental Process*. New York 1951
Tucker, G.N. *The Canadian Commercial Revolution, 1845-1851*. New Haven 1936
Tulchinsky, G. *The River Barons: Montreal Businessmen and the Growth of Industry and Transportation 1837-53*. Toronto 1977
Underhill, F. *In Search of Canadian Liberalism*. Toronto 1960
Unger, I. *The Greenback Era: A Social and Political History of American Finance, 1865-1879*. Princeton 1964
Urquhart, M.C., and K.A.H. Buckley, eds. *Historical Statistics of Canada*. Toronto 1965

Waite, P.B. *Canada 1874-1896: Arduous Destiny*. Toronto 1971

Warner, D.F. *The Idea of Continental Union*. Lexington 1963

Whitaker, R. *The Government Party: Organizing and Financing the Liberal Party of Canada 1930-58*. Toronto 1977

Whitelaw, W.M. *The Maritimes and Canada before Confederation*. Toronto 1966

Wilson, A. *John Northway, Blue Serge Canadian*. Toronto 1963

Wilson, R.G. *Gentlemen Merchants: The Merchant Community in Leeds, 1700-1830*. Manchester 1971

Winks, R. *Canada and the United States: The Civil War Years*. Baltimore 1960

Wismer, L.E., ed. *Proceedings of the Canadian Labour Union Congress: 1873-77*. Ottawa 1951

Wood, L.A. *A History of Farmers' Movements in Canada*. 2nd ed. Toronto 1975

Wynn, G. *Timber Colony: A Historical Geography of Early New Brunswick*. Toronto 1981

ARTICLES

Acheson, W. 'The National Policy and the Industrialization of the Maritimes, 1880-1910.' *Acadiensis* 1 (1972): 3-28

– 'The Great Merchant and Economic Development in St. John, 1820-1850.' *Acadiensis* 8-2 (1979): 3-27

Ankli, R. 'Canadian-American Reciprocity: A Comment.' JEH 30 (1970): 427-31

– 'The Reciprocity Treaty of 1854.' *CJE* 4 (1971): 1-20

Ankli, R., and W. Millar. 'Ontario Agriculture in Transition: The Switch from Wheat to Cheese.' JEH 42 (1982): 207-15

Babcock, R.H. 'Economic Development in Portland Me., and St. John N.B. during the Age of Iron and Steam 1850-1914.' *American Review of Canadian Studies* 9 (1979): 3-37

Barber, C. 'Canadian Tariff Policy.' CJEPS 21 (1955): 512-30

Barnett, D.F. 'The Galt Tariff: Incidental or Effective Protection?' CJE 9 (1976): 389-407

Bertram, G.W. 'Historical Statistics on Growth and Structure of Manufacturing in Canada, 1870-1957.' In Canadian Political Science Association, *Conference on Statistics*, 1962 & 1963, 93-146. Toronto 1964

Bland, W.R. 'The Location of Manufacturing in Southern Ontario in 1881.' *Ontario Geography* 8 (1974): 9-39

Blyth, J.A. 'The Development of the Paper Industry in Old Ontario, 1824-1867.' OH 62 (1970): 119-33

Böhme, H. 'Big Business Pressure Groups and Bismarck's Turn to Protectionism, 1873-79.' *The Historical Journal* 10 (1967): 218-36

Bradbury, B. 'The Family Economy and Work in an Industrializing City: Montreal in the 1870s.' Canadian Historical Association, *Historical Papers* (1979): 71-96

Burgess, J. 'L'industrie de la chaussure Montréal: 1840-1870: le passage de l'artisanat à la fabrique.' *Revue d'histoire l'Amerique français* 31 (1977): 187-210

Careless, J.M.S. 'Aspects of Metropolitanism in Atlantic Canada.' In M. Wade, ed., *Regionalism in the Canadian Community*. Toronto 1969

– 'Mid-Victorian Liberalism in Central Canadian Newspapers, 1850-1867.' CHR 31 (1950): 221-36

Chambers, E.J. 'Late Nineteenth Century Business Cycles in Canada.' CJEPS 47 (1964): 391-412

Chandler, A.D., Jr. 'Anthracite Coal and the Beginnings of the Industrial Revolution in the United States.' *Business History Review* 46 (1972): 141-81

Chapman, S.D. 'British Marketing Enteprise: The Changing Roles of Merchants, Manufacturers, and Financiers, 1700-1860.' *Business History Review* 53 (1979): 205-33

Clark, A.H. 'Contributions of Its Southern Neighbors to the Underdevelopment of the Maritimes Provinces Area, 1710-1867.' In R.A. Preston, ed., *The Influence of the United States on Canadian Development: Eleven Case Studies*. Durham, NC 1972

Clark, P.B., and James Q. Wilson. 'Incentive Systems: A Theory of Organizations.' *Administrative Science Quarterly* 6 (1961): 129-66

Clark, S.D. 'The Canadian Manufacturers' Association: A Political Pressure Group.' CJEPS 4 (1938): 505–23

– 'The Canadian Manufacturers' Association and the Tariff.' CJEPS 5 (1939): 19-39

Craven, P., and T. Traves. 'The Class Politics of the National Policy.' JCS 14-3 (1979): Creighton, D.G. 'Economic Nationalism and Confederation.' Canadian Historical Association *Report* (1942): 44-51

– 'George Brown, Sir John Macdonald and the "Workingman."' CHR 24 (1943): 362-76

Davidson, R.I.K. 'John Taylor.' DCB, vol. 10,671-2. Toronto 1972

Davies, P.N. 'The Development of the Liner Trades.' In K. Matthews and G. Panting, eds, *Ships and Shipbuilding* (St John's 1978)

den Otter, A.A. 'Alexander Galt, the 1859 Tariff and Canadian Economic Nationalism.' CHR 63 (1982): 151-78

Deschênes, L. 'William Price.' DCB, vol. 9, 638-42. Toronto 1976

Doucet, M.J. 'Working Class Housing in a Small Nineteenth Century Canadian City: Hamilton, Ontario 1852-1881.' In G.S. Kealey and P. Warrian, eds, *Essays in Canadian Working Class History*. Toronto 1976

Dubuc, A. 'William Molson.' DCB, vol. , 517-25. Toronto 1972

Dyster, B. 'John William Gamble.' DCB, vol. 10, 299-300. Toronto 1972

Faucher, A. 'The Decline of Shipbuilding at Quebec in the Nineteenth Century.' CJEPS 23 (1957): 195-215

– 'Some Aspects of the Financial Difficulties of the Province of Canada.' *CJEPS* 33 (1957): 617-24

Fingard, J. 'The Winter's Tale: The Seasonal Contours of Pre-Industrial Poverty, in British North America 1815-1860.' Canadian Historical Association *Historical Papers* (1974): 65-94

Forster, B. 'The Coming of the National Policy: Business, Goverment and the Tariff, 1876-1879.' *JCS* 14 (1979): 39-49

– 'A Conservative Heart: The United Empire Club 1874-1882.' *OH* 78 (1986)

Forster, B., M. Davidson, and R.C. Brown. 'The Franchise, Personators and Dead Men: An Inquiry into the Voters' Lists and the Election of 1891.' *CHR* (forthcoming 1986)

Fowke, V.C. 'The National Policy – Old and New.' *CJEPS* 18 (1952): 271-86

Galambos, L. 'The Emerging Organizational Synthesis in Modern American History.' *Business History Review* 44 (1970): 279-90

Gates, L.F. 'The Decided Policy of William Lyon Mackenzie.' *CHR* 40 (1959): 185-208

Hansen, A.H. 'Economic Progress and Declining Population Growth.' *American Economic Review* 29 (1939): 1-15

Harley, C.K. 'On the Persistence of Old Techniques: The Case of North American Wooden Shipbuilding.' *JEH* 33 (1973): 372-98

Hecht, I.W.D. 'Israel D. Andrews and the Reciprocity Treaty of 1854: A Reappraisal.' *CHR* 44 (1963): 313-29

Hinton, M.N.A. 'The Growth of the Canadian Cotton Textile Industry 1844-1873: "A New Industrial Career."' Unpublished paper 1981

Kindleberger, C.P. 'The Rise of Free Trade in Western Europe, 1820-1875.' *JEH* 35 (1975): 20-55

Klassen, H.C. 'Luther Hamilton Holton.' *DCB*, vol. 10, 354-8. Toronto 1972

Lawr, D.A. 'The Development of Ontario Farming, 1870-1914: Patterns of Growth and Change.' *OH* 44 (1972): 239-51

Lee, D. 'The Dominion General Election of 1878 in Ontario.' *OH* 51 (1959): 172-90

Longley, R.S. 'Peter Mitchell, Guardian of the North Atlantic Fisheries, 1867-1871.' *CHR* 22 (1941): 389-402

McCalla, D. 'The Commercial Politics of the Toronto Board of Trade, 1850-1860.' *CHR* 50 (1969): 51-66

McCann, L.D. 'Metropolitanism and Branch Businesses in the Maritimes, 1881-1931.' *Acadiensis* 13 (1983): 112-25

– 'Staples and the New Industrialism in the Growth of Post-Confederation Halifax.' *Acadiensis* 8 (1979): 47-79

MacDonald, L.R. 'Merchants against Industry.' *CHR* 56 (1975): 263-81

McDougall, D.M. 'The Domestic Availability of Manufactured Commodity Output, Canada, 1870-1915.' *CJE* 6 (1973): 195-6

McInnis, M. 'The Changing Structure of Canadian Agriculture 1867-1897.' *JEH* 42 (1982): 191-8

McKee, S., Jr. 'Canada's Bid for the Traffic of the Middle West: A Quarter Century of the History of the St. Lawrence, 1849-1874.' Canadian Historical Association *Report* (1940): 26-35

MacNab, J.E. 'Toronto's Industrial Growth to 1891.' *OH* 47-2 (1955): 67-80

Mainer, G. 'William Hamilton.' *DCB*, vol. 10, 330-31. Toronto 1972

Masters, D.C. 'A Further Word on I.D. Andrews and the Reciprocity Treaty of 1854.' *CHR* 17 (1936): 159-67

– 'A.T. Galt and Canadian Fiscal Autonomy.' *CHR* 15 (1934): 276-82

Michell, H. 'The Grange in Canada.' *Queen's Quarterly* 22 (1914-15): 164-83

– 'Notes on Prices of Agricultural Commodities in the United States and Canada, 1850-1934.' *CJEPS* 1 (1935): 269-79

Morrison, R.J. 'Henry C. Carey and American Economic Development.' *Explorations in Economic History* 5 (1968): 132-44

Muise, D. 'The Federal Election of 1867 in Nova Scotia: An Economic Interpretation.' Nova Scotia Historical Society *Collections* 36 (1968): 327-51

– 'Parties and Constituencies: Federal Elections in Nova Scotia, 1867-1896. Canadian Historical Association *Historical Papers* (1971): 183-201

North, D.C. 'Ocean Freight Rates and Economic Development 1750-1913.' *JEH* 18 (1958): 537-55

Officer, L.H., and L.B. Smith. 'The Canadian-American Reciprocity Treaty of 1855 to 1866.' *JEH* 28 (1969): 598-603

– 'Canadian-American Reciprocity: A Reply.' *JEH* 30 (1970): 432-4

Overman, W.D. 'I.D. Andrews and Reciprocity in 1854: An Episode in Dollar Diplomacy.' *CHR* 15 (1934): 248-63

Panitch, Leo. 'Corporatism in Canada.' *Studies in Political Economy: A Socialist Review* 1 (1979): 43-92

Phelps, E. 'The Canada Oil Association – An Early Business Combination.' *Western Historical Notes* 19 (1963): 31-9

Pickett, J. 'Residential Capital Formation in Canada, 1871-1921.' *CJEPS* 29 (1963): 40-58

Piva, M.J. 'Continuity and Crisis: Francis Hincks and Canadian Economic Policy.' *CHR* 66 (1985): 185-210

Pomfret, R. 'Capital Formation in Canada 1870-1900.' *Explorations in Economic History* 18 (1981): 84-96

Presthus, R. 'Interest Groups and the Canadian Parliament: Activities, Interaction, Legitimacy and Influence.' *JPS* 4 (1971): 444-60

Reid, R. 'The Rosamond Woolen Company of Almonte: Industrial Development in a Rural Setting.' *OH* 75 (1983): 266-89

Remiggi, F.W. 'La Lutte du Clerge contre Le Marchard de Poisson: A Study of Power

Structures on the Gaspé North Coast in the Nineteenth Century.' In L.R. Fischer and W.W. Sager, eds, *The Enterprising Canadians: Entrepreneurs and Economic Development in Eastern Canada*, 1820-1914. St John's 1979

Rice, R. 'Measuring British Dominance of Shipbuilding in the 'Maritimes,' 1787-1890.' In K. Matthews and G. Panting, eds, *Ships and Shipbuilding in the North Atlantic Region*, 109-55. St John's 1978

Risk, R.C.B. 'The Nineteenth-Century Foundations of the Business Corporation in Ontario.' *University of Toronto Law Journal* 23 (1973): 270-306

Ryan, S. 'The Newfoundland Salt Cod Trade in the Nineteenth Century.' In J. Hiller and P. Neary, eds, *Newfoundland in the Nineteenth and Twentieth Centuries*. Toronto 1980

Sager, E.W., and L.R. Fischer. 'Atlantic Canada and the Age of Sail Revisited.' CHR 63 (1982):

Sager, E.W.; L.R. Fischer; and R.E. Ommer. 'The Shipping Industry and Regional Economic Development in Atlantic Canada, 1871-1891: Saint John as a Case Study.' In L.R. Fischer and E.W. Sager, eds, *Merchant Shipping and Economic Development in Atlantic Canada*, 3-59. St John's 1982

– 'Landward and Seaward Opportunities in Canada's Age of Sail.' In Fischer and Sager, eds, ibid.

Salisbury, R.H. 'An Exchange Theory of Interest Groups.' *Midwest Journal of Political Science* 13 (1969): 1-32

Saunders, S.A. 'The Maritime Provinces and the Reciprocity Treaty.' In G.A. Rawlyk, ed., *Historical Essays on the Atlantic Provinces*. Toronto 1967

Slaven, A. 'The Shipbuilding Industry.' In R. Church, ed., *The Dynamics of Victorian Business: Problems and Perspectives to the 1870's*. London 1980

Tallman, R. 'Peter Mitchell and the Genesis of a National Fisheries Policy.' *Acadiensis* 10 (1975): 66-78

Tulchinsky, G. 'William Workman.' DCB, vol. 10, 717-18. Toronto 1972

Tulchinsky, G., and Brian Young. 'John Young.' DCB, vol. 10, 720-7. Toronto 1972

Underhill, F.H. 'The Development of National Parties in Canada.' CHR 16 (1935): 367-87

Urquhart, M.C., et al. 'New Estimates of Gross National Product Canada 1870 to 1926: Some Implications for Canadian Development.' Kingston, typescript, 1984

Walker, D.F. 'The Energy Sources of Manufacturing Industry in Southern Ontario, 1871-1921.' *Ontario Geography* 9 (1971): 56-66

– 'Transportation of Coal into Southern Ontario, 1871-1921.' OH 63 (1971): 15-30

Watkins, M.H. 'A Staple Theory of Economic Growth.' CJEPS 29 (1963): 141-58

– 'The Staple Theory Revisited.' JCS 12 (1977): 83-95

THESES

Beaven, B. 'A Last Hurrah: Studies in Liberal Party Development and Ideology in Ontario, 1878-1893.' PH D thesis, University of Toronto 1981

Bliss, J.W.M. 'A Living Profit: Studies in the Social History of Canadian Business, 1883-1911.' PH D thesis, University of Toronto 1972

Burgess, J. 'L'industrie de la chaussure à Montréal: 1840-1870: le passage de l'artisanat à la fabrique.' MA thesis, Université du Québec à Montréal, 1978

Burley, David G. 'The Politics of Business: Frederick Nicholls and the National Policy, 1874-1895.' MA thesis, Trent University 1974

Cowan, A.W. 'The Canandian White Pine Trade with the United Kingdom, 1867-1914.' MA thesis, Carleton University 1966

Donovan, K.J. 'New Brunswick and the Federal Election of 1878.' MA thesis, University of New Brunswick 1973

Fraser, R.L. 'Like Eden in Her Summer Dress: Gentry, Economy and Society: Upper Canada, 1812-1840.' PH D thesis, University of Toronto 1979

Graham, W.R. 'The Alexander Mackenzie Administration, 1873-1878: A Study of Liberal Tenets and Tactics.' MA thesis, University of Toronto 1944

– 'Sir Richard Cartwright and the Liberal Party.' PH D thesis, University of Toronto 1950

Hale, A.W.C. 'The National Policies of Canada: Myth and Reality, 1867-1900.' PH D thesis, Wales 1979

Inwood, K. 'The Decline and Rise of Charcoal Iron: The Case of Canada.' PH D thesis, University of Toronto 1984

Langdon, S. 'The Political Economy of Capitalist Transformation: Central Canada from the 1840's to the 1870's.' MA thesis, Carleton University 1972

McDonald, R.H. 'Nova Scotia Views the United States, 1784-1854.' PH D thesis, Queen's University 1974

Muise, D. 'Elections and Constituencies: Federal Politics in Nova Scotia 1867-1878.' PH D thesis, University of Western Ontario 1971

Phelps, E. 'John Henry Fairbanks of Petrolia (1831-1914): A Canadian Entrepreneur.' MA thesis, University of Western Ontario 1965

Pinchin, H.M. 'Canadian Tariff Levels 1870-1959.' PH D diss., Yale 1970

Sutherland, D.A. 'The Merchants of Halifax, 1815-1850. A Commercial Class in Pursuit of Metropolitan Status.' PH D thesis, University of Toronto 1975

Swainson, D. 'The Personnel of Politics: A Study of the Ontario Members of the Second Federal Parliament.' PH D thesis, University of Toronto 1968

Walkom, T.L. 'The Daily Newspaper Industry in Ontario's Developing Capitalist Economy: Toronto and Ottawa, 1871-1911.' PH D thesis, University of Toronto, 1983

Index